ASTROLOGY

For Gabriel Thompson Oliva

A manu patrini tui

ASTROLOGY

From Ancient Babylon to the Present

P.G. MAXWELL-STUART

AMBERLEY

First published 2010

Amberley Publishing Plc
Cirencester Road, Chalford,
Stroud, Gloucestershire, GL6 8PE
www.amberleybooks.com

Copyright text and illustrations © P.G. Maxwell-Stuart,
2010

The right of P.G. Maxwell-Stuart to be identified
as the Author of this work has been asserted in
accordance with the Copyrights, Designs and Patents
Act 1988.

ISBN 978 1 84868 107 1

British Library Cataloguing in Publication Data.

A catalogue record for this book is available from the
British Library.

Typeset in 10.2pt on 13.5pt Adobe Caslon.
Typesetting and Origination by Fonthill.

Printed in the UK.

Contents

Observers of Times. These I take to be some who, by correspondence with an evil spirit, declare such and such days or times to have a particular fatality so that no business which was undertaken on that day could prosper; and this part of the Black Art may take in such as carrying on the study of judicial astrology to the extreme, and to the gates of Hell, ascribe events of things to the governance and influence of the stars, and that influence to be so, or so directed for good or evil, according to the particular position, conjunction or situation of those stars or planets in differing houses, as if these could be the directors of the fate of persons, families, and nations; and that the events of things were directed by them, and by the seasons and times of their stations here or there in the course of their ordinary motion, whether direct or retrograde. In a word, the practice of judicial astrology, though not a dealing with or by the help of the Devil, is condemned here as being a plain robbing Divine Providence of its known glory in directing and disposing both causes and events in all things relating to the government of mankind, or indeed of the whole world, and of ascribing that to the poor, innocent, unconcerned stars or planets, which is singly in the disposition of Him that made them.

Daniel Defoe, *A System of Magick* (1727)

I have no desire to offend any class of men by putting forth this work. I do not know whether I should not respect even prejudice, for the sake of peace, were it not that I cannot conscientiously consent to abandon truth in the effort. I am callous to the puny efforts of critics who may desire to pour on me the waters of vituperation or ridicule, having already passed through a flood. After many years' experience, I have found the laws of astrology unfailing, and as I can discover no prohibition of its practice in the Word of God, I am prepared to defend it against all the foolish attacks of those who falsely declare that it upholds fatality, or is opposed to the providence or the revelation of the Deity.

'Zadkiel', *An Introduction to Astrology by William Lilly* (1881)

Author's Note

Astrology has been much honoured and much derided throughout its history and its practitioners both consulted as wise counsellors and prosecuted as rogues and charlatans in almost equal measure. For most of the two and a half millennia here briefly reviewed, however, astrology was, along with its twin, astronomy, from whom it was separated only late in their double existence, a science at the forefront of intellectual speculation. We should now, in the unhappy jargon of our time, call it 'cutting edge'. What follows, therefore, is neither a traipse through technicalities nor a succession of anecdotes unencumbered by explanation, but an attempt to show astrology as a serious intellectual undertaking in its changing historical contexts, subject to renegation and defence as circumstances and necessity persuaded. In the history of astrology we see a science testing hypotheses, bending and adapting to fresh facts, and rejecting ideas which do not work in practice, just as one expects any discipline calling itself a 'science' to do. It can be said that astrology has left its mark on modern vocabulary – consider, disaster, influential, martial, jovial, mercurial, saturnine, and lunatic are all words rooted in the science of the stars – but perhaps more importantly one should draw attention to the universality of astrology since, whatever the scepticism of the modern West, (and this is less deeply rooted than may appear at first glance), in the world beyond western boundaries astrology flourishes now much as it did in earlier times. Approaching the subject with scorn or limp curiosity is therefore to deprive oneself of an opportunity to watch the human mind grapple with important questions of existence and meaning and relationship, and to deny oneself the pleasure and instruction of being intrigued.

Some Astrological Terms

Ascendant: The degree or sign of the zodiac rising over the horizon at the time and place of someone's birth.

Aspect: The angular relationship between two planets.

Astrology: The study of the influence of celestial bodies on the earth and its inhabitants.

Conjunction: The close relationship between two planets as they appear in the zodiac.

Constellation: A group of fixed stars supposedly forming a particular picture or pattern.

Exalted: A planet is said to be exalted when its position in the zodiac is such that its influence will operate at its most powerful.

Horoscope: Originally the ascendant, from the eighteenth century the word was increasingly used of the chart itself.

House: One of the twelve sections of the zodiac. Each house represents a particular aspect of life.

Judicial astrology: Astrology which offers an opinion. It may be subdivided into (i) casting and interpreting horoscopes for individuals, based on the querent's time of birth; and (ii) horary, which consists of drawing a chart for the particular moment a question is asked and then interpreting the data with a view to answering that question.

Motion: A planet's movement. A motion may be direct, retrograde, or stationary. 'Retrograde' means that when observed from the earth, a planet appears to reverse its former direction of movement.

Natural astrology: Interpreting the effect of astral influences on natural phenomena such as the weather and agriculture.

Planet: A star which moves rather than remaining fixed. Before the eighteenth century, the planets were considered to be moon, Mercury, Venus, sun, Mars, Jupiter, Saturn. The eighteenth century added Uranus, the nineteenth Neptune, and the twentieth Pluto.

Sign: One of the twelve divisions of the zodiac, each occupied by a particular constellation. The signs in use in the West are Aries, Taurus, Gemini, Cancer, Leo, Virgo, Libra, Scorpio, Sagittarius, Capricorn, Aquarius, and Pisces.

Triplicity: A group of three zodiacal signs governed by one of the elements. Fire = Aries, Leo, Sagittarius. Earth = Taurus, Virgo, Capricorn. Air = Gemini, Libra, Aquarius. Water = Cancer, Scorpio, Pisces.

Zodiac: An imaginary belt running round the earth, occupied by the twelve constellations.

I

The Land Between the Rivers
c.800 BC–c.600 BC: Interpreting Portents

In March 669 BC, King Esarhaddon of Assyria received information from one of his astrologers that Mercury was going to rise the following month. Since the planet was the harbinger of rain and flood, King Esarhaddon would have been anxious to ascertain whether the astrologer's prediction was accurate or not; so he wrote to one of his principal Court astrologers, Ishtar-shumu-eresh, for reassurance on this important point. Such an exchange was common. We have letters from Ishtar-shumu-eresh to the King, answering other queries. For example:

> To the King, my lord, [from] your servant. Good health to the King. May the gods Nab and Marduk bless the King, my lord. The 20th, 22nd, and 15th are good days for taking the oath; [and] We watched for Mars two or three times today, but we did not see it. It has set. Perhaps the King, my lord, will say as follows: 'Is there any ominous sign in the fact that it has set?' I answer, 'There is not.'

Ishtar-shumu-eresh therefore replied to Esarhaddon, dismissing with the words of a proverb the unnamed astrologer's information as a mistake – 'an ignorant one frustrates the judge, an uneducated one makes the mighty worry' – having said which, he went on to make unrelated remarks about Venus. The King, who either read the letter too hastily or listened with only half an ear as it was being read to him, latched on to the passage about Venus and thought that Ishtar-shumu-eresh was telling him that it was Venus, not Mercury, which was rising. Naturally somewhat puzzled by what he thought was this answer to his question about Mercury, Esarhaddon wrote to two other astrologers, Nabu-ahhe-eriba and Balasi, and asked them for their opinion. Nabu-ahhe-eriba was scathing:

> He who wrote to the King, my lord, 'The planet Venus is visible, it is visible in the month Adar, [*the last month of the year*]' is a vile man, an ignoramus, a cheat! And he who wrote to the King, my lord, 'Venus is … rising in the constellation Aries' does not speak the truth either. Venus is not yet visible. Who does anyone so deceitfully send such a report to the King, my lord?

Balasi's reply was equally dismissive:

Regarding the planet Venus about which the King, my lord, wrote to me, 'I am told it has become visible', the man who wrote this to the King, my lord, does not know what he is talking about ... Who is the man who writes so to the King, my lord? I repeat, he does not understand the difference between Mercury and Venus.

Needless to say, Ishtar-shumu-eresh was not going to take peaceably this traducing of his capabilities – a reduction based on the King's mistake, not his own, although naturally it would have been impolitic to point this out. So he met or sought for Nabu-ahhe-eriba in the palace and had an argument with him. The outcome was to some degree satisfactory, for we are told, 'Later at night, they went out and made observations. They saw it [*presumably Mercury*] and were satisfied.' 'All' is an odd word to use of just two people, so it may be that Balasi and perhaps others accompanied them. We should probably not be surprised that the dispute involved Mercury rather than any of the other planets. The first and last visibility of Mercury in the morning and evening, for example, are irregular and asymmetrical in comparison with the other planets, and this makes it very difficult to calculate accurately its heliacal phenomena – Swerdlow with reason calls them 'idiosyncratic' – so we may gather that appearances of the planet could not be predicted with certainty at this period. Astrologers' honour, then, may have been satisfied on this occasion by group scrutiny of the sky, but a Court astrologer's professional life, and with it his livelihood, depended on the reliability of both his observation and his interpretations of astral and planetary signs.

What we learn from this incident, (and it is supported by evidence from elsewhere, too), is that the King was liable to check what his astrologers were telling him by asking for a second opinion – hence, the idea that Court astrologers manipulated their answers to drive forward political agenda of their own is not very convincing – and that there was a hierarchy of experts, with a kind of inner circle at the top, upon whose specialised knowledge the King could feel free and able to call. Members of this inner circle were paid in land, in kind, and in money, although these rewards do not appear to have been generous during the later Assyrian period. 'The Chief Scribe's house is wretched. A donkey wouldn't go in there,' says one cuneiform text. Nevertheless, any reward at all depended on the goodwill of the King, goodwill which scholars tried to maintain by servile flattery such as comparing the King to the god Marduk, and if that goodwill were lost, so was the unhappy courtier. One poor man who had fallen foul of the Court and the King's favour clearly became destitute. He begged his former lord for help on several occasions, but was simply told to go and earn a living by making bricks – 'I am dying for want of food. I am forced to beg like a dog' – but what was his eventual fate we do not know.

So when *Proverbs* said, 'The wrath of a king is as messengers of death', these unfortunate astronomer-astrologers would have known exactly how true that was; and indeed we can see for ourselves this danger, recorded in the book of *Daniel*. In 624 BC, the Babylonian King Nebuchadnezzar was troubled by bad dreams. He therefore called together his Court magicians, astrologers, sorcerers, and Chaldaeans, (a special class of priest-seer learned in astrology, divination, and magic), and ordered them to interpret his dream. Naturally they asked him for details, but the King refused to comply, saying that they were to tell him what his dream was and then interpret it. They protested, of course, that they were unable to see into his mind, whereupon the King mentioned the penalty for failure – 'You will be cut in pieces, and your houses will be made a dunghill' – a threat he nearly carried out, prevented only by the timely intervention of Daniel, a man 'ten times better than all the magicians and astrologers who were in his realm'. Daniel had been brought up at Nebuchadnezzar's Court in company with others who were 'skilful in all wisdom, and cunning in knowledge, and understanding science'. He it was who proved able to do as the King wanted and was richly rewarded in consequence. (*Daniel* 2.1–48; 1.3–6, 20). Boys who showed an aptitude for the occult sciences, then, might be spotted, perhaps by the equivalent of talent-scouts, and sent for training in noble or even royal households, after which a potentially splendid career awaited them, provided they did not make mistakes. Errors, whether of ability or judgement, not to mention Court intrigue and the jealousy of one's colleagues, led straight to poverty.

Royal and professional preoccupation with celestial phenomena in particular is characteristic of all early societies, and it seems as though it was not until the advent of Judaism and Christianity, as Fr. Henri de Lubac wrote, that humankind was liberated from the dictates of Fate. For if human beings enjoyed a direct link with their Creator who was also the creator of everything else, including the stars and planets, then they were no longer in thrall to those 'countless Powers – gods, spirits, demons – who pinioned human life in the net of their tyrannical wills,' and indeed were no longer dependent on that small educated élite whose mastery of mathematics, astronomy, and astrology enabled them not only to interpret the will of those disconcerting and awful Powers, but also, by reason of their foreknowledge of that will, to circumvent it or turn it to the state's advantage. Astrology in this pre-Biblical period was thus, to use Nicolas Campion's phraseology, more managerial than predictive. But De Lubac's pertinent observation points to only two phases in the history of astrology. Once the predictive aspect of the science – and here I use the word in its Latin sense, 'branch of knowledge' – had become the dominant interest for both astrologers and their clients, astrology was subject to attack in Christian Europe and the various Muslim countries, principally on the grounds that it seemed to place limits upon the absolute power and will of God; and then in the West, emerging acceptance among the learned classes of a post-Copernican solar system threw astrology into a degree of confusion with which it struggled to cope, a confusion not made less by the later discoveries of Uranus, Neptune, and Pluto which then had to be accommodated into the celestial system on which prediction rested. Accommodate, however, it did and managed to do so successfully, quite after the fashion of any of the other sciences. These, one may note, operated and still do operate, at least in theory, under a series of challenges to their assumptions, which cause them to discard those data which no longer seem to be valid and to adopt others, modified or entirely new, which appear to answer the combative reservations. Since astrology was doing just the same, it will probably be as well for the historian and his or her readers to regard astrology right from the start as a coherent, rational science; otherwise its history will appear to be little more than an exercise in the study of a quaint byway of superseded misapprehensions, an interpretation of this historico-scientific endeavour which could not be further from the truth. [1]

We should perhaps begin at the beginning and ask ourselves why earlier peoples thought that detailed scrutiny of the sky, especially at night, was both potentially useful and significant. The sun and moon, of course, obtrude upon one's consciousness in very particular ways which very quickly make clear the existence of patterns in their behaviour. The sun's rays may be hot in summer and cooler in winter; daylight is longer in summer than in winter; without sunshine crops and fruits ripen slowly, or do not ripen at all – pattern and consequence equally noticeable. The moon appears to alter its shape from crescent to gibbous to full and back again according to a regular sequence; sometimes it can be seen in ghostly form during the day; it gives no heat, but rather presides over, if it does not actually cause, a coolness and a chilly exudation from plants and earth, which seems to last till dawn. Unlike the sun which gives light even though its face be hidden by cloud, the moon illuminates only when its face is seen. Otherwise, the night hours protract themselves in impenetrable darkness which starlight cannot lift. Pattern and consequence again, but with variation; and variation also occurs with the appearance of comets or the temporary disappearance, partial or complete, of the sun or moon during an eclipse. Human life, too, has its patterns and variations. We are born and live and die: that is a pattern. Variations occur when we fall ill or a life is cut short by accident, murder, or war. A question is therefore almost bound to arise sooner or later. Do the regularities of the heavenly bodies run parallel with the regularities of human existence, and is there some kind of correspondence between irregularities in the movements or appearance of those heavenly bodies and irregularities in the lives of human beings?

Such posited analogies between the stars and planets and the human condition naturally lead to intense and detailed scrutiny of the heavens, and to keeping such records of astral and planetary movements or appearances coincidental with notable events on earth as will serve to forewarn or foretell their reoccurrence. Keeping records supplements living memory and allows traditional expertise to be passed on and supplemented in its turn, and expertise, of course, implies the existence of experts. Watching the heavens night after night takes time; being able to write, or having secretaries at one's command, suggests that one is to some degree privileged, a member of an élite among one's society, with abilities beyond the norm, abilities which have been nurtured and developed; and this, in conjunction with the leisure to spend long periods of time in looking at the sky or checking past records of celestial events supposes a person and a group of individuals enabled by wealth or social position to develop an expertise and so belong to a particular profession, that of astronomer-astrologer. Until quite late in the modern period, these two were not distinguished from one another. Astronomy looked at the sky and recorded and measured what it saw there; astrology took that information and interpreted its significance in relation to other heavenly bodies and to earth and its inhabitants. Astronomers undertook their scrutinies in order to provide material for interpretation; astrologers used the material to produce other exegeses. The two therefore walk hand in hand for much of the history we are discussing, the one implying the other, and we should not make the mistake of separating them, or assume that one is more respectable or reliable or rational than the other.

Still, the astronomico-astrological infancy of this science reveals certain limitations in what it could, or indeed wanted to do. Watching the sky was useful for prognosticating weather, essential in a largely agricultural society, and an aspect of astrology which never disappeared, as farmers' calendars from the Middle Ages onwards confirm. But the sky itself was a parchment on which the gods and goddesses wrote or signed their pleasure and displeasure, and in consequence astrologers' scrutiny of it was inextricably bound up with state religion and the lookout for those omens which would indicate the will or mood of the principal deities. Now here it is important to recall that in ancient Mesopotamian belief there was more than one heaven. Nearest the earth was the sky, the lower heaven, while above that, according to two first-millennium tablets, there was a middle heaven in which lived 300 deities known collectively as Igigi who had once descended to earth to grow food for other gods who lived upon earth, but had soon grown tired of it and returned to their celestial place. Above that middle heaven was the abode of An (Babylonian Anu), one of the three great divine essences of the cosmos, a highest heaven remote from earth and yet not altogether detached from it. So, as one can see from this heavenly construction, the Mesopotamian universe is an ordered one, that order being maintained and directed by the gods, as is clear from a phrase describing some of them as 'the ones who draw the cosmic designs', and it is these divinities who communicate with human beings through the celestial phenomena 'written' upon the third and lowest heaven, that of the sky. In later Babylonian theogonies, however, the god Marduk was said to have settled the Igogi in the uppermost heaven and occupied the middle heaven himself, the floor of his heaven being composed of a type of blue stone called *saggilmud* in Akkadian – perhaps lapis lazuli or at any rate a stone a similar colour – and this floor in turn formed the arching blue sky of earth, upon which Marduk inscribed the planets and the stars.

Sumerian and later Babylonian astronomy-astrology was thus intimately interconnected with religion. As Francesca Rochberg observes, 'It is unintelligible to speak of the scribes' study and understanding of the phenomena, natural and invented, as distinct and separate from their study and understanding of the divine.' The scribes she mentions include those experts to whom we alluded earlier, observers of the heavens and recorders of phenomena both there and upon earth; for anything which happened in either, be it comet or human birth, eclipse or epidemic, were potential messages from the gods who used the stars and planets as their messengers. But if the gods could send messages of their own free accord, they could also surely send signs and omens in answer to human questions posed directly to them; and these signs did not necessarily need to be restricted to the heavens, but could be observable from the behaviour of birds or animals or, indeed, humans themselves. As a Babylonian diviner's manual puts it, 'The signs in the sky, just as those on earth give us signals.' Thus two broad types of interpreter began to develop, one specialising in the interpretation of omens, (called a 'scribe' or a 'scholar'), reliant upon reason or deduction to arrive at his conclusions: the other able to communicate with the gods directly, (called a 'prophet' or a 'seer'). Neither, of course, would work or be allowed to work in an ivory tower. Astronomer-astrologers could be too useful to the state to permit them the indulgence, had they even thought of wanting it, of pursuing their art for its own sake. Mesopotamian rulers, regarded as guarantors of regularity in life and its events here on earth, needed to know the will of the gods and to be forewarned of their displeasure, and hence their possible intention to disrupt or throw into chaos that desirable earthly stability; and so the most skilled astronomer-astrologers became part of the political establishment, consulted, if not quite at every turn, at least very frequently, so that danger and turmoil might be foreseen and thus circumvented. [2]

There were various records these experts might consult. Some gave simple prognostications relating to basic, but important, human endeavours:

> In the month Arahsamna, 11th day, Venus disappeared in the east. Two months […] days it stayed away in the sky. In the month Tebeti, […]th day, Venus became visible in the west. The harvest of the land will prosper; [or, more ominously], When the planet Jupiter turns his face when rising towards the west, and you can see the face of the sky, and no wind blows, there will be a famine and disaster will rule.

In each case, we see the astronomer-astrologer exercising both parts of his craft, observation and then interpretation, and we may also note the slow, painstaking construction of a tradition which saw the disintegration of several empires and dynasties – Mesopotamian, Hittite, Kassite, Elamite – before Assyria rose to take their place, (although not without its own later disorder and territorial diminution), a tradition which eventually produced the eighth-century BC great series of omen tablets known as the *Enuma Anu Enlil*, ('In the days of Anu and Enlil'), containing about 7,000 omens 'designed to cover every possible eventuality'.

The collection begins with a brief statement about the creation of the heavens and the earth, which shows clearly the fundamental view of the place and movements of the celestial bodies. The latter were divinely fixed, and stable in their motions, and in consequence any deviation from that regularity could be interpreted as an omen, that is to say, a message to humankind from the controlling deities:

> When Anu, Enlil, and Ea, the great gods, in their sure counsel had fixed the design of heaven and earth, they assigned to the hands of the great gods [the duty] to form the day well [and] to renew the month for mankind to behold. They saw the sun god within the gate whence he departs [and] in between heaven and earth they took counsel faithfully.

Simo Parpola summarised the contents of these tablets:

> primarily as a collection of signals sent by the gods to the King. They sent these signs in order to affect the conduct of the King, the actions that he should take, and these signs were there for this single purpose only – that the gods could express their pleasure or dis-pleasure with the conduct of the King.

The signs or omens described thereafter are distributed among seventy cuneiform tablets, the majority of which tend to note features or conjunctions or events which take place under the dominance of a particular planet. Thus, tablets 1–14 deal with the appearance of the moon and 15–22 with her eclipses. Tablets 23 and 24 have as their subject the appearance of the sun, 26–28 the sun's rising, (which may also be the subject matter of tablet 25), and 31–37 the sun's eclipses. Tablet 56 centres on Mars, (as may also 57 and 58), tablets 59–62 on Venus, and 64 and 65 on Jupiter. Others give warning of clouds, lightning and thunder, the fixed stars, (that is, those which do not wander about the sky, as the planets do), and certain constellations, such as the Pleiades. Now, while it is true that the sky was considered to be a book whose contents related principally to the King, this is by no means true of every observation. For example:

> If Venus becomes visible at daylight: men's wives will not stay with their husbands, but run after their men; if Venus rises in the morning and does not set: the Lamastu demon will seize infants; if the dawn Venus rises at sunrise, and the nightfall [Venus] at sunset: the father will expel his son, and the mother will bar her door to her daughter. [3]

But political thrust, however important to readings of the sky, was thus not the only impetus behind astronomy-astrology, and indeed one can see it gradually making room for more general significations relating to the people as a whole. This is partly because broader applications of the divine messages were a natural development inherent in the nature of such readings, and partly because astrology was not the only divinatory science among these ancient peoples. It had to contend with all kinds of other omens whose meanings were clearly directed at everyone regardless of rank or status. The appearance of newborn children, for example, could be revealing of individual fates. 'If a woman gives birth to a male dwarf – troubles: the house of the man will be scattered'; 'if a woman gives birth to a blind child – the land will be disturbed: the house of the man will not prosper'; 'if a woman gives birth to a deaf child – that house will prosper outside its city'. Extispicy, (examining the entrails of a ritually slaughtered animal or bird), and hepatoscopy, (examination of a liver similarly extracted), were complex divinatory techniques which took into account markings, colour, and abnormalities of these body-parts, and interpreted them for the inquirer. 'If on the right side of the liver there are two finger-shaped outgrowths … it is an omen of a period of anarchy'. But if the reading proved thus ominous, suitable prayers could be offered to mitigate the effects of the unhappy prognostication:

> You great gods of the night, whom Anu and Enlil have created, you efface the evil signs that have arisen [for me]. You remove from the man's house the ill-portending features that occurred in [my] extispicy. Remove from me the evil sign that occurred in [my] house. Let that evil pass me by, and I shall sing your praises as long as I live.

Dreams, too, provided opportunities for the gods to communicate with human beings:

> If a man, while he sleeps, dreams that the entire town falls upon him and that he cries out and no one hears him: this man will have good luck attached to him. If a man, while he sleeps, dreams that the entire town falls upon him and he cries out and someone hears him: this man will have bad luck attached to him.

Almost anything, in fact, could serve as a vehicle for omens – the surface of oil poured upon water or water poured upon oil in a divining bowl, the behaviour of smoke rising from an incense-brazier, the flight of birds or insects, the unexpected or unguarded remark overheard in the street. So astrology was by no means the only, or at first even the pre-eminent way for humans to discern what the gods were trying to tell him. Slowly, however, it demoted extispicy which had long been the preferred learned divinatory technique, and from that time onwards its own special position among the occult sciences was assured. [4]

Now, it is noteworthy that although the astronomer-astrologers of the Land between the Rivers knew perfectly well the difference between the planets (which they called 'wild sheep' because they wandered about and kept changing their positions in the sky) and 'fixed' stars, not every planet played as important a role as the others when it came to divination. Here, the moon, the sun, and Venus appear to have been considered the planets of particular significance. Between them they account for 46 of 66 tablets of the *Enuma Anu Enlil*, (nos 67–70 having no dominant identified as yet). The moon, or rather the moon god, was masculine, father of the divine twins, Venus and the sun, and may have had different names when he was full and crescent. It was not only the appearance of the moon which was important, though. Its relationship with other heavenly bodies was also significant. 'If the moon keeps setting while the sun rises,' wrote one astrologer to the King, 'the reign of the King will come to an end. There will be years of struggle and his country will experience severe famine'. The astrologer Mār-Ishtar noted, 'If, at the appearance of the moon, Scorpio stands by its right horn, in that year locusts will rise and consume the harvest,' and Ishtar-shumu-eresh, whom we have met before, reporting that the planet Jupiter stood behind the moon, quoted a relevant observation from the records that this predicted hostility in the country. Should the King have any doubts about this, he added, 'the side of the moon should be shown to one of the eunuchs who has a sharp eye'.

Eclipses, of course, were highly significant, although not necessarily worrying. 'The King should not be afraid of this eclipse,' wrote the astrologer Balasi, a judgement his colleague Nabu-ahhe-erība endorsed, adding that the eclipse in question threatened another land altogether. Still, precautions would be no bad thing, so Mār-Ishtar advised the King to have apotropaic rituals performed, along with chants, and ceremonies designed to ward off malaria and plague. [5] One of the apotropaic rituals entailed having a substitute 'king' apparently die in place of the genuine and his heir. A burial chamber was prepared and the substitute king, along with a substitute queen, buried with all due rites, as well as many other ceremonies intended to make sure the real king survived any possible crisis. This avoidance ritual did not mean that the substitutes actually had to die. A letter from the priest Akkullānu makes it clear that statues could be used as substitutes instead of people, although it was also possible, under similar circumstances, that the gods would take the life of someone else in place of the king. 'If the planet Jupiter is present in the eclipse, all is well with the King. A noble dignitary will die in his stead.' Sure enough, on the occasion which caused Akkullānu to write to the King, less than a month passed by after the eclipse before the Chief Judge of the kingdom was dead.

Clearly, then, the appearance (or disappearance) and movement of celestial bodies was of first importance to kings, who required their astronomer-astrologers to offer regular commentaries on such events. Nabu-ahhe-eriba said in a letter:

As regards the report on the lunar eclipse about which the King, my lord, wrote to me, they used to receive and introduce all astrological reports into the presence of the father of the King, my lord. Afterwards, on the river bank, a man whom the father of the King, my lord, knew, used to read them to the King … Nowadays it should be done as best suits the King, my lord.

These reports, however, may have been delivered only when the time for hearing them was propitious. Nabu-ahhe-eriba wrote:

Since this is a gloomy day, I did not send the introductory blessing. The eclipse swept from the eastern quadrant and settled over the entire western quadrant of the moon. The planets Jupiter and Venus were present during the eclipse until it cleared. With the King, my lord, all is well. It is evil of the Westland. Tomorrow I shall send the King, my lord, a report concerning the lunar eclipse.

Why not send it immediately? Was it not yet fully prepared? This sounds somewhat inefficient and would surely not impress a monarch who was quite capable of expressing his displeasure in ways which might be most uncomfortable. If the day were ill-omened, this would explain any delay in sending a full report, and if inefficiency was indeed the reason for the astrologer's tardiness, it could be covered by this plausible excuse.

But not all mentions of eclipses were monitory. Some were merely observational in tone – 'a lunar eclipse took place on 14th of the month Simannu during the morning watch. It started in the south of the moon and cleared up in the south. Its right side was eclipsed' – and astronomer-astrologers were clearly in the habit of communicating such observations to one another. 'As regards the lunar eclipse about which the King, my lord, wrote to me, it was observed in the cities of Akkad, Barsip, and Nippur. What we had seen in Akkad corresponded to the other observations.' Observations of solar eclipses seem to be fairly unworried – 'A solar eclipse of two fingers' magnitude took place during sunrise. There is no apotropaic ritual against it. It is not like a lunar eclipse. I'll write down the relevant interpretation and send it to you' – and indeed frequently mention of a solar eclipse is made merely to say that it has not happened. But whether this non-event came as a relief or was being recorded as a fairly neutral observation is not altogether clear from the often fragmentary nature of the cuneiform tablets.

Mention of the planets offers the same mixture of astronomical impartiality. 'Venus has now taken a nice course'; 'the planet Venus will reach the constellation Virgo'; 'the planet Mercury … is bright, clothed with brilliance'; 'after Jupiter has become visible, I shall write again to the King, my lord. I am waiting for it. It will take this whole month'; 'the planet Mars has gone on into the constellation Capricorn, halted there, and is at present shining very brightly'. We also hear evidence of the difficulties people encountered when looking for the elusive Mercury. 'As regards the planet Mercury about which the King, our lord, wrote to us, "I have heard it can be seen in Babylon", he who wrote this to the King, our lord, may really have observed it. His eye, however, must have fallen on it'. [*That is, he must have seen it by chance*]. 'We ourselves have kept watch but have not observed it.' But at any moment the astrologer will take over and interpret the planetary or astral sighting. 'When the planet Mars comes out of the constellation Scorpio, turns, and re-enters Scorpio,' wrote Ishtar-shumu-eresh, 'its interpretation is this' – and he proceeds to quote part of an oral tradition to say that the King should not venture out of doors at this time because the omen is evil. This advice he reinforces with an observation he describes as 'uncanonical', that is, which did not come from the official records. 'When Mars turns from the head of the constellation Leo and afflicts Cancer and Gemini, its interpretation is this: the end of the reign of the King of the Westland.'

The remains of a Babylonian astrologer's handbook pull together the various aspects of observation and interpretation in a manner clearly intended to make the tablets useful as a short reference work or teaching guide, and consist of two lists of omens and a set of instructions for their user. 'If in the town or its surroundings one observes a strange-looking bird which has a beard like a human being, and a mouth, and if it is perched on tall legs or flying around, and if it opens its mouth and words come out'; 'if the sky is constantly covered with a haze'; 'if the planet Venus becomes stationary in the morning and on its critical dates'. This mixture of omens, some natural, some meteorological, some astronomical, is not accompanied by what the individual omens mean. For interpretations, the astrologer must obviously rely on other texts, or his own memory of what tradition has to say about such omens, or his own intuition. But then the manual makes a number of general statements which are designed to be helpful: 'Sky and earth both produce portents. Although they may appear separately, they are not separate, because the sky and earth are related. A sign which portends evil in the sky is evil on earth as well, and one which portends evil on earth is evil in the sky.' Next come practical instructions. 'When you look up a sign [*in the omen catalogues*], either one in the sky or one on earth, and if it is confirmed that that sign has an evil portent, (referring, for example, to an enemy or disease or famine), check the date of the sign. If no other sign occurs to counteract or annul [*its evil aspect or effect*], you cannot make it pass by. Its evil consequences cannot be removed and will happen.' But, says the text, if one wishes to try to dispel those evil effects, one must undertake detailed research to find out the exact state of the stars and planets in order to determine whether one's forecast is indeed accurate or not. There are twelve months and 360 days in a year.

> Check in the records for the timings of the disappearances, the visibilities, and the first appearances of the stars ... the first appearance of the sun and the moon in the months Addaru and Ulūlu, the risings and first appearances of the moon as observed each month. Watch the opposition of the Pleiades and the moon. All this will give you a proper answer.

After this, having ascertained the validity or otherwise of his observations, the astrologer cam presumably give appropriate advice about whether it will be worthwhile arranging apotropaic rituals or manufacturing an amulet or offering prayers to particular deities or not. [6]

The mathematical achievements producing the observations which make these interpretations possible are quite remarkable, sufficient, indeed, to induce Swerdlow to say:

[The Babylonians] have left no record of their theoretical analyses and discussions, but to judge from the works they have left us, the Diaries and ephemerides, the goal-year texts and almanacs, the discussions of two scribes of *Enuma Anu Enlil* contained more rigorous science than the speculations of twenty philosophers speaking Greek, not even Aristotle excepted.

The 'diaries' to which he refers are more or less daily accounts, dating back to the eighth century BC, of celestial and meteorological observations, along with remarks on noteworthy events here on earth; the 'almanacs' record the positions of the moon, the sun, the other planets, particular stars such as Sirius, Antares, and Vega, and constellations – Aries, Cancer, Virgo, Scorpio, are noted – as they appear on the first day of each month throughout the year; and an astronomical compendium known as the *Mul Apin* catalogued such phenomena as the names of certain stars and constellations, their rising and setting in relation to the sun, stars in the path of the moon, appearances and disappearances, visibility and invisibility of the five planets apart from the moon and sun.

All these texts, and several more surviving, give clear evidence of an orderly ancient approach to observing the sky and movements or signs within it, and this order took the form of dividing the sky into regions of equal size (to facilitate observation) and creating an imaginary belt, the zodiac, around the earth, extending about 8° north and south of the ecliptic, (the annual path of the sun relative to the fixed stars). The zodiac itself was divided into twelve equal parts known as 'signs', and to begin with, it was the passage of the moon through these which was held to be particularly significant. Only after the rise of Greek as the international language of astrology after the fourth century BC did the passage of the sun supplant that of the moon in horoscopic importance. It is thus a lunar zodiac which is presumed in the records of the *Mul Apin* with a list of eighteen constellations which 'stood in the path of the moon', twelve being those we now designate by Latin names – Taurus, Gemini, Cancer, Leo, Virgo, Libra, Scorpio, Sagittarius, Capricorn, Aquarius, Pisces, and Aries. Groups of fixed stars (constellations) and individually moving planets, then, were observed in relation to these divisions of the sky and the zodiacal belt, and the relationships thus created used to facilitate interpretation of the omens stemming from them. [7]

To Mesopotamian astronomer-astrologers, therefore, we owe detailed scrutiny of the sky and its heavenly bodies, sophisticated mathematical mapping of the location and behaviour of these observed phenomena, along with their periodicities and variants, and calculation and prognostication of events by means of their accompanying omens. This last, prognostication, is important. If mathematics could become the key to unlocking the future movements of stars and planets, and observers could predict, with greater or lesser accuracy, what those movements, appearances, visibilities, and invisibilities were likely to be, the intimate connection between the gods and celestial bodies would dissolve. Instead of being signs of divine will or anger or favour, or mirroring in heaven events here upon earth, the planets and stars would themselves become major fountainheads of influence, (quite literally sources of 'in-flowings'), dire or benign, and this in turn would mean that celestial phenomena would no longer be seen as messages directed principally to kings and states, but rather as sources of potentiality in their own right, transmitting their characteristic qualities to humankind in general or to each individual from the moment of birth or conception. [8]

As always, however, the workings of astronomy-astrology were complex and would never yield themselves to the kind of rigorous self-contained categorisation beloved of post-industrial science. Even if, for example, the overt ties between deities and heavenly bodies were considered broken, or at least considerably weakened, the planets continued to derive their supposed characteristics and powers from their original association with particular gods and goddesses – the moon with Sin, the sun with Shamash, Mercury with Nabu, Venus with Ishtar, Mars with Nergal, Jupiter with Marduk, Saturn with Ninurta – and while these divinities may have had circumscribed lives, their names passing into history as the empires of their worshippers fell to conquerors, certain of those original associations persisted regardless. So, since Marduk was (or became) king of the gods, Jupiter (and through his influence, the Jupiterian personality) embodies those functions and provinces considered characteristic of kingship – authority, law, expansion, intellect, religion, philosophy, generosity – and these remain to this day the positive astrological associations of that planet. Moreover, if we think of one activity much influenced by astrology, namely medicine, we can see further evidence of this ambiguity about the exact origin of powers, causes, and effects. Medicines often had to be administered at certain times of day, 'facing the sun', or exposed to the stars overnight to be irradiated or influenced by them in some way. 'If a man's left temple hurts him and his left eye is swollen and tears, you crush dates, Telmun-dates, *ašû*-plant, and cedar resin in myrrh oil. You expose it overnight to the stars. In the morning, without eating, you daub his eyes with it,' or, 'You expose the emetic overnight to the stars. He drinks it and will vomit.'

So who or what causes such irradiation to be effective? Is it a god or goddess, or is it the star itself? In some instances there can be no doubt that it is the action of a deity which imparts the curative action. Thus, the Goat constellation (Lyra) is the heavenly manifestation of Gula, the goddess of healing, and we find one prescription which tells the physician to leave a concoction of herbs, aromatics, and beer to stand overnight in front of the Goat star, (that is, the goddess Gula), while another text gives the prayer to be addressed to an unnamed star. 'You, star, who illuminates … the midst of heaven, who surveys all four regions, I, N son of N, prostrate myself before you this night. Decide my case. Give me a verdict. Let these herbs wipe away the evil which affects me.' On the other hand, there are texts which describe illness as 'raining down from the stars', and which attribute specific ailments to specific planets, such as those of the spleen to Jupiter and those of the kidneys to Mars, and in these texts both the malign and the curative actions seem to belong to the planets or constellations both named and unnamed. [9]

These ambiguities over the exact nature of the source of planetary and astral power were transmitted along with the rest of Mesopotamia's astronomico-astrological tradition to other lands and later centuries, and one can hear echoes of them in Mediaeval and early modern controversies over the relationship between God and the stars, the balance between God's will and the inclination to certain forms of behaviour caused (or not caused) by the influence of the stars and free will and predestination. Indeed, they summarise the essential paradox of Babylonian astrology. On the one hand, the stars and planets were signs of the whims, the moods, the purposes of gods and goddesses, and were therefore likely to be unstable, if not in their motions, at least in their meanings. On the other, it was clear that the stars and planets appeared to obey some kind of regular laws, since they and their passages across the sky formed consistent patterns, and their movements were therefore largely predictable. Was the universe essentially stable or unstable? Here was a question of fundamental importance apparently passed over by the Babylonians, but which Greek (one should say 'Greek-speaking') philosophers took up and mulled over with momentous consequences for the future of astrology.

2

Greece & Rome c.600 BC–50 BC: The Religious Zodiac

Swerdlow's comment about the superiority of the Babylonian mathematical and observational sciences over Greek philosophical musings on the nature of the universe may be provocative, but it is undoubtedly true in so far as Greek theories and discoveries were not constructed or made *in vacuo* but depended, often heavily, on the work of their Middle Eastern predecessors and contemporaries, although by the fifth and fourth centuries BC Greek speculations were making their way into the huge expanse of the Persian Empire, aided by the growing use of Greek as a lingua franca in whole swathes of those dominions. If we take the vexed question of who invented the zodiac, for example, it has been argued that Oenopides of Chios in about the middle of the fifth century BC introduced the notion of the zodiac to the Greeks, several decades earlier than the appearance of the twelve zodiacal signs in a Babylonian text, and that in consequence this notion spread from the Greeks to the Babylonians, not the other way round. What made Oenopides think of it? Controversy among certain sixth and fifth century Greek philosophers about the structure and shape of the cosmos, to which Oenopides, an excellent geometer, made more than one significant contribution. In favour of a Babylonian origin, however, it has been suggested that 'before the introduction of the zodiac, the Babylonians used a number of constellations to locate bodies in the sky … By the fifth century BC this had been reduced to 12 constellations. Finally, shortly before 400 BC these 12 constellations were replaced by the 12 equal divisions of the ecliptic into the signs of the zodiac', while the twelve months of the Babylonian year were so intimately connected with those signs that in a number of texts the name of the month and the name of the sign were actually interchangeable.

Clearly both Greek and Babylonian concepts of the zodiac were, relatively speaking, late in making their appearance, either not long before Plato or during his lifetime, (late fifth – early fourth century BC), well within a period of mutual interchange between the Greek mainland and islands and the western coasts of the Persian Empire. So the concept could have flowed either way, and attribution of its 'discovery' could justly be awarded to either civilisation or both. What needs to be borne in mind – a much more important point than who invented what first – is that the word zodiac can and does refer to more than one such idea. The ecliptic represents the sun's path across the sky and is marked by a number of constellations, groupings of stars which appear to be fixed in certain patterns to which are given names – the Plough, Orion, the Pleiades, and so on. The sun's path round the ecliptic was probably divided first of all into four – the four seasons marked off from each other by the two equinoxes of spring and autumn, and the two solstices of midsummer and midwinter. The Mesopotamians were more interested in the moon than the sun, and so noted particularly the constellations which lay in the path of the moon as it travelled from horizon to horizon. In consequence, the word 'zodiac' refers both to a division of space and to a division of time, and is applied to what became standardised as twelve sectors dividing the ecliptic and also to the twelve divisions or 'months' of the year.

Now, differences between types of zodiac creep in depending on when these months and their corresponding constellations are judged to begin. Thus, 20 or 21 March marks the day of the vernal equinox when day and night are of equal length, and on this day the sun is said to be entering the sign of Aries, that is, the division of the zodiac associated with that constellation. Aries is followed by Taurus (20 April – 21 May), and Taurus by Gemini (21 May – 21 June), and so forth until the sun has entered and traversed all twelve signs in months which vary in length between twenty-nine and thirty-one days. This is the so-called 'tropical' zodiac which recognises twelve temporal divisions of roughly equal length, but also takes into account that its starting-point, the vernal equinox, moves slowly backwards through the constellations at the rate of $1°$ in 72 years and that therefore the tropical longitudes of the fixed stars also move at the same rate – hence its name. This was the form of the zodiac adopted by Greek and Roman astrologers. Astronomers view things differently and, while allowing the same twelve constellations or signs, create 'months' of unequal length: Aries = 27 days, Taurus = 38, Gemini = 30, and so on, which means that their divisions of the zodiac are also unequal. The 'sidereal' zodiac, however, as opposed to the tropical or astronomical, employed exactly equal divisions – twelve months of 30 days each, twelve constellations each $30°$ long – and this was the zodiac used or preferred by the Babylonians.[1]

What, then, caused the Greeks to switch to the tropical zodiac, and was the change advantageous to astrology or not? It is generally agreed that the Greeks benefited from Babylonian and Assyrian advances in both astronomical and astrological speculation – they borrowed, for example, Babylonian methods of calculating planetary positions – and, to go back even further, we can see that Homer's verses in the *Iliad* describing the constellations which decorated Achilles' shield were taken straight from a Babylonian hymn to the gods of night. Nevertheless, whereas in Mesopotamia the stars were identified with deities and treated as manifestations of them, the Greeks believed quite the opposite and kept their divinities earthbound and their stars in the sky, so that their stars were never worshipped or placated or cajoled as were those of the Land between the Rivers, in spite of the fact that several Greek myths contain personified cosmological or stellar components: the sun as Helios, the sun's light as Apollo, the moon as Selene, the dawn as Eos, and Phosphoros and Hesperos as Venus just before sunrise and just after sunset respectively. What a number of Greeks from the eighth to the fifth century devoted their attention to was speculation, based on current and earlier theories, about the structure of the universe and the manner of its working, their speculation being balanced and informed by close observation. They envisaged the cosmos as a sphere whose poles, tropics, equator, and ecliptic could be measured and mapped, thus giving it a specific conceptual form from which it could be visualised and described in mathematical terms; and yet in spite of the attractions provided by the geometry of this coherent model, its relative simplicity was intellectually insufficient and gave rise to questions which may be divided very broadly into two groups. First, is there a single source from which or from whom everything is produced and to which everything will return? (Anaximander). Secondly, is the observable cosmos real and knowable, or an illusion and unknowable? (Xenophon Philosophus). From these further grew further questions. If one accepts it as real and knowable, how is it ordered and what kind of relationship does humanity either in general or individually have with this order? (Heraclitus of Ephesus). Order implies harmony which in turn implies mathematical proportion. (Pythagoras). What is the physical structure underlying this order and harmony? Fire or water, earth or air? Or could it be a balance between all four? (Empedocles).

These speculations and their conclusions were pulled together and given coherent theoretical form by Plato and Aristotle during the fifth and fourth centuries BC. Plato argued for a universe which was intelligent and ordered, whose intelligence stemmed from its Prime Cause, God, and its order from its inherent stillness and stability. But the observable world of phenomena is unstable and, in the light of divine realities, an illusion, which means that knowledge gained by observation of its phenomena is likely to be unreliable. Nevertheless, the stars and planets do reveal something of the invisible, intelligible world which lies beyond or is concealed by the illusory world, since the stars maintain exactly the same positions in relation to each other, (even though they seem to circle the earth once a day), and thus demonstrate after their fashion that motionlessness which is characteristic of perfect cosmic order; and the planets, (while moving in a less orderly manner than the fixed stars, as their name 'wanderers' indicates), still travel regularly from east to west and so reveal and demonstrate a little of that same harmonious order. So together the stars and planets act as a kind of bridge between divine stability and regularity, and non-divine instability and chaos. God, then, being the First Cause, the stars and planets act as His ministers, revealing truths not only about the nature of Heaven, but also about humanity itself; for 'when He had compounded the whole [universe], He divided it into souls equal in number to the stars, and each individual soul He assigned to one star … [and] explained to them the nature of the universe and told them the laws which had been allotted to [the stars]'. (*Timaeus* 41D–E). Before it was born, each soul chose a life and then, after having its choice ratified and woven by two of the Fates, fell asleep and dropped down Creation to its birth, descending through the planetary spheres as it went. So, in the words of Nicolas Campion, 'every human being contains something of the divine, is made of the same stuff as the rest of the universe, and is linked to a star'.

One essential contrast between the world of God, the Prime Mover, and the worlds below consists of the difference between perfection and imperfection signified by varying degrees of motion. God's world is perfect and therefore motionless. Once motion sets in, perfection begins to be lost, for motion implies change and therefore deviation, more or less, from perfection. The planets illustrate this. Saturn, the slowest of the planets, is less imperfect than Mercury which moves so quickly in the sky, while the sun and moon which not only move even more rapidly but change their appearances, too, are more imperfect even than Mercury, although the earth, which is stable, seems to contradict this proposition. The problem presented by its apparent motionlessness was, in fact, never fully resolved although, since the surface of the earth is so subject to change from the seasons of the year, the variations in climate, the rise and fall of empires, and so on, it may be said that the earth actually typifies motion, change, and instability, and does so to such an extent that it almost embodies the notion of imperfection. [2]

But it is to Aristotle that we owe a clear theory of causation stretching from God to humanity. In his cosmology, a more or less spherical earth lies motionless at the centre of a universe round which rotates the perpetually-moving sky. This cosmos can be divided into two regions: celestial, which extends from the orbit of the moon outwards to the extremities of the universe, and terrestrial, which occupies the space between the moon's orbit and the earth. Everything within the celestial region is perfect, immutable, incorruptible, orderly, and regular, and is made, not from the four elements of earth, air, fire, and water, but from a fifth, a quintessence known as *aithēr* which has no qualities such as hot, cold, dry, or wet, but remains unchanging. Originally meaning 'pure air', *aithēr* was differentiated from the other elements and given its special function by Plato, after whom Aristotle elaborated the suggestion and posited that *aithēr*'s movements are circular and therefore, because it carries the spheres of the planets and stars within itself, the orbits of celestial bodies must be circular, too. *Aithēr* also affects the nature of these bodies, making them both intelligent and divine, perhaps because they are perfect, immutable, incorruptible, orderly, and regular. Everything within the terrestrial region, by contrast, is the opposite, although movement in this region, for example, is not random but 'natural', in the sense that it is the nature of fire to move upwards and of earth to move downwards. As Simplicius, a sixth-century AD commentator on Aristotle, wrote, 'If a thing has a natural motion, it either moves by nature as the so-called "natural" bodies such as earth and fire do, or as so-called "self-moving" bodies which are moved by the soul within them.' So were stars and planets lifeless bodies being carried round mechanically by the movement of the *aithēr*, or did they, as Plato maintained, possess immanent souls which consciously directed that movement? It is a question to which Aristotle did not provide a satisfactory answer, at least not in his treatise *De caelo* ('The Universe') which contains his fullest expression of arguments formulated during a personal research programme which did not remain static or reach a final conclusion.

Taking into account his other expressed views and conjectures, however, we may tentatively say that for him the universe was a purposeful organism and the planets signs of the way an individual might have his or her potentiality and function revealed. While Plato's astrology gave humanity the means to co-operate with the Divine and provided, (as did Babylonian astrology), ways of recognising the proper days for sacrifice to the gods and the performance of other duties essential to the welfare of the state, Aristotle emphasised the physical relationships between heavenly and terrestrial bodies, and thus gave an intellectual framework to the proposition that humankind is an integral part of the physical universe which has been given its ultimate purpose by the First Cause and Prime Mover, God. Thus, between the fifth and fourth centuries, we find a gradual shift in astronomical-astrological outlook, which fixes within flexible bounds a theoretical model for the universe and its working, and so allows more confident prediction both of future astronomical events such as eclipses and of astrologically-influenced outcomes such as personal behaviour and social characteristics. [3]

We now have to add one more philosophical strand to the weave of astrology during this period. Zeno of Citium moved to Athens from Cyprus in c.311 BC and founded a school of philosophy known as 'Stoicism'. From this, astrology inherited two broad propositions: (i) all things are connected by similarities in their essential qualities, connections later called 'sympathies', a word referring to fellow-feeling between individuals or the harmony produced from a musical instrument by chords vibrating together; and (ii) since the universe is governed by an ordered reason one can call 'God', nothing can happen which is not concordant with that reason, and therefore what happens is fated, in the sense that it takes place in accordance with that sequence of connections or sympathy which is set in motion the moment someone is conceived or born, or something is created. Hence it follows that the universe as a whole obeys one set of divine laws, and this means that the connections or sympathies between the various parts can either be seen or worked out, and that because of this, comment can be made on the individual conditions of those various parts by taking into consideration the nature and type of the sympathy between each one and the rest. Consequently, the stars and planets may be held to have connections with and therefore an influence upon human beings, just as they also have connections with plants and stones and minerals, whose suitability for the cure of illness or protection of humans or animals or dwelling-places can be gauged from the sympathies existent between these objects, the relevant heavenly bodies, and the persons or things to be cured or brought under protection. If neither proposition was entirely original to Stoicism – the first owes much to Plato, the second to astral magic – both nevertheless gave an intellectual coherence to astrological theory and so helped to make astrology attractive as a science, that is, Latin *scientia*, 'a body of knowledge, particularly expert knowledge'. '[The Chaldaeans]', wrote Cicero, referring either to professional astrologers in general or to astrologers from Babylonia-Assyria in particular, 'are thought to have achieved expert knowledge (*scientiam*) of the stars by observing them every day, with the result that it is possible for them to predict what is going to happen to anyone, and with what allotted destiny anyone has been born'. In his book on divination, cast in the form of a dialogue with his brother Quintus who takes the role of supporter of astrology, Cicero the sceptic summarises the traditional arguments of those who accepted the Babylonian-Greek-Stoic theories favouring the science:

> In the star-bearing sphere which is called 'zodiac' in Greek, there is an energy of such a kind that every single part of that sphere moves and changes the sky in a different way according to whatever stars are in these and neighbouring parts [of it] at any time. This energy is set in motion in various ways by those stars which are called 'wanderers' [*planets*]; and when they have come into that part of the sphere in which a person is born, or into that which has some close association or harmony [with it], [astrologers] call these stars in 'trinal' or 'squared' aspect with it. Now, since so many big changes and alterations in the seasons and the sky happen because of the progressive and retrograde motion of the stars, and since these [changes] are made to happen by the energy of the sun, as we ourselves

observe, [astrologers] think it is not just likely but actually true that, just as the air has been modified this way, so children in their earliest stages [4] are endowed with a specific temperament and given a particular appearance, and from this someone's character, disposition, mind, body, and course of life are moulded, as well as what happens to him and the way that turns out.

But not everyone accepted the validity of astrological propositions, and among both Platonists and Stoics there were several voices raised in query. A number of these – Carneades, Diogenes of Babylon, Panaetius – came to Rome during the second century BC and introduced the Romans to Stoic thought. It would simplify things too much, however, to suggest that they also taught the Romans to be sceptical about astrology, for there is evidence that sceptics already existed. One such was the poet and playwright Quintus Ennius (239–169 BC) who has a character in one of his plays dismiss a whole range of interpreters and diviners:

> I don't consider the Marsian man who studies the flight of birds worth anything at all; nor villagers who interpret the entrails of sacrificed creatures or portents, or thunder and lightning; nor astrologers from the race-course; nor the devotees of Isis who interpret omens; nor the interpreters of dreams. [Why not? Because they are] superstitious prophets and shameless soothsayers who are either without any kind of technical skill or mad or ruled by destitution; who don't know which byway they themselves should take, but point out the highway to the other fellow; who promise riches to those from whom they themselves beg a silver coin.

Another sceptic was the politician Marcus Porcius Cato (234–149 BC) who wrote a manual on farming, a short work packed with advice and country lore, in which he advised his reader not to let the farm bailiff seek the advice of 'anyone who interprets the entrails of sacrificed animals or omens or thunder and lightning, anyone who interprets the flight of birds, any diviner, or any astrologer (*Chaldaeum*)'. What these two writers note in common is the social status of their targets. Ennius's character is sneering at the lower classes, at poverty-stricken practitioners of the various interpretive arts who are one step (and that one small) above common beggars, people without skill or techniques (*inertes*), no better than charlatans; while Cato directs his strictures in the direction of the *vilicus*, the farm manager who might well be a slave and therefore (it is implied) quite likely to turn to superstition instead of using the common sense and accumulated experience of a solid Roman citizen.

It was a strain of intellectual snobbery which continued well beyond the second century BC. The poet Juvenal, who was writing at the turn of the first and second century AD, draws the attention of a young man, Postumus, to the dangers of getting married. He cannot be sure, says Juvenal, how his wife will turn out. She may, for example, be one of those extremely superstitious types who will believe anything anyone tells them. 'Their confidence in astrologers (*Chaldaeis*) is even greater than their trust in soothsayers,' he warns. 'Whatever an astrologer (*astrologus*) says they will believe has come from the

source of [the Egyptian god] Ammon.' What is more, astrologers are shady characters
– 'no astrologer (*mathematicus*) without a criminal record will have talent or inspiration'
– and the silly woman does not actually understand what he is saying to her. 'She knows
nothing about any threat made by the grim planet of [the god] Saturn, which sign means
that Venus is showing herself to be propitious, which month will bring about financial
losses, and which conditions material gain.' But if an ignoramus is bad a know-it-all is
worse. Watch out for the woman who carries a tatty almanac round with her. She won't go
anywhere if her astrological calculations say she shouldn't:

> When she has a notion to be driven a mile outwith the city, she picks the right time from
> her book. If the corner of her eye itches after she has rubbed it, she looks carefully at her
> birth-horoscope before demanding eye-salves; and even though she is lying ill in bed, no
> moment seems better for taking food than the one prescribed by [the Egyptian astrologer]
> Petosiris. The lower orders and women: so untrustworthy. [5]

But Stoics and other 'university' men did have other, more substantial reservations about
the validity of at least some astrological theses. Panaetius, for example, seems to have raised
a question which would return over and over again in hostile argument: if two children
are born at the same time, how can they have different destinies? Moreover, since children
clearly derive their physical characteristics from their parents, how can one say this is not
so, and that those characteristics are determined by the phases of the moon and the control
exercised by the sky; and if the stars cause children to be born with physical defects, how
is it possible that those defects can be cured by medicine or surgery? Answers to these
objections were provided, of course, the most common being the astrological dictum that
the stars incline rather than determine, and there was the well-known attempt by Nigidius
Figulus, refuted by St Augustine, to explain the different fates and characters of twins:

> He spun a potter's wheel as vigorously as he could and, while it was going round, he struck
> it twice with ink very quickly indeed in what he intended to be a single place. Then, as the
> movement began to stop, the marks he had contrived were found quite a distance apart
> on the very edge of the wheel. 'There you are!' he said. 'The sky [revolves] so rapidly that,
> even if the second [twin] is born after the first as quickly as I made my second mark on
> the wheel, in relation to the distance travelled by the sky the distance is very great. This,'
> he said, 'produces whatever great dissimilarities there are in the characters and fortunes of
> twins.'

St Augustine, of course, was having none of it, but still found himself having to account
for the remarkable differences between the Biblical twins Esau and Jacob, thus engaging
in the kind of battle between sceptic and proponent which was to go on for centuries, and
to which we shall return in due course.

But we must actually be chary of accepting Roman scepticism too much at face value,
for while the Romans may have been much influenced by the intellectual endeavours
of the Greek scholars they read, it was also common practice to affect to despise them.

'*Little* Greeks', sneered Cicero himself, 'people more keen on impassioned disputation than the truth'. Yet in the heat of real life, as opposed to the cool of the study, celestial omens exerted genuine power at times of particular crisis. When a lunar eclipse took place on 21 June 168 BC while a Roman army was encamped overnight and preparing for battle the following day, the soldiers were terrified and, *in accordance with established custom*, tried to stop the fading of the light by clashing together their bronze cooking pots and pans, and snatching burning sticks and logs from their camp-fires and holding them up to the sky. Their commander, Lucius Aemilius Paulus, 'who was not deaf and was not entirely without experience of the irregularities of eclipses', knew the reason for the moon's temporary disappearance, but was also very devout, 'a lover of sacrifices and divination', and as soon as the moon started to emerge from earth's shadow, he sacrificed eleven heifers to her. Cicero's version of this incident in his *Republic* has one of Aemilius Paulus's officers try to explain the astronomy behind the eclipse in a speech to the soldiers next day, and adds a disdainful comment by one of the speakers in his dialogue. 'Are you telling me he was able to instruct men who were more or less country clods, and had the nerve to say this kind of thing in front of ignoramuses?' Two points become clear from these two accounts. First, whatever scholarly theories the educated upper classes may have read and absorbed, the majority of people still believed that celestial phenomena had the power to bring about effects here on earth, and that steps could be taken to meet or counteract those phenomena; and secondly, a knowledge of scholarly theories did not necessarily produce scepticism in their students. [6]

Now, it is worth observing that the word 'superstitious' is frequently bandied about in connection with the Romans, (in contrast to the 'rational' Greeks – a hangover of nineteenth-century historical perception), whereas they should more accurately be described as 'religious'. But Rome was not Athens, and while the populace at large undoubtedly took careful note of omens, whether observed in the sky or elsewhere, the sophisticated techniques of astrology developed in Babylonia and Greece and thence imported into Rome, tended to be seen as something of a foreign innovation, and these external origins of the science marked it out in the eyes of many of Rome's republican and then imperial rulers as dubious at best, unwholesome and potentially subversive at worst. Thus, in 139 BC, an edict was issued ordering astrologers 'to leave the City and Italy within ten days, because through their lies by means of fallacious interpretation of the stars, they were fomenting in unstable and shallow minds an ardour from which they themselves were profiting financially'. The original edict has not survived and this version comes from a source dated about a century and a half after the event, but there seems to be no good reason to doubt its authenticity, and its sentiments agree with those expressed in several later orders for the expulsion of astrologers. It is worth noting that this same decree also removed Jews from Italy on the curious grounds that they were trying to persuade Romans to worship a syncretic deity called 'Jupiter Sabazius'. The passage appears in a work by Valerius Maximus as part of a section entitled 'Superstition'. By superstition, however, the Romans meant religious activities not authorised or sanctioned by the official state religion, and this gives us a good indication of the motives which lay behind the expulsion of both the astrologers and the Jews. They were foreigners, or at least importers of foreign cults – it is significant that one very common Latin term for astrologers is *Chaldaei* ('Assyrians') – and therefore, in the eyes of the state, more or less undesirables. We should also not discount certain experiences which would have made those same authorities nervous of star-interpreters. Not quite forty years after this wholesale expulsion, a slave-revolt broke out in Sicily. One of its leaders was a Cilician called Athenion who had great skill in astrology, (*astromantikē*, 'prophesying from the stars'), and used this to win over more than a thousand to his cause. He was elected 'king' of the rebels and 'pretended that the gods were giving him a sign via the stars that he would be king of the whole of Sicily'. *Pretended* is the recording historian's word. The revolt was a serious one and was not easily put down, so the mixture of slave, foreign soil, revolt and astrology was one almost calculated to set Roman teeth on edge.

Still, official disapproval could not prevent non-Roman cults from establishing themselves in Rome, despite the occasional wide-ranging expulsion – witness the temples of Isis and, later on, the churches of Christians – and neither could the disdain of a number of Roman intellectuals for astrology prevent others from taking it seriously. Even a sceptic such as Cicero was able to describe one enthusiastic amateur, Lucius Tarutius, as 'our good friend, well-instructed in the business of astrological calculations', while at the same time dismissing his science as a delusion:

> He made several attempts to discover our city's date of birth, taking as his starting-point the Feast day of Pales, which is when (we have been told) the City was founded by Romulus; and he used to say that Rome was born when the moon was in the constellation Libra, and he had no hesitation in prophesying [Rome's] destiny.

Cicero's younger contemporary, the historian Posidonius (*c.*135–*c.*50 BC), would have approved of that last. It was his belief that Rome was destined by Fate to rule the world, and that divination as a whole can be traced back to three sources: God, Fate, and Nature. By 'Fate' he meant 'an orderly succession of causes in which one cause is intertwined with another and out of itself gives birth to something real'. Hence, if you know the cause of something, you can predict its effect and therefore its future. [7]

The possibility of accepting a governing role for the stars was thus available to educated Romans (along with their Greek instructors and admirers) as well as to the lower classes, and both groups came together in that most powerful of melting-pots, the Roman army. The vehicle was an imported religion, Mithraism. Its origins are obscure. It may have begun during the first century AD in northern Syria where the Romans came into contact with it, and it is probably no coincidence that one of the densest concentrations of evidence for the existence of Mithraic temples or *mithraea* is in Ostia, the port of Rome, where there are remains or traces of a large number of such cult-centres, since ports are one of the most natural gateways connecting one distant place with another. Mithras himself is identified on the one hand with the sun and on the other, perhaps, with Saturn in his role of governor of time. His worship, commonly but not invariably, took place in *mithraea* which seem to have been intended to resemble a natural cave, while the notion of the cave itself symbolised the vault of the sky. Members of the cult passed through seven hierarchical grades, each of which had a special symbol and a guardian planet:

1. Raven – Mercury
2. Bridegroom – Venus
3. Soldier – Mars
4. Lion – Jupiter
5. Persian – Moon
6. Sun-courier – Sun
7. Father – Saturn

Archaeology also provides evidence for linking these grades with the days of the week and with signs of the zodiac – Scorpio, Libra, Virgo, Leo, Cancer, Gemini, and Taurus – and it has also been argued that the arrangement of zodiacal signs on some Mithraic monuments can be seen further as illustrations of certain technical aspects of astrology, such as decans (one 10° division of a 30° zodiac sign, each division being ruled by a planet) or exaltations (the sign or degree of the zodiac in which a planet exerts its most powerful influence). Since members of this cult kept its liturgy and activities secret, however, we are not in any position to offer a definitive explanation either of the individual ranks of the Mithraic hierarchy or even the goal or goals of the cult itself. [8]

But its complex iconography remaining in paintings, mosaics, and sculptures from the surviving *mithraea* suggests some kind of drama illustrating the passage of souls from this life to the next via the planets and stars; and this is reminiscent partly of one important aspect of Egyptian astrology which saw the decans pictured in drawings and texts on coffin lids as early as the third millennium BC, and partly of Plato's view that the souls of the good are permitted to ascend to the stars. As Nicolas Campion expresses it, 'This is plausibly a democratisation of Egyptian cosmology in which only the Pharaoh and his queen had a guaranteed spiritual presence in the stars; for Plato, in spite of his elitist instincts, every soul belonged in the starry heavens.' Certainly this is the interpretation of the Mithraic mysteries intimated by Celsus in the late second century AD:

> These truths are obscurely represented … by the mystery of Mithras [in which] there is a symbol of the two orbits in heaven, the one being that of the fixed stars and the other that assigned to the planets, and of the soul's passage through these. The symbol is this. There is a ladder with seven gates and at its top an eighth gate. The first of the gates is of lead, the second of tin, the third of bronze, the fourth of iron, the fifth of an alloy, the sixth of silver, and the seventh of gold. They associate first with Kronos (Saturn), taking lead to refer to the slowness of the star; the second with Aphrodite (Venus), comparing her with the brightness and soft-ness of tin; the third with Zeus (Jupiter), as the gate that has a bronze base and is firm; the fourth with Herms (Mercury), for both iron and Hermes are reliable for all works and make money and are hard-working; the fifth with Ares (Mars), the gate which as a result of the mixture is uneven and varied in quality; the sixth with the moon as the silver gate; and the seventh with the sun as the golden gate, these metals resembling their colours.

But while this may seem to provide us with important insights into Mithraic symbolism, it looks as though, in certain respects, the account is badly mistaken. The order of planets does not make sense, for example, and the links between the planets and metals is mostly eccentric, for while sun = gold, silver = moon, Saturn = lead are standard associations (as in alchemy which was an occult science well known to the Roman world of the second century AD when Celsus was writing), the others are correspondences quite different from the norm. To be sure, Roger Beck argues that these oddities are paradoxes rather than eccentricities, and that Celsus has given his readers a partial truth, in tune with what one expects of revelations made to non-initiates. Similarly, when the relationship between the planets and the days of the week, as Celsus records them, seems to give the planets in the reverse order of the usual correspondence of the planet with the weekday, Beck proposes that this merely intimates the initiate's triumph over time. But both interpretations one may think are a little forced, smacking just a touch, perhaps, of a late nineteenth or early twentieth-century occultist approach to somewhat obscure symbols nowadays viewed, perforce, without knowledge of their full context. Somewhat more successful, perhaps because less strained, is the suggestion made by Richard Gordon during his discussion of the *mithraeum* at Sette Sefre in Ostia. There, in the arrangement of the zodiacal signs on the surviving benches he sees a series of correspondences between the four annual seasons and the planets and signs of the zodiac.

Sun (Mithras)

SPRING	Aries			Pisces	WINTER
	Taurus	Jupiter	Saturn	Aquarius	
	Gemini		Venus	Capricorn	
SUMMER	Cancer	Mercury		Sagittarius	AUTUMN
	Leo			Scorpio	
	Virgo	Moon	Mars	Libra	

This sequence of signs is in accord with that of ancient zodiacs, and the designation of (a) Aries – Virgo and (b) Libra – Pisces as (a) northern signs and (b) southern signs also agrees with the majority of ancient astronomical-astrological writers. Moreover, the further division of the signs between the four annual seasons is also to be found in ancient astrological writers, so Gordon's proposal seems not only to agree with these but also to fit surviving archaeological remains rather better than other suggestions. If he is right, it means that the initiatic journey made by worshippers in a *mithraeum* was deeply imbued with astrological significance, the day and night halves, (Spring and summer, autumn and winter respectively), representing the night just before creation and then the day of creation itself, with the figure of Mithras-Sun maintaining the pivotal position between the two, joining 'a sign which is a lunar domicile (Aries) with a sign which is a solar domicile (Libra), in a union of opposites'; and hence, 'the mysteries of Mithras constitute an entirely rational reformulation, in terms taken from current beliefs about the constitution of the cosmos, of the traditional theme of immanence'. [9]

So in answer to the question, how can the individual soul reach God? the Mithraic mysteries answered, via the stars. As long ago as Plato there existed the proposition that God had blended and mixed the Soul of the Universe and then, having completed this stage of the creative process, 'divided [that Soul] into souls equal in number to the stars, and each several soul He assigned to one star; and, setting them each as it were in a chariot, He showed them the nature of the universe and declared to them the laws of destiny'. (*Timaeus* 41 D–E). Then each good soul became the 'motor' which drives round not only the sum total of sun, moon, and other planets and stars, but also each star and planet individually. (*Laws* 10.898C–D). Thus, contemplation of the heavens becomes an exercise in moral meditation, as the gazer learns therefrom both the mind and intention of the Creator, and his or her place in the cosmos as an embodiment of that divine will and purpose, and progression through the Mithraic mysteries turns into an enactment of the journey of the soul after death as it passes through the planets and reintegrates with the divine Potter who first gave it form and individuality.

3

Hellenistic & Roman Egypt
50 BC–c.AD 100: Personal Horoscopes

A long gap intervenes between Cicero's strictures on astrology and the rise and spread of Mithraism, a gap which was filled by a remarkable amount of speculation, observation, and condensation of astrological lore and increasingly sophisticated mathematics in the work of a series of influential practitioners and scholars. But not in Rome. The focus of much astrological activity had moved from its Middle Eastern birthplace in the Land between the Rivers to Egypt where it had found a home in Alexandria whose library had long been the largest and most comprehensive in the Classical world. Egypt, of course, had a long history of its own with regard to the stars and planets. The earliest Egyptian pictures of planets date from *c*.1473 BC. The Egyptian state itself mirrored the realm of heaven, and Egyptian religion connected the individual human being, (first the Pharaoh alone, then every person), to the stars in a relationship which was at once a deeply emotional and at the same a quotidian experience. Hence the Egyptian legacy to later astrologers involved ideas both of cosmic order and of personal relationship with the stars and planets, ideas which, as we have seen already, were bound to influence the astrological speculations of those several peoples with whom Egypt had contact, through trade or war, in subsequent centuries.

The library at Alexandria, however, does not seem to have included books in the Egyptian language; only those in Greek or Latin were bought or copied, and of these the great majority were in Greek. It is likely, for example, that the library had a copy of the historical compendium *Babyloniaca* by Berossus, a third-century BC Babylonian astrologer who had moved from his native city to the Greek island of Cos where he had set up a school of astrology. This work now survives only in quoted fragments, but it contained much astronomical-astrological information which passed hence to the Greeks and from them into Macedonian Egypt. His information included a prediction of certain natural catastrophes:

Berossus … says that these happen because of a passage of the planets. Indeed, he is so positive about this that he assigns a date for the conflagration and the flood. Things on earth will burn, he maintains, when all the planets which, at the present time follow different orbits, come together in Cancer, so situated with one immediately behind another in the same track that a straight line can pass through all their spheres. The flood (he says) will happen when the same set of planets meets in Capricorn. [1]

It is also possible that the library had a copy of works attributed to two Egyptians, Nechepso and Petosiris, a Pharaoh supposedly from the seventh or sixth century BC, and a high priest of Thoth from about the fourth. The attribution is undoubtedly false, the actual author being an astrologer-diviner from about the second or first century BC. The fragments of these works, like those of Berossus surviving only in quotations by much later authors, suggest they had four principal themes: (i) astral omens used to give general predictions or indications of future events; (ii) the record of a vision in which Nechepso learns the truth of horoscopy; (iii) an essay on astral botany directed towards the use of plants in medicine, and (iv) essays on numerology. Thus, we are told, during total eclipses, the colour of the moon was regarded as significant:

> The colour black signifies the death of the ruler, humiliation, famine, and change. Bright red [signifies] misfortune of the land; whitish, famine and death to flocks and herds and travellers or merchants; violet, war and famine; golden appearance, deadly infection and death.

Equally, if the sun or moon suffer an eclipse while they are in Aries during the month of April, many evils will fall upon places in Egypt and Syria, assassination plots and rebellion will be hatched against the rulers or important people in those places, army camps will be set on fire, and Libya will see invasions of unruly mobs and danger to its ruler from violent friends. It may be thought it is interesting to detect in these and so many more passages of a similar kind what appear to be the major preoccupations of ancient societies: lack of stability and orderly government, famine, disease, and war. But actually in these scholarly works we are listening to the voices of a very select group of people, highly-skilled practitioners of a complex science, whose business is to interpret the sky's signs and omens largely for the benefit of another select group of people, the rulers and the politico-religious class whose principal concern is to maintain a stable society, feed the populace, and endeavour to keep the peace with their neighbours. Doubtless these were also of concern to the people in general, of course; but for the moment, at least, when we hear astrologers speak, they are mainly in conversation with their peers or political masters.

It was not long, however, before they began to draw maps of the heavens for particular individuals below and beyond that charmed circle, and interpret their meaning in relation to those new clients. In the work of Dorotheus of Sidon, for example, we find someone speaking directly to that well-known cliché, 'the man in the street'. Dorotheus's work is laid out in the form of a poem, the *Carmen Astrologicum*, which gives us plenty of detailed insight into the concerns of ordinary men and women. Internal indications suggest that Dorotheus, who calls himself 'King of Egypt', but by the testimony of Firmicus Maternus and Michael Italicus actually came from Phoenicia (Lebanon), flourished between *c.*25 and *c.*75 AD. The version we have of the *Carmen* has come down to us via Arabic, which means that it is likely to contain later interpolations, but the majority of the work is original and is noteworthy because it offers us not only the earliest surviving treatise to discuss horary or electional (catarchic) as well as natal (genethliacal) astrology, but also some of the earliest known horoscopic charts. Genethliacal astrology is based on a map of the sky at the moment of a person's birth, from which prognostications about character and future events may be made. Catarchic astrology is about 'beginnings' and uses a sky-map, drawn at the time of asking a question, to offer advice about the advisability of starting some activity – a journey, a new job, an engagement to marry, and so forth. This is the astrology discussed in Book 5 of Dorotheus's *Carmen*, following four Books which deal with nativities, and it tells the reader both how to proceed with his or her proposed enterprise and which aspects or positions of which heavenly bodies should receive particular attention beforehand:

> Look concerning the commencement of every matter at the ascendant and the moon. The moon is the strongest of what is [possible] if it is above the earth, especially if this is at night. The ascendant is the strongest of what is [possible] if the moon is under the earth by day … It is best to lay the foundations of a building if you build it when the moon is getting bigger and lighter and is in the middle of the zone which is the equator, ascending towards the north while Jupiter or Venus is with the moon, or aspects the moon from a strong position. If Saturn is with the moon, or aspects it from a strong position, there occurs in this work difficulty and dissension and slowness, or trouble and misery. If Mars is with the moon, or aspects it from a strong position, a conflagration or injury from fire will reach that building … If you want to sell something or buy it, look at the position of the moon, because the star with which the moon conjoins indicates the buyer and the price, and the star from which the moon flows indicates the seller. The moon indicates the commodity which you sell or buy. So look at the moon and at the star from which the moon flows or with which it conjoins. If you find the malefics [*unlucky signs*] with the moon or with the star from which the moon flows, or with which it conjoins, or if the malefics aspect it, it indicates that misfortune or misery occurs in the matter which is attributed to the moon, or to that star from which the moon flows or with which is conjoins. If the benefics [*lucky signs*] happen to be in one of these positions, joy and happiness and success in his desire occur to the master of that action which is attributed to this star or to the moon, if God wishes. [2]

Taken as a whole, the subject matter of the *Carmen* lets us see the kind of questions an astrologer might expect to be asked and therefore the various aspects of life his client considered important. Book 1 concentrates on natal horoscopes and lays stress on the client's family background before turning to his or her private life:

> If you wish to consider the parents of your client, look for his father from the sun and the lord of its triplicity, because from these planets are known the lineage of the father and his livelihood … Look concerning the matter of his mother from the moon and, in lineage, from its place and its term and its right side and its left side and from its place in the south.

Parental condition – social, economic, fortunate or unfortunate – is thus important when one comes to consider the prospects of the offspring: not so different, in fact, from the kind of consideration one might expect a modern doctor or judge or social worker to take into account in certain circumstances. Further possible questions refine the astrologer's knowledge of his client and aim at satisfying the client's particular inquiries. Are the father and mother lucky or unlucky? Which parent will die before the client? Will he inherit his father's property? How many other children will his mother have? (An important question, since it will affect his inheritance). 'Saturn and the sun indicate older brothers, Jupiter and Mars indicate middle ones, Mercury younger ones the moon older sisters, and Venus younger sisters.' Are the brothers likely to get on with one another? – the chart Dorotheus includes at this point indicates a situation in which the querent has three brothers, two older, one younger, and one older sister – and only at this point does Dorotheus turn to discussing the client's personal luck and health.

The majority of this first book, then, has been directed towards the client's astrological inheritance, (we might talk about his or her genes), and his or her prospects in relation to the family's property and since the astrological inheritance clearly has a bearing on the latter, we are likely to form the impression that questions of inheritance would loom large in any sessions with the astrologer. This is scarcely surprising. In societies without state pensions or state welfare to provide some kind of safety-net for the poor or unfortunate, one's prospects of inheriting wealth or property, (not to mention one's tendency to be lucky), are bound to assume great importance, the more pressing in the event of a parent's ill health or impending death and the existence of older siblings who may expect legally to come into the greater portion of whatever there is to be shared. Thus, with two older brothers, the client in Dorotheus's exemplar could expect only a limited share of the family fortune, such as it might be.

Book 2 is devoted to questions about marriage and children:

> If Venus is with Jupiter while Venus is in a good place, this indicates marriage to an agree-able wife. If you find Venus [descending] and Mars and Jupiter aspecting it by day while the lords of its triplicity are in mid-heaven, they indicate that the wife will be a whore, well known in the mouths of the majority of men.

Compare this with Dorotheus's near contemporary, Anoubion, whose astrological poem, like that of Dorotheus, was immensely influential in later centuries. 'When Venus is in mid-heaven together with Saturn, in her own signs, without the presence of Mars, she gives a wife who is neither poor nor old ... but certainly not a maiden, either.' So it will be important for the client to know about a potential bride's astrological background, how this marriage is likely to turn out, whether he will marry more than once – 'mark off from mid-heaven to Venus. Whatever number of planets is between these two, that is the number of wives he will have' – and, of course, there is the crucial business of children. How many will he have? What will their fortunes be, good or bad? How many will be male and how many female? 'If you find Saturn in opposition to Mercury, it indicates the death of the children. If you find Venus while Saturn is in opposition to it, without the aspect of Jupiter, he will be sterile or have few children ... If Saturn injures Venus without the aspect of Jupiter, it indicates grief on account of children; or they will have children but will not enjoy them; or no children will be born to him'. Here the influence of Saturn is obviously baleful, and

Dorotheus devotes a lot of attention to what the querent may expect from the planets as they appear in his or her chart:

> If Venus aspects the moon from opposition, there will be no good in his marriage and no children. Even if there were, they would die. He will be disgraced and beaten because of women. If Mercury aspects the moon from opposition, it indicates quarrels and affliction from groups of people, and great slander, and he will be a coward in speaking.

Anoubion agrees with Dorotheus's conclusions. 'If Saturn and Venus dwell together in a setting sign, women will be born barren and men without issue.'[3]

Dorotheus also takes into account the possibility that both the man or the woman concerned may prefer to have sex with someone of their own gender. 'If Venus is in the cardinal point of the west in opposition, and the moon is in the ascendant, then, if the querent is female, it indicates she will be desirous of women; if the querent is a male, he will be desirous of males.' Certain relationships between planets will make this 'worse', or indicate that the man will be effeminate or that the woman will be butch. What does Dorotheus mean by 'worse' in this context, if indeed 'worse' comes from his text and is not part of an Arabic interpolation or addition? It is not likely to bear the burden of moral disapproval. While it is true that the world of the first century AD in which Dorotheus was living disliked and condemned or made fun of the passive partner in male same-sex intercourse, there is no real sense that this passage is condemnatory of men or women on any ground other than practical. For it is worth noting that the section in which 'worse' occurs comes directly after his sections on marriage and directly before his sections on the client's prospects of children from the marriage; so 'worse' here may be referring to the effect of same-sex preferences on the likelihood of the marriage's producing children. The more ingrained the same-sex preference, the less likely the prospect of children and they, after all, are one of the principal reasons for wanting to marry in the first place.

Book 3 deals with the querent's expected length of life, but is the most heavily interpolated part of the *Carmen*, and Book 4 describes further technicalities, so we reach the final Book before detailed questions affecting the client's fortunes in everyday life are taken up again. This Book, it will be remembered, turns largely from questions relating to the natal chart to those anent particular problems facing the client at a particular moment. Hence, 'if you find the ascendant is a twin sign, it indicates that the action which he commences at that hour will not be finished until an action different from this occurs in it, and [the second action] will be finished before the first action is finished'. What kind of actions does Dorotheus go on to discuss? Building, demolishing, buying, selling, asking a favour, marriage – 'If the marriage takes place when the moon is in Aries, the marriage will have no good in it ... If the moon is in Gemini in the first half, it will not be good; but if it is in the other half, it will be good. Avoid marriage when the moon is in Cancer.' This section on marriage is very detailed. It answers questions about the dowry, the parties' respective prospects for happiness or unhappiness, the woman's faithfulness or otherwise, the man's recklessness with money or otherwise, the prospect of children, love or hatred within the marriage, who will fare better in the marriage, the woman or the man, quarrelling, discord, reconciliation. After marriage comes partnership in business, debt, travel, buying or building a ship and journeys by sea:

> If the moon is under the earth with Saturn while Saturn is in its station and is with the moon in the same sign at the hour when [the sailors] start to row the boat, it indicates that great pains and a great, severe misfortune will happen to them. A hideous fear will fall on them, and strong waves, until water enters the ship, and the people on board for whom death and loss in dampness or water were predicted will be lost in those waves while the moon is under the earth.

On the other hand, a different alignment of the earth and the moon and Venus means the people will not drown and their voyage will end in profit and good fortune.

Travel also implies messages of one kind or another and the planet of Mercury, messenger of the gods, naturally plays a leading role in Dorotheus's remarks at this point. But then comes a sudden jump to questions dealing with imprisonment, leading to illness and prospects of recovering from it, increase or loss of property, court cases, exile, and theft – a long section whose various disasters remind us of how dangerous travel of any kind could be in the ancient world. Individuals, or even small groups of people, might easily find themselves attacked on the road by well-armed bands of robbers who might well think themselves safe from reprisal by any authorities. Tainted water, infected food, the bite of unexpected insects could fell the traveller with illness, and lack of effective remedies might prevent his recovery for a long time, during which, where would he be able to stay in either comfort or safety? Without those modern resources which help identify an individual as the person he or she claims to be, a traveller might fall under suspicion of being a thief or murderer or rapist when he entered unfamiliar territory, in which case arrest and imprisonment and trial and (who knows?) execution could be his unexpected lot.

Included in this section, therefore, is important astrological information about how to identify a thief. For example, if the planet which indicates the thief's characteristics is Jupiter, the thief will be pale-skinned and fat. He will have big eyes whose whites are unusually small, and his beard will be round and curly. Saturn, on the other hand, will indicate an ugly thief with very dark or black skin, and a hang-dog look. Mars means he will have red, lank hair, fat cheeks, and a highly sociable disposition. The Venus thief will be handsome with a full head of hair, large dark eyes, and a pink and white complexion, while Mercury will indicate he is a slippery character, slim to the point of being extremely thin and bald, but with a beard which suits his face. These indicators are further refined by reference to the signs of the zodiac. Sagittarius, for example:

> indicates that the thief is long-legged and wide-thighed. If he turns his back, he is more comely than face-on. Lank in his beard, long in it but small in it, red in his colour, clever, agile, delicate, a runaway slave, a marksman. He works with his hands. He is a profiteer, a wastrel, a generous man. There are some of them whose craving is for animals, and some who are bald or have no hair.

Such indicators were discernible in the horoscope because of the complex relationship between the planets and between the planets and the signs of the zodiac. We have come across several in the quoted passages from the *Carmen*. 'Lord of triplicity', for example, refers to the ruling planet of a group of three zodiac signs which, as a group, relate to one of the four elements. Thus, Aries, Leo and Sagittarius constitute a fire triplicity which is ruled by the sun (their 'lord') during the day, and by Jupiter at night. Taurus, Virgo and Capricorn make an earth triplicity ruled by Venus during the day and the moon at night. Gemini, Libra and Aquarius form an air triplicity ruled by Saturn during the day and Mercury by night; and Cancer, Scorpio and Pisces make a water triplicity ruled by Venus during the day and by the moon at night. 'Aspects' refer to specific angular relationships between planets and other celestial bodies and are known by separate names according to the angle – symbolic rather than geophysical – they have with another body. Thus, 'opposition' means 180°, 'trine' 120°, 'square' 90°, 'conjunction' 0°, 'sextile' 60°, and so forth. 'Ascendant' is a term used to describe the degree of the zodiac arising on the eastern horizon as marked on the astrologer's chart. Hence, 'If it is Saturn which aspects the moon and the ascendant, it indicates that the thief has used tricks and has deceived and has misled so that he may steal.'

Would these indications have been useful at a time when there was no forensic science to provide clues to a criminal's identity and when people were recognised largely by distinctive physical marks or traits, and their habitual clothing? Possibly, but it should be noted how closely these indicators follow contemporary expectations of astrologically-defined characters. Mars, (the most obvious example), must surely produce someone with red hair; but there was a well-established perception among both the Greeks and the Romans that red hair or a red complexion were undesirable traits in anyone. Pseudo-Aristotle said that it indicated a bad character, and likened red-heads to foxes. Adamantius noted that red hair unmixed with other colours belonged to people who were animal-like, shameless and greedy. The playwright Plautus had his lying slave full of tricks (Pseudolus) described as having red hair, a pot belly, thick calves, a swarthy complexion, a big head, sharp eyes, a ruddy face, and huge feet. The poet Martial addressed a stinging epigram to an unprepossessing individual – 'Red-haired, swarthy-faced, short-footed, boss-eyed: it's a great achievement, Zoilus, if you are a decent chap' – and an anonymous physiognomist remarked that thick watery-red hair indicates a violent man. No wonder, then, that the tradition lasted well into the Middle Ages. 'Rote hare, Gott bewahre' ran a popular German saying which reflects the belief that Judas Iscariot, the ultimate undesirable, had had red hair. [4]

Next, Dorotheus turns to another kind of lost property, the runaway slave. Here he uses astrology to indicate the direction in which the fugitive is going: 'If the moon is in the ascendant, it indicates that the runaway is headed towards the east. If the moon is in the mid-heaven, it indicates that the runaway is headed towards the south.' One must remember that the horoscope to which this refers is horary or catarchic, that is, cast with reference either to the particular time at which the question is put, or to the time a particular incident is thought to have begun: hence the reference to the moon's being 'in the mid-heaven' which, presumably, means that the client thought his slave had run away during the middle of the night. Other celestial signs and relationships tell the querent that the runaway has shed blood while he was away, or that he has been recaptured, or will hang himself, or has lost the goods he stole when he ran away, or will drown, or suffer some other unpleasant death such as crucifixion, or will return to his master of his own accord, or that the master will die before the slave comes back. Finally, Dorotheus includes one or two disparate topics – the best time to exorcise a poltergeist, or undertake treatment for stomach upset or an eye infection – and closes with various observations on how long an illness is likely to last and, rather ominously, the best time to make a will.

Many of the topics he covers in this fifth Book can be counted as those common to almost any age and society – business, marriage, and health – but there are three which indicate particular concerns of Dorotheus's period. Travel, especially travel by sea, was clearly regarded as a potentially hazardous undertaking. Pirates, weather, wind or lack of it, high seas, and shipwreck were the most obvious dangers, and in Dorotheus's text he emphasises high waves, unspecified calamities, and 'hideous' fear. That word 'hideous' appears frequently in the passage: 'hideous matter', 'hideous and worse', 'violence and hideousness', 'misfortune whose condition is hideous', 'the hideousness will increase'. There are also indications of a battle at sea and 'difficult surgical operations' and a breaking of [people's] 'joints'. An early fifth-century Christian writer, Synesius, gives us a good idea of what in his personal experience some of these meant:

> The men groaned, the women shrieked, everybody called upon God, cried aloud, remembered their dear ones. Only Amarantus was in good spirits, thinking he was going to get out of paying his creditors … I noticed that the soldiers had all drawn their swords. I asked why and learned that they preferred to belch up their souls to the open air, on deck, rather than gurgle them up to the sea. True descendants of Homer, I thought, and approved of the idea. Then someone called out that anyone who had any gold should hang it round his or her neck. Those who had, did so, both gold and anything else of the value of gold. The women not only put on their jewellery but handed out pieces of string to anyone who needed them. This is a time-honoured practice, and the reason for it is this: you must provide the corpse of someone lost at sea with the money to pay for a funeral so that whoever recovers it, profiting by it, won't mind giving it a little attention.

Tracking down thieves and runaway slaves was also a difficult matter. It depended on birthmarks, scars, pockmarks, tattoos, and skin colour. Thus, on 31 January AD 49, Metrophanes sold Pasion, a female slave. She was about twenty-five years old, of middle height, and had skin the colour of honey – whatever that means, since honey may appear in different shades of brown according to its type and consistency. Interestingly enough, the certificate of sale includes descriptions of both seller and buyer, too. (Such documents, however, regularly provided descriptions of all the parties concerned).

Metrophanes was aged about fifty-eight, of middling height, with a honey-coloured complexion, a long face, and a scar on his left forearm, while Pasion was about six years younger, of similar height and complexion, with a scar on his left wrist. We find the same comprehensiveness again in the sale of a nineteen-year-old slave who had a slight squint and a scar on his forehead. The seller, a woman called Statoria Philoxena, was aged about fifty and had a scar on her right wrist, while the buyer, Lucius Valerius Severus, aged about forty-four, had a scar in the middle of his nose. When slaves ran away, therefore, it was easy for the authorities not only to verify the accuracy of the descriptions supplied by their owners from these certificates of sale, but also the true identity of the owner who was making the complaint. Runaways were liable to be identified by the clothes they wore as well as by physical markings:

> If any person has found a slave called Philippos, about fourteen years old, white (pale)-skinned, hesitant in speech because he cannot pronounce certain letters properly, broad-nosed, wearing a thick woollen tunic dyed various colours and a well-used belt, he should [take him] to the army guardroom.

Another notice from the same period gives even more information:

> An Egyptian … knows no Greek, tall, lean, his head closely shaved, with a slight wound on the left side, honey-coloured complexion, sallow, with a skimpy beard and no hair at all near it, smooth-skinned, narrow in the jaw, long-nosed. A weaver by trade. He walks around as if he were somebody important, chattering in a shrill voice. He is about thirty-two years old. He wears undyed, ragged clothes. [5]

Astrology, then, was able to combine with legal documentation to provide extra information which would be useful to owners and the authorities: a description of the thief, if the thief were unknown, his direction of escape – and it seems the thief was always 'he'. One wonders if thieves really were exclusively male or whether it was assumed that women would not steal from their owners or employers – and the likelihood of his being caught or not. But what is notable about Dorotheus's descriptions of the thieves or runaways is that, unlike the specific descriptions of individuals contained in legal documents, these astrological portraits are closely tied to types formed by the influence of the planets. Hence according to the first-century AD astrologer, Teucer of Babylon:

> Mars by nature is fiery and burning and drying. Anent parts of the body: it rules the heat, the seat, the genitalia, the bile, the blood, the excretion of faeces, the hinder parts. It also signifies middle brothers, and injury and sickness, violence, malice, war, robbery, arson, adultery, banishment, captivity, seduction of women, miscarriage, cutting and dissolution, attack by soldiers or armed robbers, trickery, lies, theft, perjury, burglary, grave-robbing, and things similar to these. It belongs to the night, is red in colour and sharp-smelling. Among metals, it is linked with iron, and in common with Mercury it governs the mouth.

Key words here are red, blood, violence, robbery, and sure enough we find that when Mars 'rules' the thief, the thief has a florid complexion, red hair, goes out of his way to be violent and do harm to others, and that violence in the form of imprisonment, agony, misery, and misfortune await him. If the subject is a runaway, Mars in conjunction with the moon means he will have lost blood during his arrest or, under other astrological conditions, that he will be burned to death or knifed, or suffer beating and imprisonment.

Reading individual characteristics and an individual fate from the generalities of planetary associations and influences may thus combine intuition and ingenuity, a legitimate combination of skills in the hands of genuine practitioners, but opportunities for lucrative fiction in those of unscrupulous manipulators. It is also possible, of course, to read back astrological characteristics from the legal documents. The pale complexion of the first runaway may connect him with Mercury and his broad nose with Scorpio, while the tall, lean second runaway suggests Aries, and his sallow complexion, scanty beard, long nose, and tendency to be self-important all indicate Mercury in one or other of its aspects. A skilful astrologer who was given the legal document and asked to derive further useful information from it could therefore easily do so, and might also call upon the related science of physiognomy which concentrated on people's external features as means of commenting upon their character or destiny. Indeed, even Cicero could not prevent himself from calling upon physiognomy when his professional career in the law-courts could benefit from his doing so. He exclaimed of a man called Chaerea:

Doesn't that head of his ... don't those closely-shaved eyebrows seem to stink of an evil disposition and plainly indicate his craftiness? From the tips of his fingernails to the very top of his head – if the 'silent' shape of his body helps people to come to any kind of con- clusion! – doesn't he appear to be composed entirely of fraud, tricks, and lies?

Cicero, of course, is playing with theatrical rhetoric, but his sarcastic appeal to the 'silence' of Chaerea's body depends for its meaning and effectiveness upon his audience's recognition and assumption that the body does indeed 'speak' through the condition and appearance of its several parts, an assumption which was also closely allied to the astrological relationship between the bodies of living creatures and the seven planets. Plutarch, for example, noted that humans consist of three parts: the body, furnished by the earth, the soul, provided by the moon, and the mind, contributed by the sun; and Pliny the Elder observed that some people are subject to the malignant influence of a star or planet, that the moon affects the growth of shellfish, the entrails of field mice, the severity or otherwise of eye-disease in cattle, and the increase and decrease of blood in human beings. He also quotes the astrologer Thrasyllus to the effect that 'when the sun is in Cancer, snakes feel extreme pain'. Claudius Ptolemy, a second-century AD astronomer-astrologer living in Alexandria, was more specific, suggesting that the moon rules the taste, stomach, womb, and left-hand side of the body; Mercury rules speech and thought, the tongue, liver, and buttocks; Venus, smell, liver, and 'flesh'; the sun, sight, brain, heart, sinews, and right-hand parts of the body; Mars, the left ear, the kidneys, veins, and genitals; Jupiter, the sense of touch, the lungs, arteries, and semen; and Saturn, the right ear, spleen, bladder, phlegm, and bones.

These were associations which were to have a profound effect on the theory and practice of medicine once they entered the mainstream of astrological practice, and it is starting to become clear with how much covert speed astrology had penetrated the fabric of the physical world and was thus influencing people's perception of themselves and of the world around them. Seneca, in fact, objected that astrologers used only five planets ('stars'), along with the sun and moon, in their calculations:

> Goodness me, do you think that so many thousands of stars up there are shining to no practical purpose? Moreover, what else is there to cause experts in birth-horoscopes to make a really big mistake other than the fact that they allocate us a small number of stars, when all [the stars] above us lay claim to a part of us for themselves? It may be that those which are lower down direct their force more directly upon us, along with those which look at us first one way, then another, because they move about quite frequently. But even those stars which are motionless, or seem to be motionless stars because their speed is the same as that of the universe, are not beyond exercising power and control over us.

From the parts of the body to living creatures as a whole, to countries and continents, to the earth and its climate, to the universe itself, the stars and planets were seen as the origins and transmitters of influxes which promoted or checked virtually every aspect of physical existence and, through bodies whether animate or inanimate, the essential characters of those individual bodies, producing in them signs whereby those characters might be known at once and accurately. It was a development which had the result of tying astrology yet more firmly to religion and the concept of a Divine Being who directed, though not in the manner of a tyrant, the unfolding composition of His universe and the course of events springing endlessly from agent to agent to agent throughout the cosmos. [6]

4

The Imperial West c.100–c.200: Political Quicksands

There is an interesting parallel between the regal and imperial Courts of the Land Between the Rivers and that of Rome. The former made use of astrologers, leaned upon them for advice, and punished them, (as far as we know), only for inadequacy or as a result of Court intrigue against them by jealous, ambitious colleagues. Rome, too, paid varying degrees of heed to her astrologers, openly exploiting their interpretations in political propaganda, but never quite managing to shake off suspicions that these 'foreign' experts would, without hesitation, engage in conspiracy against the legitimate government of the day, in an effort both to destroy the Emperor and, with wider intent, to subvert and poison the traditional virtues which had made Rome what it was. In spite of this combination of leeriness and mistrust, however, the astrologers and the Imperial government rubbed along and, provided the Emperor himself did not find it personally satisfying or politically expedient to take hostile and violent steps to get rid of them, astrologers could expect to pursue the practice of their science without over-much hindrance from the scepticism of the sneering classes.

When it came to Imperial propaganda, though, no scepticism was allowed to stand in the way, as the initial reign of Octavian Augustus illustrates. Stories about prodigies and portents accompanying his birth began to circulate within his lifetime. Julius Marathus, his freedman secretary, wrote a *Life of Augustus* which noted that a few months before the future Emperor was born, Rome was rife with gossip about a portent which was interpreted to mean that a male child born that year would become King of the Romans. Other stories – his mother dreamed she had mated with Apollo in the form of a serpent, and that her intestines were carried up to the stars and were spread out over the entire circumference of the earth and sky; his father dreamed that the brilliance of the sun had risen from his wife's womb – will have been told *post eventum*, although how much later is not clear because the dates of Asclepias of Mendes who recorded them in his *Theologoumena* ('Inquiries into the Nature of the Gods') are not known. But we are also told that when the astrologer Nigidius Figulus first learned of Octavian's birth, he declared – 'as is well known and much talked of' – in open Senate that the ruler of the world had been born. He was well-equipped to know what he was saying. The historian Dio Cassius noted:

This man [Nigidius], could distinguish better than any of his contemporaries the orderly arrangement of the vault of heaven and the differences between the stars – the kind of things they produce when they are in opposition to each other, and the kind of things they produce when they join forces in association with each other.

Whether Nigidius actually predicted greatness for Octavian on the very day of his birth is, of course, open to question. It is not impossible, given Nigidius's reputation for skill as an astrologer, that he did indeed do so, but we have no idea whether the story was foisted on him by later historians precisely because of that reputation, or whether he himself told the story in later years to enhance his fame and magnify his skill.

One also needs to bear in mind that this is by no means the only recorded instance of an astrologer's predicting great things for Augustus. Suetonius, a keen collector of Imperial tittle-tattle, (but not necessarily for that reason unreliable), noted that in 44 BC Octavian, then Master of Horse for Julius Caesar his adopted father, was sent to Apollonia, a town about sixty miles north of Corfu on the Illyrian coast. It was to be a quiet retreat before the rigours of civil war caught up with him again. He was accompanied, we are told by Nicolaus of Damascus, a contemporary historian, by men of his own age, and friends. These included Marcus Agrippa who went with him one day to the *pergula* belonging to the local astrologer, Theogenes. (*Pergula* here probably refers to some kind of upper storey to the main house, suitable for making observations of the night sky.) Agrippa had his consultation first and was told that great, almost incredible things awaited him. This made Octavian nervous. He did not want his future to be any less brilliant, so he was reluctant to disclose the time of his birth (*genituram*), essential information if Theogenes was to draw his horoscope. Finally, however, and with a great deal of hesitation on his part and encouragement from Agrippa and Theogenes, he revealed the day and hour. At this point Suetonius is so eager to reach the climax of his story that he allows Theogenes no time to make his calculations and draw the chart. Instead, Theogenes no sooner hears the *genitura* than he jumps up and pays Octavian homage. *Adoravit* may mean several things, but at its most intense it refers to paying someone divine honours. As a result, Suetonius tells us, Octavian had such faith in the destiny predicted for him that he published the horoscope Theogenes either then or later produced, and issued a silver coin stamped with the sign of Capricorn 'under which he was born'.

Now, it is well known that this narrative contains a problem. According to modern calendrical reckoning, Octavian was born on 23 September 63 BC and at this stage the sun is in Libra, not Capricorn. The discrepancy has teased astrologers and historians since at least the sixteenth century, and several solutions have been proposed, including recalculating the birth-date in accordance with the calendar prior to Julius Caesar's reformation of it; drawing a horoscope based on the likely date of Octavian's conception rather than birth – a chart which will indeed see sun, moon, and Mercury in Capricorn; and giving preference to the moon rather than the sun, as the moon is in Capricorn in Octavian's *natal* chart. Tamsyn Barton, however, has pointed out that astrology during this period allowed the practitioner great flexibility both in drawing and interpreting the chart. 'The last thing astrologers worried about was contradiction … The art of astrology consisted of finding more and more ways of answering the same question.' Thus, 'when the hour of the birth was not exactly known, as must frequently have been the case, the astrologer was quite prepared to look for a horoscope *appropriate to the circumstances of the client*', (Barton's italics). What, then, were these circumstances in Octavian's case? He was, despite his youth, one of the most eminent men in Rome, pausing in Apollonia for a period of reflection and study before going on to the City where, it was perfectly clear, he would play a prominent role in the new regime Julius Caesar was bound to inaugurate. It would therefore have taken little effort on Theogenes' part to realise enough of this to see that an extraordinary future awaited Octavian, and react accordingly.

But why was Capricorn considered to be so fortunate a sign in this imperial, or rather pre-imperial horoscope? An enormous time-marker (*horologium*) in Rome, described by Pliny the Elder, showed a specific connection between Capricorn and the point where the sun began to rise again after the darkness of night. According to the contemporary astrologer Manilius, Capricorn is the sign which rules over the West; and Nigidius Figulus, who supposedly told Octavian's father that his son would rule the world, wrote a commentary on the sign. This links an Egyptian myth about the defeat of Typhon, a monster who had opposed the legitimate rule of the gods, by a stratagem devised by Pan who was then rewarded by the grateful deities with a place among the stars as Capricorn. Hence the great play Augustus made of Capricorn in his imperial propaganda – a large number of glass-pastes and cameos, coins, terracottas, sculptures, and paintings dating from his reign underline the connection – when he received the title 'Augustus' and other honours on 13 January when the sun was in Capricorn. [1]

Despite this enthusiasm for the political advantages afforded by astrological symbolism, however, Augustus became very suspicious of individual consultations and in AD 11 issued an edict forbidding diviners (a category which undoubtedly included astrologers) from foretelling the future to anyone in a private consultation, or foretelling death even if there were others present. He may have felt nervous about his own end, since 'the sky in many places seemed ablaze and numerous comets appeared at one and the same time', portents of the death of princes, and Rome's secret police were increasingly on the lookout for behaviour among individuals which might be interpretable as treason. Manilius, who completed his lengthy work on astrology a few years after Augustus's death, seems to have been a Stoic who regarded the universe as a kind of machine whose workings were predictable. 'The Fates rule the world, everything remains firmly fixed by its dependable law and the long ages are stamped with events which are bound to happen. We die as we are being born, and the end is based on the beginning.'

Yet his enthusiasm for Augustus's propitious birth never seems to have provided him with any official status at Court, unlike Tiberius Claudius Thrasyllus (died AD 36), a personal friend of the Emperor Tiberius who occasionally practised astrology himself and told the future Emperor Galba, 'you, too, one day will have a taste of empire'. Thrasyllus wrote an astrological textbook (*Pinax*) and perhaps a tract on divination as well, and it was while Tiberius Caesar was in exile on Rhodes during Augustus's reign that Thrasyllus taught him the science, following which Tiberius developed the grisly habit of consulting astrologers and having them thrown off a rocky outcrop if he doubted their abilities or thought they were fraudulent. Tiberius's villa in Rhodes stood at the top of a cliff and was reached with difficulty, since it had no proper path or roadway leading to it. The historian Tacitus in his account of Tiberius's reign says:

Thrasyllus was brought via these same crags and, after he had stirred the feelings of his questioner by skilfully revealing that he (Tiberius) would be Emperor, and [other] things which were going to happen, he was asked if he had investigated his own horoscope as well. What kind of year did it contain on that occasion? What sort of day? He drew the positions of the stars and measured the distances between them. First he stopped dead and froze; then he started to become alarmed. The more he looked closely [at the chart], greater and greater grew his apprehensive astonishment and fear. Finally he cried out that a dangerous situation which could be interpreted in more than one way and was near its critical stage was threatening him. At that point Tiberius embraced him and congratulated him on foreseeing his dangers and escaping them, accepted what [Thrasyllus] had said, as though it had come from an oracle, and considered him as one of his closest friends.

Again, as in the case of Theogenes, we cannot be sure whether Thrasyllus was being skilful or adroit or both. Tiberius's custom of having some of the island's astrologers thrown off a cliff to their deaths will scarcely have escaped Thrasyllus's notice, and his summons to the villa must therefore have caused him a good deal of alarm. But he had time to prepare himself, mentally at least, and his prediction of a brilliant future for Tiberius, with an unspoken acknowledgement of the crises which had met some other astrologers, may have helped to preserve him. After all, was he to be accounted incompetent for predicting that Tiberius would be Emperor? Surely not: and if he was not incompetent, why would Tiberius have him killed? The fear, the panic, above all the hesitation in Thrasyllus's manner must have reminded Tiberius of what fate he had inflicted on other astrologers and why he had inflicted it, and these very symptoms would surely have served to steer Tiberius away from his murderous thoughts. If, then, Thrasyllus's behaviour was a ploy, it was a very dangerous one, but it worked.

Thrasyllus survived and so did his son, Balbillus, also an astrologer, who withdrew from Rome when Tiberius died, seeking refuge in Alexandria where astrology and astrologers were less likely to be the target of Imperial moods. He was wise to do so, for the short reign of Gaius known as 'Caligula' was barbarous and bloody, although it must be said that when the Emperor consulted an astrologer, Sulla, and was told a violent death awaited him in the near future, he does not seem to have punished the intrepid diviner. Perhaps the prediction was all too likely to be true. Gaius was succeeded by his uncle Claudius, and this restored Balbillus's confidence, because he and Claudius had known one another and been on friendly terms for years. He was given important academic appointments in Alexandria – Head of the Museion (University) and Library – which may have provided him the impetus to write an astrological treatise, *Astrologoumena*. It was a highly technical work, if we may judge from epitomes of it, and his apparent concentration upon the mathematical aspects of the science may have influenced one of Claudius's proclamations in which the Emperor explained that there was going to be an eclipse of the sun on his birthday, the eclipse was going to take place at such and such a time, would last for such and such a period, and people should not take this as an evil omen because it was an entirely natural and predictable phenomenon.

Claudius, however, like Augustus, was quite capable of being in two minds about astrologers, if not their science, for in AD 52 he renewed earlier expulsion orders which banished astrologers from Rome and Italy. The impulse for this action came from a political trial, that of Furius Camillus Scribonius and his mother Vibia, who had been consulting astrologers about the possible date of Claudius's death. Nor were they the only ones to have been engaged thus. If we are to believe Seneca, astrologers had been predicting the Emperor's death for some time already. 'Let astrologers tell the truth some time,' says the god Mercury to the Fates in Seneca's satirical dialogue, *Apocolocyntosis*. 'They have been burying him every year – every month! – since he became Emperor.' (3.2). Regardless of the decree, though, Balbillus's influence at Court does not seem to have been affected. Indeed, it proved baleful on at least one occasion, for when a comet appeared in AD 64 and Nero, then Emperor, sought Balbillus's advice about its meaning, Balbillus told him that when comets portended evil, it was the practice of kings to deflect that evil from themselves by executing a number of important people, an observation which Nero proved all too willing to translate into immediate action.

Nero, of course, has a remarkably unpleasant reputation, and it seems likely that when his mother, Agrippina, decided to murder her husband, the Emperor Claudius, in order to clear the way for her son's accession to Imperial power, the astrologers in her coteries – one of whom was almost certainly Balbillus – after casting a horoscope for the appointed day, advised her on the best time to make the public announcement that Claudius, who had seemed to be ill for a while, had finally died. Agrippina, Tacitus informs us, issued frequent bulletins that the Emperor's state of health was improving, her motive being 'to allow time for the favourable moment suggested by the astrologers to arrive'. (*Annales* 12.68). Alas, however, the crucial horoscope was not actually propitious. From what the astrologers saw, the sun, Venus and Mercury were in Libra, the moon in Leo, Saturn and Jupiter in Aries, and Mars in Scorpio. Now, on the face of it, this could be interpreted to mean that a new Golden Age was about to begin. But this arrangement of the planets with each other tell a different story, for according to astrological theory, 'Saturn opposite Mercury and Jupiter opposite the sun-Venus conjunction seem to foretell Nero's wretched end' – death at the hands of a slave because he himself was unable to face committing suicide. These minatory signs in fact reflect the baleful omens of his birth-chart which on the one hand predicted he would become Emperor and on the other, that he would murder his mother, as indeed he did. No wonder, therefore, his birth horoscope was never published in his lifetime. As for the one cast at the time of Claudius's murder, Agrippina's delay seems to have been caused by the presence of those evil portents we have noted, which the Court astrologers were seeking to interpret in such a way that the good would be emphasised, the unfortunate minimised, and the passage of hours move the planets out of their frightful relationships into ones more happy for the reign which was about to begin. [2]

The political nature of the work Balbillus and his colleagues were expected to do is thus amply illustrated, and as Nero's time in power progressed, threading a way through the mantraps of those perilous years turned into an even more delicate business. The advent of Poppaea Sabina, for example, and that of her husband's favourite astrologer, Ptolemy Seleucus, to positions of influence with Nero, the former in his bed, caused Balbillus much agitation, for both were much opposed to his dominance at Court. Juvenal later commented on the fevered atmosphere at Court:

> Even greater faith is placed in astrologers. Whatever an astrologer says [people] will believe ... Chief among these was one who was often in exile, and because of his 'friendship' and his notebook which was for hire, the great citizen dreaded by Otho died, [i.e. the Emperor Galba]. Consequently, no astrologer who has not been found guilty by a court of law will be reckoned to have talent and inspiration in his art.

In other words, Ptolemy was available to provide any interpretation of the stars which his employer of the time wanted to hear, and in this case Ptolemy had attached himself to the future Emperor Otho and encouraged him to aim at the Principate, (an aim which would inevitably mean the death of the current incumbent, Galba), in spite of the fact that Otho actually had misgivings about the enterprise. 'The diviners and astrologers who were always round him,' says Plutarch, 'especially Ptolemy, would not let him abandon his hopes.'

It comes as no surprise, then, to find that many did not approve of the role they played. Astrologers, and these astrologers in particular, according to Tacitus, are 'a species of human being not to be trusted by those in power and mislead those who entertain hopes ... the worst possible instrument for the wife of an Emperor'. [3] By 'wife', Tacitus meant Poppaea Sabina whom Nero married in AD 62 and killed three years later, a domestic murder which removed her supporter Ptolemy from the Court and banished him to Lusitania. After all this blood-stained excitement, Balbillus seems to have needed a respite from constant tension and retired from Rome to watch, from a safer distance, the death of Nero, the rise of Galba, Otho, and Vitellius as short-lived emperors, and the accession of Vespasian in AD 69. All four, we are told, had had their glittering futures predicted by astrologers, but while others had their brief moments in the Imperial sun, Vespasian particularly favoured Balbillus, perhaps in part because of Balbillus's useful family connections with the royal house of Commagene, a client-kingdom which rebelled against Rome in AD 72 but was then defeated and treated with unusual lenience by the Emperor. Frederick Cramer links this lenience with Balbillus's possible role as a negotiator between Rome and Commagene. If this did indeed happen, it helps to explain Vespasian's granting Balbillus a unique favour, that of acceding to his request to allow the city of Ephesus to celebrate sacred games, which were then named in Balbillus's honour, the *Balbillaea*. [4]

Royal blood and Imperial favour thus combined to make Balbillus an unusually eminent practitioner of the science, but by this time he was near the end of his life and we assume he died in *c*.AD 79–81, at about the same time as, or not long after, his Flavian patron. Titus and his brother Domitian, the next two emperors, continued their father's trust in astrology, Domitian to the point of terror since, we are told, 'he had certain knowledge about the year and day of his death – even, indeed, the hour and manner of it'. Perhaps this is what lay behind his sending Metius Pompusianus into exile and then having him executed, because the man's horoscope promised he would one day become emperor. Nor was Pompusianus the only one to suffer such a fate:

Domitian had not failed to take careful note of the days and the hours when the leading men [in the state] had been born, and therefore began to destroy in advance no small number of men who did not even hope to attain [Imperial] power. But his precautions were in vain. On the day before he expected to die, he remarked aloud that 'tomorrow the moon in Aquarius will be stained with blood and something will happen which people all over the world will talk about'.

An astrologer, Ascletarius, was brought before him on a charge of treason, probably predicting the Emperor's death. 'What about yourself?' asked Domitian. 'What fate awaits you?' The astrologer replied, 'I shall shortly be torn to pieces by dogs.' And so indeed he was.

To disprove his prediction, Domitian ordered that he be executed at once and buried. But his body was placed on a funeral pyre in accordance with usual custom, and when a sudden storm put out the fire, a pack of dogs appeared, pulled the corpse from its place, and quickly tore it to pieces.

Next day, the predicted day of the Emperor's death, yet another astrologer was brought into the Imperial presence. Larginus Proculus, 'an astrologer and sorcerer', was accused of foretelling Domitian's demise and, if the charge against him was genuine, he would have had the satisfaction of hearing that his prophecy had been fulfilled; for on the day and in the hour that death had been predicted so long ago, Domitian was stabbed several times while trying to relax in a bath, and thus astrological science appeared to have enjoyed a major justification.

With Imperial favour and consultation, and these recorded triumphs, (no doubt doctored in places to fit what the historian considered to be a significant pattern of events), one might expect to find astrology in more or less all its manifestations accepted in every social circle as a valid and credible discipline. Some people appear to have done so. The poet Persius expressed the relationship between himself and a close friend, Cornutus, in astrological terms:

> Please have no doubt that our lives are in harmony because of the firm bond [between us], and that they are guided by a single star. Either a Fate clinging fast to Truth has hung the duration of our days upon a similar Balance [*Libra*] [5], or the hour when faithful [friends] are born has divided our two like-minded destinies between the Twins [*Gemini*] and we break in pieces [the influence of] ill-omened Saturn by means of [the influence of] Jupiter whom we both share. However it may be, it is a fact that your star is in harmony with me.

Petronius Arbiter gives us a notion not only of how an outrageously vulgar and snobbish freedman regarded astrologers, but also provides us, admittedly through the freedman's mouth, with a scrap of consultation.

Trimalchio, the freedman, is explaining to dinner-guests how he became astonishingly rich and was encouraged by:

> an astrologer who had come to our place by chance, a little Greek effort, Serapa was his name, someone who knows the gods' intentions. This chap told me even things I'd forgotten.

He explained everything to me in great detail. He was thoroughly acquainted with my intestines and the only thing he didn't tell me was what I'd had for dinner the day before. You'd have thought he'd always lived with me. Habbinas, I'm asking you – you were there, I think – 'You acquired your lady-wife at the expense of those things [we know about]. You haven't much luck with your friends. No one is ever as grateful to you as he should be. You are in possession of large amounts of property. You are nourishing a viper in your bosom' … and he also said – I shouldn't really tell you this – that as from now I have thirty years, four months, two days left to live. Oh, and before long I'm going to receive a legacy. This is what my destiny says!

One notices the vagueness of the astrologer's predictions in this case, and the contempt (in imitation of his social betters), with which Trimalchio calls him a *Graeculus*, possibly an affectionate, but more likely a dismissive diminutive. The astrologer's name, Serapa, however, is reminiscent of 'Serapis', a Graeco-Egyptian god originating in Alexandria; so it is possible we are to understand that he had come to Rome from Egypt to practise his science and earn a living from wealthy, gullible clients. Some Romans were happy enough to trust astrology, but only in relation to its astronomical content and its forecasts in relation to weather. Pliny the Elder wrote:

The essential character of the heavens, which are intertwined with the world and ingrained in its texture, is eternal. But their influence as far as earth is concerned is highly relevant, and because of their effects, brilliance, and size we have been able to get to know them in great detail.

The poet Lucan went further, putting in the mouth of a priest addressing Julius Caesar a list of planets' and stars' effects on earth's climate:

Various powers were assigned by the first law of the universe to those stars which, without anyone or anything else, regulate the rapid movement of the sky and run contrary to it. The sun divides time into periods and exchanges day for night. With his powerful rays he prevents the stars from moving and, from his post, checks the progress of their wandering orbits. The moon mingles the sea and the earth by means of her phases. Frozen ice and the belt of snow submit to Saturn. Mars has command of the winds and random strikes of lightning. Under Jupiter is climate and air which is never turbulent. Venus controls the fruitful seeds of the physical world; Mercury settles the behaviour of boundless water.

This, however, is scarcely predictive astrology, and several writers of the late first century BC – early first century AD expressed reservation or open hostility to it. Farmers have to take into account the stars and the sky, admitted Columella, but he also pointed out that he had written a book against astrologers on the grounds that they say that changes in the air happen on specific, predictable occasions. On the other hand, if Pliny, Lucan, and Columella could spare a little time for astrologers, others spared none at all. Lucilius, a Greek epigrammatist, wrote several stinging poems about the inadequacies of astrologers and their clients.

Aulos the astrologer drew up his own birth-chart and said that his doom had arrived, [although] he still had four hours to live. When the fifth came along and he had to go on living after he had perceived nothing, he was ashamed of Petosiris and hanged himself. [Now], hanging in the air, he is dying, but he dies understanding nothing.

All those who take note of Mars and Saturn while they cast their horoscope are all worthy of a single drum-roll. Perhaps I shall see them not long hence actually realising what Taurus does and what Leo is capable of doing.[6]

Doubtless attitudes towards astrologers varied from social class to social class, those in the set closest to the Emperor anxiously sniffing the air to see which way the wind of Imperial favour or disfavour was blowing, and those further away tempering their notions according to whether astrologers of their acquaintance or those in the eye of gossip were successful in their predictions, adequately near the mark, or simply wrong. A poet such as Marcus Manilius, for example, whose lengthy work, *Astronomica*, is the earliest Latin treatment of the subject to survive more or less intact, found it difficult to attract a wide readership during his lifetime. *Astronomica* is in five Books. The first two were written during Augustus's reign, the third and fourth similarly or perhaps under Tiberius, and the fifth under Tiberius, and one is inclined to suggest that since the verse itself is not intolerably bad, the reason for people's reluctance to read the work, or at any rate to possess a copy of it, lies in the vagaries of the Imperial temperament at the time. Tiberius's treatment of astrologers on Rhodes would scarcely have passed unremarked by the gossips of the capital and a certain discretion anent one's library be observed in consequence.

Yet the poem itself cannot be regarded as revolutionary or threatening or, indeed, especially novel. Book 1 begins by explaining that the god Mercury was responsible for revealing to human beings that destiny is written in the stars, after which prooemium Manilius lists and discusses various theories about how the universe came into being. His favoured explanation turns out to be the Stoic view that everything was created from the four elements, and that a divine spirit governs them and maintains their harmoniousness. Next Manilius describes the constellations which are amazing in their stability and regularity:

Nothing in this mighty edifice is more wonderful than its design and the obedience of everything to immutable law. Nowhere does confusion do harm; nothing in any of its parts moves randomly to enlarge or shorten its course or change the order of its movement … All this is not the result of chance, but the plan of a God most high. (1.478–81, 531).

After this we are treated to technicalities dealing with various celestial circles including the zodiac, and finally a passage on comets which Manilius introduces at this point to complete his picture of the physical heavens before he proceeds to the powers of the stars and the laws by which they are governed.

Book 2 deals with the signs of the zodiac, starting with those which are masculine, (Aries, Gemini, Leo, Libra, Sagittarius, Aquarius), and followed by the feminine, (Taurus,

Cancer, Virgo, Scorpio, Capricorn, Pisces); then the relationships between the signs – 'they affect our destinies through their agreements with each other, for they rejoice in alliances and co-operate with one another according to their natures and locations', (2.271–2) – then, after a brief digression, the allotment of parts of the human body to the influence of zodiacal signs:

Aries – head	Libra – buttocks
Taurus – neck	Scorpio – groin
Gemini – arms	Sagittarius – thighs
Cancer – chest	Capricorn – knees
Leo – sides	Aquarius – legs
Virgo – stomach	Pisces – feet.

The Book ends with further technicalities related to these zodiacal relationships – the subdivisions (*dodecatemories*) of the signs of the zodiac, the subdivisions of the planets, five of which are allotted to each zodiacal subdivision – and finally the framework of the horoscope itself divided (i) into quadrants dominating infancy, youth, adulthood, and old age, and further (ii) into twelve parts or 'houses' in modern astrological parlance, corresponding to the twelve signs of the zodiac.

Book 3 discusses a subsidiary set of 'houses' relating to home, warfare, business, law, marriage, length of life, dangers, social class, children, character, health, and success; and Book 4 the qualities and skills given to those born under each sign of the zodiac. Thus Sagittarius:

> in the stars of this constellation the human form is blended with a beast's and placed above it. Wherefore it has lordship over beasts. And because it carries a shaft poised on drawn bow, it imparts strength to limb and keenness to the intellect, swiftness of movement, and an indefatigable spirit. (4.238–42).

These individual 'geographies' are succeeded by terrestrial, a description of the various races of the world, followed by accommodating countries and regions to particular signs of the zodiac: the Hellespont, Propontis, Syria, Persia, and Egypt to Aries, for example, or Scythia, Asia, and Arabia to Taurus, and so forth. Finally, Manilius notes the effect of eclipses upon the earth and ends with an affirmation of the rightness of the astronomer-astrologer's craft:

> God grudges not the earth the sight of heaven, but reveals His face and form by cease-less revolution, offering, nay impressing, Himself upon us to the end that He can be truly known, can teach His nature to those who have eyes to see, and can compel them to mark His laws. Of itself the firmament summons our minds to the stars, and in not concealing its ordinances shows that it would have them known. Who then would deem it wrong to understand what is right for us to see? (4.916–22).

Someone else might have stopped at this point. Manilius himself says so at the beginning of Book 5, but he decided to make a thorough job of his astronomical survey and so ventures to constellations beyond those of the zodiac, which he describes in some detail before gaps in the text make understanding of what he has to say about further planetary influences a matter of conjecture. The Book, and therefore the whole poem, then comes to a somewhat unexpected and slightly odd end with a description of the various magnitudes of the stars in constellations such as Orion and the Pleiades. It fizzles, but fizzles out, and one is left wondering whether Manilius had tired of his task and left it unfinished, or whether, since Book 5 had probably been composed during the more feverish days of Tiberius's principate, sheer nervousness caused his pen to falter and give up the ghost.

It is interesting, then, to compare the fate of the *Astronomica* with that of another astrological poem, a paraphrased Latin translation of a Greek poem, *Phaenomena* by Aratus of Soli, dating from the third century BC. This version, *Aratea*, attributed to Germanicus Caesar (15 BC–AD 19), nephew of the Emperor Tiberius, (or sometimes to the Emperor himself), made its appearance at about the same time as Manilius's *Astronomica*. But in spite of its many differences by omission or expansion from Aratus's original, it actually has less to offer the reader, since Germanicus consciously abandons Aratus's picture of a cosmos governed by a providential and beneficent deity whose nature and will are revealed by celestial and meteorological phenomena, in favour of a more literary and Ovidian set of myths and erotic themes intended for diversion rather than instruction or explication. The *Aratea* was thus always more likely than the *Astronomica* to be a relatively popular work. Written by a member of the Imperial family and refashioned for distinctly pleasurable reading, how could it fail to capture the attention of *ce-pays çi*, the circle of families at the peak of Roman society, whose interests were bound to be governed by political rather than merely intellectual considerations? In this regard, its opening lines are significant: 'Aratus began with mighty Jupiter. My poem, however, claims you, father, greatest of all, as its inspirer. It is you I reverence; it is to you I am offering sacred gifts, the first fruits of my literary efforts.' The 'you' is Augustus to whom the whole poem is addressed and dedicated, and if the Imperial author knew that a patron is best approached on one's knees, it can scarcely be doubted that his upper-class readership was fully aware of that, too. Nor may it be an accident that Manilius, Germanicus, and several of their successors chose to write their *astronomica-astrologica* in verse rather than prose. For verse provides opportunities to digress, to indulge in rhetorical flourishes, and to allude to myth and folktale, which are not so readily available to the writer of a scholarly tome or practical handbook, and in as far as a verse-author can take wing every so often from prosaic discussion or exposition, so he can provide distance between himself, his audience, and any potentially difficult intellectual propositions which, in the cold light of prose, might seem to have unwelcome political or theological interpretive possibilities. [7]

5

Jewish Traditions, Demons & Manuals c.100–c.200: An Astrological Legacy

If emperors decreed the expulsion of astrologers from Rome, (along with magicians, diviners, and other groups seen as undesirable), their official disapproval could not fail to infect everyone's attitude to the science and its practitioners, if only temporarily; and it is a point worthy of note that, in spite of their using astrologers and consulting them on several occasions at least, every single Julio-Claudian and Flavian emperor from Augustus to Domitian either approved a senatorial decree or issued one of their own banishing astrologers from the capital and, most often, from Italy as well. To be an astrologer in first-century Rome and Roman territory was thus a potentially hazardous business, and astrologers had to wait for the greater political calm of the second century AD to enjoy a certain respite. Now, among the minorities who were liable to find themselves caught up in the net of expulsions from the capital were Jews and Christians, both of whom had astrology woven in some form or another into their religious and allied texts. The Jews were forbidden to worship the sun or the moon or any of the host of heaven (*Deuteronomy* 17.3), and the prophets treated the practitioners of astrology with contempt. 'Thou art wearied in the multitude of thy counsels,' said Isaiah, apostrophising Babylon. 'Let now the astrologers, the star-gazers, the monthly prognosticators, stand up and save thee from these things that shall come upon thee.' (47.13). Yet from time to time the Jews, surrounded as they were by the worshippers of astral deities, yielded to temptation. 'Ye have borne the tabernacles of your Moloch and Chiun your images, the star of your god, which ye made to yourselves,' (*Amos* 5.26); and they were not always sorry to have done so, as they explained to the prophet Jeremiah:

> As for the word that thou hast spoken unto us in the name of the Lord, we will not hearken unto thee. But we will certainly do whatsoever thing goeth forth out of our own mouth, to burn incense unto the Queen of Heaven, and to pour out drink-offerings unto her, *as we have done, we and our fathers, our kings and our princes, in the cities of Judah and in the streets of Jerusalem.* (44.16–17, my italics).

The Queen of Heaven is, of course, a reference to Ishtar-Astarte, the goddess associated with the planet Venus, and it is probably no accident that Isaiah refers to Babylon and Jeremiah to Egypt, for the Jews suffered exile in both places at different times, and in both places came into contact with the worship of astral deities, interpretations of omens, and the notion that the stars and planets expressed the will of or conveyed messages from invisible gods or goddesses. So while *Psalm* 104 describes God as creator and absolute master of the cosmos, *Job* 38.7 ('the morning stars sang together') and *Psalm* 148.3 ('Praise Him, sun and moon: praise Him, all ye stars of night') personify the celestial bodies as though they were living entities in their own right; and *Judges* 5.20 ('the stars in their courses fought against Sisera') and *Psalm* 19.1 ('the heavens declare the glory of God, and the firmament sheweth His handiwork') strongly suggest that they could be regarded both as signs that there was a God who had created them, and as influential players in a drama which was likely to have an effect on human affairs. These are points taken up by commentators in the Babylonian *Talmud*, although it is a moot point how far some of the Talmudic commentators were influenced by astrology and how much by fatalism. James Charlesworth points out that in *Shabbat* 156a, for example, the claim that a person's character is determined by the day of the week on which he or she was born preserves a belief in fatalism, not astrology:

> Nevertheless, the thought may have evolved out of a compromise between astrological fatalism … which claims that a man's character is shaped by the position of the zodiac at the time of birth, and the Biblical beliefs that man's destiny is determined either by God or by his own actions.

On the other hand, Rabbi Hanina bar Hama, significantly enough a native of Babylon, taught that a person's character is determined by the constellation of the hour in which she or he was born, that the planets influence wisdom and wealth, and that 'Israel stands under astrological influence': to which Rabbi Johanan bar Nappaha in effect replied, 'Phooey!'

Belief in possible connections between one's birth sign and one's character and appearance can perhaps be seen to yield to the doubts of Rabbi Johanan and those who thought like him in an astrological document from Qumran, written in code, which connects astrology-physiognomy in the kind of way we were examining earlier. A man born 'in the foot of Taurus', it says, will have long, thin thighs and long slender toes, while someone else whose sign is not given, (the manuscript is in a fragmentary condition), has thick fingers, fat thighs covered in hair, and short tubby toes. Clearly there are strong links between this and Hellenistic texts which reflect not only the belief that the signs of the zodiac influence the shape and appearance of the human body, but also that people's physiognomy can provide a clue to the ascendant – that part of the zodiacal sign rising at the moment of birth – pertaining to a given individual. Hence, as Mladan Popović has suggested, it may be thought that this document 'was originally an elaborate physiognomic catalogue, listing entries for every division of the twelve zodiacal signs, in order to determine people's ascendant signs'. The text also mentions spirits relating to 'the house of light' and 'the house of darkness', that is, the areas above and below the horizon. There is debate over the exact meaning of the Hebrew word used here for 'spirit', but it seems likely that it refers to those spirits, good and bad, which Jewish tradition allotted to the signs of the zodiac, and the implication of the text seems to be that 'the more parts of a zodiacal sign that have ascended, the more powerful the radiating sign and spirit on the people who were born at that moment'. Such rapport between this text and its Hellenistic counterparts one may think makes it odd that such a document should be found in the library of the Essenes who were well known to adhere strictly to Jewish Law and therefore to distance themselves from pagan beliefs and practices. But Matthias Albani has wondered whether it may have served as a piece of useful evidence in combating those very beliefs and practices, which were gaining ground among certain groups of Jews. Hence its being written in code – 'not only a means of literary style for marking the esoteric character of such contents, but … also … a 'prohibition sign' for unauthorised readers'.

Rabbinical exchanges, however, merely illustrate a long-standing debate within Judaism about the validity of astrology and its impact on the belief the omniscience and omnipotence of God, a debate which was to be renewed centuries later during the confessional quarrels of the reformation. Thus, in the Babylonian *Talmud*, the blessing bestowed on Abraham by God was interpreted as the gift of astrology; Jethro supposedly advised Moses to use astrology to help him govern the Children of Israel; and two people born under the same star have a special relationship, (one thinks here of Persius and Cornutus), because humans, although not animals, are under planetary influence. The planets themselves might be personified, not as divinities but as messengers from God – and with the development of this point of view we enter the realm of magic where the sympathetic and antipathetic relationships between created entities and things and influxes flowing from one to another, are open to manipulation and control by human beings.

Various pseudepigrapha show the intimate interconnection between astrology and these beliefs. The *Testament of Solomon*, a work containing elements traceable to the first century AD, has King Solomon describing how he conjured demons among whom were:

> Thirty-six spirits, their heads shapeless like dogs, but in themselves they were human in form: with faces of asses, faces of oxen, and faces of birds. And I, Solomon, on hearing and seeing them, wondered, and I asked them and said, 'Who are you?' But they, of one accord with one voice, said, 'We are the thirty-six elements, the world-rulers of the darkness of this age … We present ourselves before thee like the other spirits, from Ram and Bull, from Twin and Crab, Lion and Virgin, Scales and Scorpion, Archer, Goat-horned, Water-Power, and Fish.'

In other words, these are the *decans*, each a ruler of 10 of the 30° of a zodiacal sign, but conceived as evil-intentioned spirits who can inflict harm on human beings. 'The second said, "I am called Barsafael, and I cause those who are subject to my hour to feel the pain of migraine. But if I merely hear the words, "Gabriel, imprison Barsafael", I retreat at once.'

Every one of the decans gives Solomon his name, details of the pain he causes and, significantly, the name of the angel who is more powerful than he and can therefore stop the human's suffering.

Control of demons was a major aspect of magic and here it is being linked specifically with astrology, just as it is in the *Sefer Ha-Razim*, a third-century AD text which repeats identification of the decans with non-human beings, this time angelic, and explains how 'to master the investigation of the strata of the heavens, to go about in all that is in their seven abodes, to observe all the astrological signs, to examine the course of the sun, to explain the observations of the moon'. It also provides ritual words and actions intended to manipulate the influence of planets upon each other and upon human beings. Similarly, the *Epistle to Rehoboam*, a work probably stemming, like so many others, from Alexandria, and addressed to King Solomon, gives instructions for exploitation of the powers of the planets. The first section makes clear what the *Epistle* is about; the second lists the hours and days of the astrological week so that the magical practitioner can see which time will be best for which activity; the third lists the angels and demons who rule over each hour of the week; the fourth and fifth provide invocations to each of the planets and ways of constructing magic symbols to intensify the power of the invocations to engage the attention of the planetary ruler; and the fifth and sixth list the plants sympathetic with the zodiacal signs and planets, and give instructions on the way to gather and use them.

Jewish astrology of the last century BC and the first AD was thus permeated by Hellenistic-Egyptian ideas, symbols, and beliefs to such an extent that it was perfectly possible and acceptable for zodiacal reliefs to be incorporated into the floors of some synagogues, and for its pseudepigraphical literature to include works synthesising astrology, magic, and religion. But it is also notable that Judaism's distinctive trait of monotheism remains untouched by the polytheism or Gnostic theories of immanence by which its forays into astrology were always liable to be affected. This can be seen, for example, in the fragments of the *Astronomical Book* found at Qumran, whose priestly author describes the visibility and illumination of the moon during its various phases. The intention of the book is clear: to compute a schematic lunar year, to show how astronomical knowledge is linked with prevision of future events, and to show that study of astronomy-astrology does not necessarily lead to idolatry. The Creator, says this tradition, is the Creator and Governor of all things, and His permission has to be sought before anyone embarks upon the perilous sea of planetary invocation:

> O King of kings and Lord of lords, the one who existed before creation, possessor of everlasting power, inconceivable illumination and limitless light, the only rich provider and supplier of mercy, visit us by granting favour and kindness that we may be able to subjugate the passing planet, the sun, and possess his power.

The prayer, whatever its subsequent divagation into magic, thus begins with an acknowledgement that God is supreme and everything, no matter how powerful, is subject to His will – an acknowledgement which was inherited by Christianity and preserved throughout the later centuries of Christian astrology and Christian magic. [1]

On 20 March 6 BC, a minute after sunset in Jerusalem, the moon occulted Jupiter in Aries. When two planets move so closely together that they appear to touch, the one is said to 'hide' (occultate) the other, an event which ancient astrologers regarded as one of high significance. 'If Jupiter comes into aspect with the waxing moon,' wrote the third-fourth century AD astrologer, Firmicus Maternus, 'this will create men of almost divine and immortal nature. This happens when the moon is moving towards Jupiter.' That the occultation should have taken place in Aries was also noteworthy, because ancient astrology associated specific regions or countries upon earth with signs of the zodiac, and

Aries, according to the astrologer Claudius Ptolemy, governed Coele Syria, Idumaea, and Judaea. Hence, to any skilled astrologer of the time in the Middle East, it would have been clear that a great birth had taken place or would take place, in the region of Syria-Palestine at the time, with Judaea the most likely location. A lunar month later, on 17 April, the occultation was repeated a little after noon. That one such indication of a divine birth should have happened was important and intriguing enough; to have it confirmed so soon afterwards was astonishing. But here, if Michael Molnar is correct, we have the initial 'star' which signalled to the Magi that a divine human being or god in human shape had been or was to be born quite probably in Judaea, so remarkable a celestial message that it sent them to Jerusalem, (perhaps the most obvious first stop in their quest for the new divinity), where they saw unmistakable confirmation that the advice of local astrologers that they go to Bethlehem was undoubtedly correct. [2]

The star of Bethlehem continued to exercise Christians for several centuries after the event, partly because of what it represented rather than because of what it was. If the stars are signs of divine will, for example, and the Bethlehem star genuinely foretold the birth of Christ, did it follow – as the anti-Christian Celsus appears to have suggested – that Christians must now acknowledge the validity of pagan astrological interpretations, even though the cosmos had changed into a new, re-ordered Christian universe; and did this also imply that Christ could not have failed to be born because He was powerless to resist the ineluctable development of an already fated cosmic plan which was greater than His own will? Did this significant role for a star in the birth-story mean that Christians were more or less obliged to condone astrology; and what did the star have to say to both Jews and Christians about the relationship between astrology and prophecy? In fact, did the coincidence between the appearance of the star and the fulfilment of prophetic verses from the Old Testament mean that astrology might now be regarded as a legitimate form of foreknowledge? Different Christians had different answers. Some (a few) clearly yielded to the prevailing circumambient climate of acceptance and incorporated astrology in various ways into their beliefs and practices. The Phibionites and Marcosians, for example, were said to venerate divine beings associated with degrees of the ecliptic; a community known as the Peretrae believed that the stars were powers of destruction; and Faustus of Mileva, against whose ideas St Augustine wrote at length, taught that Christ Himself was actually composed of astral material. This last may illustrate how one attempt to dissociate Christ from subjection to astral fatalism was pressed to an extreme, for at least two early Christian theologians, Ignatius of Antioch and Theodotus, suggested that Jesus and the Bethlehem star were essentially identical and that in consequence this unique event had destroyed the old astral order (thereby rendering all pagan astrological interpretation henceforth invalid), and established a new, fundamentally Christian cosmic order.

Argument did not cease, although it gradually settled down into a general pattern along the lines of 'the stars act as signs of what is to come', (Clement of Alexandria); 'the stars do not influence anyone's birth, still less that of our Creator', (St Augustine); and 'the old form of knowledge (*scientia*) has been supplanted by a new one, and so now interpreting horoscopes is wrong', (Tertullian). For Christians of at least the first four centuries, then, the star of Bethlehem was significant in a host of ways, and whether we ourselves regard it as an occultation, conjunction, miraculous appearance, or literary device, we cannot be in any doubt that the role it played in early Christian disputation reveals a readiness on everyone's part to acquiesce in one form or another in the ancient supposition that the sky could speak if God allowed it to do so.

This alliance of astrology and a new religion whose initial variants were sometimes wild and quite extraordinary should been seen especially against the background of Alexandria, partly because that city was the centre of speculative and practical advances in astrology at this time, and partly because it was such a melting-pot of religions, cults, and sects that virtually nothing could not be proposed or actually practised in the name of some divinity or other.[3] Arising out of this ferment during the last century BC and the first two centuries AD there emerged a series of texts known collectively as *Hermetica* or *Corpus Hermeticum* because supposedly they came from the pen of a divine or semi-divine figure known as 'Hermes Trismegistus'. These disparate writings were to find favour among scholars of many different kinds for a millennium and a half, on the grounds that they, and therefore their wisdom, were older even than the writings of or attributed to Moses, and in consequence their influence on more than one of the occult sciences was profound. This *Corpus* embodied the religious syncretism of Ptolemaic and Roman Alexandria, blending Greek, Egyptian, Platonic, and Christian religious notions in such a way as to produce a distinctive kind of theology of its own, and while they do not betray such direct astrological content, there is reason to suppose that the surviving tracts which make up the *Corpus* were edited down from a much larger body of work by Byzantine scholars who omitted a good deal of material of which they disapproved.

As it stands, then, it is Tract 16 which contains most of the *Corpus*'s astrology. 'The sun,' we are told, 'is situated in the centre of the cosmos, wearing it like a crown.' This is an image reminiscent both of Mithras and of the later god, the Unconquered Sun (*Sol Invictus*), with whom Christ Himself was to be aligned or identified. 'Like a good driver, it steadies the chariot of the cosmos and fastens the reins to itself to prevent the cosmos from going out of control.' These reins are 'life and soul and spirit and immortality and becoming' by means of which a constant spiral of transformation is created among mortal beings. 'Around the sun are many troops of spirits looking like battalions in changing array ... They have been assigned the territory of humankind, and they oversee human activity.' It is the business of these spirits to punish human irreverence towards the gods by sending 'torrents, hurricanes, thunderstorms, fiery alterations and earthquakes ... famines and wars'.

These spirits (*daimones*) refer to beings intermediary between humankind and the gods. In Classical pagan contexts this means that they are not essentially evil or hostile to human beings, as their derivative 'demons' might suggest; but in Christian contexts the writer, or indeed the reader, might find it all too seductive to understand them in this entirely negative light, and the following section of the Tract illustrates what one may call an intermediate stage of interpretation in which the spirits are good or bad according to their essential energies:

(13) The sun sets in array the troop, or rather troops of spirits (*daimones*), which are many and changing, arrayed under the regiments of stars, an equal number of them for each

star. Thus deployed they follow the orders of a particular star, and they are good and evil according to their natures – that is, their energies. For energy is the essence of a spirit. Some of them, however, are mixtures of good and evil.

(14) They have all been granted authority over the things of the earth and over the troubles of the earth, and they produce change and tumult collectively for cities and nations, individually for each person. They reshape our souls to their own ends, and they rouse them, lying in ambush in our muscle and marrow, in veins and arteries, in the brain itself, reaching to the very guts.

(15) The spirits on duty at the exact moment of birth, arrayed under each of the stars, take possession of each of us as we come into being and receive a soul. From moment to moment they change places, not staying in position but moving by rotation. Those which enter through the body into the two parts of the soul twist the soul about, each towards its own energy. But the rational part of the soul stands unmastered by the spirits, suitable as a receptacle for God.

(16) Thus, if by way of the sun anyone has a ray shining upon him in his rational part, (and the totality of those enlightened is few), the spirits' effect on him is nullified. For none – neither spirits nor gods – can do anything against a single ray of God. All others the spirits carry off as spoils, both souls and bodies, since they are fond of the spirits' energies and acquiesce in them … So, with our bodies as their instruments, the spirits govern this earthly government. Hermes has called this government 'Fate'.

(17) The intelligible cosmos, then, depends from God and the sensible cosmos from the Intelligible; but the sun, through the intelligible cosmos and the sensible as well, is supplied by God with the influx of good, in other words, with His craftsmanship. Around the sun are the eight spheres which depend from it: the sphere of the fixed stars, the six of the planets, and the one which surrounds the earth. From these spheres depend the spirits, and then, from the spirits, humans. Thus all things and all persons are dependent from God.

(18) Therefore the father of all is God; their craftsmanship is the sun; and the cosmos is the instrument of craftsmanship. Intelligible essence governs heaven; heaven governs the gods; and spirits posted by the gods govern humans. This is the army of gods and spirits.

(19) Through them God makes everything for Himself, and all things are parts of God.

It is not so much the stars themselves which are of consequence, then, but their tutelary spirits under the command of the sun, although the sun himself is not the spirits' ultimate ruler – he acts merely as general of their army. The ultimate ruler is God who is the source of all delegated creating power. So here is provided a cosmic system which fits easily into the Christian concept of what such a thing might or should or actually does look like. The spirits are presented in a not entirely ambiguous way. They may be good or bad according to their energies, but it is obvious they veer more to the bad than the good, and one is reminded of one well-established Christian tradition which ascribed the origin of human knowledge of astrology to the instruction of specifically evil spirits – the indifferent *daimones* of Classical pagan religion now become the demons of Christianity. The second-century Tatian wrote:

Men became the subject of the demons' apostasy, for they showed men a chart of the constellations, and like dice-players they introduced the factor of Fate – a very unjust one – which brought both judge and prisoner to where they are now. Murderers and their victims, rich and poor, are children of Fate, and every birth-chart gave entertainment as in a theatre to the demons.

This impression of a humanity under the complete control of hostile spirit-forces is underlined by the *Corpus*'s observation that the spirits can enter into the very fabric of the human body and from there exercise an almost irresistible force upon the soul itself. With certain modifications, this is close to the popular perception of diabolic possession, the only consolation for the human being the proviso that 'none – neither demons nor gods – can do anything against a single ray of God'. Such a view, which sees the universe as a battle-ground between good and evil forces, with the latter pressing very hard indeed upon humankind whose safety lies in the single fact that God is stronger than anything in His creation. Reliance upon Him can therefore prevail in the battle with spirits and demons, bringing in its wake at least one important consequence – the desire to use whatever power or powers may be available to control the otherwise near-ineluctable pressures to which humans are normally subject. Hence, as we have seen already and shall see again, the intimacy which grew up between astrology and magic. [4]

Meanwhile, however, astrologers largely based in Alexandria either as students or practitioners were flourishing during the second to fifth centuries AD, preparing *omnium gathera* for the benefit of a wider audience, or refining the technicalities of the science for their own satisfaction. Perhaps the most obvious initial examples are those of Claudius Ptolemy (*c.*100–178) and Vettius Valens (*c.*120–175). Ptolemy, about whom not a great deal is known, certainly lived in Alexandria for a while and produced the two works for which he is famous, *Syntaxis* or *Almagest*, which is a compendium of Greek astronomy, and *Tetrabiblos*, which is an abridged and somewhat deviant version of the standard Greek astrology of the time. The *Almagest* has been described as a criminal deceit:

> All of his own observations that Ptolemy uses in the *Syntaxis* are fraudulent, so far as we can test them. Many of the observations that he attributes to others astronomers are also frauds that he has committed. His work is riddled with theoretical errors and with failures of comprehension … Thus Ptolemy is not the greatest astronomer of antiquity, but he is something still more unusual: he is the most successful fraud in the history of science. [5]

It is not an auspicious verdict if one wants to consider his immense reputation and influence, since inevitably the researches (of whatever kind) he undertook in astronomy will have had their effect on his application of these to astrology; but because that reputation was indeed immense and long-lasting, we are obliged to take into account his principal themes, if not each individual assertion or opinion.

He begins by saying that his *Tetrabiblos* is intended to answer astrology's critics, those who 'are of the opinion that what is incomprehensible to themselves must be equally so to others', (1.1), and then, after pointing out that heavenly bodies have an effect upon those below, of whatever kind, argues (or asserts) that astrology is useful to human beings in as much as while the movements of stars and planets may be mathematically determined, human lives are not necessarily bound to a similar determination:

> The heavenly bodies alone are regulated in their courses by this immutable divine law, but the effects they produce are only of a secondary nature, and merely a series of accidents arising each from its respective cause … Those events only, whether general or particular, whose causes are so powerful that nothing can withstand them, can happen by necessity; but the effects of the weaker causes may be prevented. (1.3).

Life is thus potentially complicated, and to interpret horoscopes with greater accuracy, the astrologer should take into account such things as family background, place of birth, and education:

> He who does not add these causes to the effects of the [changing sky] will only involve himself in difficulties; for although celestial causes are the most powerful, all others being subject to them while they themselves are subject to none, yet those who judge from the effects of [the sky] alone, without adding these other considerations, can never hope to succeed, (1.2) … Persons, therefore, who foretell events should do it from a thorough knowledge of Nature and not from any silly opinions of their own. (1.3).

With these rules established – not that earlier astrologers would have found anything novel about them – Ptolemy proceeds to a description of the planets, the stars, the constellations, and their effects, their natures, and their relationships, before entering upon Books 2 and 3 which deal with what he calls 'general prediction', (relating to countries, seasons, and major events), and 'particular or genethliacal prediction', relating to individual people, their natures, characteristics, and prospects. Here we are on familiar territory, for Ptolemy weds astrology and physiognomy in ways we have seen before:

> Jupiter. Ruling and oriental, gives a fair, handsome complexion, moderate quantity of hair, full eyes, excellent stature and dignified appearance, the temperament inclined to heat and moisture. If occidental, the complexion is fair but not uniform, lank hair, the forehead or crown of the head bald, a middle stature, and the constitution more moist. (3.16).
>
> There will be blindness of one eye when the moon is in either of the [horizontal] angles, [*i.e. east or west*], exactly at 0°, or at the full; or with any other configuration if she applies to any of the nebulous parts of the zodiac, for example, the little cloud in Pisces or the Pleiades of Taurus, the head of the arrow in Sagittarius, the Scorpion's sting, the parts about the plaited hair of Leo, or the water part of Aquarius. (3.17).
>
> If Jupiter alone governs the mind and be well situated, he renders men noble-minded, agreeable, pious, revered, comfortable in life, courteous, honourable, candid, just, dignified, venerable, attentive to their own concerns, merciful, learned, beneficent, very affection-ate, and fit to govern. If badly situated, the same propensities are imprinted on the mind, but more faintly and with less energy. Thus, they will be prodigal instead of generous;

superstition will be substituted for piety, timidity for a becoming reserve, pride for dignity, folly for good breeding, love of pleasure for love of business, negligence for ease, and indifference for candour. If he [*Jupiter*] have familiarity with Mars well placed, he renders men rough, warlike, good soldiers, impetuous, hating subjection, hot-headed, bold, free speaking, active, fond of disputes, contentious, imperious, high-minded, honourable, hasty tempered, judicious and fortunate. If ill-disposed, he makes men mischievous, careless, cruel, unfeeling, seditious, quarrelsome, stubborn, slanderers, arrogant, covetous, rapacious, unsteady, shallow, unsettled, rash, faithless, indiscreet, turbulent, worthless, dissatisfied, lustful, contemptible, and wholly without any steadiness or rule of action. (3.18).

Mars brings death by continual fever, semi-tertian [fevers], sudden infections, stone and gravel, blood-spilling and haemorrhage, abortion, childbirth, erysipelas, and in short, by whatever originates in excessive heat. (4.9).

Ptolemy thus offers his readers a practical guide to the interpretation of horoscopes, (although sometimes his text reads as though he had merely swallowed the equivalent of a thesaurus and thrown in every synonym and near-relation he could think of), and a careful set of stepping stones between the rigid determinism implied by a purely Stoic view of the universe and the Hermetic cosmos teeming with spirits, through which humankind was supposed to negotiate its daily progress; and he was sufficiently successful in steering clear of either extremity, and producing a theoretically consistent system based on an Aristotelian model, to enable his work to be taken up by Christian Europe and be both cherished and taught as though he were the complete master of his astrological craft.

In certain ways, of course, he was; but if we compare his *Tetrabiblos* with the *Anthologiae* of his near-contemporary, Vettius Valens, we can see the limitations of his approach. Valens was a dedicated practising astrologer. Born in Antioch, he moved to Egypt in his mid thirties in order to perfect his knowledge of the occult sciences, and from that point willingly allowed astrology to absorb his entire attention and energy. This willingness seems to have arisen partly from viewing astrology as a bulwark against whatever pains and disappointments life might throw at him, and to some extent because he saw it as an integral part of his religious life.

For him, astrology is a mystery. He himself is a *mystes*, as are those who, like him, have been initiated into the *mysteria* of the astrology of initiates. He holds initiates into the mysteries in honour and ranks them as philosophers. These mysteries, whose fruit is a true understanding of the sky, sacred and immortal contemplation, divine and venerable, are a gift of God. Knowledge of them is transmitted by tradition. Vettius Valens searched long for the truth about the stars, until one day the will of God in its kindness let him obtain the tradition. The effect of this vision is union with God. As in Hermetic literature, this union is owed to Higher Wisdom. The soul is transported to the higher plane, it climbs up the sky and mingles with the divine choirs. Thus, in uniting humankind with the gods, heavenly contemplation makes it divine.

The 'tradition' to which Valens refers is that derived from his predecessors in the science, whom he frequently quotes – fortunately for us, since often he thus preserves fragments from works which have been lost or from authors about whom we should otherwise know nothing. So sacred is this tradition that Valens thought his own students should take an oath to keep its secrets inviolate from the unworthy or uninitiated:

> I adjure them by the sacred circle of the sun, by the varied paths of the moon, by the powers of the five other stars, and by the circle of the twelve signs to keep these matters secret, never to share them with the ignorant or the uninitiated, and to remember and to honour the one who inducted them into this art. May it go well for those who keep this oath and may the aforesaid gods grant them what they wish. May the opposite happen to those who foreswear this oath. (*Anthologiae* 7.2).

But while Valens acknowledges his predecessors, he does not always gloss over their shortcomings and he also criticises the abilities and failings of some of his contemporaries. As a corrective to these negatives, therefore, he offers readers a clearly-written, comprehensible treatise with examples of horoscopes fully worked-out for the better instruction of his students; and it is the inclusion of over a hundred of these that makes the *Anthologiae* especially useful and intriguing as a record of Valens's own experience as well as offering us a glimpse of the procedures whereby an astrologer of the period could calculate, and draw and interpret individual horoscopes with accuracy and flair. This is his version of the chart for a child who was born on 14 August 158 and who died in May 161:

> Sun, Mercury and Venus in Leo, moon in Virgo, Saturn in Libra, Jupiter in Capricorn, Mars in Aries, the ascendant in Cancer … I interpreted from investigation into these periods and since it was an infant, I counted months instead of years. For at the end of the 8th month and during part of the 9th he was subject to convulsions lacking little of being dangerous. Libra indicated the 8th month Saturn being located there … and there were indications for the other months being controlled by the maleficent stars, and he was afflicted by eruptions and eczema, namely in the 15th and 17th and 23rd month, and in the rest, but especially about the 27th month … The 17th was indicated by Mars in Aries and the moon in Virgo … Then from the 28th month he lived precariously, for the rising time of Libra and the period of Saturn in Libra coincided. And in the 32nd month he was dangerously ill and was in convulsions … And in the 33rd month he died. (*Anthologiae* 7.5).

Now, Valens was particularly interested in how to determine the length of a subject's or client's life and its critical periods (*klimaktēres*), those years during which the subject is likely to suffer a crisis. The way the former was calculated depended on measurements involving a particular arc of the zodiac. One point – usually the sun, moon, or planet in the ascendant – is fixed as a 'starter' and another as a 'destroyer', and the distance between the two, not more than 90°, represents the length of life. (3.3). Each planet had a certain period associated with it, and Valens uses these figures in his calculations:

> Sun in Taurus; Mercury in Taurus; moon in Pisces; Saturn in Scorpio; Jupiter, Mars and Venus in Aries; ascendant in Gemini. The rising time of Gemini in the second klima is 28.

Mercury in Taurus adds Taurus's rising time, 24, plus Mars in Aries, 15. [Therefore the client] died in his 67th year.

As for climacterics, these quickly found their way into medicine which regarded multiples of seven or nine as especially significant. 'Greetings,' wrote the Emperor Augustus to his grandson, 'I hope you have celebrated my sixty-fourth birthday in health and happiness, for you see I have passed the climacteric common to all old men, the sixty-third year.' Astrologers, however, unlike doctors, did not confine these critical periods to health but extended them to the soul, fortune, enterprise, and so forth.

What, then, may be said of Ptolemy and Valens in relation to each other, and to their second-century contemporaries? Both are trying to be comprehensive, Ptolemy more as a theorist, Valens more as a practising astrologer. Ptolemy's book is better ordered than that of Valens who begins with a clear enough structure in his first three Books, but then allows the rest to ramble somewhat – perhaps the result of his composing the remaining Books over twenty years. Ptolemy avoids any personal references, either to himself or to other individuals; Valens fills his work with personal observations, asides, and examples, partly in the form of horoscopes, (including his own), partly by means of remarks *ad hominem* – some astrologers waste people's time, he says, lead them astray, defraud them, or 'bastardise the science with fancy words and complicated schemes' – or passages *de hominibus*, in which the status and prospects of his clients can be followed via the horoscopic details and forecasts he prepares for his readers. [6]

These contrasts, however, cannot be regarded as particularly unusual. Two other astrologers from the end of the second century exhibit similar differences. Antiochus of Athens, who wrote two astrological works, *Eisagōgika* ('Introduction') and *Thēsauroi* ('Treasuries'), concentrated on the technical aspects of the science. Thus, *Eisagōgika* deals with the planets, the signs of the zodiac, houses, exaltations, aspects, ascendants, and 'lots', (meaning significant points on the zodiac, determined by certain formulae, relating to fortune, necessity, courage, love, and so forth), while *Thēsauroi* explains why the zodiac begins with Aries, masculine and feminine zodiacal signs, oppositions, sects, decans, trine and quartile signs, lordships, and the lots again. Both works are handbooks, but strictly theoretical in their approach. Antigonus of Nicaea, on the other hand, author of a work of which only fragments survive, is notable for his collection of nativities, including that of the Emperor Hadrian, and thus comes closer to Valens in interest and intention. Three of these horoscopes are preserved in the *Apotelesmatika* of Hephaistio of Thebes, (late fourth–early fifth century). The second, it has been suggested, but not universally accepted, may be that of Licinius Sura, a prominent individual in political circles, who encouraged Trajan to grasp the Imperial power after the death of Nerva in January 98. The third is that of Hadrian's grand-nephew, Pedanius Fuscus, who was executed when only eighteen years of age. The first belongs to Hadrian himself. Antigonus begins this horoscope with the essential astrological details, followed by a few biographical observations:

[Hadrian] was born with the sun in the 8th degree of Aquarius and the moon and Jupiter and the ascendant, all three, in the 1st degree of the same sign, Aquarius; Saturn in the

10th degree of Capricorn; Venus in the 12th degree of Pisces; Mars with it in the 22nd degree; and the Mid-Heaven in the 22nd degree of Scorpio. This person was adopted by the Emperor [Trajan], a relative of his, and he himself became Emperor, too, about his forty-second year. He was both intelligent and well-educated, and he was worshipped like a god in temples and sacred places. He was united to only one woman, and from the time of her virginity he was childless. He had one sister. He came to be in rebellion and dissension against his own people. When he was about sixty-three years old, he died, having succumbed to dropsy and asthma.

The rest of the entry is filled out with astrological explanations of the details given in this first paragraph. If the horoscope was written soon after Hadrian's death, it may be asked what was the point in Antigonus's exercise? Since the horoscope leads him to praise Hadrian to the skies, we are surely not looking at a piece of political expediency, because the Emperor's death would render this superfluous, although it may, of course, have been an example of post mortem laudification. But if the horoscope had been written before Hadrian died, its tone and message at once become explicable, even more so if Antigonus was not a relatively obscure figure from the Roman provinces, but a prominent member of the Imperial Court. According to the somewhat dubious collection of anecdotes known as the *Historia Augusta*, Hadrian was known to consult astrologers – '[in the province of Lower Moesia] he heard from an astrologer [*a mathematico*] the same prediction of his future power as had been made, as he already knew, by his great-uncle Aelius Hadrianus, a master of astrology', (*Hadrian* 2.4) – and so it is reasonable to suggest that Antigonus may have held the same kind of position in relation to Hadrian as Thrasyllus and Balbillus had done in relation to the Julio-Claudian emperors. Hence Antigonus's published horoscopes would have been directed to the same end as those of Vettius Valens, to publicise his own accumulated experience and illustrate certain themes he wanted to discuss. [7]

Neither the political role of astrology nor its intimate relationship with religion, expressed in the description and workings of the cosmos and the attendant problems of fatalism versus free will reached any kind of conclusion during these early centuries. Emperors, however, whatever their personal views on divination as a whole and astrology in particular, continued the Imperial custom of issuing Greek coins with what appear to be astrological symbols on them. The principate of Antoninus Pius, Hadrian's successor, was particularly prolific in this regard: (i) zodiac with a circle of the eponymous gods of the days of the week; (ii) two zodiacs, one inside the other; (iii) Aquarius and Saturn; (iv) bust of Selene (the moon), a star in front, a crescent moon in Cancer below; (v) bust of a radiate Helios, lion below; (vi) Jupiter in Pisces; (vii) Jupiter in Sagittarius; (viii) Mars in Scorpio; (ix) Venus in Taurus; (x) constellation of the Ploughman (*Boötēs*); (xi) constellation of the Reaper (*actually the star Seginus in the constellation Boötēs*). Moreover, a relatively new building, Hadrian's Pantheon, displayed in its architectural form allusions to the cosmos. The sphere, most evident in the huge cupola over the cella, seems to represent the vault of heaven, as Dio Cassius suggested (53.27.2); its axis corresponds to sunrise on two days a year, 1 April and 16 September; and the rhythm of the recesses up through the building is expressible in terms of 7–14–28. The Romans found the number seven significant.

Aulus Gellius, referring to Varro, wrote that there were seven circles in the heavens; that the zodiac too was influenced by the number seven, 'for the summer solstice occurs in the seventh sign from the winter solstice, and the winter solstice in the seventh after the summer, and one equinox in the seventh sign after the other'. The moon completes its course in 4 x 7 days = 28; and seven extends to and affects the birth of human beings, for by the seventh day after semen has been introduced into the womb, 'it is compacted and coagulated and rendered fit to take shape', and by 7 x 7 = 49th day, 'the entire embryo has formed in the womb' – and so he goes on, piling example upon example to leave us in no doubt that seven and its multiples carried special weight in any Roman symbolical system. These multiples are common in the Pantheon – 28 vertical rows of coffers in the cupola, 28 reliefs on the façades of the intermediate block – so we are entitled to suggest that some consciously astrological considerations contributed to the design of this temple 'dedicated to the divine beings conceived as the forces controlling the universe, at the head of whom were the ancestors of the Imperial house'. Add to this the constantly turning dome representing the heavens in Nero's *Domus Aurea*, the baldachin over Domitian's throne, evoking the vault of heaven, and Septimius Severus's having his horoscope painted on several ceilings in his palace, and we gain some notion of how thoroughly the Roman official ambience was imbued by the symbolism of ruling sun and attendant planets and constellations.

Fortified by the teaching of astrological manuals on the one hand, and largely unperturbed by a long tradition of Jewish ambivalence towards the science on the other, Christianity absorbed, expanded, developed, and reinterpreted the propositions of astrology and the astral symbolism encouraged and spread by the state in so complaisant a fashion, in spite of objections from many of its own theologians, that when the Empire divided itself between west and east, supreme power flowed to Constantinople, and the Christian faith became that officially approved by the Empire, astrology held her own amid competing intellectual disciplines and continued to blossom in its new and alien soil. [8]

6

A Christian Dilemma c.200–c.500: Theological Doubts & Popular Belief

Julius Firmicus Maternus, a Sicilian of the late third and early fourth century, was a lawyer by profession and an astrologer by inclination and conviction. His principal book, *Mathesis* ('instruction'), preserves a great deal of information from earlier Greek writers, setting out the fundamental principles of the science, and references to an eclipse of the sun on 17 July, 334 suggest a rough date for when Maternus began to write it. He undertook the work ostensibly for the benefit of a friend of his, Lollianus Mavortius, a highly distinguished politician who held the office of consul in 355. The two men had once spent time together in Campania where Mavortius was governor. Maternus, he says, was ill and had to be nursed back to health, and to while away the long winter days he and Mavortius engaged in conversations during which it emerged – or at least Maternus flatteringly claims it emerged – that Mavortius had a great interest in astronomy-astrology.

In discussing these and other questions, you also asked me about the wonders of Sicily which you had learned in childhood from the Greek and Roman writers. Finally you shifted the conversation … and showed me the wide range of your knowledge. You described the uses of the nine spheres and the five zones, each with their different colouring. You mentioned the twelve signs of the zodiac and the effects of the five eternally wandering planets; the daily and the annual path of the sun; the swift motion of the moon and its waxing and waning; the number of revolutions it takes to make the greater year, which is often spoken about, in which the five planets and the sun and moon are brought back to their original places; it is completed, you said, in the 1461st year. We went on to the explanation of the Milky Way and the eclipses of the sun and moon; why the rotation of the heavens never carries the Dipper to the west or brings it back to the east; which part of the earth is subject to the north wind and which to the south; the reason the earth itself is in the centre and hangs in balance, and how Oceanus, which some call the Atlantic Sea, flows round and embraces the land like an island. You explained all those problems to me, my most illustrious Mavortius, most clearly and simply. That was the point at which I dared to make the rash, impromptu offer to write out for you what the Egyptian sages and Babylonian priests, who are so knowledgeable about the force of the stars, have handed down to us in their teaching about astrology. (*Prooemium* 5–6).

In consequence, Maternus ventured to dedicate the *Mathesis* to someone who would appreciate its subject matter. After these polite preliminaries Maternus justifies his work to a wider readership. There are many, he says, who oppose astrology and use all kinds of spurious arguments to try to destroy its credibility; but these can and must be countered, principally by laying out the subtleties of the science, which seem to have escaped so many of its critics:

> First of all I should like to ask this violent opponent of the astrologers whether he has any first-hand knowledge of the science. When he asked for a forecast did he *never* receive true responses? Or did he scorn to listen, in his narrow-minded and violent attitude? Did he expect his ears to be polluted by the answers? Did he throw into confusion with over-excited speech the basic tenets of the whole doctrine? (1.3.4).

Astrology was taught to humans by the divine Mind and this is how astrologers are able to penetrate the secrets of Nature. It is not an easy science to master, but humans have an advantage in as much as they are actually sparks from the divinity which is immanent in everything.

> Who doubts that by the same law divine Mind is transfused into earthly bodies, that descent is allotted through the sun and ascent prepared through the moon? For the divine Mind is diffused throughout the whole body of the universe as in a circle, now outside, now inside, and rules and orders all things. Conceived by self-begetting, it is preserved by everlasting fiery motion for the procreation and preservation of all things. It never lays down this duty through weariness, but maintains itself and the world and everything that is in the world with its everlasting motion. Out of this Soul the everlasting fires of the stars accomplish the swift completion of their orbits, quickened by the power of the living Mind. They bring part of this Soul to earthly bodies and in turn take it back to the perpetual fires of the great Soul. In this way, immortal Soul endows the frail earthly body with confidence in its power. The individual soul corresponds in every way to its author and source which is diffused through all living things born on earth and quickens them by divine fire. Therefore, since we are kin to the planets, we should not deprive them of their powers by impious arguments, since we are shaped and created by their daily courses. (1.5.9–12).

Historical examples show that humankind is subject to Fate, but only up to a point. 'What we do while we are alive belongs to us; only our death belongs to Chance or Fate.' (1.8.3). Nevertheless, an air of determinate fatalism hangs over Maternus's work and his examples illustrate his view of the inevitability of one's succumbing to fate in one form or another. A youth with everything to live for hangs himself, an innocent man commits suicide, a good man is obliged to live as a beggar, while a criminal rises high in society and the state. Most notable, Maternus thinks, is the example of the second-century AD philosopher Plotinus who sought, by virtuous conduct and healthy living, to avoid the decrees of Fate. Yet Fate had the last word, striking him down with a ghastly final illness somewhat reminiscent of

Job's most severe physical trials, so that 'in the end even Plotinus realised the power of Fate and accepted the fiery judgement of the stars'. (1.7.2–4, 14–22; quotation, 22).

Finally, having reviewed the various terrestrial zones and the differences in their inhabitants' appearances, Maternus ends with praise of the Emperor Constantine and a prayer, addressed to the seven planets in turn, that under Constantine's rule humanity may enjoy everlasting peace and prosperity. Thereafter, in seven remaining Books of the *Mathesis*, he turns to technicalities – signs, planets, aspects, houses, angles, significations of relationships between the celestial bodies, and the fixed stars of the extra-zodiacal constellations – and gives a number of horoscopic examples apparently drawn from real life, before ending with an exhortation to Mavortius reminiscent of that insisted upon by Vettius Valens:

> It is for you to remember the sanctity of your oath. Guard these books with a pure mind and soul, and do not reveal this science to inexperienced ears or sacrilegious minds. The nature of the divine prefers to be hidden in diverse coverings. Access to it should not be easy, nor its majesty open to all. This is what I should like to accomplish with my book – that it should be open to the religious but denied to the profane. In this way we shall not pollute the revered theories of the ancients by publishing them for the sacrilegious. Therefore hand this book down to your sons, since you have brought them up from early years in the practice of virtue. Give it to your friends, but only those who are closest to you, whom you know follow virtuous examples. (8.32.2–3). [1]

Now, the period between the second and fourth centuries AD has been characterised as 'an age of anxiety', and it is worth pausing for a moment to see why this should have been so. For a start, the physical composition of the universe suggests a disturbing antithesis between the celestial and terrestrial worlds. E.R. Dodds summarised the picture perfectly:

> The earth was a globe suspended in space at the centre of a system of concentric moving spheres. First came the envelope of thick and murky terrestrial atmosphere which reached as far as the moon; beyond the moon were the successive spheres of the sun and the five planets; beyond these again the eighth sphere, composed of fiery ether, purest of the material elements, which in its daily revolution about the earth carried round with it the fixed stars. The whole vast structure was seen as an expression of a divine order; as such, it was felt to be beautiful and worshipful; and because it was self-moving it was thought to be alive or informed by a living spirit.

The key word here is 'vast'. People came more and more to think of the earth as a tiny particle in an enormous, almost inconceivable space, and this sense of the smallness of the earth and therefore of humanity itself and the individual human life, led to the notion that God (or the gods) had created people merely for diversion or amused curiosity, and that the world was little more than a stage set upon which humans acted the parts and spoke the lines contained in God's script, without any free will other than that of playing their allotted roles well or badly. Resignation to Fate was thus the only realistic stance an intelligent human being could adopt. Moreover, the concept of planetary and stellar *daimones* quickly turned into a belief that the world was permeated by evil forces, the question being whether these evil forces were under the ultimate control of a good God, or whether they belonged to another deity altogether, an evil God engaged in constant warfare with the Good, in which case, was humanity a more or less helpless scrap of creation torn one way and another between these competing divinities or forces?

In the midst of this depression, therefore, astrology had its part to play, facing the old, irresolvable question of Fate and free will. But if Firmicus Maternus had been largely convinced that one's ultimate destiny had been planned and was thus ineluctable – an important distinction which allowed human beings to exercise a certain degree of deliberate choice before Fate caught up with them – other pagan writers were coming to agree with Christian theologians that the stars were not in themselves causative powers and did not determine fate, but fulfilled the office of signs or indicators of a superior or divine will. The clearest statement of this point of view from a Christian writer comes from Origen (*c*.185–*c*.254), a native of Alexandria and thus open to the ferment of astrological learning and speculation in that city, who turned his attention to astrology in his *Commentary on Genesis* 1.14: 'And God said, Let there be lights in the firmament of heaven to divide the day from the night; and let them be for signs, and for seasons, and for days, and years.' Scripture is quite clear, says Origen, that stars are not agents but signs; they are not, however, signs to human beings but to other powers, a notion which Theophilus of Alexandria indignantly accused him of holding in a letter to the Bishops of Palestine and Cyprus:

> Foretelling the future – which only the Saviour knows how to do – Origen attributes to the movements of the stars, in as much as from their course and changes in their appear- ance spirits (*daimones*) deduce knowledge of the future and sometimes themselves do, or sometimes command others to do, what has to be done.

In the face of this degree of misunderstanding, it is not surprising that Origen was careful to answer similar criticisms from the pagan Celsus by asserting that Christians certainly did not worship the stars but rather 'the Author of the prophecies which are in them, and the Word of God who mediates them'. (*Contra Celsum* 5.12).

As signs, then, the stars and planets are not venerable in themselves, nor do they exercise any power over human fate. Unfortunately, however, evil spirits may use their superior abilities to read those signs and, armed with this foreknowledge, act maliciously against human beings, not least by teaching them the principles of astrology in the first place and causing them to believe in its efficacy as a predictive science. Demons, for example, carefully observe the phases of the moon, then produce symptoms of epilepsy in certain people, and as a result everyone is encouraged to believe that the moon has effected the illness. Astrology is thus a highly ambiguous science. The stars may not be in charge of fate, but their behaviour can be used by spirits both to convey messages of one kind or another to humankind, (the understanding of which would be legitimate), or to mislead people into the sin of idolatry, (the surrender to which would not be legitimate). At best, therefore, Origen concedes much to astrology while seeking to temper pagan arguments about fatalism.

The Neoplatonic philosopher Plotinus (205–270) adopted a somewhat similar position. His arguments can be summarised by his essay on whether the stars are causes or not, from his principal treatise *Enneads*. People say the planets cause everything and act towards human beings as though they had feelings of liking or hostility. If the planets do not have souls, they can have only a limited physical effect upon us. If they do have souls, why would they react emotionally towards us? In fact, they cannot be said to react emotionally at all, either towards us or towards each other, regardless of their changing positional relationships. Ascribing diverse and variable conscious reactions among planets destroys the notion of the universe as an organic unity, and if the stars actually can be signs of things to come, it is because they co-operate in the workings of the universe as a whole.

> But, if the stars announce the future – as we hold of many other things also – what explanation of the cause have we to offer? What explains the purposeful arrangement thus implied? Obviously, unless the particular is included under some general principle of order, there can be no signification. We may think of the stars as letters perpetually being inscribed on the heavens or inscribed once for all and yet moving as they pursue the other tasks allotted to them: upon these main tasks will follow the quality of signifying, just as the one principle underlying any living unit enables us to reason from member to member, so that for example, we may judge of character and even of perils and safeguards by indications in the eyes or in some part of the body. If these parts of us are members of a whole, so are we: in different ways one law applies. All teems with symbol. The wise man is the man who in any one thing can read another, a process familiar to all of us in not a few examples of everyday experience.

Each person is compounded of an ensouled body and a higher soul. The higher soul transcends the physical universe and is beyond the reach of its 'necessary' laws. When the lower soul enters the human body, it is subject to an influx from the stars, an influx which has various, principally negative effects because 'what comes from the stars will not reach the recipients in the same state in which it left them ... [and] all these things become evil in us, though they are not so up in heaven'. (11). These planetary influences are sometimes in harmony with the purpose of the organically whole universe and sometimes opposed to it, but while nothing can bring about change in the fundamental pattern of the universe, secondary less important factors may be altered because these do not affect that basic pattern. The stars thus either give signs of an existing situation or have a limited role to play in helping to produce that situation. So, if someone is rich by inheritance, the stars merely announce he is rich. If the wealth has come from elsewhere – hard work, sharp practice, and so on – the factors which contributed to making him work hard or cheat or discover buried treasure quite by chance must be taken into account as well as any possible planetary influence. (This is the now common requirement that the astrologer take every circumstance into account, not merely astral patterns and relationships, before interpreting any situation for his client).

The 'lots' are woven together by the Fates into multifarious patterns; some people rise above them, others do not, and in dealing with the challenges constantly presented by the changing circumstances of life, the soul is 'like a farmer who, when he has sown or planted, is always putting right what rainstorms or continuous frosts or gales of wind have spoiled'. (16). Those people who live through their lower soul will be subject to planetary influences, but those who live through their higher soul will not. Evils are a necessary part of the universal pattern. If evils did not exist, the Whole would be imperfect; but as long as higher principles exist, they too will flow into the lower soul, just as while the sun exists, all its rays will shine from it upon everything else. All things, then, are part of the great Unity, but individual parts of that Unity react in different ways to the constantly changing circumstances which manifest in that region of mutability at whose centre are placed the earth and its human inhabitants. Some things happen because of the movements of the stars, others do not, and in consequence the effect of the stars upon mutable beings is limited. [2]

While Christian and pagan thus agreed in attributing some power to the stars, though power of a much restricted kind, it seems that people during this period were still eager to consult astrologers even when those consultations might prove dangerous to both parties. They were eager, apparently, to know about the lives, (that is, the deaths), of the Emperors, as Tertullian tells us in his *Apologeticum*. This was probably written in autumn 197 or later in 198 during the aftermath of an unsuccessful revolt by Clodius Albinus in Gaul against the Emperor Septimius Severus, and possibly at the time Caracalla, described as a monster by two contemporary historians, Dio Cassius and Herodian, became co-Emperor with his father Severus. In 197 Caracalla was given the title 'Caesar', and it may be significant that Tertullian expresses his monitions against diviners at this particular point:

> Even those who are now daily revealed as the accomplices or abettors of criminal factions, the gleanings that still remain after the vintage of parricides, how they decked out their doors with the freshest and most luxuriant bay trees, how they darkened their porches with the tallest and brightest lamps, with what elegant and splendid couches did they divide up the marketplace among themselves, not that they might celebrate the joy of the people, but that they might now learn private prayers in a ceremony connected with another and might install both a copy and a picture of their hope, while changing mentally the name of the Emperor! These same dutiful services are paid also by those who consult astrologers and soothsayers and augurs and magicians about the lives of the Caesars, which arts, as having been introduced by the apostate angels and forbidden by God, the Christians never employ even for their own concerns. [3]

Like most emperors, Severus had used astrologers when it suited him. After his first wife died, 'he made inquiries about the horoscopes of marriageable women, being himself no mean astrologer (*mathēseos peritissimus*)', and studied carefully the birth-chart of one of his sons, Antoninus Geta, remarking to his Prefect of the Guard, 'It seems extraordinary to me, my dear Juvenalis, that our Geta is destined to be a deified Emperor, because I see nothing Imperial in his horoscope'. On the other hand, as a result of so many plots against him, he eventually put to death numerous individuals on the grounds that they had asked astrologers (*Chaldaeos*) or soothsayers how long he was going to live, and it looks as though

Tertullian had just such activities in mind when he wrote his warning against these or similar consultations.

At roughly the same period as Tertullian was writing, Hippolytus, Bishop of Pontus, produced a comprehensive work entitled *Philosophoumena*, in Greek, or *Refutatio Omnium Haeresium*, in Latin. Book 4 is devoted to a refutation of the Greek astrology of the time, and although the first chapters of the Book are missing from the only surviving manuscript, the rest provide a fairly thorough dismissal of astrology as a valid science. For a start, horoscopes, says Hippolytus, cannot be drawn because neither the time of the deposit of semen nor the child's conception nor its time of birth can be fixed exactly, and therefore one cannot know which planet or zodiacal sign is in the ascendant at the crucial moment. Secondly, it is ludicrous to associate signs of the zodiac with a person's looks or temperament:

> For example, they say that he who is born under Leo will be courageous, and he who is born under Virgo straight-haired, pale-complexioned, childless and bashful. But these things and those like them deserve laughter rather than serious consideration. For according to them, an Ethiopian can be born under Virgo and, if so, will be white, straight-haired, and so forth. (4.6).

Hippolytus also notes the close connection between astrology and physiognomy, and lists the zodiacal signs and the types attributed to their influence:

> Those born in Cancer are of the following description: not large in stature, blue-black hair, reddish complexion, small mouth, round head, narrow forehead, greenish eyes, beautiful enough, slightly irregular limbs Their disposition: evil, crafty, skilled in plots, insatiable, stingy, ungracious, servile, unhelpful, forgetful. They don't give back what belongs to someone else, but they don't ask for what belongs to them to be returned. Useful in friendship. (4.18).

What twaddle all this is! he exclaims before going on to describe and condemn various magical practices apparently common at the time. By using the names of animals to designate constellations and extrapolating human physical, psychological, and behavioural characteristics from these, he concludes, heretics hope to deceive people who put too much faith in astrologers into constructing a religious system quite at odds with the truth. Therefore we should be aware of how absurd are the bases of their speculations, and not allow ourselves to be misled by them. (4.50).

How justified was Hippolytus in implying that belief in the validity of astrology was widespread even among Christians at the time? Bardaisan of Edessa (c.153–222), 'a prominent philosopher and theologian who eventually came to identify himself as a Christian', developed a complex system of teaching which included the notions – none original to him – that humans are both free and unfree, able to exercise their own wills but subject to Nature and their horoscope. God placed the seven planets in the firmament whence they influence people's lives, especially at the moment of birth when, as a result of the position of the planets at that instant, various qualities are imparted from them to the newborn child whose soul has travelled downwards to the body through the seven planetary spheres. Edessa itself which Stephen Ross has described as 'a laboratory in which the thinking of philosophers including Marcion, Bardaisan, and Mani was further developed and then propagated', therefore presented local Christians, who were vying for adherents with many different pagan and heretical cults strongly influenced by astrological ideas, with a bewilderment of theological problems and a constant impendence of temptation.

But this kind of situation did not obtain merely in Syria, as Tertullian shows, nor only in the second and third centuries. For in Spain, the late fourth-century unorthodox theologian Priscillian, (if we are to believe his critics), affirmed the validity of astrology and taught that the signs of the zodiac were to be assigned to various parts of the body – a notion which was neither new nor particularly heterodox, since it rapidly became a cliché of western medical theory – while at more or less the same time the historian Ammianus Marcellinus was inveighing against:

> [those] who deny that there are higher powers in heaven, do not appear in public or eat a meal or think they can, with due caution, take a bath until they have critically examined the ephemeris and learned where, for example, the planet Mercury is, or what degree of the constellation of the Crab the moon occupies in its course through the heavens.

If we turn to North Africa, we find a similar situation. St Augustine's *Confessions* (397), for example, make it clear that during his younger days he had not hesitated to consult astrologers (*mathematicos*), and not even Nebridius a close friend of his, who scoffed at the whole business of divination, could persuade him out of it, because Augustine was quite convinced at the time that no one had proved beyond any doubt that what astrologers accurately foretold to their clients had happened merely by accident or chance rather than being the result of the stars' particular movements or influences which the professional skill of the astrologer then revealed. In his older years, however, St Augustine repudiated his youthful fascination and in Book 5 of his *De Civitate Dei* ('The City of God'), written between 413 and 427, he tackled the problem of fatalism, beginning with outright condemnation:

> Those whose opinion it is that the stars determine what we do, or what goods we may have, or what evils we shall suffer, independently of the will of God, must be refused a hearing by everyone, not only by those who hold to the true religion, but also by those who choose to be worshippers of gods of any kind, even false ones. (5.1).

He then proceeded to consider three separate but interlinked points. First, some people say that things happen by chance or Fate. If by 'Fate' they mean the will or power of God, they should say so distinctly because in popular parlance the word 'Fate' is used to mean 'nothing other than the force exerted by the position of the stars when anyone is born or conceived'. (5.1). Secondly, some say that the position of the stars depends on the will of God and that the stars dictate a person's character and future course of life. This, says

St Augustine, not only detracts from the supreme power of God, but also presumes that He decided to hand over part of that power to stars to act as independent authorities – a proposition which, it could be argued, will make Him, through them, an author of human sin and crime and, of course, absolve human beings of responsibility for their actions.

Thirdly, one might say that the stars merely signify human fate and character and are not the causes of them; but this, in practice, is often no more than sloppy speech – 'the astrologers do not usually say that, for example, "Mars in this position *signifies* a homicide". Rather they say "*causes* a homicide."' But even if we grant this point, it must still be said that astrologers have signally failed to offer satisfactory explanations for why twins grow up to be completely different individuals with lives entirely different from each other. This St Augustine now discusses at length in four chapters, providing examples from the Bible (Esau and Jacob) and his own experience – 'I have known twins who not only had different occupations and migrated to different places, but who also suffered different kinds of illness', (5.2) – and arguing that because astrologers are obliged to take into account such tiny intervals of time when it comes to birth, or indeed conception, of twins, that their calculations can never ensure entirely correct prediction. Moreover, 'if conception at the same moment permits twins to have different fortunes in the womb, why does birth at the same moment not permit any two other persons also to have different fortunes on earth?' (5.5).

Next St Augustine turns to another branch of astrology. Up to this point he has been dealing essentially with considerations relevant to birth-charts. Now he discusses 'electional' astrology which deals with the best time to begin a new course of action:

> If it is only people who are subject to the constellations, and not everything which lies under heaven, why do people choose certain days as propitious for the planting of vines or trees or corn? … People suppose that the choice of days is important in these matters because they believe that the position of the stars, as it changes according to the different moments of time, has dominion over *all* earthly bodies and living things. (5.7).

Here St Augustine is fudging his argument. By saying 'if it is only people who are subject to the constellations', he is setting up a straw man which will be easy to knock down, especially if he insists – as his subsequent argument shows he does – on treating electional astrology as though it were the same as genethliacal. 'Who is such a fool as to venture to say that all trees, all beasts, snakes, birds, fish and worms have each a moment of birth?' So, if astrologers deny that non-human creatures are subject to the stars, they will imply that only human beings can be so governed or influenced, and then St Augustine will be able to raise the objection that humans possess free will and so their lives cannot be entirely determined by outside forces. If, on the other hand, astrologers concede birth-charts to non-human creatures, they can be dismissed as fools or charlatans; and it is at this point St Augustine introduces an interesting observation relating to the tests with which some clients apparently tried astrologers' skill:

> Men customarily bring to the astrologers, to test their skill, the horoscopes of dumb animals which they have discovered by diligently observing their birth at home. And they

praise those astrologers above all others who, having inspected the constellations, pronounce that it is not a man, but an animal, which has been born. They even dare to say what kind of an animal it is: whether it is suitable to give wool, or to be ridden, or for ploughing, or for guarding the house. They are even tested by questions about the fates of dogs and their answers are greeted with great shouts of astonishment. (5.7).

All in all, therefore, he concludes, astrology cannot be valid because God has given human beings free will and this means they cannot be subject to any decrees of or predetermination by the stars; and if astrologers are capable of giving remarkable answers to people's questions, it is because they are prompted thereto by evil spirits 'whose care it is to sow and establish in people's minds these false and noxious opinions concerning the influence of the stars on our fate'. [4]

These points for theological debate, however, were confined to the educated and professional classes who tended to take what one might call a relatively intellectual attitude towards the business of reading and interpreting signs in the heavens. The rest of society was not so refined. In c.400, for example, Maximus, Bishop of Turin, gave evidence in one of his sermons of the more robust reactions of those living outwith the ivory tower to the dramatic warning of an eclipse:

When, a few days ago, I accused many of you of avaricious greed, that same day around evening such a great shouting arose among the people that its irreligious sound penetrated to the heavens. When I inquired what the shouting meant, they told me your shouting was intended to help the moon in her travails and assist her with their yells when she was eclipsed.

Such inclinations among the majority may go some way to explain why Zeno, Bishop of Verona in the late fourth century, felt able to address newly-baptised converts to Christianity with a reinterpretation of the zodiac along Christian lines which he clearly felt they would understand and appreciate:

I am well aware you are eager to know more. Your old life has been replaced, and because you won't be allowed to live it any more, perhaps you want me to tell you in what nativity and sign your mother [*i.e. the Church*] bore you – so different, so many, so dissimilar that you are – in a single birth. I shall indulge you as I would small children and very briefly reveal the secrets of a sacred horoscope. So, brethren, this is your birth-chart.

First, the one who condemns nobody who believes in Him – not Aries, but the Lamb – has taken you under His protection. He has clothed your nakedness with the snow-white brilliance of His fleece. He graciously pours out his blessed milk upon your lips when they cry like a baby. The same person, not a Taurus with swollen neck and grim forehead and menacing horn, but the best of calves, sweet-natured, affectionate, and mild, reproves you so that, not looking for any portents while you are doing anything, going under His yoke without ill-feeling, and making the soil of your flesh fertile by subduing it, you may bring in a happy harvest of divine seeds in heavenly granaries. He also gives warning by means of the Twins (Gemini) who accompany each other – that is, salvation by means of the two Testaments which are growing grey with age – so that you may make it your principal business to flee idolatry, unchastity, and greed which is an incurable Cancer.

But our Leo, as *Genesis* bears witness, [5] is the lion-cub whose holy sacraments we celebrate. He lay down and fell asleep so that He might conquer death, and woke up so that He might confer upon us immortality, the gift of His blessed resurrection. Appropriately enough, Virgo follows him and heralds Libra so that, through the Son of God who became incarnate and came forth from the Virgin, we might know equity and justice upon earth. Whoever has resolutely maintained this [justice] and administered it, I shall not call a Scorpio but, as the Lord says in the Gospel, 'he will tread down every snake completely without injury to the sole of his foot'. [6] Nor will he ever be afraid of the Devil himself who is truly a most relentless Sagittarius, armed with various fiery arrows and every moment stripping down the hearts of the whole human race. Because of this, the Apostle Paul says, 'Clothe yourselves with the armour of God so that you can stand firm against the villainies of the Devil, once you have received the shield of faith by means of which you will be able to extinguish all the arrows of the Evil One, which are full of fire.' Sometimes he discharges against unfortunate people an ugly-visaged Capricorn who springs forth with his horn, his discoloured, spiteful lips bursting with foaming veins, and, while his quivering captive collapses, vents his rage on every part of his body. Some people he deprives of their minds, some he makes mad, some he turns into murderers, some into adulterers, some he makes commit sacrilege, some he turns blind with greed.

Details take a long time. He has various and innumerable ways of doing harm. But our Aquarius, overflowing with a curative stream, habitually destroys all of them without much trouble. The two Pisces follow Him in one closely-related sign: that is, two peoples from the Jews and the Gentiles who live by means of the water of baptism, marked with one sign [to become] the single people of Christ.

Astrology, then, was firmly fixed in the public consciousness, whether that public were pagan or Christian, and for the most part nothing anyone might say against it seemed to make much difference. Astrologers still plied their craft and sought to reassure clients nervous about the future, as we can see, for example, from three horoscopes from the 470s, drawn up, it appears, *post eventum* either for the instruction of students or as a client's record kept out of interest or as insurance against possible future complaint. The first tells us that someone set out on a sea voyage, leaving Caesarea in Palestine at 11 a.m. on 1 October 474. The moon had come within Saturn's territory 'in the place of the evil demon', and was moving slowly, a configuration which caused a storm and held back the progress of the voyage. Mars in Aries was in opposition to Mercury in Libra, so the tillers were damaged and fights broke out on board. But the traveller in question later managed to disembark, whereupon a woman fell in love with him – 'because the moon was in a quartile aspect with a beneficent planet [*Venus*] situated in a terrestrial sign' – after which he embarked on another ship bound, almost certainly, for Constantinople.

It is an interesting vignette of some of the difficulties and dangers attendant upon sea travel, and one which is supplemented by the other two horoscopes, both catarchic inquiries about whether a ship would safely survive its journey. '16 July 475, about 8 a.m.', wrote the astrologer. 'First and foremost I looked for the Lot of Fortune which I found in the 12th House [*that of the evil spirit*] in a very moist sign [*Cancer*].' This was not good. It betokened 'fear, danger, harm, foreign travel, and quadrupeds'. Because of the presence of Venus in the horoscope, and the fact that the moon was contiguous with Jupiter, the people on board were saved after about a fortnight. (The reference to quadrupeds appears to have been correct, for among other goods the ship was transporting camels). Finally, the astrologer offered his clients good news. 'I told them that when the moon was in Sagittarius or Pisces, the ship would arrive' – and, sure enough, it did. The third horoscope, dated 14 July 479, at about 9 a.m., tells a similar story. Saturn and Mars in Virgo meant that the ship in question had encountered a great storm, but after the crew and passengers had transferred themselves and their cargo – caged birds, books and paper, bronze objects (perhaps kitchen utensils), and medical ingredients – to another ship, they all arrived safely at their destination.

Nevertheless, in spite of the clear harmlessness of such inquiries which constituted the majority of business conducted in astrological consultations, every so often both state and fledgling Church felt obliged, for their own individual reasons, to condemn astrology as a science and astrologers as a group. Hence Emperor Constantius II outlawed all forms of magic and divination in 357; and seven years later the Council of Laodicea forbade anyone in holy orders to be 'magicians, enchanters, or astrologers', (Canon 36), a prohibition echoed by the First Council of Toledo in 400, by the Emperors Honorius and Theodosius in 409, who ordered all astrologers to burn their books in the presence of a bishop, and as the *Theodosian Code* repeated in 438–9:

> We decree that astrologers be expelled not only from the city of Rome but also from all cities, unless they are ready to burn the books containing their errors under the eyes of the bishops and convert to belief in the Catholic religion, never to return to their original error. If they do not do this and are found in any city in violation of our wholesome decree, or if they teach the secrets of their error and belief, they shall merit the punishment of deportation.

Perhaps not surprisingly, therefore, someone such as Firmicus Maternus reacted with a plea to his fellow and future astrologers to behave in such a manner as to make their character and reputation henceforth unassailable:

> Since you have received the whole knowledge of this divine science and are now endowed with the secrets of the stars and have learned the first principles of the art, shape yourself in the image and likeness of divinity, so that you may always be a model of excellence … Study and pursue all the distinguishing marks of virtue and, when you have trained yourself in these, be easy of access, so that if anyone wishes to consult you about anything, he may approach you without fear. Be modest, upright, sober, eat little, be content with few goods, so that the shameful love of money may not defile the glory of this divine science. Try with your training and principles to outdo the training and principles of worthy

priests … Beware of replying to anyone asking about the condition of the state or the life
of the Roman Emperor … In fact, no astrologer is able to find out anything true about
the destiny of the Emperor, for the Emperor alone is not subject to the course of the stars,
and in his fate alone the stars have no power of decreeing … Have a wife, a home, many
sincere friends. Be constantly available to the public. Keep away from all quarrels. Do not
undertake any harmful business. Do not at any time be tempted by an increase in income
… Employ peaceful moderation in all your dealings with other people. Avoid plots, at all
times shun disturbances and violence. (*Mathesis* 2.30).

It is an idealised portrait seeking to distance the actual practitioner from the uncomfortable
fact that his socially self-conscious peers and the few Imperial clients tended to regard
him as little more than a kind of astrological domestic who could be called on when
convenient to provide directions for the future, and sacked without recourse if the quality
of his services no longer proved acceptable or his honesty fell under suspicion. But of
course intermittent Imperial anathemas also reflect, in their own way, the uncertainties
of the world which produced them. The early Church was engaged in constant battles,
often violent, to establish an orthodox body of teaching and an authority which would
be able to defend that orthodoxy on the one hand, and oppose heterodox opinions on the
other. In 330 the Emperor Constantine formally dedicated his new city of Constantinople,
(ancient Byzantium), which then started to become the eastern, and more powerful capital
of a divided Empire. Slowly but perceptibly over the succeeding centuries Greek was
lost to western scholars, and since so much astrological learning was expressed in Greek,
learned astrology-astronomy was much more difficult to maintain in the Latin half of
the Empire and its preservation and advancement became largely an eastern pursuit.
Moreover, as Roman culture itself in the bulk of Europe retreated before an essentially
German replacement which knew little or nothing of Classical horoscopic astrology, what
astrological-astronomical erudition did survive remained in the hands of the Church, and
the Church was to quite an extent successful in supplanting the rule or direction of planets
and constellations with the rule and direction of God alone, leaving the cosmos alive with
multifarious non-human entities who were far from autonomous and acted, if act they did,
entirely at the will and by the permission of almighty God. [7]

7

Islamic Speculation c.600–c.900: Fresh Insights, Transmission & Astral Magic

With the arrival of the seventh century came a new religion out of Arabia, quickly establishing itself in many parts of what had been the Roman Empire and regions immediately adjacent. Persia, which had long been open to intellectual and cultural influences from the Hellenistic world and from India, as well as being a repository of learning from the ancient past of Babylon: and Syria, whose cities had seen much lively ferment of ideas springing from its heterodox Christian communities, both converted (though not entirely) to nascent Islam and thus provided its expounders and scholars with philosophical challenges they proved both willing and able to meet. One such challenge could be found in astrology and was to all intents and purposes the same challenge which had long faced Christian theologians: how does on reconcile the theory of astral influence upon earth and its inhabitants with the omnipotence and oneness of God?

Justification for the pursuit of astronomy-astrology could be found in the Qu'ran: 'He has pressed the night and the day and the sun and the moon into your service: the stars also serve you by His leave. Surely in this there are signs for men of understanding', (16.12); 'We have decked the heavens with the zodiacal signs and made them lovely to behold. We have guarded them from every cursed devil', (15.16-17); 'Surely in the heavens and the earth there are signs for the faithful'. (45.3). The stars are personified – 'Do you not see that those in heaven and earth, and the sun and the moon and the stars, the mountains and the trees, the beasts, and countless men, all do homage to God', (22.18) – and act as repellers of demons: 'We have decked the lower heaven with constellations. They guard it against rebellious devils', (36.6–7); 'We have adorned the lowest heavens with lamps, missiles with which to pelt the devils'. (67.5). [1] Armed with such texts, many a Muslim scholar could feel he had permission to pursue inquiries into the working of the heavens and to take from non-Muslim sources such information as might prove useful to his work.

These non-Muslim sources can be well illustrated from Sasanian Iraq where a wide mixture of pagan, Gnostic, Christian, and later Muslim communities lived side by side, heirs, after their separate fashions, to the astral traditions and beliefs of the earlier Land Between the Rivers which asserted that events on earth were caused by the natural revolutions of the heavenly bodies, although now the old gods and their imported Hellenistic and Iranian counterparts might be downgraded to the status of demons. But not always. Persian Magians worshipped Zurvān, a divinity who personified infinite time and became identified with foreordained destiny – that of the world in general and of each person individually. He was also the father of Ahura Mazda, the personification of Good, and of Ahriman, the personification of Evil, both of whom, along with their spirit-forces, were continually at war with one another and each of whom was assisted in his struggle by some of the heavenly bodies. The signs of the zodiac supported Ahura Mazda and were therefore agents of good fortune; the seven planets were on the side of Ahriman and thus brought evil luck. So knowing how to read the stars was essential so that one could foresee one's ineluctable fate. But there was at least consolation in the knowledge that, since the stars were predictable, techniques for unravelling their meaning were available to any who wished to master them, and so forewarned might indeed turn out to be forearmed. Hence the translation into Middle Persian and Syriac of Greek astrological texts which provided useful and welcome additions to indigenous information, and helped introduce these fruits of foreign learning to Middle Eastern society from as early as the third century AD.

One of the most notable centres of astral worship, astrology, and (in the ninth century) translation of astrological texts was to be found at Harran, a city twenty-five miles south of Edessa and a community with a very long history of adherence to pagan rites and cults even after the advents of Christianity and Islam, both hostile to those beliefs and forms of worship. The anonymous late fourth-century *Doctrine of Addai* urged the citizens of Edessa not to be led astray in the manner of some of their neighbours:

> Behold there are those among you who worship Bath Nikkal, as the inhabitants of Harran, your neighbours, do; and Tar'atha, as the people of Mabug; and the eagle, as the Arabians; also the sun and moon, as the rest of the inhabitants of Harran, who are as yourselves. Do not be led away captive by the rays of the luminaries and the bright star, for every one who worships creatures is cursed before God. Be ye indeed far away from … magic arts, which are without mercy, and from soothsaying and divination, and fortune-tellers and from fates and nativities [*horoscopes*], in which the erring Chaldaeans boast, and from planets and signs of the zodiac, in which the foolish trust. [2]

These admonitions had little effect. Conversion to Christianity or to Islam did not necessarily mean that a person abandoned his or her personal adherence to concepts of demonology, astrology, magic, or fatalism, and we find, for example, in the mid-seventh century a heterodox bishop, Severus Sebokht, using information he had gathered from followers of Bardaisan who had made their way into Iraq, 'carrying a tradition of scientific astrology and proclaiming the power of the planets and the zodiac', to assist his writing a treatise on the constellations.

Severus is an important figure in the history of the transmission of Greek natural philosophy to western Syria and thence to other Middle Eastern communities. He wrote his own commentaries on Aristotle and translated others into Syriac, praised Indian mathematics, especially 'their valuable methods of computation', by which he had in mind partly the numerical symbols used by Indian mathematicians, and made two major contributions to astronomy-astrology. [3] The second was the work on constellations, just mentioned. Written in 660 and showing evidence of Severus's acquaintance with the works of Ptolemy, Aratos, and Theon of Alexandria, the parts which survive discuss the origin of the constellations and maintain – an old argument – that they do not appear by nature in what seem to be the arrangements accorded them by astrologers, but that human imagination has attributed these patterns to them. Moreover – another old argument – astrologers' claims anent planetary and astral influences intrude upon the doctrine of free will.

> They maintain that things here are determined according to destiny and the distribution of the seven stars and the twelve signs of the 'zodiac', (as they call it); and some [*planets*] are named 'dominating', and others [*the signs*] are their 'houses', with 'exaltations' and 'lowerings' … According to their 'beholdings', their 'testimonies', and the corresponding figures, life and death are given to human beings, as well as health and disease, riches and poverty, lordship and servitude, and everything which happens in the dwelling of humankind. Because they say that if (what they call) 'good stars' are present in their exaltations, trigons, and tetragons of the sphere – namely in (the east) or in (the west), or in the 'middle of the sky', or in the region below which they call 'Parents' – when they are seen by stars of the same influences, (or other influences if they are among the good ones), [*these good stars*] arrange for good things for those who were born at this hour: they will be rich and powerful, masters and lords, and have a happy life. But when 'bad stars' are present in these places, in their 'places of exaltation' and in their trigons, as astrologers say, and the good stars and their influences have gone astray and are in humbler places, then the weak and the sick, the poor and the subject, and loose livers are born.
>
> (Astrologers) say many things of this kind, full of ineptitudes and chattering without end, and they intermingle and imagine figures, situations and fates, beholdings and testimonies in the signs of the zodiac which are more appropriate to them, in the most appropriate places and figures, according to the 'astrology' which they have created. Thus they try to suppress among themselves the freedom and free will which God has given humankind, with the result that they destroy the search for perfection and the voluntary tendency of each person towards evil, because according to their theory there is no reward for good deeds or punishment for evil ones; and therefore intellectual life and all the control which results from the free will of people who, according to the holy and true word, were created in the image of God, no longer have any point, and people are reduced to animal instinct and an unintelligent life. (*Treatise on the Constellations* 5.1–2).

Thereafter, his treatment of the constellations is what we should term 'astronomical' rather than astrological, and includes noting the most brilliant stars which appear in the various astral groupings. (6.5). It is possible that Severus's approach to these signs and stars is a natural consequence of his earlier *Treatise on the Astrolabe*, also written in 660 and so very fresh in his mind. An astrolabe is an instrument for use in astronomy-astrology and consists of four parts, usually made of metal. One, a large circular disk, calibrated in degrees and sometimes hours round its rim, holds a second disk engraved so as to represent the sky. A third is an openwork disk known as the *rete* ('net'), whose openings allow the user to see through to the disk below. The rete carries star-pointers and is also engraved with a representation of the ecliptic, the sun's annual path through the sky. Finally, a ruler or pointer, the alidade, pivots on a pin and enables the astronomer-astrologer to make various measurements, such as the altitude of a celestial body. All these several parts can pivot concentrically in relation to each other and so, by adjusting them accordingly, the user is able to perform a number of different calculations: the position of celestial bodies, the altitude of any object over the horizon, the time of sunrise on a particular date, and so forth. The astrolabe was thus invaluable for mullahs (to find the direction of prayer towards Mecca), architects (to survey land), soldiers (to calculate the height of a building), mariners (to help navigate), and astrologers (to cast horoscopes), and the speed with which its moveable components could be set to reveal the visible and invisible sky on a specific date at a specific time meant that its user was able to solve quickly all kinds of questions which would otherwise have taken many hours of complex calculation to resolve.

The Muslim historian Ya'qūbī (died 897) attributed a work on the astrolabe to Ptolemy who, according to a humorous Islamic tale, discovered the astrolabe by chance when he dropped a celestial globe and the donkey he was riding stepped on it and flattened it. But Ptolemy was discussing projection rather than embodying it in an instrument, and the first indication that such an instrument had been invented comes from Theon of Alexandria (late fourth century AD) who wrote a treatise on it. The earliest descriptions of actual astrolabes come from John Philoponos of Alexandria (*c*.490–*c*.570) and Severus Sebokht who incorporated into his treatise much material from Theon of Alexandria. Severus's version is as follows:

> Its material is brass, its form round and flat, and it is composed of three or four tablets. If these are raised, one finds they are round, flat, and equal to each other. They are placed one on top of another within one which encloses them all. This last has a rim, like a case [*anulus*], which encloses and contains all of them. Above all these, and within, is placed a circle called the 'zodiac' because the *zōdia*, (that is to say, the signs of the zodiac), are marked on it, with their names and degrees, which are 30 in number for each sign. The astrolabe … bears the names of the signs and, all round, the names of the most brilliant and best known of the fixed stars of the celestial sphere, their names being written above them. The [natural] philosopher who constructed the astrolabe called this structure of the signs of the zodiac of the fixed stars *arakhnē*, that is to say 'spider' because the attachments of its grooves are like the filaments or threads of a spider's web.

There follow chapters on, among other things, how to find the position of the sun, the position of the moon and the other planets, the ascensions of each sign of the zodiac, the declination of each sign from the equator, how to verify whether one's astrolabe is giving a true or false reading, and very much more, including the instrument's ability to ascertain the length of daylight during the course of a year, finding the geographical latitude and longitude of different cities, and observing the ecliptic and declination of the sun. [4]

These mathematical practicalities owed much to Greek learning, but Greek was not the only source from which astronomical-astrological principles and models flowed into Atabic, Iranian, and Syriac treatises.

The Indians transmitted interrogational astrology, together with their version of military astrology and certain other elements they had added to the Greek science, to the Sasanians of Iran in the fifth and sixth centuries. To their resulting mix of Greek and Indian astrology ... the Sasanians added Zoroastrian millenarianism to produce historical astrology in which conjunctions of Saturn and Jupiter over the millennia provide a structure for accommodating the histories of religions, dynasties, and individual rulers. [5]

A series of texts whose titles begin with zīj ('cord'), infused with both Indian and Iranian materials, began to appear in the fifth century, although it was the eighth which saw them burgeon. These were compendia providing data and formulae for calculating planetary motions, the timing of eclipses, geographical latitudes and longitudes, and a large number of other astronomical-astrological requirements, with the earliest texts in Arabic actually coming from north-west India and Afghanistan. (The *Zīj al-Jāmiʿ* and the *Zīj al-Hazūr*, for example, were written in Kandahar not long after 735, and contained material based on Sanskrit computation, while the *Zīj al-Harqan* (742) reflects Indian and Iranian methods of computation).

These zījes, however, were essentially handbooks of astronomy although, obviously, their contents proved invaluable to astrologers as well, and it took a little longer for Indian astrological works to make their way via translation into Iran and thence eventually to Constantinople and a Greek-speaking readership. The new centre for astrological studies was Baghdad, and an academy to teach the subject was founded in 777 by a Jewish astronomer-astrologer, Jacob ibn Tariq, who is supposed to have travelled to Ceylon (Sri Lanka) specifically for the purpose of collecting books on astronomy. The city itself was founded on the astrologically-determined favourable 30 July 762 [6] on the advice of three astrologers assembled for that purpose by Caliph Abu Jaʿfar, al-Mansūr. These three included a Persian Jew from Basra, Māshāʾallāh (*c*.720/30–*c*.810), who entered the service of the Abbāsid Caliphs while he was still a young man, and went on to write twenty-eight astrological treatises, some based on Dorotheus of Sidon, Theophilus of Edessa, Hephaistio of Thebes, and Rhetorius of Alexandria, and one, *De scientia motus orbis* ('Understanding the movement of the world'), which seems to take its cue from at least some of the teachings of Harran. Several of his books contained horoscopes, and we can see from them the kind of questions which were preoccupying his clients. One, for example, seems to have been asking about somebody's (not necessarily the client's) prospects of advancement in the army, and another about success or failure in a war:

Also one of the fixed stars is in 27° and 40′ of Taurus; also another in 4° and 4′ of Cancer; a certain one in 5° and 40′ in Gemini; another in Pisces in 21° and 30′, of the second power. The others are of the first. All are in the south and in the situation where the influences of Mars and Mercury are mixed. Any one of these in the ascendant or mid-heaven, especially in a nocturnal activity, will clearly indicate the leader of an army. He will be magnanimous, prudent, circumspect in every enterprise. He will enjoy boys and maidens and will rejoice in perjury. When the nativity is diurnal, it will make him prompt, impious, a liar, irritable, lacking friends, crafty, lazy, a mocker, infamous, a murderer, an enchanter; and he pursues every evil deed of this sort.

If you are asked about a war … look for [the questioner] in the ascendant and its ruler, and for his enemy in the opposite sign and its ruler. Then make the planet from which the moon is receding a helper for the opposite sign and its ruler. Then look at the two planets. Whichever of them has the better position, is more powerful in its indication, and more abundant in its aspects, is the victor. Be aware that the superior planets are more powerful than the inferior.

Māshā'allāh is also notable, however, for having written a work, *Book on Conjunctions, Faiths, and Religions*, based on the proposition that millennial passages of time are marked by the occurrence of conjunctions of Jupiter and Saturn in Cancer and Capricorn, a Greek theory modified by Zoroastrian astrologers to allow for a cosmic lifetime lasting for twelve such millennia corresponding to the twelve divisions of the zodiac, and partly for being a popular and widespread influence on astrological studies during the Mediaeval period in Europe because of the Latin translations made of some of his works, among which were 'Book on the Aims of the Secrets of Astronomy', 'A Letter' (dealing with eclipses, conjunctions, and the revolutions of the planets), 'Prices' (with a late fourteenth-century note to the effect that Māshā'allāh wrote it on behalf of a merchant-friend with whom he had gone into business), three books on horoscopes, and one on the properties of the stars. [7]

Almost contemporary with Māshā'allāh, but older, was another non-Muslim adviser to a caliph, the Christian Theophilos of Edessa (*c*.695–785). Theophilos was another astrologer who owed some of his learning to a period of study in Harran, and seems to have been proficient in Pahlavī and Greek, since he gives evidence of knowing elements of Indian military astrology through Pahlavī translation, and provided his own Syriac versions of works by Aristotle and Galen, although one later Muslim scholar commented that these were absolutely dreadful. This, of course, may be an indication that his first language was actually Greek rather than Syriac, and if so, in the late 770s he may have used that superior ability to compose one of his best-known works, *Labours Concerning Military Initiatives*, in Greek in order to make it inaccessible to some of his potential rivals at the Court of Caliph al-Mahdī. It is a significant book in as much as it is the only Mediaeval treatise we have which is devoted to military astrology, that is to say, an adaptation of astrological techniques to questions specifically dealing with the outbreak, conduct, and likely outcome of war, a system of astrology in which Indian astrologers had specialised hitherto. Before settling to the meat and purpose of his treatise, Theophilos addresses a few general remarks to his son, Deucalion. The energies of the stars, he says, do not necessarily concentrate on providing a single type of influence, although their nature is indeed specific. Thus, Mars is associated especially with war, but this characteristic energy may then diversify into arson, plague, drought, and famine. Skilled astrologers are aware of this and of the complexities brought about by the planets' and stars' relationships with each other, and are careful to take everything into account when drawing up a horoscope. Bearing this last point in mind, says Theophilos, he has applied methods taken from genethliacal and horary systems of casting horoscopes to military questions, something not often done by the ancient astrologers who constitute his sources, and it is this approach which informs the rest of his book. [8]

Novelty and usefulness characterise this period in Islamic astrology. Between the eighth and tenth centuries in particular, there seems to have been a remarkable number of astrologers whose work proved to be significant in one way or another to the history and development of the science. Sahl ibn Bishr (Zahel), like Māshā'allāh, was a Jewish astrologer originally from Iran. His work now survives in a thirteenth-century Latin translation by Guido Bonatti and shows, in company with much other ninth-century Islamic astrological material, an interest in and careful use of technical questions involving such important details as cusps, (imaginary lines which separate one sign of the zodiac from another), and houses, (the twelve segments of the zodiac). But more important is a younger contemporary, Abū Ma'shar (787–886), known in the West as Albumasar. He was born in Balkh, a city in Khurasan which in his day was a huge territory east of Iran. Balkh, as David Pingree says, 'had once been seen as an outpost of Hellenism in Central Asia, and had then become a centre for the mingling of Indians, Chinese, Scythians, and Graeco-Syrians with Iranians … Its religious communities included Jews, Nestorians, Manichaeans, Buddhists, and Hindus, as well as Zoroastrians'.

So Abū Ma'shar was born and brought up in a highly diverse and eclectic set of communities, a feature of his childhood and youth which may help to account for the diversity of the sources he later used for his writings. Beginning as a student of religion, when he was thirty-eight he turned his attention to mathematics and astronomy-astrology and thereafter wrote copiously, evincing a special interest in that branch of astrology which had so fascinated Māshā'allāh – the periodic return of all heavenly bodies to their place of origin in a time-span known as the World Year, and on the effects of the planets and stars on terrestrial events and hence the development of the historical process.

Abū Ma'shar summarises his treatment of this at the beginning of the first chapter of his *Kitāb al-Milal Wa'd'duwal* ('Book of Religions and Dynasties'), written some time after 869. The first part discusses how to foretell from planetary conjunctions the appearance of prophets and successful military leaders; the second, the changing fortunes of kings and royal dynasties; the third, the connection between planetary relationships and terrestrial events, (by which he means dynastic changes, outbreaks of disease, conflicts, the occurrence of widespread use of magic, lawsuits, adulteries, and so on), after which the remaining five parts elaborate in various ways upon the technicalities of the third. But Abū Ma'shar's expertise embraced much more astrological subject matter than this, and some fifty books bearing his name – it is perhaps a matter of nice judgement whether they all come from his pen or whether, as was so often the case, some were attributed to him with the aim of borrowing his lustre – give an indication of the breadth of his learning. Sayings of earlier astrologers on nativities; explaining dreams from the stars; magic and astrology, and how to predict from the numerical equivalents of proper names; meteorological astrology, ('Book of Rains and Winds and Changes in the Weather'); mundane astrology, (astrology limited to drawing up charts to predict and explain national trends: a subdivision of historical astrology), exemplified by his *Book of Flowers*, (i.e. 'choice extracts'), which offers interpretations of the separate planets as rulers of the year, their natures, their appearance in triplicities, their movements within the zodiacal signs, and the significance of comets. The book-list also contains a description of the planetary temples of the Sabians of

Harran, and *Sayings of Abū Ma'shar on the Secrets of Astrology*, a collection made by one of his pupils, which gives fascinating glimpses into the practice of astrology in contemporary Baghdad.

Records of Abū Ma'shar confirm, (as one might expect), his status as one of the foremost astrologers of his day:

> [Abū Ma'shar] said, 'We were with the army of the Cumans and many of us astronomers were sitting in a tent and someone was approaching. One of the astronomers said, 'Let's see what he is going to say.' So we observed the ascendant, which was Sagittarius in the termini of Mercury, and the moon was there at that hour in an empty course. I said, 'He is full of idle talk and is a useless fellow.' We questioned him when he arrived and he talked a lot of nonsense, and all the astronomers marvelled at my great experience.

Not everyone, however, was pleased with his performances. On one occasion, we are told, he was thrown into prison and promised his liberty if a prediction he had made came true, and execution if it did not. Fortunately for Abū Ma'shar, it turned out true in every respect, but one can see why he gave advice to a fellow astrologer that 'if the King summons you to serve him in astronomical [*i.e. astrological*] science, don't give an opinion when Scorpio is in the horoscope … or Mars is in an angle, because the opinion will be wrong. Scorpio is a sign of mendacity'. But one story about him suggests he had a sense of humour:

> [Abu Sa'īd Shādhān] said that, although his master Abū Ma'shar was very rational and supreme in science, whenever the moon was diametrically opposite to the sun, he fell down and shook. He had no record of his nativity but had made a universal interrogation. Virgo was the ascendant of the interrogation, while the moon was in Scorpio diametrically opposite to the sun and configured with Mars. Such a figure signified epilepsy. He was accustomed to having fruit and anything he liked put in front of him, and ate once a day and drank wine for the rest of the day. He had a marvellous thirst. He told me, 'If I could stop drinking wine for one year, I would be cured of epilepsy.'

Abū Ma'ashar's significance in the history of astrology lies in his efforts to explain to his audiences philosophical and historical justifications for the science, and for this his diverse background, which had evidently produced a very wide reading in Pahlavi, Greek, and Indian astronomico-astrological traditions had equipped him well. He and his colleagues in the ninth-century Islamic world were, in fact, responsible for astrologising the Abbasid Caliphate's adoption of Greek science and philosophy, and thereby causing a growth of serious interest in the science, especially in intellectual circles. A particularly potent influence upon Abū Ma'shar in particular, however, was the astral theology developed in Harran which posited three levels of being: divine, ethereal, and sublunar. The human soul has descended from the divine to the sublunar level and its goal is to return whence it came; but it cannot do so without the assistance of spirits belonging to the ethereal level – the rulers of the planets and constellations – acting as intermediaries on its behalf. Relationships and congruities between the ethereal and sublunar levels therefore assume an immense importance, and in Harran's religious philosophy these relationships happen not simply because the *movements* of the former have an effect upon the latter, (which was Aristotle's view), but because *each* of these two levels possesses an innate ability to affect the other in certain specific ways: certain celestial bodies can affect certain terrestrial ones, and certain terrestrial bodies have the potentiality of being affected by certain celestial ones. Hence, the elaborate system of associations between planets, signs of the zodiac, and the great variety of people, animals, plants, and inanimate objects on earth receives a better-founded explanation and justification than reliance upon posited likenesses and sympathies whose arbitrariness opponents of astrology had long been criticising. Abū Ma'shar further buttresses his arguments by turning to history to show that in the transmission of knowledge from many different sources, one can find evidence of the truth about how humankind has come by its understanding of the workings of Nature – divine revelation. In this way, scientific philosophy complements its religious counterpart, the oneness of learning is allowed to mirror the oneness of God, and a justification for learning in harmony with Islamic principles is provided. [9]

While Abū Ma'shar was very influential on both Muslim intellectual and social history and, via Latin translations, upon the intellectual and social life of Western Europe and Byzantium, too, it cannot be said he was a particularly original thinker. Perhaps that designation is better attached to the man who, we are told, drew him into the study of astrology – the remarkable scholar al-Kindī (*c.*801–66). Born, or at least educated in Iraq, al-Kindī completed his studies in Baghdad and went on to enjoy royal patronage for a while as tutor to the son of Caliph al-Mu'tasim, before falling out of favour and spending his latter years in relative isolation. The range of his interests and expertise was enormous. Apart from astronomy-astrology, to which we shall return, he wrote a copious number of fairly short but complex works – Pinella Travaglia lists 94, the late tenth-century bibliographer, Ibn al-Nadīm, listed 260 – dealing with philosophy, cosmology, physics, mathematics, meteorology, medicine, pharmacology, alchemy, mineralogy, optics, music, and divination. He also seems to have undertaken technological studies relating to the making of clocks, astronomical instruments, and swords. His approach to all these subjects was more or less the same, as Jolivet and Rashd point out:

> to work through the legacy of ancient science and then to transcend it in furtherance of his twofold aim of advancing both scientific paedagogy and research. His method always combined an empirical strain with a mathematical tendency that led him to seek geometrical or numerical relationships between phenomena.

Al-Kindī's works on astronomy-astrology include short treatises on obtaining distances by use of the astrolabe, the construction and use of the six armillary spheres, (skeleton celestial globes consisting of hoops representing the equator, the tropics, the arctic and Antarctic circles, and so on), the revolutions of the years, an introduction to judicial astrology, and the application of astrology to medicine. But the treatise which had a profound effect on Western astrology, once it became known through Latin translation, was *Risāla fī shu'ā'āt* ('Letter on Rays') which offers an explanation for the way celestial bodies affect terrestrial.

There exist, he says, cosmic rays which not only enable stars to transmit their nature or essence into the sublunar world, but also to cause the elements which make up the world to transmit rays in their turn, thereby conveying both stellar and elemental qualities to whomsoever or whatsoever receives them; and because the stars are constantly moving into new positions, the criss-crossing of their rays produces an infinite variety of influxes and effects. These propositions flow from al-Kindī's unorthodox 'attempt to explain creation as an incessant outflow from the ultimate source', and led him to offer a theological and scientific justification for the practice of astrology – 'whoever has acquired the knowledge of the whole condition of the celestial harmony will know the past and the present and the future' – as well as for astral magic which depends on the existence of vehicles for the transmission of sympathies and antipathies between beings, both animate and inanimate. Once of these vehicles, of course, is the voice, and al-Kindī suggested that the human imagination formed concepts and emitted rays which were transformed into action by the muscular movements involved in utterance. Hence both incantation and, indeed, prayer were capable of producing the effects intended or mentally visualised by the speaker. Now, whether al-Kindī intended his theories to support either the theory or practice of magic is open to question. If by 'magic' one means 'natural magic', that is, an understanding and manipulation of the laws of Nature to produce effects which are not at all arbitrary but appear and work in accordance with those laws, then the likelihood is that al-Kindī, who never actually mentions magic as such in his treatises, would have been prepared to acknowledge 'natural magic' as a valid descriptive term for what he was describing. [10]

Nevertheless, in thus providing a 'natural' explanation for the operations of astrology, whether he wished to or not, al-Kindī had also opened the door to explaining why magic as a whole might work, whether that magic were 'natural', ritual, or indeed demonic in kind, and here we should turn our attention to the Harran connection. As we have seen, Theophilos of Edessa studied there for a while and Māshā'allāh appears to have been influenced by some of its teachings. But just how distinctive these could be may be gauged from part of an anonymous late ninth-century work, *Kitāb al-nawāmīs* ('Book of Laws'), which was later translated into Latin under the title *Liber Vaccae* ('The Book of the Cow'), referring to the first of its magical attempts to join soul with matter in order to produce a separate being:

[Hunayn says]: I have seen that they could never accomplish this unless they worshipped the stars and constructed temples, all of whose doors they placed to the east so that they might face the great light which is the light of the sun, from which comes the light of the day and its splendour, and unless they suffumigated in these temples with suffumigations of great exaltation, brought sacrifices to them, lit candles and lamps in them, built oratories in them, and illuminated their gods, the stars, within them, whom they address with words appropriate to one who is worshipped, praying for them to fulfil their needs. They also question them about someone who is absent, about things already done and things to be done in the future; and when they happen, they make them tell about each thing separately; and they ask about life, death, health, truthfulness, food, and drink, about all things over the knowledge of which stands none but their Creator. Therefore the stars caused people to have knowledge by means of whatever power people possess which enables them to address the stars, until any one of them has come to the point at which he may be in Rome and perambulate Africa in the same day, or may be in Scythia in the morning and walk about the vast west in the evening. For the earth is rolled up for them, and they are carried about in the air and walk on the waters. They know before its birth whether the foetus is male or female, and whether or not it will live.

But with all this, they disagree in their intentions, their laws, and their sciences, so that some of them worship the sun, others the moon, and some of them the stars one by one; and they worship both fire and darkness. Those who worship fire said that it is the eye of the sun, but it is not as they thought it is. Because there is no day except from the sun, and as we do not discover the splendour of creation without it, they said, 'This is our deity.' They lit candles and lamps to it, and this was sufficient so that they became endowed with the genius to build buildings which do not decay, and to make candles which do not burn out over the extension and passage of time … [and] they were inspired to make for their gods those seven luminaries which do not burn out, which are the candles which do not cease, but which remain for ever.

I remember the torches which are not extinguished in water, and the suffumigations into whose smoke they look when there is a query about something, and they hear the answers. For when the magicians are properly positioned in the temple designated for the stars, then the nature of benefit descends into them, and they do nothing which does not bring some benefit. For whenever one of them tries this and asks about something, small or large, as if the god were standing on his altar, holding the suffumigation in his hands, that magician addresses his star with the words and prayers appropriate to the star.

Now, this 'Book of Laws' was supposed to have been written by Plato, an attribution which reminds us that the Sabians of Harran had developed a very particular form of esoteric Neoplatonism which laid emphasis on the study of the stars they worshipped and therefore encouraged research in astronomy, astrology, alchemy, and medicine – the last two because of the connection between astral influxes and the properties of the elements, and the growth and development of minerals, metals, and plants. These Harranian teachings then drifted out of the city via scholars who studied there, or treatises influenced by them, and so made their way into the much wider fields of Islamic and then Western European scholarship.

One such channel was Thābit ibn Qurra, a money-changer, translator, and scholar who was born in the city in 836, but was brought to Baghdad by a patron who had been impressed by his linguistic abilities in Greek and Syriac, and paid him 500 dinars a month to retain his services. Like so many of his contemporaries he wrote voluminously: about 150 works in Arabic and 16 in Syriac. From one of the latter comes a passage in praise of the legacy of Greek learning which Ibn Qurra was helping to transmit to the Arabic-speaking world:

We are the heirs and the transmitters to our heirs of heathenism, which is honoured glo-riously in this world. Lucky is he who bears the burden with a sure hope for the sake of heathenism. Who has made the world to be inhabited and filled with cities except the good men and kings of heathenism? Who has constructed harbours and canals? Who has made manifest the occult sciences? On whom has dawned the divinity which gives divination and teaches the knowledge of future events except the wise men of the heathen? It is they who have pointed out all these things, and have made to arise the medicine of souls, and have made to shine forth their redemption; and it is they also who have made to arise the medicine for bodies. They have filled the world with the correctness of modes of life and with the wisdom which is the beginning of excellence. Without these products of heathenism, the world would be an empty and a needy place, and it would have been enveloped in sheer want and misery.

Among his many translations and contributions to the Harranian legacy, Thābit ibn Qurra produced one of astrological magic, known in its Latin form as *De imaginibus*. It describes how to create talismans and tune them to the positions of the stars and planets:

When you want to make an image of a man who wants to become the head of a city or province, or judge of a prefecture or a town … carve the head of the image when the Caput Draconis is in the ascendant, and let the lord of the ascendant be a benefic, free from the aspect of the malefics. Carve the body of the image under whatever rising sign the moon will be in; carve the shoulders and breasts with Venus in the ascendant; the haunches with the sun rising in one of its dignities; the thighs with Mercury in the ascendant, but not retrograde or combust or afflicted, and in one of his fortunate places; and the feet under the ascendant of the moon in conjunction with Venus … See that the ascendant and its lord and the tenth house be fortunate, and that the malefics be far away from the ascendant and its lord; and let the lord of the eleventh be one of the benefics, in aspect of the ascendant and its lord; and let the lord of the tenth be in conjunction with the lord of the ascendant in a friendly conjunction, or with complete mutual reception. When you have done this and made the image in this manner, he will obtain what he desires from his king, and be given the post he seeks. Preserve the image as I have told you, and it will do the work, if God wills.

Now, it is easy to assume that these topics, including astral magic, were the domain of the learned; but it is important to see them in a wider and more general context. During the tenth century, for example, Ibn Wahshiyya is said to have translated a book on Nabataean agriculture ('Al-Filāha an-Nabatiyya') from Syrian into Arabic. It contains quite a lot of information about *popular* magical practices, including some related to image magic similar to that described by Ibn Qurra. Farmers, it says, were accustomed to carve statues from myrtle to represent a man or a woman whom they wished to harm in some way. The name of the individual depicted was added, along with the likeness of some noxious creature such as a lion, a snake, or a scorpion, with all the carving done 'at a particular time with the stars in a certain constellation'. Once completed, the statue would then cause the person named on it to suffer nightmares or madness, or at least some damage or misfortune. A simple cane could also be made into an instrument of magic by leaving it out overnight under the open sky to absorb influxes from the stars, and then storing it away from sunlight. To operate the magic, one used the cane as fuel to burn some snakes, and then one cast the ash into the wind. Wherever the ash might fall would be protected from hailstorms. Stellar influxes were also important in some simpler operations. For example, if one wanted to stop the decrease of water in a subterranean or open fountain which served as the source for a stream or river, one could take 'sweet' salt, mix it with an equal amount of river sand, leave the mixture out overnight to absorb influxes from the moon and stars, and then throw it into the well or sprinkle it at the foot of the spring, 'seven handfuls a day, thrown with the right hand'.

These magical practices which look to the planets and stars for their power to work stemmed from that paganism praised by Ibn Qurra's Syriac source, which recognised the seven planets as deities. Jupiter and Venus were seen as particularly beneficent, Saturn and Mars as maleficent, while the sun, with the help of the beneficent planets, constantly worked hard to mitigate the nefarious influences of Mars and Saturn. Prayers combined with magical intent could be addressed to their deities:

> If you take seven olive stones and stand in front of the sun and throw them, one by one, towards the sun with all your might, saying, 'O god of gods, be merciful towards me and make an end of my illness,' then that illness will end by permission of this god, even if it had continued for years. This must be done seven times, so that you make use of forty-nine stones.

To cure what seems to have been the common cold, Persian folk lore magic recommended taking two strings of different colours, measuring the height of the patient, tying seven knots in those strings, blowing certain prayers on them, and then hanging the strings round the patient's neck. If the distinction between prayer and magic here is not altogether clear, one must recollect that the social context in which this amalgam was being used was imbued with magic of all kinds. Resort to magical operations, simple or complex, without the accompaniment of religious supplication, was an entirely natural, (one might almost say automatic), reaction to a problem, large or small, which one was keen to solve. Children who limped were thought to lack some of their vertebrae, so one found a donkey and whispered the child's deficiency into its ear. Incantations were blown upon someone directly, or upon a handful of dirt or salt which was then thrown at him or her. Popular magic can also be found embedded in romances. In the eleventh-century *Vis o Rāmin*, Vis's nursemaid renders Vis's husband impotent by making two small figures from copper and bronze, binding them back to back with iron wire, and burying them in a river bank at dawn. Society, learned or not, thus regarded magic as a regular way – one among many – of tackling a difficulty, exerting one's will, achieving one's desire, and circumventing or otherwise avoiding adversity; and astrology sophisticated or not, provided relevant information which might or might not be used in conjunction with magic to enable the individual to manage his or her life, or attain a particular goal. [11]

With this in mind, we shall not be surprised by the compilation of perhaps the most famous treatise in Arabic, *Ghayāt al-Hakīm* ('The Aim of the Sage'), better known in the

West by its Latin title, *Picatrix*. Neither the date nor the author of the book is certain, the former depending in large extent upon the latter. The historian Ibn Kaldūn attributed *Picatrix* to Maslama ibn Ahmad al-Majrītī, a Muslim mathematician living in Spain during the late ninth century, but the attribution is not generally accepted, partly because at least two of the sources used by the author can be dated to the end of the tenth century. Maribel Fierro has suggested that the author may have been Maslama ibn Qāsim al-Qurtubī (906–64), a religious scholar of suspect opinions, an alchemist, and a magician, 'a man of charms and talismans', as the biographer and historian, al-Faradī, puts it. He was born and then studied in Cordoba after which he travelled widely in North Africa and the Middle East before returning to Andalusia. Originally composed in Arabic, *Picatrix* was translated into Spanish in 1256 and then, at some unknown later date, into Latin. [12] It is a somewhat disorderly piece of work, but basically it is a grimoire composed from Arabic texts on a variety of occult scientific subjects, largely written in Syria and Mesopotamia during the previous two centuries. These texts themselves clearly contained material derived from Greek astrological and magical treatises, and it is also possible to detect Indian practices (mediated through Pahlavi sources) in *Picatrix*'s application of catarchic astrology to the making of amulets, as well as the influence of the Harranian astrological philosophy which seems to have been pervasive during this period. Taken as a whole, *Picatrix* thus sums up a remarkably long history of astral magic and, as Frances Yates observed, provided 'a most complete textbook for the magician, giving the philosophy of nature on which talismanic and sympathetic magic is based, together with full instructions for its practice'.

That philosophy is founded upon the proposition that magical powers are derived ultimately from God, and that they flow from Him via a complex concatenation of stages ranging from God Himself to the seven planets to the elements which make up matter. These powers are conveyed or transmitted via rays by angels and spirits who exist above the sublunar world, and it is these entities human beings contact when they wish to avail themselves of the powers of magic. There are various ways in which contact can be made: indirectly, when by drawing or creating images the human operator opens up a channel for the powers to descend in astral rays; and directly, when the magician invokes planetary deities, (and indeed not just planetary deities, but celestial spirits from every constellation, visible and invisible), and induces them to send their angels or spirits to do the magician's bidding. Hence, the teaching of *Picatrix* is both theoretical and practical, and this makes it a most desirable handbook of certain types of magic.

The whole is divided into four Books. Book 1 begins with bibliographical material relating to the Spanish translation and attributes the treatise to a very wise philosopher called 'Picatrix' who wrote it in order to reveal to those whom the wise consider worthy of profiting by them the secrets of what he calls 'nigromancy', by which he clearly means astral and talismanic magic. Investigation of Nature, he says, is entirely compatible with religion:

> To know is a very lofty and noble thing, and you must study every day in God, (that is to say, in His commandments and His goodness), because knowledge, understanding, and goodness proceed from Him. His spirit is a noble, profound light, and whoever sets out

to study in Him must despise the things of this world, because they come to an end and there is no stability in them. From Him, as from the world on high, descends the human spirit, and therefore it must desire to return to the place from which it came and where it had its origin. From there it will know what the world is like, how it works, and how it came into being through its Creator. This reason for knowing [things] is true wisdom. Be aware that God is the maker and creator of the whole world and everything which exists in it, and that this world and everything which exists in it were created by Him, the Most High. The reason for this is too mysterious and too potent to be understood, and as much of it as can be understood is employed with ardour and earnest application; and to devote one's energies to knowing and finding out is the greatest gift God Himself has given to humankind. (1.1.1).

Having established this point, the author goes on to define 'nigromancy' – 'all the things a human being performs, as a result of which sensations and spirits follow at every stage, and [which he or she does] for the sake of the wonderful things by which he operates, because sensation follows these things when one concentrates upon them and marvels at them', (1.2.1), a definition which, of course, could open the way to accusations of involvement with demons. Magic, says 'Picatrix', can be divided into two parts, theoretical and practical. The first deals with the fixed stars, constellations, and the way the planets project their rays while they are moving, all of which provides the information one needs to make magical images; and this includes the spoken word, because 'words have in themselves the power of nigromancy'. Practical magic consists of knowing the physical composition of 'the three Natures', that is, the animal, vegetable, and mineral kingdoms, and the power of the fixed stars with which they are infused. Chapter 3 explains why the sky is shaped as a sphere and draws attention to the distinction between this higher plane and the sublunar world; the superior knows no change or corruption, so the perfection of its form never changes, and from this region spring the powers of spirits. The sky can be divided into 360° and has the same number of 'figures', (that is, representational images associated with the zodiac), which are used in astrology. When the planets pass through these, they exert various influences upon the world below. Thus, Saturn affects things which are cold and dry; Jupiter those which are hot and moist; Mars those which are hot and dry; Venus things fairly hot and very moist; Mercury things slightly hot and very dry; the moon things which are cold and moist. Variations on these themes take place, however, as the planets move out of one degree into another and so alter their relationships with the sky and with each other.

Making talismans successfully means one must have a correct and comprehensive knowledge of the constellations, and the author now concentrates on these and on the lunar mansions, arcs of 12° 51′ roughly corresponding to the daily mean motion of the moon through the ecliptic, assigning to each mansion its proper talisman. The talismans are described, but not in that detail which would provide the reader with the exact operation whereby they acquire their astral potency:

A talisman to cure scorpion stings. Make an image of a scorpion on a bezoar-stone. Do this when the moon is in the second decan of Scorpio while Leo, Taurus, and Aquarius are in the ascendant. Fix this stone in a gold ring and, under the foresaid constellation, mark a softened piece of incense with it. Give the person who has been stung a drink containing one of these marked pieces of incense, and he or she will be cured instantaneously and the pain will die down. (1.5. 25).

The end of Book 1 overlaps with the beginning of Book 2. 'Picatrix' talks about the relationship between human beings and the rest of creation and the correspondences between earthly creatures and their celestial archetypes, and says distinctly that 'the roots of magic are the movements of the planets', at which point he interrupts his discourse to explain how he became a practising magician:

I want to provide an example which I learned from a sage who spent his time working in these branches of knowledge. He told me, 'I lived for a while in the royal palace in Egypt, where there was a young man who had originally come from India and who had also devoted himself to the foresaid [studies]. While the young man and I were talking to each other, we heard the voice of a man wailing that he had been given a poisonous sting by a scorpion and was going to die. When the young man heard him, he took out of his purse a piece of cloth in which he had wrapped a large number of seals which, to judge by their smell, resembled incense. He said one of them should be given to the man in a drink and he would be cured at once. Now I, wanting to learn further, and in order to put it to the test, got to my feet, took the seal out of his hands, and gave it to the man in a drink, as he had suggested. Straight away his cries and pains died away and he was saved. I looked closely at the seal. It had the figure of a scorpion on it. I asked [the young man] what he had used to mark it, and he showed me a gold ring with a bezoar-stone which bore the figure of a scorpion. I quizzed him about the figure, what it was and what were the secret influences which had brought about [the cure]. He replied that the figure was made when the moon was in the second decan of Scorpio, and this was the secret and the power of that ring.' This is [the story] the sage told me. So I myself made an image with that figure at the foresaid time, and with it I marked incense, as well as anything else which could receive an imprint; and with these I began to work the wonders at which everyone was astonished. (2.1.2).

The coincidence between the details of this anecdote and those of the talisman we recorded earlier suggest that the other talismans recorded by the author in this chapter may also have sprung from his own experience, in which case *Picatrix* would be more than simply a scholar's amalgamation of extracts from earlier sources.

Technicalities follow derived from Abū Maʾshar, Ibn Wahshiyya, and Theon of Alexandria, among other sources. Then in chapter 5 we learn that the branch of knowledge (*scientia*) he is discussing can be divided into three parts: magic, which is the special province of the Sabaeans (of Harran); worshipping the stars with incense, sacrifices, prayers, and written charms or supplications, which is the particular interest of the Greeks; and the same kind of astral religion conjoined with invocation of spirits, that being associated with Indians, certain people from the Yemen, and the Copts of Egypt. [13]

Once again, too, we are reminded that, in the opinion of the Greeks at least, 'the science of astrology is considered as the root of the whole science of magic'. This brings 'Picatrix', (after one or two divagations into divination and prophecy), to the way in which talismans work. They derive their power, he says, from that of their dominant constellation and from the special qualities (*virtutes*) of the substances from which they are made. These special qualities reinforce the diverse effects of the stars:

> and I tell you that a single planet produces different effects, effects which are separate and distinct from each other, just as fire does when one boils honey. When it is boiled in the proper way at an even temperature, it acquires a good taste, better than the one it had to begin with; but if it is boiled too hard, it may be burned and acquire an unpleasant taste. (2.6.3).

This is followed by discussions on the sphere of the fixed stars and its influence, the relative effects of the planets in relation one another – 'when the moon is in conjunction with Saturn, its action will be feeble and hidden. This is because the special quality or power (*virtus*) of Saturn is stronger than that of the moon', (2.6.7) – the significance of lines, surfaces, time, place, words, and numbers in relation to talismans, and the results to be expected from forming combinations of the qualities hot, cold, moist, and dry.

Chapters 9 and 10 describe the signatures of the zodiacal signs to be inscribed on talismans, the metals to be used, the signs of the planets, and the images of the planetary deities, about which 'Picatrix' records variations in opinion:

> The figure of Saturn according to the wise 'Picatrix' is that of a person with the face of a crow and the feet of a camel, seated upon a high-backed chair, holding a spear [or staff] in his right hand, and a lance or dart in his left … The figure of Saturn according to the wise Mercurius [*i.e. Hermes*] is that of a person standing upright, his hands raised above his head, holding a fish, with a [creature] resembling a lizard under his feet.

To these observations 'Picatrix' adds instructions on the making of planetary talismans, and it is possible, in view of his overt acknowledgement of different sources for his descriptions of the planetary images, that he has culled these instructions from a variety of sources, too. Book 2 ends with two chapters dealing with the 36 decans, their images, and their patron-planets; a reprisal of the decans, this time according to Indian astrological teaching, an extract from a book on talismans by al-Razi, a thirteenth-century physician and alchemist, and a note on what appears to be Brahmanic practices related to the stars:

> When [certain of their sages] seek to attain and arrive at the level of the high caste men who have established their laws, they first mortify their bodies and cleanse themselves from all impurities. They would begin this in the first hour of Sunday, a day and hour properly attributed to the sun. They would refrain from eating meat for forty days, and follow a régime consisting of products from the earth, grains, and plants. Each day they would diminish the amount of food up to the fortieth day when what they ate on that day

would be a fortieth of what they had eaten on the first. Throughout all this they would practise abstinence, and afterwards make use of medicines which take away the desire to eat and drink, without suffering any inconvenience at all. When they were doing all this, they would find a refinement and acuity of intellect in their spirits; they would understand what they wanted, and keep hold of and increase their wills and physical senses. The earthly and heavy parts which were in them began to diminish, and a refinement and acuity in them conspicuously appear; there would appear a taste and instinctive desire to ascend to a higher world and to the place from which the spirit is brought forth, and [the sages] would detest the savours, the inactivities, and the delights of the world. When they did this, the inevitable consequence was that they then attracted the special qualities and powers of the sky, for they would say and do wonderful things, and achieve what they wanted in the past or future by knowing the stages of their life. They used to have the power of making laws at will, and the spirits of the stars would obey them. (2.12.53).

Book 3 is a curious mixture of detailed instructions on how to make talismans – the required planetary images, the colours and materials of robes to be worn while worshipping the planets, formulae for special inks, the effects of the planets on various regions and countries, the characteristic of a number of animals and human superiority in the structure of the living world, and (to some extent) the theory and practice of a certain type of magic. This first, somewhat chaotic half of the Book gives way to a rather more coherent second half which concentrates, (as much as the author ever concentrates), on the details of astral magic, and here 'Picatrix' is clearly echoing the practices and usages of Sabaeans from Harran. A list of planets is provided, along with the groups of people whom they may be expected to influence:

> From the sun, make petitions which are appropriate to him, such as requests to kings, sons of soldiers and kings, people of importance who love justice and truth and hate falsehood and violence, who seek a good reputation and strive for people's praise; [requests to] officials, clergy, physicians, philosophers, people of importance who are humble, intelligent and noble in spirit, powerful brothers, fathers, and so forth. (3.7.3)

Also listed are the ceremonies, ritual paraphernalia, and prayers to be used in planetary worship, as well as details of a child's initiation into a cult devoted to Mars:

> In a month when the sun lingers in Scorpio, they take a child, bring him to a secret, specially decorated house where this performance is to take place and stand him on his feet. They bring in a handful of tamarisk and burn it in a censer made from latten [*mixed yellow metal*]. They say words pertaining to Mars over the child and clothe him in the [red] garments of Mars. If the fire touches the boy's back, they regard him as unwanted for this performance, unsuitable and untrained as far as the performance is concerned. But if the fire touches him in front, they claim he is suitable and fitted for it. In this case, they take him to their prayer-house and there inspect him to see if he is sound in every part of his body, and then they take him to another secret house and veil his eyes. A priest gets himself

ready in front of him and puts a staff made of red tamarisk on top of him. They clothe him in an animal skin and put a censer full of fire next to his feet on the right, and another censer fill of water on his left. Then the child's mother comes with a cockerel in her hands, and sits in the doorway of the house. The priest takes a pot full of flaming fire in his hands, makes [the child] swear an oath, and by this binds him never to reveal the secrets [of this performance]; and he really terrifies him so that he will not reveal it to anyone, saying that if he does tell anyone what has happened, he will die at once. When all this is done, he unveils the child's eyes and [tells him] to open them. His mother comes, with the cockerel. The priest takes it into his hands and cuts its throat over the child. Immediately his mother throws a piece of red cloth over him and leads him out of the house; and as soon as the child leaves the house, she puts on his index finger a ring with the image of a monkey on it. (3.7.37).

There follow prayers to Saturn and the sun, taken from Ibn Wahshiyya's version of *Nabataean Agriculture*; details of the spirits of each planet and, again, the ways in which they should be worshipped; then back to a talisman, this time for protection against poisons, recipes for a large number of potions to ensure success in love – magic without references to planets or constellations: 'Take an equal quantity of black cat's brain and human urine. Mix them together and give them in food to whomever you want. His or her spirits and inclinations will be roused towards you,' (3.11.8) – and similar non-astral protections: 'Join together a human eye and a wolf's eye. Whoever carries these two will not be obstructed by an evil eye or an evil tongue.' (3.11.61). Recipes for poisons come next, and then manufacture of 'a wonderful stone against poisons', followed by examples of the magical arts of Egypt and India. Most of the early recipes are taken from books attributed to Aristotle – hence, perhaps, the lack of astrology in their composition – and Book 3 ends with a further borrowing, this time from Aristotle's *Metaphysica*, allowing 'Picatrix' to discuss what is meant by the word 'natura', a discussion which continues in the early part of Book 4.

After this excursus, however, he returns to his subject with instructions on what to do when the moon is in each of the twelve signs of the zodiac:

When the moon is in Scorpio and you want to attract her influence and power, get up while the moon is in the 13th degree of Scorpio and go to a place in which there are several trees growing very closely together and where there is plenty of water. Draw a square on the ground and cover it completely nut-tree leaves and leaves from the quince and pine. Drench the whole thing with rose water. Next, place nine silver censers in front of you and put a piece of aloe wood in each one of them and as much storax and incense as you can [manage]. Then clothe yourself in cloth which is completely white, and take care there is absolutely no mixture [of weave] in it. Once you have done this, place in front of you two earthenware censers full of water. Take a small earthenware jug and use it to pour water from one censer into another. Sprinkle this water over your sides and back, and make your sacrifice from animals relating to [the moon]. After all this has been done, get to your feet and prostrate yourself four times on the ground, and during each of the prostrations, say,

'Seraphs, Seraphs!' and stay where you are. Throw aloe wood and storax into the heart of
the fire, and put storax into each of the nine censers. Then prostrate yourself again four
times, as before. Then there will come to you a person in seemly and complete shape, [14]
whom you may ask whatever you want; and what you desire will be fulfilled. (4.2.9).

There follows a mélange of observations and extracts from other authors: an account of
the house of the sun, built by 'Hermes', how to make oneself invisible, astrological and
magical aphorisms, an extract from a pseudo-Aristotelian treatise on talismans, taken from
a translation by Hunain ibn Ishāq, two extracts on death and the effect of music on the
soul, attributed to Plato, and a disquisition on love with further apparent quotations from
Plato. Chapter 6 goes over ground by now familiar – recipes for suffumigations appropriate
to the seven planets, which are attributed to Indian practice; chapter 7 contains extracts
from Ibn Wahshiyya's *Nabataean Agriculture*, and explanations of the magical properties
of certain plants:

If anyone takes a vessel made from crystal or clear, transparent glass, fills it with good, clear
olive oil, and holds it up to the sun every morning early, on an empty stomach, constantly
looking at his shadow and fixing his eyes on that oil, his sight will be invigorated and every
weakness of the vision and the eyes will go away. His heart and inclination will rejoice, and
he will be loved by everyone who sees him, and approved of in the very best way. (4.7.13).

We then learn a variety of recipes for different purposes – to raise a storm, to get rid of
animals which harm one's vines, to kill mice, to make poison, and so forth – and read
about the trees of various countries. 'In France is found a tree which will cause the death
of anyone who stands under it for half an hour, and if anyone touches it or handles any
part of it, he or she will die at once'. (4.7.55). Finally, two chapters tell us about the special
qualities (*virtutes*) of all kinds of things in Nature and relate these to the manufacture of
a wide range of talismans, before ending with a reversion to astrology in a discussion of
'the twenty-eight mansions of the moon according to Plinio'. This source has not been
identified and is certainly not the first-century AD Roman encyclopaedist, Pliny the Elder.
Nor does this section appear in the Arabic original.

This Latin version of the *Ghāyat al-Hakīm* exercised a considerable influence on
Western magic although, apart from short fragments and extracts, we have to wait until
the sixteenth and seventeenth centuries to see its influence at full tide. It was then copied
many times from what appear to be two originals, one from the region of Liège late in the
fourteenth century, and one from Italy in the middle of the fifteenth, and among those
familiar with it were Marsilio Ficino and Cornelius Agrippa, both of whom we shall
meet later, and the seventeenth-century English astrologer, William Lilly, who owned
a manuscript copy given to him by Sir Richard Napier, grandson of Richard Napier, a
famous astrological physician. One of the difficulties it presented to potential readers and
users was that it contained formulae for making talismans, some of which did not depend
on 'demonic' assistance, and some which did; and if we look at an incomplete Polish
transcription – interesting because it is the only one to contain illustrations – we can see

that it appears to stop short at the point where a non-demonic interpretation of the work ceases to be possible, a hesitation which actually persisted even in later readers and users who were prepared to familiarise themselves with the whole work. [15]

In short, then, the contents of the book may vary considerably in interest, and its chaotic structure, (if that is not too specific a word), make it rather difficult to read, but *Picatrix* is a good example of the way certain aspects of both popular and learned astrologico-magical traditions from the past and the compiler's present, and from disparate geographical areas, were collected and transmitted to cultures other than their own, and linked in vivid, seductive fashion the two occult sciences of astrology and magic, thereby perpetuating if it did not create a bond which, though not always visible in later centuries, would lurk beneath their apparently disparate surfaces.

8

Byzantium & the Jewish Diaspora c.900–c.1200: Agreements to Disagree

Needless to say, the enthusiasm of the ninth and tenth centuries for astrology in its various forms could not last, and in fact a reaction set in as early as the tenth. Al-Fārābī (*c*.870–*c*.950), for example, was one objector on religious grounds, supporting the notion of human free will against the implicit doctrine of astral determinism, although he also provided a condescending defence of image-making, which (had he not been lucky) could easily have been used by others as a defence of talismanic magic:

> Image making and imitation by means of similitudes is one way to instruct the multitude and the vulgar in a large number of difficult theoretical things, so as to produce in their souls the impressions of these things by way of their similitudes. The vulgar need not conceive and comprehend these things as they are. It is enough if they comprehend and intellect them by means of what corresponds to them.

But it was mathematicians in particular who resented popular perception of their discipline as more or less synonymous with astrology and sought to distance themselves from the science. Indeed, their embarrassment reached a point where they preferred to use ink and paper for their work rather than the traditional dustboard. 'This,' said 'Uqlidisi of Damascus in 952, 'is because many a man hates to expose the [dustboard] between his hands when he finds the need to use this art of calculation, for fear of the misinterpretation of the attendants or whoever may see it. It belittles him, for it is seen between the hands of the misbehaved who earn their living by astrology in the streets' – an interesting side light on the popularity of astrology among the people at large, whatever the learned might think. Al-Bīrūnī (973–*c*.1048), who was respectful of Indian astronomy, even though he had reservations about its methods in comparison with those of the Greeks, was clearly irritated by what he saw as the unjustified pretensions of astrologers. He wrote in his *Chronology of Nations* (1029):

> It is the same set of people who excite suspicion against, and bring discredit upon, astronomers and mathematicians, by counting themselves among their ranks, and by presenting themselves as professors of their art, although they cannot even impose upon anybody who has only the slightest degree of scientific training.

While it is true al-Bīrūnī wrote a manual on the elements of astrology, he did so at the request of a female patron and closes with remarks which clearly express his impatience at the efforts of some astrologers to go beyond the boundaries of what he considers the science is capable of achieving:

> There are, however, astrologers who increase the range of horoscope inspection by claiming to elicit the past life of the questioner. Hashwiyite astrologers, inclined to falsification when such a question is asked, bid their clients return and sleep on the matter for three nights and concentrate their attention on it during the day, and then question them. After satisfying myself as to their writings, I know of no method of dealing with them except insisting on exposing their vicious decrees and the way they lead the questioner into crime by the bad advice given him.
>
> Khabi' refers to hidden objects (concealed in the hand) and Damair to secret thoughts reserved by the questioner. What greater ignominy is likely to be the part of astrologers than that resulting from hasty dealing with such questions, and in comparison how numerous are the lucky hits of magicians who keep up a patter while they are on the lookout for telltale indications and actions!
>
> Now we have arrived at a point of the science of the stars which I have regarded as sufficing for the beginner; anyone who exceeds the limits set out above exposes himself and the science to derision and scorn, for such are ignorant of the further relations of the art, and especially of those which have been ascertained with certainty.

Here, of course, he is objecting not so much to astrology itself as to the way it was being practised by certain groups of professionals, and so we should not really include him among the number of those who condemned the science root and branch. Much more critical were two remarkable contemporaries, Ibn al-Haitham (965–c.1040) and Ibn Sīnā (980–1037), known respectively in the West as Alhazen and Avicenna. Ibn al-Haitham rejected the astronomical system taught by Ptolemy and envisaged an altogether new model of planetary movements and relationships, one which would have thrown into doubt and confusion the whole system upon which astrological interpretation was founded; while Ibn Sīnā objected that astrologers' methods depended upon conjecture rather than empiricism, maintaining that the science of contemporary astrologers (as Henry Corbin expresses it) 'travesties its real task, fails of its end and its raison d'être through the ridiculous insufficiency of its data and its hasty schematisations'. According to Ibn Sīnā's *Refutation of Astrology*, there is at least one kind of knowledge with which a self-respecting savant will not deign to bother himself, and that is knowledge which is both base and invalid, such as magic, divination by scapulomancy and haruspicy, and astrology. Any savant with eyes in his head and some degree of experience knows that any part of this last lacks any sold basis, and, wrote Ibn Sīnā, because one of his close friends was troubled by the possibility that there might be something in it, he composed his *Refutation* to set the man's mind at rest, an aim in which he claims to have been successful.

Al-Ghazali (1058–1111) was in full agreement. Both magic and astrology were to be regarded as coming under the heading of reprehensible knowledge, and astrology in particular seemed to have the extraordinary ability to pull wool over people's eyes, an ability he remarked in his *Al-Munqidh min al-Dalāl* ('Deliverance from Error'):

> [You can say to somebody], 'Isn't it the case that the horoscope varies according to whether the sun is in the ascendant, in the ecliptic, or in declension? And in their horoscopes, do [astrologers] make this variation the basis of the difference of treatment, and of length of life and hour of death? Isn't there a distinction between declension and the sun's being in the ecliptic: and likewise, between sun-*set* and the sun's being *toward* setting? Is there any way to believe this?' If it were not that [the person] hears it in astrological terminology, he would probably have experimentally observed its falsity a hundred times. Yet he goes on habitually believing in it, so that if an astrologer says to him, 'If the sun is in the ecliptic and star A confronts him while the ascendant is in star B, then, should you put on a new garment at that time, you will be killed in that garment,' he will not put on the garment at that time, even though he may suffer from extreme cold, and even though he hears this from an astrologer whose falsity he has acknowledged a hundred times.

Once again we have an opportunity to note the distance between learned dismissal and what al-Ghazali tells us is popular superstition, the tone being one common to a number of scholars who find themselves superior to others by reason of personal opinion and do not hesitate to say so. Nevertheless, al-Ghazali may not have been substantially wrong. Homing in on the possible weaknesses of pavement astrology was perfectly legitimate, and noting that failure to observe the heavens with due care rendered the popular practice of and faith in astrology, particularly judicial astrology, an uncertain and unreliable business cannot be dismissed. Nor is the criticism that the alliance between astrology and talismanic magic runs counter to the precepts of religion entirely invalid. Defenders of astrology therefore had work to do, and it is probably no coincidence that many of them were influenced by modes of thinking imported from outwith the Qu'ranic tradition. The tenth-century Abū Ya'qub al-Sijistānī, for example, clearly owed much to the Neoplatonism of Plotinus when he conceived God as the One beyond both Being and non-Being. God created Intellect by His fiat, and it is the ability of human beings to participate in Intellect which makes them superior to the rest of created entities. Access to Intellect may be had in more than one way, and here prophecy and revelation can be seen to be particularly important, for prophets converse with angels, read the book of the heavens, and reveal what is unseen. Thus, for al-Sijistānī, the true astrologers were those *nutaqā'* ('speaking prophets'), imams, and their initiated pupils, precisely because, inspired and assisted thereto by angels, they knew how to read the celestial book and could therefore gain knowledge of the present and the future. He wrote:

> With regard to the word written in the stars ... originating with the munificent [Soul], and in collaboration with the *nātiq*, it consists of psychic movements which manifest themselves in the spheres and stars. In each movement of the celestial bodies of these spheres, in every shift which brings them nearer or further away from each other, there are properties and natural actions; and they (I mean the spheres), along with the shining stars with which they are sprinkled, have, for men endowed with an extreme sensitivity, a configura-

tion resembling the form of letters. For there one finds a figure in which there is a point in the extension of its height, like an *alif* [*Arabic letter*] ... or [one finds] a star which is like a point similar to that of the *bā* [*letter b*] or the *tā* [*letter t*], and so on for all the letters. But there is no way of managing [to do this successfully] without the *nātiq* who is assisted by inspiration to decipher this writing and to know how to interpret it at each cycle, how the celestial bodies speak at each epoch, what they ordain, and what they allow and forbid. He who has the privilege of the 'mission' reads all this as though he were looking at a book and reading it. Such is the divine word coming from the stars.

This view, of course, may limit the role of the 'true' astrologer to a few privileged individuals, but it also endows the stars with an equally privileged role, that of revealers of the divine intention and will, and if the stars can be regarded in this light, it means that astrology itself has a valid, not to say necessary place in God's scheme of things, no matter whether the practice of the science is distorted or degraded by 'false' astrologers plying their inadequacies in the market place.

Criticism of astrology, then, could be countered, but not always without difficulty, and there was also one further consideration which had a notable effect on the developing history of the science within Islamic society, the fact that it was not indigenous to that society but came as an essentially alien tradition, mainly pagan and Greek, from sources other than Arabic or Islamic. This inevitably meant that there would be an additional impulse to check the credentials of this foreign tradition in all its diverse aspects, before admitting it to participation in that wholeness of wisdom which springs from the oneness of God. Hence the constant practice of Islamic scholars to examine, criticise, comment upon, and correct the work of earlier astronomer-astrologers such as Ptolemy, during the course of which they made remarkable advances in knowledge of mathematics and astronomy. Hence, too, the increasing separation of astronomy from astrology as scholars sought to clarify and expand their understanding of how God's cosmos actually operates, although of course advances here, in turn, helped to fortify astrology by giving its predictive arts a more solid and reliable astronomical basis. No wonder, then, if a mood of self-confident optimism pervaded scholarly Islamic circles at this time, a mood which is caught by the assurance of al-Asturlābī (died *c*.1139):

> The ancients distinguished themselves through their chance discovery of basic principles and the invention of ideas. Modern scholars, on the other hand, distinguish themselves through the invention of a multitude of scientific details, the simplification of difficult problems, the combination of scattered information, and the explanation of already exist-ing material in coherent form. The ancients came to their particular achievements by virtue of their priority in time, and not on account of any natural qualification and intelligence. Yet how many things escaped them, which then became the original inventions of modern scholars, and how much did the former leave for the latter to do! [1]

From astrology's point of view, then, hostile criticism was not entirely without its uses, and even potential abrasion between itself and religion could be overcome, or at least overlooked, when clergy themselves were practitioners of the science. Such was the situation in ninth-century Byzantium when the Patriarch of Constantinople, John VII (known as 'The Grammarian'), predicted future events for the Emperor by inspecting and interpreting images seen on the surface of water in a basin, and happily employed a form of image-magic in which three men were instructed to strike a three-headed statue in the Hippodrome with enormous hammers at precisely the same time as the Patriarch uttered a magical formula which transferred the effects of the battering to the three leaders of an invading army which was threatening the capital. The magic was successful, for the three leaders turned against one other; two were destroyed and the third retreated in disorder with the army. John's cousin, Leo the Mathematician, briefly Metropolitan of Thessalonica, saved that city from famine by accurately foretelling the end of a drought; in 907–8 Emperor Leo VI asked the Metropolitan of Synada to interpret an eclipse of the moon; and while Leo the Deacon did not agree that it was astrologers who provided scientific explanations for earthquakes, he did connect the many natural and military disasters of the 970s and 980s with unusual celestial phenomena. The historian, Michael Psellos (*c.*1017–*c.*1078), too, had no qualms about combining religion with astrology, and although he is careful to distance himself from it by claiming not to believe that the stars direct human affairs, it is perfectly clear both from this and the extract following this that he had given a great deal of time and effort to studying it and becoming proficient in its practice. Not long before 1055, he became a monk and wrote in his *Chronographia*:

> Owing to the fact that I took this step shortly before [Emperor Constantine IX] died ... many persons surmised that I had previous knowledge of the event. According to them, I knew he was going to die and for this reason changed my manner of life. It is a fact that most people give me credit for more learning than I actually possess. Because I have dabbled in geometry, they imagine I am capable of measuring the whole heavens, and since I have devoted a certain amount of study to the phenomena of the celestial sphere, they insist I must also be acquainted with the phases, the obliquity of the ecliptic, eclipses, full moons, cycles and epicycles. They even claim I can predict the future, despite my repudiation of books written on these subjects.
>
> Another thing in which I have been interested is horoscopy, far enough to learn something of the nonsense which derives from it. The truth is, my education was so wide and the questions of those who consulted me so diverse, that there is no science which I was not induced to study. Because of this interest in horoscopes, I find myself inevitably subjected to troublesome inquiries about them. That I have applied myself to the science in all its aspects I admit, but at the same time none of these studies, forbidden by the leaders of the Church, has been put to improper use. I know the theory about the lottery of Fortune and about a presiding evil genius, but I certainly do not believe that the positions or the appearance of stars affect what goes on in the sublunary world. To blazes with all those who tell us there is a spiritual life, and who then declare that its direction lies in the hands of their new-fangled gods! These are the folk who deny the unity of human life, for while, according to them, life owes its origin and birth to the Creator in Heaven, and derives from Him alone, they also insist that the stars, which have no power of reasoning, are liv-

ing beings, and they give them a dwelling-place in every part of the human body before it lives, grafting on to it, so to speak, the power of thought afterwards.

As in Imperial Rome, then, astrologers continued to play a part in public life, and Psellos gives an example of their operating at the highest levels. The reigning Emperor, Michael V, decided to banish his mother, the Empress Zoe, in 1042, but before embarking on this action he consulted various people to see what advice they would give him. '[One such group] thought the astrologers should be consulted: he ought first to assure himself that the time was propitious for the enterprise; some aspect of the heavens might be unfavourable.' Michael listened to everyone and decided he should indeed ask help of astrology:

> At that time there was a group of distinguished men engaged in the study of that science, men with whom I myself had dealings. These gentlemen were not specially concerned with the position or movements of stars in the celestial sphere, (actually they had no training in the proof of such things by the laws of geometry, and certainly this power of demonstration was not acquired by them before they studied astrology); they confined themselves rather to the setting up of astrological centres, the examination of the rise and fall of the zodiacal signs above or below the horizon. Other phenomena connected with these movements also became the object of their study – the ruling planets, the relative positions and limits of the planets, together with those aspects considered favourable and those which were not propitious. Certain predictions were then offered to persons who asked for advice and their questions were answered. I say this because I myself have some knowledge of the science, a knowledge acquired after long and diligent study, and I have been of some assistance to many of these men and helped them to understand the planetary aspects. Despite this, I am no believer in the theory that our human affairs are influenced by the movements of the stars.
>
> Let us return to the reigning Emperor. Without disclosing the nature of the deed he had in mind, he submitted a vague inquiry to the astrologers. The only information he asked for was this, whether the heavenly aspects were inauspicious to a man who took a great risk. Observations were taken and the general position of the stars was carefully examined at the proper moment, and when the astrologers saw that everything portended blood and sorrow, they warned him to give up his enterprise. The more circumspect among them advised him to put off the deed until some later occasion. At this the Emperor burst into a loud laugh. He mocked their science, calling it a fraud. 'To blazes with you!' he said. 'And as for your wonderful knowledge, my daring venture will make child's play of it.'

The Emperor's confidence was entirely mistaken, since he was later deposed and blinded; but that did not stop others from following his example, for Michael VII, too, just before he fell, was noted as giving an attentive ear to 'astronomers, tellers of portents, prophecies from statues, obtained by the performance of rituals, and superstitious demagogues'; and Manuel I (1118–80) not only employed astrology in his political dealings, but actually wrote a defence of it, which he addressed to the current Patriarch of Constantinople, even though, (as the hostile historian Niketas Khoniates observed), the astrologers upon whom the

Emperor relied proved to be incompetent on at least one critical occasion. Nevertheless, we must not see these emperors and churchmen as either 'superstitious' or misguided. There was a remarkable renaissance of all kinds of knowledge during the twelfth century wherein a great deal of translation from Arabic into Greek provided the stimulus to the study and acceptance of astrology as a valid science, and it is in this context that Manuel's interest in and advocacy of the subject must be viewed. We also need to be aware that Khoniates, who chronicled his reign, is a hostile witness who found the Emperor's support of Court astrologers both ridiculous and dangerous.

But Khoniates was by no means the Emperor's only critic. At some point during the 1170s, Manuel received a letter from the Patriarch. It had been written by a monk of the Pankrator monastery and asserted that astrological teachings amounted to nothing less than heresy. Since the Emperor was, by virtue of his office, Defender of the Faith, he could not let this challenge to his orthodoxy pass without reply, and so he composed a defence, maintaining that, on the contrary, astrology was entirely compatible with Christian doctrine, as he would show. Manuel made three principal points: (i) some types of astrology – for example, those used in connection with astral magic – are indeed impious and should be condemned; but (ii) the stars are part of God's creation and are therefore good in themselves, and He employs them as His messengers to humanity: they must be regarded as signs, not causes; and (iii) there have been many worthy people in the past, (and Manuel gives examples), who have endorsed astrology and who cannot be regarded in any way as heretical. Manuel was answered by Michael Glykas, a conservative theologian, probably after the Emperor's death, since there do not appear to have been any repercussions either from his temerity in contradicting the Faith's defender, or from the manner in which he did so – Paul Magdalino calls this manner 'patronising sarcasm', which sums it up exactly. The manner is conveyed through the means, and the means quite simply refute Manuel's scholarship, calling it into question at almost every point and thereby implicitly casting doubt on the Emperor's intelligence and integrity. It is interesting, however, that, like Psellos, Glykas clearly knows a great deal about the subject and so must have studied it in some detail, as did Anna Komnena (1083–1153), daughter of Emperor Alexios I. During her history of her father's reign, she suddenly remarks in the middle of a passage critical of astrology, 'I myself once dabbled a little in the art, not in order to make use of any such knowledge (Heaven forbid!) but so that being better informed about its futile jargon I might confound the experts.'[2]

A degree of hypocrisy can thus be detected in the Imperial, clerical, and scholarly circles of Byzantium during the eleventh and twelfth centuries. Still, one should not press this far, because during those same centuries Byzantium was enjoying an extraordinarily rich intellectual life whose notable characteristic was polymathy fed by acquaintance with a wide range of sources both ancient and modern, Greek, Arabic, Pahlavi, and Indian. The learned eleventh-century Jewish physician and astrologer, Symeon Seth, mentioned by Anna Komnena in her digression on astrology, for example, probably produced a dietetic text which contained material from Persian, Arabic, and Indian sources, and he certainly did translate into Greek an Arabic version of a Pahlavi version of an Indian collection of animal fables, *Panchatantra*. This rich life was badly damaged by the disastrous capture and sack of Constantinople in 1204 by crusading armies from the west, but picked up again at the end of the thirteenth and beginning of the fourteenth century, gaining a fillip, as far as astronomy-astrology was concerned, from the introduction of Persian astronomy into the Byzantine world. It came partly via Gregory Khioniades who, as George Khrysokkokes from the mid-fourteenth century tells us:

> had been raised in Constantinople [and] fell in love with mathematics and other sciences. After he had mastered medicine, he wished to study astronomy. He was informed that, in order to satisfy his desire, he would have to go to Persia. He travelled to Trebizond where he was given some assistance by the Emperor Komnenos, and thence proceeded to Persia itself, where he persuaded yet another Emperor to aid him. He eventually learned all he wished to know and returned to Trebizond, bearing away from Persia a number of astronomical texts which he translated into Greek.

From the start, this Perso-Byzantine astronomy kept close contact with astrology. George Khrysokokkes, for example, included with his version of a *zīj* by Nasīr ad-Dīn at-Tūsī a defence of astrology, explaining that the stars have energies given to them by God, and that these energies enable them to act as signs of the present and the future within the created cosmos. In order to be able to offer accurate predictions, an astronomer-astrologer needs to be master of the technicalities of his craft, and if his predictions turn out to be inaccurate, the fault lies with him, not the methods of astrology itself. The only other reason for apparent error may be that God has chosen to break or ignore His rules and work a miracle for reasons of His own. Thus, as Nikephoras Gregoras expressed it in summer 1330, 'It is by no means forbidden to derive from this science a clear indication of facts here below. Why? Because we know the book of God, that heavenly ornament, where everything there is and will be is written.' Gregoras may also have composed a defence of astrology, *De astrologia dialogus*, (although the work is anonymous and has also been attributed to John Zacharias, chief physician to Emperor Andronikos II). He ends it with a panegyric:

> I congratulate on his good fortune the man who eagerly devotes himself to this science. I bless him, and to him alone I give the title 'savant' and (if you let me) 'philosopher'. This man tries to give explanations of chance happenings, which take their nature into account. He has made an effort to purify his mind from passionate attachment to worldly things, but is always inquisitive and has a good memory. He is accustomed to let his intelligence roam the heavens, and he wants to be like God, (in as far as that is possible), in having to some degree the ability to know and predict things before they happen. I don't particularly blame those who deliberately despise this [science], because they don't understand something they have not engaged in. How can they adhere to something of which they have no knowledge? Let me not even hesitate to say that from these things alone, or these things first of all, one examines and gets to know the Creator and contemplates the nature of everything He has brought into being: all the manifest parts of the cosmos, and the secret powers within it, wherein sympathy between the different parts of the cosmos lies concealed, and, furthermore, the universe's connections, inexpressible and expressible, by

means of which the Final Things are joined to the First, and both to those in between. Hence one will see simply and purely, and will be able to appear in one's own person in the presence of the Father and Creator. Then one will regard the words of scholarship as fictitious, since one will be living and sharing in absolute knowledge and absolute truth in the light of things as they are, and beholding celestial signs perfect and unmoving in a spotless brilliance … It is because of this kind of knowledge that we very much have the advantage over others. The person who sets out on that mission without [astrology] probably does so in vain and is, in all likelihood, stupid, because he has no knowledge of a path which will allow him to approach it with ease. [3]

This is astrology as an aid to ecstatic contemplation of creation in the presence of God, as is made clear, among other things, by the reminiscence of St Paul – 'Now we see through a glass darkly: but then, face to face' – an interesting parallel to a mystical practice towards the same end, verging upon the magical, which was noted by Rabbi Hayya Gaon (died 1038):

Perhaps you know that many of the sages were of the opinion that whoever is suited in various specified respects, when he wants to see the Chariot and to glimpse the palaces of the celestial angels, there are techniques for him to perform, (namely) that he should fast a certain number of days and place his head between his knees and whisper to the earth many specified hymns and praises. Then he looks within himself and his chambers, as if he sees with his eyes seven palaces, and visualises as if he proceeds from one palace to the next, and sees what is in it.

But this kind of claim, noble and compelling as it may have been within its own relatively limited terms, was not allowed to dismiss or conceal the reservations which others were expressing. One such objector was Theodore Melitoniotes, Director of the Patriarchal Academy in Constantinople, whose commentary on Ptolemy, (*Astronomical Tetrabiblos*), is both clear in its exposition and exhaustive in its pursuit of detail. Melitoniotes rejected astrology and its claims altogether in favour of a study of the stars, untrammelled by any connection with the justifications flowing with and from the Persian works then popular in the Empire. So Byzantine experience of astrological studies followed the see-saw pattern familiar to us from our brief review of the science in Islamic tradition. On the one hand, religion viewed it with suspicion as a branch of knowledge and a craft which obtruded upon the omniscience of God and His gift of free will to humanity. The state, too, was equally nervous of its claim to be able to foresee and foretell future events, and therefore of its ability to lay bare in advance changes of political fortune and the advent of Imperial death; and many, both religious and secular, also despised and condemned the astrology of the street corner, the simple predictions of how everyday concerns might turn out, answers to questions posed by common folk. On the other hand, Biblical texts could be found to support study of the heavens, and since no one could deny that the sun, the moon, the other planets, and the stars had been created by God, it was obvious that He had created them for a purpose. Inquiry might therefore legitimately be undertaken to ask what that purpose was, at which point questions arose regarding the nature of these heavenly bodies. Were they merely signs of God's will, or were they possessed in some fashion of powers or energies which could and did influence the very fabric of creation itself through a network of interacting sympathies and antipathies? These concerns were too important to be suppressed, and as the purely astronomical and mathematical aspects of the science underwent change, refinement, and sophistication, so the criticism that astrology's methods and presumptions were too crude and too inaccurate to provide reliable interpretations of the evidence lost at least some of its hostile force. Hence astrology survived its opponents and continued to flourish and blossom in learned, religious, and political circles, in spite of its continuing association with magic, as well as among society's less exalted ranks. [4]

The Byzantine Empire did not exist in a vacuum, of course. There were others: that of Islam which stretched into Spain and remained there for several centuries; that of the Christian West in the form of the Holy Roman Empire, a gradual amalgamation of territories, centred upon Austria and the German states; and that of the Western Church whose domain was spiritual rather than secular, but whose non-material geography encompassed, if only in a theoretical claim, the vast spread of Europe to the very borders of Islam and Orthodoxy. Within these contingent and sometimes overlapping empires a constant migration of minds and manuscripts brought change and consolidation, innovation and condemnation to learned circles whose debates eventually made their way into and round the competing powers. A good example of how intercourse spread novelty wide can be found in the dispersed Jewish communities living under these various régimes. As early as the tenth century, the physician Shabbetai Donnolo from southern Italy, wrote two influential works: *Sefer ha-Mirkahot* which summarises his forty years' experience as a doctor-pharmacist, and *Sefer Hakhmoni*, a commentary on the Kabbalistic *Sefer Yetzirah*. In these, which indicate that he knew both Greek and Latin as well as Hebrew and Italian, he promoted the notion that humanity is a microcosm reflecting the created universe which is the macrocosm, and that therefore everything in the physical individual corresponds to some phenomenon in the cosmos:

God made for [Man] a spherical head, like the firmament of heaven which is above the firmament of this world. He gave him the upper palate above the mouth, in which the teeth and jaw are planted, in the likeness of the firmament of this world above us. And just as He separates this firmament which is above us between waters – between the upper waters and the lower waters – so too does the upper palate of the mouth separate between the humour of the head and that of the upper digestive tract called the stomach. Similarly, just as God rested His holy presence in the upper heavens which covered the waters, as it says in Scripture, 'He who roofed the waters with His rafters' (*Psalm* 104.3), so too He placed the animated soul, knowledge, and discernment in the membrane of the brain, which is wrapped around the brain and its humour. This is evident, because if the brain is ruptured, a person will die immediately for there resides the life-force … [Further], just as God place the two lights … in the heavenly firmament, so too He put two eyes in a man's head. The right eye is like the sun and the left resembles the moon … And just as God made the celestial dragon in the universe and stretched it out over the firmament, from east to west, from end to end, as well as the stars and the constellations and everything in the universe which is branching from it, so too He made the spinal cord inside the vertebrae, extending from the brain to the pelvis.

It is not surprising, therefore, to find that Donnolo was an enthusiastic proponent of astrology, maintaining that non-Jewish astrology was actually derived from Jewish sources – an important point if he was to rescue the science from its association with idolatry in many Jewish eyes – and that the relationship he saw between the macrocosm and the microcosm allowed physicians a better understanding of human physiology and pathology. Donnolo thus took the sting out of potential religious criticism of astrology by aligning the science with God in the acts of creation, while at the same time emphasising God's ultimate power, and allowing astrology its due role alongside astronomy as the 'other' aspect of a dual observational and interpretive science. Unease about the relationship between religion and astrology, however, would not go away, and in the early twelfth century Abraham Bar Hiyya from Barcelona, for example, felt obliged on the one hand to mount a defence of astrology after he was criticised by a colleague for insisting that a Jewish wedding be postponed because astrologers had deemed the moment inauspicious, and on the other to emphasise that the stars could not, of themselves, affect events unless permitted to do so by God. But the criticism had bitten deep:

> From my youth until this day, I taught myself the science of the stars and I involved myself, investigated and sought it out, considering myself an acquirer of wisdom and thought, sinless and innocent. But now when I observed that righteous and modest sages who are themselves wise and knowledgeable do not agree with my opinion, I detested my craft. Furthermore, I stated that in the days of my youth and adolescence they would judge me by the honour which I acquired before princes and queens. But now in my old age, this has become my indictment … Perhaps the force of [my critics'] words will convince me to follow after them.

Nervous about allowing astrology to intrude upon religion, some scholars sought to mask their support for a magic-astral interpretation of Jewish sources under condemnation of astrology's practitioners Thus, in his *Sefer ha-Kazari*, a philosophical-religious dialogue, Judah Ha-Levi (*c*.1045–1141), a Spanish physician and poet, put in the mouth of his Rabbi interlocutor a passage which acknowledges the science – 'Do we reject the idea that heavenly spheres influence terrestrial matters? We do not' – but finds fault with astrologers: 'We do not know the precise details of [how astral influence works], while the astrologer pretends to know the particulars. But we deny he has this knowledge and categorically declare that no mortal possesses it.' That said, however, Ha-Levi includes in the same work a discussion of the golden calf set up and worshipped by the Israelites during their enforced nomadism in the desert (*Exodus* 32.3–6). He apparently blames them for listening to bad counsel – 'They did [this] on the advice of astrologers and builders of talismans, who had thought that their actions, as dictated by reason, would be more correct than true deeds' – but in fact it becomes clear that he regards their real fault as taking the initiative in making such an effigy without waiting for God to direct them, not as making the effigy itself. For in his view, the golden calf was meant to attract the spirituality of the stars and zodiacal signs and act as a focal point for them. Recently liberated from slavery, stranded in a frightening desert, and seemingly abandoned by Moses who, having gone to Mount Sinai, had not returned, they took matters into their own hands and hoped to work an operation of astral magic which would draw down the protection they obviously felt they needed. Hence, in Ha-Levi's eyes, the magic of images made for legitimate purposes, and the astrology which both made their manufacture possible and explained and legitimised their working, were of equal value – a novel theological interpretation which would certainly not satisfy orthodox Jewish opinion, but one which was entirely consistent with certain strands of contemporary astrological speculation.

A similarly radical theology couched in an allusive style is to be found in the writings of Abraham ibn Ezra (1092/3–1167) who spent much of his life wandering in North Africa, Iraq, Italy, and France. He wrote voluminously – Biblical commentaries, linguistics, Hebrew grammars, poems, and short works on astrology. The latter were all later translated in Latin by Pietro d'Abano and thus made available to Western European scholars. Ibn Ezra agrees with Ha-Levi in two important respects: (i) it is possible to make images which will attract astral influences, such as Gentiles' drawing down the power of the scorpion if they want to heal someone who has been stung – a form of astral magic we have met already in *Picatrix*; and (ii) making such images without express command or permission from God may be regarded as tantamount to idolatry. Nevertheless, it is obvious that Ibn Ezra accepts the reality of such astral magic in spite of the roundabout way he expresses himself and his ostensible rejection of views which regard it as possible, since his exposition of the Temple and the Tabernacle, for example, sees their constituent parts as images to attract 'supreme power', by which he means the ability of the stars to affect the terrestrial world through emanation of their individual energies and characteristics. 'Everything in the lowest world receives power from the middle [*i.e. celestial*] world, each thing according to the constellation of the stars.'

All this, of course, may be regarded as skating upon thin ice, and certainly the stoutest opponent of such notions was Rabbi Moses ben Maimon (Maimonides) (1135/8–1204). Steeped in Islamic philosophy and the works of Aristotle, with whom he agreed in much but from whom he also differed in certain important points, his major philosophical work, *The Guide for the Perplexed*, written tellingly enough in Arabic, mentions astrology (as opposed to astronomy) only to dismiss it:

These are the various kinds of witchcraft. In some cases all these various performances are required. Thus, the witches sometimes order: take a leaf of a certain plant when the moon is seen in a certain degree [of the zodiac] in the east point, or in one of the other cardinal points [of the horizon]; also a certain quantity of the horn, the sweat, the hair and the blood of a certain animal when the sun is, for example, in the middle of the sky, or in some other definite place; and a portion of a certain mineral or minerals, melted at a certain conjunction of sun and moon, and at a definite position of the stars. Speak then and say certain words, and fumigate with those leaves or similar ones to that molten image, and such and such a thing will happen ... The number of these stupid and mad things is great. In all of them without exception, women are required to be the agent. Witchcraft is intimately connected with astrology. Those who practise it assign each plant, animal, or mineral to a certain star, and believe that the above processes of witchcraft are different forms of worship offered to that star, which is pleased with that act, word, or offering of incense, and fulfils their wishes.

The vagueness of this account may mirror the information Maimonides had read or was given, but it also has the effect of making the astral magic itself seem to be a waffling process, an extempore affair founded on little more than the practitioner's inspiration of the moment, allied to a subversive idolatry, and therefore not something anyone is obliged to take with any seriousness. But Maimonides' principal objections to astrology can be found elsewhere, in his responses to questions posed to him by Jews apparently disturbed or worried by the astrology they found practised by the society in which they happened to be living. In *c.*1172, for example, the head of the Jewish community in Yemen asked him about several different matters, one of which was astrological. Maimonides offered a scathing answer:

> I note that you are inclined to believe in astrology and in the influence of the past and future conjunctions of the planets upon human affairs. You should dismiss such notions from your thoughts. Cleanse your mind as one cleanses dirty clothes ... I have observed your statement that science is little cultivated and that learning does not flourish in your country, which you attribute to the influence of the conjunctions in the earthly trigon [*Taurus, Virgo, Capricorn*] ... This condition is not due to the earthly or fiery trigon, as is proven by the fact that Solomon, King of Israel, lived during the earthly trigon and yet Scripture testifies that he was wiser than all men.

Using astrology to disprove astrology could have been an effective tactic, but Maimonides preferred simply to brush the matter aside. In his better known *Letter in Opposition to Astrology* (1194/5) which responds to inquiries from a group of Jews in the south of France, he deals with the basic question of whether the position of heavenly bodies at someone's birth determine the course of his or her life, and begins by offering his credentials:

> The first thing I studied is that science which is called 'judicial astrology' ... I have also read in all matters concerning all of idolatry, so that it seems to me there does not remain in the world a composition on this subject, having been translated into Arabic from other languages, but that I have read it.

Having mastered all these sources, he has come to the conclusion that judicial astrology is merely stupid. 'There are lucid, faultless proofs refuting all the roots of those assertions,' he says, although he does not say what they are, nor does he give examples. Then he takes a racial line. Judicial astrology was taken seriously by Babylonians, Canaanites, and Egyptians; sensible people, on the other hand, such as the Greeks and Persians, knew it was twaddle. What *they* took seriously was astronomy, 'knowledge of the form of the spheres, their number, their measure, the course they follow, each one's period of revolution, their declination to the north or to the south, their revolving to the east or to the west, and the orbit of every star and what its course is'. Thus Maimonides distinguishes between observation and interpretation, and so separates these two aspects of what most people regarded, and would continue to regard for many centuries, as a single science. 'But as for these assertions of stupid astrologers, they are nothing.'

Acknowledgement of this dichotomy, however, does not produce the same idea of separation a twenty-first century person might envisage, for Maimonides goes on to make clear that the active presence of God within creation exerts a unifying influence throughout the whole. Gentile savants, he goes on, have all acknowledged the existence of a Creator and Governor of the universe:

> and they are in accord that the power of the Creator flows first upon the spheres and the stars; from the spheres and the stars it flows and spreads throughout this [lower] world … Just as we maintain that the Holy One (blessed be He) performs signs and wonders through the angels, so do these philosophers maintain that all these occurrences in the nature of the world come through the spheres and the stars. They maintain that the spheres and the stars possess souls and knowledge. All these things are true. I myself have already made it clear, with proofs, that all these things involve no damage to religion.

What happens to people, say these philosophers, happens by chance – which is where Jews part company with them, for 'the religion of Moses, our master, maintains that what happens to individuals is not due to chance, but rather to judgement'. In other words, human beings have been given free will, and it is this which directs what they choose to do and become. Maimonides then provides an illustration. There are two men: Reuben, a tanner, poor, whose children have died in his lifetime, and Simon, a perfumer, rich, with living children. Gentile philosophers attribute these men's different conditions to simple chance. Judicial astrologers say that each man's situation was fixed by the power of the stars at his birth and cannot be altered. Jewish religious tradition, and rationality, both reject these two explanations. The situation in which Reuben and Simon find themselves depends from the will of God, and they are at liberty to respond to that will either well or badly. If the former, they will be happy; if the latter, they will be punished.

> The summary of the matter is that our mind cannot grasp how the decrees of the Holy One (blessed be He) work upon human beings in this world and in the world to come. [But] what we have said about this from the beginning is that the entire position of the star-gazers is regarded as a falsehood by all men of science (*madda'*).[5]

Maimonides, however, seems to have been in a minority. Moses ben Nachman (Nahmanides) (1194–1270), a physician, exegete, and Kabbalist who later became Chief Rabbi of Catalunya, also contrasted Greek 'science' with Jewish, but came to the conclusion that whereas the Greeks had only an appreciation of what can be known through the five senses, Jewish 'science' was less superficial, a more subtle and more profound acquaintance with natural phenomena, since it discerned (and was prepared to manipulate) those things the senses could not appreciate as well as those they could. He wrote:

> All these things and those like them, [*i.e. the occult sciences*] are old and true sciences, passed on in a tradition by those who received the Torah. When we were exiled, these sciences were lost with us. A few [people] still retain a distorted recollection of them, but the philosophers have [subsequently] come and denied them.

The Jews, then, are a repository of real understanding of how the cosmos works, inheritors of a spiritual science which allows the privileged individual to unlock the secrets of phenomena. Thus Nahmanides saw the ritual of the scapegoat – letting loose a goat in the desert on the Day of Atonement to carry away with it the sins of the people – in terms of astral magic, as a sacrifice to Mars (ruler of wastelands and destruction and bloodshed) whereby a salutary influence may be drawn from the stars to benefit human beings. This interpretation, as can be expected, set off a train of fresh thoughts, centring largely upon the extent of the effect of this drawing down; was it confined to the upper sephiroth of the Kabbalistic Tree, or did it come down far enough to embrace *malkuth*, the world of matter? Of course, if astral or sephirotic influxes were confined to the celestial world, neither astral nor Kabbalistic magic could be regarded as having validity, since both depended on such influxes reaching the sublunar world. So a middle way was found between the two extremes of interpretation. One could, it was suggested, ritually affect the relationships between the higher sephiroth, thus bringing them into perfect balance, and that would allow power to flow downwards into the material world. It was an argument to bridge a highly abstruse gap, but it worked to the extent that it permitted astral and Kabbalistic magic to be discussed and operated without fear of anathemata from every Jewish theologian.

It is therefore interesting to see how objection worked in practice. Nahmanides, whose principal activity was that of physician, wore a lion amulet, (that is, an amulet with the figure of a lion engraved on it, consecrated at the appropriate moment under the rulership of the zodiacal sign Leo), and used it to place over the ureter of someone suffering from kidney stones. This particular healing device was in wide use at the time, by Christians as well as Jews. In 1301, for example, the Catalan physician Arnald of Villanova treated Pope Boniface VIII for kidney stones with a lion-amulet made from gold held in place over the kidneys with a kind of girdle, and we can see what such an amulet looked like from one surviving specimen in the Kunsthistorisches Museum in Vienna, and another in the British Museum. Solomon ben Aderet (1235–1310) from the next generation of rabbinical commentators, in correspondence with Rabbi Abba Mari, defended the use of amulets for this purpose, arguing, with respect to astral powers:

> [God] placed these forces in the essences of the existence of Nature, [and they can be] discerned by inquiry, such as drugs and herbs which are known to learned doctors, or in particular natures which inquiry cannot discern … And it is not impossible that such should be the case with incantations such as there are in the matter of amulets and the like.

In other words, special properties exist in Nature, some of them occult, and can be introduced into objects either naturally, as in leaving the objects out overnight to absorb astral influences, or magically, as in making and engraving amulets during particular astrological conditions and employing incantations or Words of Power to draw down those influences by one's will and intention.

Abba Mari's difficulty lay not in the efficacy of the lion-amulet, which he accepted, but in its use – connection with the zodiacal sign Leo, he said, brought it within acts prohibited by the Bible and Talmudic injunction – to which Ben Aderet in essence replied that as long as amulets were not idolatrous, they were not forbidden. But was the use of an astrologically-empowered amulet not a recognition of the force of the star to which it had been aligned and thus a tacit form of star-worship? asked Abba Mari. Ben Aderet demurred:

> The Lord (blessed be He) divided the lands among the constellations and gave them dominion over the earth, so that a certain star will control a certain place, and so the different countries and places are divided in their faiths, one worshipping a certain image and one worshipping another, and whoever worships the star which controls that place is not considered an idolater provided he knows and realises that that star and its dominion derive exclusively from the Lord (blessed be He) who gave it the ability to rule that land.

What is more, he added, Jews have a distinct obligation to maintain their health, and by imposing a limit on the ways in which they might seek to do so, Abba Mari was contravening that obligation. Besides, Abba Mari was being very selective in his choice of grounds for objection. Jewish doctors had an imperative to heal the sick and that gave them a very wide range of possible legitimate choices, including the use of astrological amulets.

Abba Mari's linking astral magic with idolatry was, in fact, the argument which had been used by Maimonides, and we can see from these examples that the principal concern of Jewish theologians and exegetes was not so much the validity of either astrology or magic or both – this they seemed to have accepted – as the use to which these occult sciences might be put. Nevertheless, there could still be tension between the constituent parts of astronomy-astrology as individual interest impelled by individual understanding of theological conundrums drew scholars one way or another to lay stress on, say, astronomy rather than astrology. One such was Rabbi Levi ben Gershom (Gersonides) (1288–1344) whose approach to the double subject tended to emphasise the former rather than the latter. This is because knowledge of the workings of the cosmos was, for him, a way of attaining immortality, and the most important branch of knowledge in this respect was astronomy, and there can be no mistaking either his enthusiasm or his novel contributions to the science. For in pursuit of a clearer understanding of the heavens, Gersonides not only criticised Ptolemy's model, but invented new instruments to help him in his observations and calculations, including the 'Jacob's staff', a square rod about three or four feet long with a cursor which slid up and down the staff and enabled the user to measure the distance between stars or planets, and the altitudes and diameters of the sun and moon. He also made detailed astronomical observations from c.1320 and recorded them in part of an enormous work, *The Wars of the Lord*, which took twelve years to write and was finally completed in January 1329. Here he notes that the sublunary order of things continues to exist only because celestial bodies are stable and unchanging, and their influxes into the lower world allow the constant change of terrestrial things to be regulated and given sufficient order to keep them in being. Otherwise these lower things would change themselves out of existence. The spheres and stars were created with the very purpose of imparting their effects to the sublunary world, and the diversity of the stars' influences mirrors the diversity of their movements in relation to the spheres, to each other, and to the earth. Thus, the action of a given planet will vary according to whether it inclines northwards or southwards, and its influence will be strongest when it is 'exalted' in the middle of the sky and when it is closest to the earth. Hence, of course, astronomy shades into astrology, as Gersonides himself recognised, although he denied that astrologers could foresee the fates, still less the separate events, belonging to the lives of individuals. Only the destinies of nations were genuinely open to their scrutiny. Foreknowledge of singular events belonged, not to astrologers but to prophets. Gersonides' position, then, can be summarised as follows:

> [In Gersonides' opinion, astrology was] founded on the metaphysical doctrine of the dependence of all earthly occurrences upon the heavenly world. The general connection imparted to the prophet by the active intellect is the general order of the astrological con-stellation … The active intellect knows the astrological order, from the most general form of the constellations to their last specification, which in turn contains all the conditions of occurrence of a particular event. Thus, when a prophet deals with the destiny of a particu-lar person or human group, he receives from the active intellect a knowledge of the order of the constellations, and with sufficient precision to enable him to predict its fate in full detail … His astrological determinism has only one limitation. The free will of man could shatter the course of action ordained for him by the stars; prophecy could therefore predict the future on the basis of astrological determination only in so far as the free will of man does not break through the determined course of things. [6]

This modifiable astral determinism therefore meant that magic was unlikely to work in the sense in which a magician would explain it. If someone made images and subjected them to the usual processes intended to imbue them with astral forces, the only actual result would be psychological, a concentration of the operator's imaginative faculty which might, of course, produce the desired effect, but would do so only by nature and not through preternatural intervention. In this, Gersonides was in agreement with Maimonides. But for the majority of Jewish exegetes the magic was both real and legitimate, and their interpretation of Biblical and Talmudic sources sang in tune with the popular view that not only did the stars and planets affect all manner of terrestrial creation of their own accord, but that they could be made to do so in harmony with deliberate human will, and with the tacit permission and blessing of God, their Creator and Governor.

9

Mediaeval Europe c.1200–c.1300: The Inheritor of Traditions

Contact with Arabic texts in the Iberian peninsula, southern Italy and southern France, as well as the Crusader kingdoms, stimulated Western European interest in astrology and led to the production of new works by Western scholars. The Jewish writers we have just been discussing, despite the internal nature of their disagreements, nevertheless formed a conduit for passage of astrology to the West during the twelfth–fourteenth centuries. Judah Ha-Levi came from Toldeo, Abraham bar Hiyya from Barcelona, Maimonides from Cordoba, Nahmanides from Gerona, Solomon ben Aderet from Barcelona, Abba Mari from Lunel near Montpellier and Gersonides from Languedoc, and if some of them wandered, sooner or later they based themselves once again somewhere in that Mediterranean bridge between the Byzantine Empire and the European north-west. The twelfth century in particular was very rich in translators. Plato of Tivoli and John of Seville both translated Abu Ali al-Khaiyat's *Book of Birth* into Latin the former in 1136, the latter in 1153, and Adelard of Bath (*c*.1080–*c*.1152) translated Abu Ma'shar's *Abbreviation of the Introduction to Astrology* and the *Book of Talismans* of Thābit ibn Qurra. (Adelard's versions are especially interesting in as much as they show him struggling with Arabic and testing his own understanding of the original by trying out what he hopes are the Latin equivalents of Arabic technical terms). Herman of Carinthia (*c*.1100–*c*.1160) translated the sixth book of an astrological treatise by Sahl ibn Bishr, the first five having been already put into Latin by John of Seville, Abu Ma'shar's *Introduction to Astronomy*, and, perhaps in collaboration with Robert of Kerron and Hugo of Santalla, a collection of works by various Islamic astrologers. Hugo himself was of major importance to Westerners in providing a translation of *The Book of Aristotle: containing every single question relating to nativities as well as to circles and orbits, taken from 250 books of the Indians*. This, which had nothing to do with Aristotle and little with Indian astronomer-astrologers, nonetheless provided its twelfth-century readers with an extensive bibliography; astronomical terms such as 'planetary latitudes', 'stations', 'heliacal risings', and so forth; astrological material derived from Dorotheus of Sidon and Rhetorius of Egypt; and discussions anent the signification of the twelve astrological places – length of life, money, prosperity and happiness, the number of siblings to be expected, which family member will die before the others, illnesses, marriage prospects, sex, travel, jobs or professions. Here, as we can see, the range of interest and anxiety is familiar from that of the ancient world, and although this is primarily because much of the book's material goes back to Dorotheus, Rhetorius, and Vettius Valens, human nature being what it is one can scarcely be surprised that these topics continued to be as important in the twelfth century as they had been in the first, second, and sixth. [1]

At some time in the 1170s or 1180s, Daniel of Morley (*c.*1140–*c.*1210) returned to his native England after a period of study, first in Paris where he thought that those occupying the professorial chairs were so ignorant as to be childish and, indeed, gross enough to be called 'brutish' (*bestiales*), after which he went, much more profitably, to Toledo. His time there had brought him into contact with a number of distinguished scholars, including Gerard of Cremona to whom we shall return later, and he had either acquired sufficient Arabic or read enough new Latin translations to be able to transmit some of the Greek and Arabic learning whose allure had brought him to Toledo in the first place. [2] Much of this acquisition is incorporated in his *Philosophia* or, as it is called in one manuscript, *Liber de naturis inferiorum et superiorum*, ('A Book on the Natures of Things Below and Things Above'), a work which leans on three sources in particular: the *Rudiments of Astronomy* by al-Firghānī, the *Rise of Knowledge* by al-Fārābi, and the *Introduction to Astronomy* by Abu Ma'shar. It is from al-Fārābi, however, that he derived his interesting view of astronomy-astrology as a branch of knowledge which is directly related to several other, apparently disparate subjects, a relationship which gives it an over-arching importance:

> With regard to its high standing, one finds that, according to what savants have said, it has eight principal parts: prognostication, medicine, necromancy which is in conformity with natural philosophy, agriculture, magical illusion, alchemy, (which is the science of how to transform metals into something else), magical images, (knowledge of which comes from the well-known, comprehensive *Book of Venus* published by Thoz the Greek), and mirrors, a science which is much broader and wider in scope than the others, as Aristotle makes clear in his book, *The Burning Mirror*. [3]

This view of astrology as a kind of *omnium gatherum* is not altogether unusual for the period – William of Conches, for example, in a work also entitled *Philosophia*, discusses God, demons, the elements, the stars, the seas and the earth, and human beings, but constantly returning to astronomy-astrology as the web linking everything into a comprehensible whole. 'The savants of this world have divided the cosmos into two parts. The upper [part], which extends from the circle of the moon as far as the immovable heaven, is active. The other [part], from the sphere of the moon downwards, is passive.' Hence his assertion that control of creation is exercised from above, superiors always dominating inferiors, both stems from and underlines the principal role of the stars in the working of the cosmos.

An equally striking view of the importance of astrology was voiced by Bernard Silvestris (floruit 1143–8). His *Cosmographia*, written in both verse and prose, and drawing upon such earlier works as *Asclepius* from the *Hermetic Corpus*, pseudo-Aristotle's *Universe*, Macrobius's *Dream of Scipio*, and Martianus Capella's *Marriage of Philology and Mercury*, is a complex vision of the universe and contains a description of what the human soul may expect to see during its descent to incarnation upon the earth. Two goddesses, Urania and Natura, experience that descent:

So that they might gain the express consent of the heavenly powers, and their guidance for the descent, now that the course of their solemn and sacred task had been determined, they entered the realm of pure and uncontaminated light, far removed and wholly distinct from the physical world. Here, if you were to express it in theological formulation, is the secret abode of supreme and super-essential God. The heavens on either hand are inhabited by ethereal and divine Powers; their ordered ranks are themselves arranged in order, and each single Power of the highest rank, the intermediate, or the lowest, understands the principle of his assigned function, the value of his special task. For a single spirit pervades their several realms, conjoined with one another and arranged in unbroken succession, and imparts sufficient power to them all. But they do not receive a uniform power from this uniform spirit. Those who are most nearly privy to the deliberations of the Godhead are drawn, at times, when His will reveals itself openly and directly, even closer to the inner mind of God. Others, by virtue of being more distant, retain only a reduced and incomplete vision, and partake more sparingly of the sight of God and knowledge of the future …

Far below this level resided the [ruler] of Saturn, an old man everywhere condemned, savagely inclined to harsh and bloody acts of unfeeling and detestable malice … He was still vigorous, and with a strength not yet impaired, and whenever there was no one whom he might devour, he would mow down with a blow of his sickle whatever was beautiful, whatever was flourishing. Just as he would not accept childbirth, so he forebade roses, lilies, and the other kinds of sweet-scented flowers to flourish. By the spectacle he presented he prefigured the hostility with which he was to menace the race of men who would come by the poisonous and deadly propensities of his planet …

As [the two goddesses] came into the pleasant atmosphere of [Jupiter's] delightful orb, they beheld two vessels, placed at the very threshold of Jupiter's abode, one full of bitter absinthe, the other of sweet honey. Souls were clustering about each vessel in turn, to taste of them, against the time when they should assume bodies. All life in the universe is subject to this condition imposed by Jupiter – that if any cause for joy arise from temporal life a cause for sorrow will occur as well. Seated in his council chamber, Jupiter shone in regal majesty, wielding in his right hand a sceptre, and suspending from his left a scale, in the balance of which he determined the affairs, now of men, now of the higher powers …

As they approached the sphere if Mars, lying just below, with its curved but distorted bands, they were greeted by a murmur like that of water cascading down a steep slope. When, drawing nearer, they could see clearly, Natura recognised by its seething and sulphurous waters the river, Fiery Phlegethon, which issues from the sphere of Mars. But at this time the fiery orb of Mars, emboldened by the favouring position of Scorpio as well as aroused by his own native propensities, shot out menacing beams into the fourth and seventh signs [of the zodiac], and sought a way of breaking out of his orbit, so that, transformed into a comet, he might appear, blood-red and terrifying, with a starry mane …

Now, the 'Helian Highway' in which the sun is borne on his annual journey was not everywhere the same, but consisted of four diversely coloured segments. The first quarter of the circle flourished green as verdant Egypt with the buds of diverse flowers under the renewing influence of Spring. The second, raging against Spring's tenderness, with fiery vapours, grew dry and parched with the aridity of Summer. The third presented an appearance compounded of the gold green of Autumnal ripeness. The fourth, too, extended through the breadth of these signs. On its surface shimmered a thin film of water which the chill of Winter had hardened into solid ice. That the single journey of this single power, so often reiterated, might present a more imposing spectacle, as he was borne through the fourfold change of his orbit he underwent a fourfold change of countenance, passing from boyhood through pubescence into youth, from youth to manhood, from manhood gradually assuming hoary age through the interspersal of white hair. These various appearances the sun assumed as it was borne through the upper, lower, and intermediary stages of its journey around the slanting circle of the zodiac …

Mercury travels around the orbit of the sun on a closely contiguous path, and thus is often heralded by the very power whose herald he is. Because of the law which governs his orbit, he rises at times above the sun, and sometimes lurks beneath him. Compliant and indecisive, Mercury does not point to the coming of misfortune in the affairs which he governs by his stellar clarity. Rather, his relations with other powers vindicate or corrupt him. Joined with the madness of Mars or the liberality of Jupiter, he determined his own activity by the character of his partner. Epicene and sexually promiscuous in his general behaviour, he has learned to create hermaphrodites of bi-corporeal shape …

Venus, while she touches the orbits of Mercury and the sun at certain points, encompasses both with the fullness of her own. Maintaining a median climate between the extremes of heat and moisture, she draws forth by the largesse of her own nature the fruits of budding plants, and inspires the renewal of all creatures by her generative impulses. Lending her authority to the evidence of favourable stars, she brings to a more tender fruition those births over which she presides. Astrologers believe that whatever incites the human longing for pleasure becomes vehement through the influence of Venus's star. The radiant countenance of Venus gives great delight to her beholders …

In the regions below were disposed the more turbid properties of the atmosphere, whose volatile appearance is altered whenever some chance occurrence offers to its passions the material they demand. So humankind, inhabiting this unquiet region, the very image of the ancient chaos, must needs be subject to the force of its upheavals … The moon, travelling her divisory and lowly course, is crude and heavy of body by comparison with the other spheres. Feeding upon the divine and immortal vitality of the heavenly fires, she transmits 'Aethericon', (the essence of bodily growth), to the lower world. Her gleaming body which shines with the reflection of the sun's brilliance is consumed and restored by a regular and unvarying flow of substance … Constantly passing through the same course of withdrawal and return, with ceaseless and unwearying speed, she can claim the most immediate power over the affairs and destiny of humankind. [4]

Bernard depicts the influence of the planets upon the human soul as almost ineluctable – he writes of 'laws', 'inexorable destiny', and 'necessity' – and although he acknowledges the parts played by 'determination of will' and 'uncertain accident', his commitment to the notion of astral determinism is strong. 'By the laws of the firmament, Man is assigned at birth his term of life and the means of its final disposition … The stars are not permitted to lie.' These views, not distinctive in themselves, perhaps, since they had long been current among many astrologers and debated by theologians, are interesting partly because of the way they are expressed and partly because of Bernard's attempt to construct a picture of cosmic order which he sees as a continuous process, endlessly coming into being from its primordial elements, evolving, and, every so often, being subject to renewal, each stage of this process (he maintains) being predictable from the stars. Bernard builds his *Cosmographia* round three major principles: order, creativity, matter. The 'order' is that of hierarchy in all parts of creation; the 'creativity' is that of God Himself radiating His creative energies throughout the order of His cosmos; and 'matter' is not so much a set of passive substances out of which things (*creaturae*) can be made by external Powers or forces, as substances containing within themselves an impulse to be given form and thus possessing an urge to co-operate with creative energy. It can therefore be seen that within this whole process astrology plays an important role, for it not only enables human beings to foresee the various stages of that process, but also opens their intellectual and imaginative faculties to the process itself, thereby enabling them to imitate the creative and improving elements of that process within their own physical and intellectual spheres of action.

How far such a concept of creation and the relationship between its constituent parts would have been possible without the influence of the explosion of translated texts which was bursting upon Western Europe at this time is open to debate. Toledo, as we have seen, was a major centre of this activity, and scholars working there included Gerard of Cremona (1114–87) whom we mentioned earlier. He, along with Domingo Gundisalvo (floruit 1150), Archdeacon of Segovia, helped to formulate a translation programme whose aim was to translate into Latin original Arabic works, and to restore ancient learning, much of which was already available in Greek but needed to be rendered into Latin to make it accessible, especially as much of it had been modified and improved over time by Islamic scholars. In these aims, both men were successful. Gerard's Latin version of Ptolemy's *Almagest*, for example, was the one most extensively used in Europe, but it is his version of the *Tables of Toledo*, based on the work of an eleventh-century astronomer, al-Zarqālī from Cordoba, which was of particular astronomical-astrological importance. The *Tables* were a set of ephemerides containing such information as tables for right and oblique ascensions, mean motion and equation for the seven planets, conjunctions, eclipses, a star catalogue, aspects, planetary visibility, and very much more – invaluable for astronomers and astrologers alike.

They were not, however, perfect, and after perhaps a century needed revision to correct anomalies. The result was the *Alfonsine Tables*, prepared between 1252 and 1270 for Alfonso X of Castile, (and originally appearing in Castilian, not Latin), by a team of Jewish and Islamic scholars. Alfonso (1221–84) was known as 'The Learned' and 'The Astronomer-Astrologer', partly because of his own scholarship and interests, and partly because of his encouragement of astronomy-astrology in particular. From the very start of his reign, he gathered Jewish, Christian, and Islamic scholars at his Court, mainly with a view to providing translations of Arabic texts into Castilian, sometimes with a Latin version as well. These Latin versions reveal some of the linguistic difficulties Alfonso's scholars encountered. They are literal rather than elegant, and every so often one can see the translator struggling with technical terms; but the new books thus produced quickly became

set texts in a number of European universities – Paris, Bologna, Oxford – where they made
a notable difference to the curriculum. Sometimes a single book delivered more than one
might think. The *Libros del saber de astronomía*, published by Manuel Rico y Sinobas, for
example, contained fifteen Arabic treatises dating from the ninth to the twelfth centuries
and covered such subjects as identification of various stars and constellations, and the
construction of instruments such as the astrolabe and the quadrant. Others concentrated
on astrology, such as Yehuda ben Moshe's Castilian version of a work by the tenth–eleventh
century astrologer, Abī-l-Rijāl, *Kitāb al-barī' fi akhām al-nujūm*, ('An Excellent Book on
Horoscopes from Constellations'), and another, (the reformulation of an earlier work), by
'Ubayd Allāh al-Istijī (eleventh century), now generally known by its Spanish title, *Libro
de las cruces*. This last presents its readers with very straightforward systems for predicting
such crucial pieces of information as the occurrence of rain or drought, and is so simplified,
indeed, that it is possible to cast a horoscope according to its rules by knowing only in
which signs are found Saturn, Jupiter, Mars, and the moon.

Alfonso's emphasis upon Castilian as the primary language of translation leads one
to ask why he should have given it preference over Latin, the scholarly lingua franca
of the time. Was he hoping to open up astrology to the common people and free them
from dependence on learned professionals? Was his intention to circumvent frauds and
ignoramuses posing as professionals by stripping astrology of some of its mysteries and
thus putting the practice within everyone's reach? The relative simplicity of *Libro de
las cruces* might suggest something of the kind. Equally, of course, it may merely reflect
Alfonso's personal interest in the vernacular, an interest he had inherited from his father,
Ferdinand III, who was one of the earliest rulers to use it for public documents, and one
which suggested he write his own works in Castilian rather than Latin. The fact that these,
apart from his poetry, tended to be works of collaboration may also reflect the disparate
religious persuasions of his collaborators. For the Jews, the ritual language was Hebrew, for
Muslims, Arabic. Only for Christians was it Latin. So everyone may have found it easier
to communicate with each other through Castilian and this, in turn, would ensure a wider
audience for those same writers' endeavours. [5] In the rest of Europe, however, tradition
and practicality demanded translation into Latin, just as the eighth–tenth centuries had
seen works in Greek, Aramaic, Syriac, Sanskrit, and Pahlavi translated into Arabic in
a programme largely centred on Baghdad. By 'works' one tends to mean those dealing
with astronomy-astrology and medicine, although philosophy also received its share of
translators' attention – this is true of the Latin as well as the Arabic programme – and the
building of an extensive corpus of knowledge in these fields had the profound effect not
merely of extending scholars' understanding and repertoire, (not to mention their linguistic
abilities), but also of consolidating what they knew, or thought they knew already; and
this double benefit of greater expertise and confirmation of traditional outlooks and
assumptions attracted the patronage scholars needed to fund their endeavours. It also
had the effect of extending knowledge in certain areas while restricting it in others. Thus,
greater sophistication in mathematics improved the astronomical quality of astronomy-
astrology, but had no effect on the fundamental premises upon which interpretive astrology
rested.

Debates of the thirteenth century can illustrate this point. There was general agreement in theological as well as secular circles that the movements of celestial bodies had an influence upon and were significant in regard to those on earth. That the moon had some consequence upon tides, that the configuration of stars at the time of someone's birth affected his or her temperament, and that astral conjunctions could assist in determining the outcome or helping one to explain the meaning of historical events were premises more or less taken for granted. What had never been so widely acknowledged was whether the stars acted as signifiers or as causes of events. Adelard of Bath, for example, had been explicit in his opinion. In one passage he depicts astronomy-astrology as a woman wearing a garment full of eyes, with a teacher's pointer in her right hand and an astrolabe in her left:

[She] sketches the shape of the world, as contained in her teaching, the number and size of the circles, the distances of the orbs, the courses of the planets, the positions of the signs of the zodiac. She paints in the parallels and colures; with thoughtful reason she divides the zodiac into twelve parts; she is aware of the size of the stars, the opposition of the two poles, the axis stretching between them. If anyone could take her to his wishes, he would be confident in declaring not only the present condition of lower things, but also their past or future conditions. For those higher and divine animate beings are the starting-point and causes of the lower natures.

This was a view highly contentious at the time, and proved to be even more so in the following century when astrological debate reached its peak in 1277 at the University of Paris with the publication of 219 propositions which, under pain of excommunication, should henceforth neither be believed nor discussed. They were produced largely at the instanced of the Bishop of Paris, Etienne Tempier (died 1279), who was deeply troubled by the Aristotelianism taking root in Europe's universities, a plant he regarded as inimical to Christianity; and, needless to say, since astronomy-astrology was widely considered to be the fountainhead of so many other disciplines, a number of Tempier's condemnations were launched in that direction. They included propositions:

That by different signs in the heavens there are signified different conditions in human beings, both of their spiritual gifts and their temporal affairs.
That our will is subject to the power of the heavenly bodies.
That Fate, which is a universal disposition, proceeds from the divine providence not without any intermediate agent, but by mediation of the movement of the heavenly bodies.
That anyone attribute health and sickness, life and death, to the position of the stars and the aspect of Fortune, saying that if Fortune is well-aspected to him he will live, and if not, he will die.
That in the hour of the begetting of a human being in his body and consequently in his soul, which follows the body, because of the way superior and inferior causes are arranged, he gets in him a disposition which inclines him to such and such actions and events.

In other words, to believe that human destiny and character are moulded by the stars which act as mediators between God and human beings, and that human free will is subject to limitation by the power of the stars is incompatible with the Christian faith. But these considerations brought many other questions in their wake. For example, are these stars actually transmitters of God's intentions, either as signs or causes, and if so, are they sentient or merely mechanical instruments of His will? Therein lay the substance of further disagreement.

Antiquity had believed that the stars were either divine or at least alive, and Aristotle had agreed with this latter notion, while the Christian Fathers took the opposite line. 'Let no one think that the sky and the heavenly bodies are alive,' wrote St John of Damascus, 'because they are inanimate and lack sense.' It was in *c*.1100, however, that a fresh debate opened on the nature of God's power. Was He entirely omnipotent all the time, or could He willingly curb that power in the light of promises made to human beings so that they could count on the regularity of cosmic order, the continuance of the moral principles He had laid down, and the assuredness of His plan of redemption? Was such a voluntary curb compatible with God's ability to suspend all three – in the working of miracles or the manifestation of wondrous signs, for example? Moreover, if God had manufactured a cosmos complete in itself, why would there be any need for any exterior Force or Power to interfere in its working? Could it be that superior parts of creation, such as the stars, had been given power to regulate and direct the inferior parts? If so, one can understand Adelard's final sentence in the quotation above: 'Those higher and divine animate beings are the starting-point and causes of the lower natures.' God, in effect, created everything and thereafter let it alone to operate in accordance with its own, diverse nature, a view which implied, among other things, of course, that the movements of the heavenly bodies were likely to be mechanical rather than directed or self-aware.

In *c*.1185, and Islamic astronomer, Nūr al-Dīn al-Bitrūjī, wrote a treatise on these movements, clearly implying that they were indeed entirely mechanical. His book was translated into Latin by Michael Scot (*c*.1175–*c*.1235), a Scottish scholar who, like so many others, had taken himself to Toledo where he contributed to the programme of translation running there, and thus the book became available to European participants in the current astronomical-astrological debate. After *c*.1227, however, Scot became Court astrologer to the Holy Roman Emperor, Frederick II, and as a result of what became his best-known books, *Liber Introductorius*, *Liber Particularis*, and *Liber Physionomie*, gained a great reputation, (although not everyone was in agreement about the extent of his abilities). These works deal with large subjects: God, the nature of humankind, the hierarchies of angels and demons, and the various kinds of divination. Scot's main contribution to the astrological debate was his conclusion that the celestial bodies, with whose movements he was intimately familiar owing to his translation of al-Bitrūjī's treatise, do not cause events but merely indicate them, much as a tavern sign on a building indicates that wine is sold therein without actually producing wine itself, or causing the person who sees the sign to go in and drink.

So, for Adelard of Bath the stars were causes, while for Michael Scot they were indicators, each man supporting a position a position seemingly irreconcilable with the other in an intellectual battle which would not, in fact, be decided by the 1277 Condemnations of Paris, but would continue, although sometimes in muted struggle, for a long time after that. Proponents of the 'signs' side of the argument, however, tended to dismiss other aspects of the science. Thus in c.1235, Robert Grosseteste (c.1168–1253) referred to the celestial bodies as 'signs' but was thinking principally of the observation of these bodies in terms of meteorology and the Last Days when 'the sun will turn to blood and the moon will not give her light'. These are truthful signs. Observation of the heavens for the purposes of judicial astrology, however, was both illicit and useless because the mathematics involved cannot be applied with that certainty judicial astrology requires. Therefore 'it is not possible for the astronomer (*astronomus*) to judge and pronounce on the details of a chance event, or on the character or even the physical constitution of a child by referring to the constellations'. Nor do the stars have an effect on human free will, since this is entirely subject to God. As for the argument that the stars affect human bodies, human bodies affect the soul, and therefore the stars affect the soul, it implies that the soul is not strong enough to resist the body, and this is evidently false. A well-ordered reason, too, is quite capable of resisting any effects which, say, Saturn or Mars may have upon the body. Moreover, traditional medicine can deal better with ill effects impressed on anyone by the stars. Free will also means that people cannot be pre-disposed to do something wicked. Therefore 'we want to give warning that judicial astrologers of this kind have been led astray, and lead [others] astray in their turn. What they teach is impious and irreligious, and has been written at the Devil's dictation. In consequence, their books should be burned'.

But even here, scholars apparently on the same side did not necessarily come to the same conclusions. About thirty years after Grosseteste made known his opinions on the subject, a Brother Reginald wrote to his fellow Dominican, St Thomas Aquinas (c.1227–74), asking whether it was permissible to make use of judicial astrology. In reply, St Thomas made it clear that he was perfectly content to acknowledge the validity of certain aspects of astronomy-astrology:

> If anyone uses the verdicts of the stars to gain foreknowledge of physical effects – that is, of storms, the dry, bright condition of the air, the health or debility of the body, or the abundance or dearth of crops, and things such as these, which flow from physical, natural causes – he obviously commits no sin, because everyone employs some observation of the heavenly bodies with regard to effects of this kind. For example, farmers sow and reap at a certain time which is governed by the movement of the sun. Sailors avoid being at sea when the moon is full or even when it is waning. When it comes to illnesses, physicians pay particular attention to critical days which are determined by the course of the sun and moon.

The key word here is 'physical'. The stars and planets may well have an effect upon matter, but cannot do so on anything which is not material. Therefore it can be argued that neither the human intellect nor the human will can be subject in any way to influxes from celestial bodies. But, St Thomas says, because a person's intellect and will are closely connected with his or her corporeal organs, disturbance within the latter must have consequences for the former. 'Most human beings are governed by their passions which are dependent on bodily appetites, and in these the influences of the stars is clearly felt.'[6]

Some time after 1260, another Dominican, St Albertus Magnus (1193/1206–1280), wrote *Speculum astronomiae* ('A Mirror of Astronomy-Astrology') in order to defend the science as a valid branch of knowledge for both Christians and natural philosophers, and in this he tried to answer the various points which had been in debate for so long and were troubling Bishop Tempier of Paris. The debate, of course, was complex, but one can reduce most of its principal concerns to seven questions.

1. Are the movements of celestial bodies merely mechanical after being initiated by God?
2. If not, are they controlled by some order of superior spiritual beings?
3. Are the stars and planets under that kind of control, or are they animate in themselves?
4. Are the stars signs or causes? If the latter, what are the implications for divine omnipotence and human free will?
5. If the stars and planets exercise influence upon terrestrial bodies, can that influence be detected and manipulated or subverted?
6. Can human beings predict what the stars and planets are likely to do, or what influence they are likely to have, by observing their movements and relationships?
7. If such prediction is possible, is it lawful in the eyes of the Church?

St Albertus directs his attention to these. He begins by distinguishing between the astronomy which deals with celestial configurations, movements, distances, and circles, 'a single great wisdom ... [which] no one contests unless he is someone who opposes the truth', (Chapter 1). The second great wisdom, also called astronomy, 'is the science of judicial astrology which ties together natural philosophy and metaphysics', (Chapter 3). God has created a heaven which is not alive, and uses the mute, deaf stars as if they were instruments (*per stellas surdas et mutas sicut per instrumenta*). This appears to put St Albertus on the side of the mechanists, following Aristotle's theory that astral influence is transmitted via the movement of the celestial bodies rather than through the will and intention of preternatural entities such as Intelligences or angels. But this is not quite his position. Heavenly influence, he says:

> derives from many stars, many places, and spaces, and images, and rays and conjunctions, and interferences, and from various angles produced by the intersection of the rays of the heavenly bodies, and from the production of rays towards the centre in which alone, according to Ptolemy, all the powers of those bodies which are in the celestial circle are collected and concentrated. This is a middle form between the necessary and the possible; whatever belongs to the motions of celestial orbs, is, in fact, necessary, whereas whatever belongs to the matter of things which can be generated and corrupted is mutable and possible. This form produced by the celestial circle and related to things which can be generated and corrupted occupies a middle position between the [necessary and the possible].

In other words, those things which exist in that upper part of the cosmos above the orbit of the moon are not subject to change and therefore what they do is not subject to change, either. Hence, they follow their perfect orbits because their perfection compels them to do so. Those things which exist below the moon's orbit, on the other hand, are subject to change and so their behaviour may be erratic owing to their susceptibility to change and degeneration. Heavenly influxes flowing from the upper region of immutability and therefore necessary behaviour gather force from that point of balance between the two regions, upper and lower, before descending into that region where mutability is the norm. Thus, heavenly influence neither compels (through necessity) nor allows (through possibility). Instead, it brings about changes by which human beings may be affected, but with which they may choose to co-operate or not. 'The stars have the power to alter the elements, to change temperaments and people's states of mind and, in addition, the way [people's] circumstances incline in relation to the things they do, and even the outcomes of battles.' But, 'the stars are by no means the *reason* for our actions, because we have been endowed with free will by the Creator and are masters of our acts … The stars have the force of a *sign* with regard to things which exist in matter which is capable of changing from one state into another, and even with regard to those things which are connected to it'. Hence the stars, their positions, and their relationships can and may licitly be read, and this reading constitutes the science of astrology.

From this point, the *Speculum* deals with a variety of different but related topics: the technicalities of astrology and bibliographies for the reader's benefit; 'nativities' (that is, birth horoscopes); 'interrogations' (questions concerned with the outcome of events), again with bibliographies'; and the business of image magic which, of course, is condemned, along with the relevant books (which St Albertus helpfully lists). His inclusion of these bibliographies is an essential part of his purpose in writing the *Speculum*, as he explains in his *prooemium*. There are several books in circulation, he says, which are rightly suspect by lovers of the Catholic faith, and there are others, perfectly harmless, which have unjustly received hostile criticism. Therefore he has decided to provide readers with a list of titles and authors, 'so that the permitted ones may be separated from those which are illicit', and so that readers who wish to look at the former may be assured 'not even a single word is found in them, which may or may seem to be contrary to the honour of the Catholic faith'.

St Albertus is thus not altogether clear about how far the stars' movements are mechanical or not, but he does say they are signs provided by God for humankind and are therefore under His direct control. Their movements are such that they can be observed and predicted, and they do indeed exercise influence upon matter in the region below the moon. Authors who have written on these matters have done so in complete conformity with Catholic teaching, and so it is indeed possible to postulate astral influence and observe and predict planetary and stellar movements without acting illicitly in the eyes of the Church. In many respects, then, St Albertus addresses the seven questions we posed earlier. So, after a quite different fashion, does the Franciscan, Roger Bacon (*c.*1214–92). Bacon lectured first in Paris and then in Oxford where, from *c.*1247 onwards, he devoted his energies both to the cultivation of a wide variety of subjects including astronomy-astrology, optics, and alchemy, and to 'experimentation', a word we must not misunderstand since it does not imply that Bacon was in any twenty-first century sense a 'scientist'. In any case, many of his experiments were described as theoretical possibilities rather than as operations he had carried out in physical or practical form. By 1266 he had written to Pope Clement IV, outlining a most ambitious programme of recording human knowledge in the shape of a vast encyclopaedia which, he said, would be beneficial both to the Faith and to the progress of learning in the universities. But so immense was the projected enterprise that it was never finished, although Bacon did complete, in a remarkably short space of time, three extensive contributions to the whole: *Opus Maius* ('The Greater Work'), *Opus Minus* ('The Lesser Work'), and *Opus Tertium* ('The Third Work'). When Pope Clement died in 1268, however, Bacon's hopes were extinguished, and although he continued to produce further work on natural philosophy, philosophy, and mathematics, at some time between 1277 and 1279 he was condemned by his fellow Franciscans 'on account of certain suspected novelties', and subjected to house arrest.

What were these novelties? Almost certainly a number of his views on astrology. He had a lofty opinion of the science. 'God, who has given philosophers the light of wisdom through which the light of truth is confirmed and strengthened, and by means of which we perceive that we are under an obligation to destroy the enemies of the Faith, is to be praised because of [astrology].' 'It is clear to everyone,' he wrote elsewhere, 'that the celestial bodies are the causes of generation and corruption in all things belonging to the lower region,' (that is, the region below the orbit of the moon). One notes he says 'causes' not 'signs'. The stars themselves are ungenerated, incorruptible, and move of their own accord, although they are subject to regulation by angelic Intelligences. They incline people to perform good or bad actions – 'inclination' leaves room for the exercise of human free will – and may be employed in astral magic for the production of amulets and images. 'If they are engraved in accordance with the aspect of the sky in the elect times, all injuries can be repelled and useful undertakings promoted.' People's physical constitutions are defined at conception or birth by the stars, and the constantly changing positions of the stars mean that astral effects may be evident at any hour of the day or night, as good physicians should know. An extreme example of this determining astral influence could be seen in a certain English woman:

> Some people have lived for a long time without nourishment. For instance, in modern times there was a woman in England, in the diocese of Norwich, who did not eat for twenty years. Yet she was plump, in good condition, and had no superfluous flesh, as [her] bishop proved by having her examined by reliable individuals. This was not a miracle but a work of Nature, because some constellation had the power at that time to reduce her elements to a stage closer to equilibrium than they were in before.

Now, none of this is particularly unconventional although many scholars would have taken issue with the suggestion that the stars were causes rather than signs, and Bacon has a great deal more to say about astronomy-astrology than the points we have mentioned here. He divided the science into three parts: (i) and (ii) discuss largely what he calls 'speculative astronomy', covering the mathematical principles of celestial motion, and 'practical astronomy' dealing with astronomical tables and instruments. What we have just reviewed is (iii), his 'judicial astronomy', and it is worth noting that in Bacon's opinion, even if judicial astronomy-astrology were to be abolished, there would be more than enough of the whole science left to constitute an immensely important subject in its own right.

But as far as the Church authorities and his own Franciscan brethren were concerned, the stumbling-block will have been some of the associations he made between astrology and religion. Conjunctions of the other planets with Jupiter, he said, following the lead of Abū Ma'shar, indicate the rise of a new religion. Thus, Jupiter and Saturn had announced the Jewish religion; Jupiter and Mars, the Chaldaean; Jupiter and the sun, the Egyptian; Jupiter with Venus, Islam; and Jupiter with Mercury, Christianity:

> For Mercury, as they say, has reference to deity and to the ocular utterances of proph-
> ets, and to belief and to prayer … They also say that the law of Mercury is harder to
> believe than the others, and contains many difficulties beyond the human intellect. This
> is in keeping with the difficult motions of Mercury, whose circuit is in an epicycle and in
> an eccentric circle and in a concentric one. For this reason, he has reference, as they say,
> to the law which contains difficult articles and hidden truths; and the Christian law is of
> this kind. But because Mercury signifies writing and writers, and depth of knowledge con-
> tained in profound books, and eloquence or sweetness of speech and tongue, oratory and
> its rapid flow, and the explanation of sentences, he indicates that this law will be defended
> by such authentic scriptures and by so many profound sciences and by such potency of elo-
> quence, that it will always remain firm in its own strength, until the final law of the moon
> shall disturb it for a time.

That final reference brings us to the conjunction of Jupiter with the moon, which will announce the advent of Antichrist and therefore the beginning of the Last Days, and so complete the cycle of conjunctions. Yet none of this would have been sufficient in itself to condemn Bacon to a period of serious punishment. The trouble almost certainly lay in his implicit suggestion that the stars and planets at the time of Christ's birth did more than simply indicate the event: they actually exerted an influence on His human nature:

> Without doubt [pagan authorities] maintain that it is impossible for God to be subject
> to a creature and that the divine work, in so far as it was from an infinite virtue and above
> Nature, in no way was subject to a celestial arrangement, but that it had merely served for
> a sign. Yet in so far as the most pure Virgin was the true and natural mother of our Lord
> Jesus Christ, and functioned according to the force of Nature in preparing in advance
> substance, and in fostering it after conception, and in like actions, they have maintained
> that the force of the heavens co-operated with the natural force of the glorious Virgin and
> aided her in so far as she functioned according to Nature, because man begets man. For if
> there was anything of a natural character in that conception through preparation of sub-
> stance and nourishment in the womb, and the like, in so far as she was a true and natural
> mother, they do not consider it improper to assume that the celestial arrangement is more
> than a sign, taking into account simply the things of Nature.

Here, if Bacon agreed with it, was a notion deeply heretical, and various saints from Augustine to Albertus had explicitly condemned it. No wonder, then, that the Master-General, having accepted that Bacon did indeed agree with the authorities to which he was referring, should not only confine him to close quarters, but also direct that his teaching be forbidden within the Order. What is more, the Master-General wrote to Pope Nicholas III, asking for Bacon's dangerous flight of intellect to be suppressed by Papal authority. Nor is it surprising to find this strict discipline enforced in the immediate aftermath of the Condemnations of Paris, since, as we have seen, these had targeted a number of astrological opinions and speculations considered detrimental to pure faith and therefore dangerous to faithful members of the Church. [7]

This scholarly wrangling, however, appears to have had little effect on the actual practice of astrology in the various worlds beyond the academic cloister. Physicians, for example, found it a necessary tool in their armoury. The theory that the human soul descended to earth from its place of origin via the spheres and other celestial bodies required that it have a vehicle in which or by which to travel, since the soul is incorporeal and is obliged to enter and reside in the world of matter. This vehicle is the astral body, composed of the same substance as the stars and spheres themselves; and because the astral body and the stars are alike in substance, the stars and planets are able to imprint their influences upon it during its downward journey. Now, medical theory (as opposed to theological or philosophical speculation) tended to confuse this astral body with 'spirits' (*spiritus*), by which are meant three kinds of very fine vapour deriving from blood and air, and so infer that the celestial influences which make impressions upon the astral body were thus given an entrée to the physical body whose various parts were continually susceptible to those same influences. We can see this at work in the various treatises of Roger of Hereford (floruit 1176–98) where each zodiacal sign has an elementary quality attributed to it, (a theory actually borrowed from Abū Ma'shar) – Leo, for example, is fiery, bilious, and lustful – and a physiognomical relationship with specific parts of the body: hence Saturn in Aries relates to the chest, in Taurus and Gemini, to the stomach; in Cancer and Leo, to the sexual organs and the lower parts of the body; in Virgo and Sagittarius, to the feet; in Libra, to the knees; in Scorpio, to the ankle; in Capricorn, to the head as well as the feet; in Aquarius, to the neck as well as the head; and in Pisces, to the shoulder, arms, and neck. The other planets follow suit, with like relationships as they pass through the twelve divisions of the zodiac.

Similarly, Bernard of Gordon (end thirteenth – beginning fourteenth century) noted in his *De conservacione vite humane* ('The Preservation of Human Life'), dated 1308, that human life has three guardians: God who watches over the will, the angels who watch over the intellect, and the stars which watch over the body. Hence, chronic illnesses follow the movement of the sun, acute illnesses that of the moon; epilepsy sometimes follows one, sometimes the other; menstruation grows and subsides according to the phases of the moon; Saturn has a dire influence on the viability of a foetus, killing it off when it has reached its eighth month of life; water may be contaminated by the power of the stars; precious or semi-precious stones engraved with the image of Aries or Leo or Sagittarius are good for fevers, dropsy, and paralysis; the Black Death of 1348 was either caused by vapours emanating from the stars which were blown long distances by the winds, or its cause was fed by planetary conjunctions – or both, which was the opinion of a physician, Gentile of Foligno, a lecturer at the University of Padua. A conjunction of Saturn, Jupiter, and Mars, he said, brought:

> poisonous material which is generated about the heart and the lungs. Its impression is not from the excess in degree of primary qualities, but through properties of poisonous vapours which have been communicated by means of air breathed in and out, great extension and transition of this plague takes place, not only from man to man but from country to country … It is no great matter in these whether it is a constellation or an earthly or antiquarian figure, if only we may know how to resist it, and that a stand be made against it lest it destroy us.

Physicians, therefore, had no doubts about the actions of the stars and planets in relation to human bodies, and the University of Bologna, pre-eminent in the training of physicians, actually employed a professor to teach students how to use astrology while making their diagnoses. Even Michael Scot, for whom the stars were indicators rather than causes, acknowledged their influence upon the development of the growing foetus, relying on the argument that, while the stars may not cause events, they do have an effect upon matter and can thus be seen as crucial factors in material objects and processes here on earth:

> The horoscope of infants enables us to say whether, once they have been conceived or born alive, they will die in the womb or while they are being born. So we know there is a great deal going on in the horoscope because of the activity of the planets whose disposition [in the heavens] organises things below in many different ways. Consequently we say that in the seventh month [of pregnancy], the moon adds a lot of moisture to the solid lump of humours, which holds in position any embryo in a woman's womb; and once this softening process has taken place, the humours descend to a lower position so that the sediment of those [humours] which lay stagnant in the womb can rise up and come out through the mouth of the uterus, either together with the embryo or after it has come out. All this happens as a result of the activity of the moon which governs every male and female. So, while the moon operates in accordance with the regular principles of nature, the foetus comes out gingerly from the loins and passes into the light of the temporal world. Therefore we say that if anyone is born before the seventh month, [a fully grown foetus] does not come out from within, in as much as the planets have not all performed their particular function in comparison with the vigorous action of the moon.
>
> If it is born in the first month, nothing comes out except humour conjoined with a great variety of solidified matter [attached to] some threads. This is because Saturn is reigning at the time, and so everything the moon has liquefied becomes solid.
>
> If it is born in the second month, blood comes out in driblets mixed with solid matter. This is because Jupiter is reigning at the time and is dominant. His activity has already changed the aqueous humour into blood and into a large number of bits and pieces of flesh, although these are not strong enough to form anything which can be considered to

constitute a complete, solidified being.

If it is born in the third month, it is rarely born alive because it is delicate and easily ripped apart in the womb, and it does not have an ability to repair itself, even though it is alive. It is also suffocated by too much heat because in this month Mars is dominant, and this produces a small gangrenous concretion.

If it is born in the fourth month, it will come out alive, and if it is alive, it will die at once because it is delicate and because the sun, which reigns over it, is far too hot.

If it is born in the fifth month, it may be alive, but when it does come out, it does not survive because Venus is dominant, and this planet is weak when it comes to females and to strength.

If it is born in the sixth month, it does not survive because Mercury is dominant and this is the planet of the strength of the community as a whole. Consequently, when [the foetus] is separated from the womb and enters into conjunction with the moon which is weaker [than Mercury], it cannot survive.

If it is born in the seventh month, it survives perfectly well and is able to survive because the moon is dominant, since through her dominance the sequence of the duties of the planets is fulfilled in a created being such as I have been describing; and with this richly endowed sequence of the working of the seven planets, which happens at the end of the seventh month, the embryo is either born and survives or, if it is not born, the foresaid planets begin to rule over it in the aforementioned sequence.

A physician's vade mecum dating from the end of the fourteenth or beginning of the fifteenth century, consists of a few pages of parchment folded in such a way that it could be hung from its owner's belt and be consulted at the flick of a finger. It contains a table of eclipses, illustrated; a table of planets accompanied by a picture of a man on the different parts of whose body signs of the influences of the appropriate planets are drawn and coloured; a section on phlebotomy with another human figure showing the veins and the ailments with which they are connected; and finally the picture of a circle of glass flasks containing urine of different colours, with interpretations of the medical meaning of those colours. Treatment is governed almost entirely by astral considerations, especially when it comes to letting blood:

ARIES: Avoid incisions in the head or the face and cut no vein in the head.
TAURUS: Avoid incisions in the neck and throat and cut no vein in these places.
GEMINI: Avoid incisions in the shoulders and arms or hands and open no vein there.
CANCER: Avoid incisions in the breast and sides, lesions in the stomach and lungs, and cut no vein or artery which goes to the spleen.
LEO: Avoid incisions of the nerves, lesions of the side and bones, and do not cut the back either by opening or bleeding.
VIRGO: Avoid opening a wound in the belly and in hidden internal places.
LIBRA: Avoid opening wounds in the umbilicus and inner parts of the belly and do not open a vein in the back or place a cup there.
SCORPIO: Avoid cutting the testicles, anus, and vesica, and do not cut the private parts

in a man or woman.

SAGITTARIUS: Avoid incisions in the thighs and fingers and do not cut blemishes or growths.

CAPRICORN: Avoid cutting the knees or the veins and nerves in these places.

AQUARIUS: Avoid cutting the legs and anywhere else as far as the heels.

PISCES: Avoid cutting the feet.

These recommendations, however, were not always infallible. In the phlebotomy section which follows these planetary injunctions, the physician is warned, 'when blood-letting is carried out from the veins in the folds of the arms, the moon should not be in Gemini'. Bernard of Gordon was aware of this prohibition, of course, but noted his own experience:

> The best authorities in astrology agree that bleeding should not be done while the moon is in Gemini, because either nothing will come of it, or [the patient] will become worse, or he or she will die. Still, I happened [once] to note down the precise time at which the moon would be in Gemini. This later slipped my memory, and I wanted to bleed myself at exactly that time. I got everything ready and then remembered, but I didn't want to give up and carried on with the bleeding. I never had a better experience!

Closely connected with medicine was alchemy, in the sense that one of the purposes of alchemy was to produce elixirs which would cure diseases and prolong life. Planetary and stellar influence marked everything in the material world and thus created a channel for power to flow downwards – this is why planetary images, inscribed upon gemstones were thought to work efficaciously, and why certain herbs were supposed to be good for the alleviation of certain symptoms or illnesses – and so when, in alchemical recipes, we find that the sun represented gold, the moon silver, Mercury quicksilver, Venus copper, Mars iron, Jupiter tin, and Saturn lead, these terms are not simply substitutes for the names of metals but also represent the celestial forces entering the processes of generation and growth, (for metals were believed to grow, like plants, in the earth), and thus contributing to the production of the metals themselves. As a fifteenth-century alchemist, Solomon Trismosin, expressed it, 'All corporeal things originate in and are maintained and exist of earth, according to time and influence of the stars and planets,' while George Ripley noted in his *Compound of Alchymie* :

> We have an Heaven yncorruptible of the Quintessence,
> Ornate with Elements, Signes, Planetts, and Starrs bright,
> Which moisteth our Erthe by suttile influence:
> And owt thereof a secrete Sulphure hid from sight,
> It fetteth by virtue of his attractive might,
> Like as the Bee fetcheth Hony out of the Flowre.

Michael Scot, not content with seeing in this process the exercise of one natural body upon another, posited the existence of preternatural entities which guided the actions of both planets and metals. Overseeing and helping the growth of metals, however, was not the only contribution the stars made to alchemy, for the stars also governed each stage of the alchemical work itself. 'If you want to secure the elixir so that it does not become unfixed,' said an anonymous fourteenth-century alchemical manuscript, 'work it from the descent of the sun towards the head of Capricorn until it rises into Aries.'[8]

The intrusion of spirits – call them angels, demons, or simply 'entities' – into some aspects of both medicine and alchemy reminds us that magic of one kind or another might not be far away from a wide variety of disciplines and practices. An interesting example of this can be found in the career of Pietro d'Abano (1250–c.1316). He was both a physician and astrologer – Professor of Medicine at the University of Padua, in fact – having first studied for many years in the University of Paris. He gained a great reputation, especially for learning in the occult sciences, as the early seventeenth-century scholar, Gabriel Naudé, recorded:

> He carried his inquiries so far into the occult sciences of abstruse and hidden nature, that, after having given most ample proofs by his writings concerning physiognomy, geomancy, and chiromancy, he moved on to the study of philosophy, physics, and astrology. These studies proved so advantageous to him that, not to speak of the two first which introduced him to all the Popes of his time, and acquired him a reputation among learned men, it is certain he was a great master in the latter, which appears not only by the astronomical figures which he caused to be painted in the great hall of the palace at Padua, and the translation he made of the books of the most earned Rabbi Abraham ben Ezra, added to those which he himself composed on critical days, and the improvement of astronomy, but by the testimony of the renowned mathematician Regiomontanus who made a fine panegyric on him as an astrologer.

Among the several treatises either by D'Abano or attributed to him are one dealing with poisons, one on the astrolabe (both genuine), and three on magic, (spurious). His principal genuine work, however, *Conciliator differentiarum philosophorum et medicorum* ('The Reconciler of the Disagreements of Philosophers and Physicians'), which was completed in 1303, consists of 210 questions relating to debatable subjects current at the time. Some involve astronomy-astrology. Disagreement 10, for example, asks whether a modern doctor can restore a sick person's health with the help of his knowledge of astronomy-astrology, and comes down on the side of the celestial bodies' being the *causes* of events here on earth, acting as mediums and instruments of God's will and initiating intention; Disagreement 104 reviews problems connected with predicting the critical days of any illness. All the planets affect morbid crises according to their various positions at any given time but, says D'Abano, because it is so difficult to achieve accuracy when predicting these movements, (especially those of the moon which ranked high in physicians' calculations of critical days), it is doubtful whether Galen, the great authority on such matters, can be trusted – an interesting instance of D'Abano's independence of thought on certain occasions. Disagreement 168 suggests that surgeons should not operate when the stars are not propitious, a standard enough opinion, but Disagreement 156 discusses whether making incantations before treatment can bring about a cure or not, thereby introducing magic into the debate, and while D'Abano actually places no faith in the words or sounds of any incantation, (this would be mere superstition), he does give examples of incantations or spoken charms which appear to have worked:

> This can be demonstrated by experience, and one can be persuaded by reason to employ an incantation. There are a good many examples of it, not just in academic theory, but the results of direct observation, as the highest sacrament of the Eucharist clearly shows, along with many others things. The divine names of the notory art of chiromancy confirm it, and there was the occasion when an enchanter felled a bull in my presence, pronounced magic words into its ear, and caused it to come alive again.

The mention of the Eucharist in this context should have been quite enough to alert the Church authorities to D'Abano's suspect opinions and sure enough it did. Naudé tells us that he was accused of practising magic and brought before the Inquisition, although apparently not on the particular point of the Eucharist, but another – that he ascribed Noah's flood to a conjunction of certain planets (*Genesis* 7.17–24), and that the subsequent confusion of languages (*Genesis* 11.1–9) was also caused by particular stars. A further charge, curious in the light of his reputation as a magician, was that he denied the existence of demons and thought they had no place in the natural order of things. Equally curious, for the same reason, is the defence offered by students whom he called as witnesses, that 'once, while he was in Constantinople, [he visited] a woman who was believed to be potent in this very [practice of] necromancy in order to make inquiries about certain secret things'. D'Abano died, we are told, before his trial ended and his corpse was later burned, an indication, surely, that he would have been found guilty of heresy had he lived, although Naudé says he was falsely accused and therefore acquitted. [9]

   The dangers of mixing astrology and religion are thus clear. Clearer still is the example of Cecco d'Ascoli (1257–1327), Professor of Astrology at the University of Bologna, whose principal works consist of an unfinished encyclopaedic poem dealing in part with astrology, *L'Acerba*, and two Latin commentaries on astrology. In these, Cecco made a number of statements and advanced several propositions which drew the attention of the Church to the potentially worrying direction in which his mind was tending:

1. The stars compel people's actions.
2. There are evil spirits in the sky, who can be coerced by incantations chanted under certain constellations to perform many extraordinary things.
3. People born under certain constellations are bound to have certain destinies, and God will not change their situation.
4. The stars control the fates of cities from the laying of the very first foundation-stone.
5. Certain 'superior' planets are especially allotted to kings, aristocrats, and magistrates while 'inferior' planets belong to the common people.
6. The stars alter the elements and therefore alter human bodies and therefore, via the

bodies, alter human souls.

7. Dreams may be prophetic because the influence of the stars allows the dreamer's soul to unite with spirits in the sky, and dreams come true when the moon is in Taurus, Leo, Aquarius, and Scorpio.

8. Images can be made according to the precepts of astral magic, which will enable the maker to receive responses from demons.

Cecco also drew Christ's horoscope to show how Libra ascending made the crucifixion inevitable, that the particular location of Capricorn at that time meant He would certainly be born in a stable, that Scorpio's position rendered Him poor, and that of Mercury made Him wise.

Now, some of these claims had either been made by others before, or were very like others' expressed opinions, and Cecco did go out of his way to deny, for example, that Christ was born under circumstances controlled by the stars, or even demons; or that the period of darkness during Christ's crucifixion was not a true miracle; or that magic and 'necromancy' are not practices contrary to the Faith and condemned by the Church. Nevertheless, his horoscope of Christ was essentially blasphemous, and he did purvey much information about magic to his students while, in spite of somewhat perfunctory acknowledgements that what he was imparting stood unconformable to Christian religion, he constantly quoted books of magic and magical authorities with apparent relish. When Zoroaster (then long regarded by Western Europe as one of the inventors of magical practice) said: 'These climates are to be marvelled at, which with the flesh of corpses and human blood give trustworthy responses,' Cecco commented:

> By this you should understand those four spirits of great power who stand at the cross-roads, that is, east, west, north, and south, whose names are Oriens, Amaymon, Paymon, and Egim, spirits who are of the major hierarchy and who have under them twenty-five legions of spirits each. Therefore, because of their noble nature, these seek sacrifice from human blood and likewise from the flesh of a dead man or a cat.

Given these pronouncements and the ambiguities attendant on his gestures towards orthodoxy, it is not surprising to find that Cecco's teachings were condemned by the Inquisition. On 16 December 1324 he was required to abjure his opinions and surrender his books on astrology, in addition to which he was deprived of his degree, forbidden to teach, and given a penance of fasting and prayer. This, as Henry Lea pointed out, made him a penitent heretic and, as such, he would have to tread very carefully in future because any subsequent lapse would bring him to the stake. Cecco decided to leave Bologna – his continued life there would be circumscribed and rather difficult, so it is easy to understand why he chose to emigrate – and went to Florence where (a mistake) he continued his life as though nothing had happened, circulating copies of his writings, and accepting the post of astrologer to Florence's Duke. All seemed well for two and a half years, but then in May 1327 he made the final mistake of making predictions anent Louis, Duke of Bavaria, who was entering Italy to assert his right to be crowned Holy Roman Emperor.

Now, either this was one exercise of astrology too far or, as has been suggested, he incurred the enmity of the Duke of Florence's chancellor, or perhaps both, and he was arrested by the Florentine Inquisition. Naturally, the Inquisitor wanted to know if Cecco had had any previous history of nonconformity, and when inquisitional papers were sent from Bologna, investigation made it clear that Cecco had violated the terms and conditions of his sentence. This meant he had relapsed into heresy, and so on 15 December sentence of death was pronounced against him by the secular arm.

He was condemned, not for astrology itself – the universities of Bologna, Padua, and Milan, for example, all had Professors of Astrology in successions unbroken between the thirteenth and sixteenth centuries – but because he had strayed well over the line which theologians had been so careful to draw between legitimate speculation about the working of celestial bodies, the extent of their influences here upon earth and inquiry into the relationship between God and the various parts of His creation, in particular the relationship between God and human beings. Preventing such divagation from orthodoxy was clearly the Church's job, and Cecco had stepped too far into nonconformity to be allowed to proceed unchecked. On the whole, therefore, Cecco might have found that a safer, though unusual, path to tread in these circumstances would perhaps have been that taken by Petrarch.

> What need is there of a soothsayer? Why does the astrologer torment himself? What does vain curiosity for a horoscope labour over? Although I am fully aware that these fellows can be annoyed by words, but not reformed, without hope of success I often attack them thus: 'Stop it, o madmen! Let the stars follow their orbits. For either the stars have no power over us, or they reveal nothing about us, or we understand nothing of this. Your lies, if nothing else, certainly reveal to the world that at least one of these possibilities is true.'

Petrarch's indignation, however, was wasted on society. For society believed that the stars could tell them something, and what that something was they wanted to know. In consequence, individual falls from grace notwithstanding, astrologers could always be assured of finding a ready audience and an eager clientele, as a broader look at the later Middle Ages will readily illustrate. [10]

10

Astrology in Mediaeval Literature, Art & Architecture c.1300–c.1500

One reason they wanted to know was that division in the Church, producing the Great Schism when several Popes and rival anti-Popes battled for recognition of their legitimacy and so split Europe into excitable camps, had stimulated questions about whether this intolerable disjunction was a sign of the coming of Antichrist and therefore the end of the world. Astrology, capable perhaps of providing an answer to this pressing question, as to others, was thus too important a science to abolish or even curtail with too much rigour, and if its speculations could be controlled and brought within the Pale of orthodox religion, there was no good reason it should not be practised and its conclusions heeded by even the most elevated members of the Church. Pierre d'Ailly, (1351-1420), theologian, astrologer, and cardinal, was deeply affected by the Schism and the question of Antichrist's coming, but he was also aware that if he wished to defend astrology – as indeed he did in a series of treatises written between 1410 and 1420 – he would be obliged to purge it of those parts which he and other Churchmen considered superstitious. There were, he noted, three main errors:

> The first belongs to those who are of the opinion that everything which happens in the future proceeds from the stars by a compelling circumstance dictated by Fate. The second belongs to those who blend a rather large number of the detestable superstitions of the practice of magic with [their] books on astronomy-astrology (*libris astronomicis*). The third belongs to those who arrogantly and superstitiously exceed the bounds of astronomical-astrological power with respect to free will and certain things which are subject only to divine and supernatural power.

When it came to answering these errors, D'Ailly essentially took the line of St Thomas Aquinas: the stars have a direct influence on the human body and an indirect influence on the soul because human beings are prone to follow the impulses of their physical senses, although the gift of free will means that they are not actually bound to do so. But every so often the Cardinal skates on what may be regarded as remarkably thin ice. He agrees with Roger Bacon, for example, that conjunctions between Jupiter and one of the other planets coincides with a change of religion, although he does not go as far as to say that the conjunction *causes* the change, at least when it comes to Judaism and Christianity, for they – unlike the religions of the Chaldaeans, Egyptians, and Muslims – are supernatural in character, that is, quite literally 'above and beyond Nature', and therefore exempt from causation originating in natural bodies such as the stars. Yet he was also able to write:

> Christ our lawgiver is said to have had a very kind temperament from birth. Therefore it is not inconsistent with the Faith, and is consistent with [our] natural reason, that He was born under a fortunate disposition of the sky or [a fortunate] constellation from which the kindliness of His temperament was able to derive in accordance with Nature.

What D'Ailly is arguing for is a distinction between supernatural and natural causes. Miracles, for instance, cannot be attributed to anything other than divine intervention and thus cannot be caused by anything within Nature itself. Hence, they have nothing to do with the stars. But in as far as Christ was man as well as God, His physicality, by definition, fell within the realm of created Nature and was therefore open to the same natural influences as that of any other human being, which is why His temperament can be said to have been influenced by the particular arrangement of stars and planets at His birth.

Critics of astrology often pointed to the impossibility of achieving the high degree of precision required by those branches of the science, judicial astrology in particular, which depended on accuracy for the validity of their predictive interpretations:

> Because on astrology [*in astrologia*] there are so many and such great difficulties when it comes to movements ... it necessarily follows that in judicial astronomy [*in astronomia de iudiciis*] the difficulties are more and greater because judicial astronomy derives from astrology and, in addition to that, presupposes many things about which it is impossible to make up one's mind ... Consequently, it appears to be human arrogance to want to attain such a foreknowledge of future chance events from conjectures of this kind; and so God is believed to have reserved such foreknowledge to Himself – at least with respect to some future events.

'Some', not 'all'. So D'Ailly protected the possibility that the astrologer might legitimately be allowed to foresee and therefore perhaps predict a limited number of *futura*, although he does not stipulate what those *futura* might be. The fact that astrology was a difficult science, too, (or rather, a science with difficulties), he maintained, did not render it entirely unworkable or useless, and experienced astrologers were able to thread their way through the problems and produce conclusions which were both legitimate and reliable:

> It is not unbelievable that some truths of this kind have been revealed to certain people by divine inspiration, especially to holy patriarchs and prophets, some of whom, we read, were skilled in the science of astronomy-astrology; and this works particularly to the praise and glorification of the truth of this science of astronomy-astrology, and to the honour and glory of the life-giving Creator of the stars, who is God, blessed for ever and ever. [1]

If some Churchmen at least were willing to validate astrology as a science, even if they were reluctant to accept every aspect of it as a legitimate discipline, secular authorities were only too eager to make full use of it, especially, indeed, those of parts most suspect to their ecclesiastical counterparts. Frederick II (1194–1250), the Holy Roman Emperor, for example, was a great patron of learning – he founded the University of Naples in 1224, and encouraged Jewish as well as Christian scholars to come to his Court. Michael Scot was one of his official astrologers and it was to him that Frederick posed a remarkable series of questions on various topics of theology and natural philosophy, the answers to which form a large part of Scot's *Liber Particularis* which we mentioned earlier:

> How many heavens are there, and who are their governors who chiefly dwell in them? How much does one heaven differ from another in relation to accurate measurement, and what is beyond the furthermost heaven, since there are so many of them? In which heaven does God exist in His essential being, and in what way does He sit upon the throne of [this] heaven?

On the whole, though, Frederick, like other rulers, tended to ask his astrologers somewhat different questions, such as whether his plans were destined for success, and when was the most propitious time for consummating his marriage to the Empress Isabella. Charles V of France, too, consulted astrologers before his marriage, although he was warned by one of his close friends that when it came to war, captains of armies must guard against 'all sorceries, signs, divination, forbidden sciences, and all astrological judgements practised in contradiction to free will, by which judgements a number of great lords have found themselves deceived'. Emperor Rudolf I seems to have been astrologically guided before being crowned Emperor and before getting married – these prenuptial precautions appear to have been shared by royal and noble persons with many of their subjects – and numerous aristocratic figures either employed or at least consulted astrologers (not to mention magicians) before undertaking any kinds of military excursion. An example of such an astrologer in such a context is Guido Bonatti, one of the most notable Latin writers on astrology from the thirteenth century, who died some time between 1296 and 1300. For most of his career he was involved one way and another in the struggles between Pope and Emperor which dominated Italy in the middle of the century, advising not only Frederick II, but also a succession of Italian warlords, Ezzelino da Romano in Brescia, Guido Novello, leader of the Emperor's supporters in Tuscany, and Guido da Montefeltro in Forlì. His advice was always practical, as can be seen in his book, *De astronomia tractatus decem* ('Ten Treatises on Astrology'), which guides the reader through a variety of questions liable to be asked by potential clients – questions about buying houses, destroying buildings, renting a house or a piece of land, planting trees, and sowing crops. Some, however, are clearly derived from his experience with the warlords. 'Will someone, Duke or anyone else, who wants to go into the army, or to war, or to begin a war, be successful or not?' and 'How to elect times for going out to war, or for fighting the enemy.'[2]

Bonatti had a high regard for his own craft and claimed:

> Everything is known to the astrologer. Everything which has taken place in the past, everything which will happen in the future – all things are revealed to him, because he knows

the effects of celestial movements past, present, and future, and because he knows when they will act and what effects they ought to produce.

It was not actually an unusual claim, as we have seen, but Bonatti was impatient of clerics – 'astrologers know vastly more about the stars than theologians do about God', was one of his dismissive comments; another referred to 'that hypocrite, John of Vicenza of the Order of Preaching Friars' who, along with some other silly fools, 'has said that astrology is neither an art nor a science' – and so perhaps we should not be surprised to find him languishing in the fourth chasm of the eighth circle of Dante's *Inferno*, among a silent, weeping crowd which includes the Greek seer, Eurypalos, and Michael Scot. 'Their faces were turned back upon their shoulders, and they approached by walking backwards, because seeing forwards was denied to them.' (20.13–15). Why was this? Because they 'aspired to see too far ahead'. (20. 106–20; 20.38).

Dante's immense triumph, *La Divina Commedia*, contains a number of passages dependent on, or referring to astrology, of which this side-swipe at Bonatti is only one, and his long essay, *Il Convivio*, has lengthy passages dealing with what are essentially astrological questions in relation to theology. But Dante does not really take a particular stance on the theoretical arguments of the day. He simply admits that both the planets and the fixed stars have a power which they are capable of transmitting, as in *Paradiso* 21.13–15 where Dante and his guide Beatrice have risen to the realm of Saturn, 'the seventh splendour which, under the breast of burning Leo, mixes its beams with his might'. Like Pietro d'Abano, Dante saw the stars as God's instruments, imposing form on matter and giving everything its special characteristic:

> Within the heaven of divine peace spins a body in whose power exists the essential being of everything enclosed within it. The next heaven which has so many things one can see distributes this essential being among various entities which are distinct from it and contained by it. The other [heavens] circulate, in various ways, the [powers] which make them different from one another, and distribute them to their goals and offspring. These organs of the universe, therefore, as you now see, advance grade by grade, so that they take from [the one] above and act on [the one] below. (*Paradiso* 2.112–23).

In other words, power flows from the motionless, perfect heaven where God dwells to the Primum Mobile, a sphere which encloses the whole of creation and in which exist the potentialities of everything else in all its variety. Within this sphere, (and therefore slightly closer to the earth), the eighth heaven is that of the stars – 'so many things one can see' – a heaven which transmits to its stars the undifferentiated power it receives from the Primum Mobile, a power which is then split up (so to speak) into various powers which are, in their turn, transmitted to individual stars or groups of stars. From this eighth heaven, transmission continues to the remaining seven spheres, each of which bears a planet, and these planets, having received differentiated and specific powers, pass them on to the *creaturae*, the created substances (human, animal, botanical, mineral) of earth so that each *creatura* may fulfil the end for which it was created. But how do these embracing spheres, each contained within another like the layers of an onion, transmit the powers they receive? They move, and this movement creates momentum, and momentum opens up a channel for transmission. What causes them to move? The action of certain angels known as 'Intelligences', themselves so ranked and graded that only the lowest act directly upon the sublunary world.

Dante's interest, however, lies not so much in how astral influences work as in what those influences affect. 'Alas, base-born, born under evil stars!' he exclaims at one point, (*Convivio* 4.27), accepting the claim that the stars influence character; or the very personal, 'O glorious stars! O light filled with great power, from which I acknowledge all my talent [comes], whatever it may be', (*Paradiso* 22.112–14); or 'Cyclical Nature which acts like a seal upon the mortal wax, exercises her skill well, but does not distinguish one lodging-house from another', (*Ibid.*, 8.127–9) – hence the differences between twins, Dante's answer to that famous objection to astrology, which had been raised since ancient times. People differ, he argues, partly because the capacities they receive from God are determined by three factors:

When the human seed falls into its receptacle, the womb, it brings with it a threefold power: that of the generating soul, that of the heavens, and that of the elements of which the seed is comprised, that is, of its own constitution. It matures and disposes the matter to receive the formative power, which is given by the soul of the male parent. The formative power prepares the organs to receive the power of the heavens, which brings the soul into life from the potency latent in the seed. As soon as this is brought into being, it receives the potential intellect from the power of the Primum Mobile ... Since the complex nature of the seed can be better or less good, and the disposition of the man who generates the seed can be better or less good, and the disposition of the heavens to bring this effect into being can be good, better, or very good, (depending on the constellations, which are in a constant state of change), it comes about that the soul which is brought into being from this seed and from these powers is of greater or less purity. (*Convivio* 4.21).

Nevertheless, if the stars imprint characteristics upon individuals, that does not mean to say they determine how each person will or indeed should act:

The sky initiates your movements. I do not say all of them, but if I did say that, a light has been given you and free will [to distinguish] between good and evil ... You are the free subjects of a greater power and a better nature, and this creates in you the mind which the sky does not have in its parish. Therefore, if the present world strays from the path, the cause is in you: let it be sought in you. (*Purgatorio* 16.73–6, 79–83).

This clearly echoes St Thomas Aquinas:

People do not acquire from birth, directly in the intellective soul, a particular disposi-tion through which they are necessarily inclined to choose a particular goal, nor [do they acquire it] from a heavenly body or from anything else, except that because of their very nature there exists in them an unavoidable appetite for their ultimate goal, that is, happiness. This does not impede the freedom of choice, because different ways remain available to the attainment of that goal. The reason for this is that heavenly bodies do not have a direct influence on the rational soul. From birth, however, in the body of a child a particular disposition arises both from the power of the heavenly bodies and from causes lower [than these in the scheme of things], namely semen and the matter which has been conceived. Through this [power], the soul is rendered in some sense prone to choose a particular thing according to which the choice of the rational soul gets an inclination from the passions which are in the sensory appetite which is a physical power derived from the various ways in which the body is constructed. But no necessity to make a choice is thereby introduced into these [passions], because it lies in the power of the rational soul to approve or even to repress the passions which spring up. (*De veritate* question 24, a.1, ad 19).

But Dante was not using astrology merely as a backdrop to his work, he employed it to indicate a link between his characters and the particular universe his poem was constructing. Richard Kay gives instances. 'The influence of each planet is also exemplified by the Pilgrim,' [i.e. Dante]. He begins his astral and spiritual journey when the sun is in Aries, the beginning of the zodiac and the ruling sign at the creation of the world, and:

> on Venus, the planet of good will he is well disposed to an unknown soul (*Paradiso* 8.44–5), while on Mars he manifests the influence of the planet in his audacity and elation (16.16–18). Beatrice, too, exhibits the influence of the place, e.g., when on Mercury, the planet of good counsel, she offers the Pilgrim '*mio infallibile avviso*' (7.19). These manifestations are obviously appropriate because the travellers have fallen under the spell of the planet they are visiting.

Astrological allusions increase, too, as Dante proceeds on his journey from Hell to Purgatory to Paradise, with their quality changing from more material the closer he is to earth, to more spiritual the closer he is to God. Thus, as Dante emerges from Hell to Purgatory, he sees Venus shining in Pisces. 'The lovely planet which prompts love/ makes the whole East smile,/ veiling the Fishes which were in her escort.' (*Purgatorio* 1.19–21). Since Pisces symbolised Christ in Christian imagery, Venus here represents a different kind of love, Christian caritas as opposed to pagan *amor* or *cupido*. Similarly, in Canto 8 of *Paradiso*, Dante again draws attention to the difference between the pagan concept of Venus and the Christian. In the former, Venus is associated with passionate love – 'the world used to believe, to its peril, that the beautiful Cyprian radiated mad love (*il folle amore*)'; in the latter, the sphere of Venus is closer to God and therefore her influences are holy, since the light is able to contain the lights (i.e. the souls) of the Blessed who have come to greet Dante and Beatrice: 'and as we see a spark within a flame … I saw within that light other lamps moving in a circle'. (*Paradiso* 8.1–3, 16, 19–20).

In sum, therefore, we may say that astrology forms a vital part of the setting for Dante's account of his vision of the three states of the soul after death and his own spiritual journey from Hell to Paradise. It also provides him with a symbolic language which enables him to communicate quickly and vividly the characters and motives of his dramatis personae; and it furnishes a vehicle for the discussion of the working of God through the stars upon Nature and humankind, a subject matter more usually dealt with in theological or philosophical treatises, but here turned into great art while losing none of its dianoetic power. A contemporary historian, Giovanni Villani, expressed a similar judgement:

> He wrote the *Commedia* in which, in polished verse, and with great, subtle questions, moral, natural, astrological, philosophical, and theological, with new, beautiful illustrations, comparisons, and poetry, he dealt with and treated in 100 chapters or cantos the existence and condition of Hell, Purgatory and Paradise as loftily as it is possible to treat them, as may be seen in this said disquisition and understood by anyone who has a subtle intellect. (*Nuova Cronica* 9.136).

On a much more parochial scale, the English poet Geoffrey Chaucer (*c.*1340–1400) used astrology for somewhat similar ends. These can be seen most obviously in his *Canterbury Tales* wherewith pilgrims making their way to the shrine of St Thomas at Canterbury entertain each other. Rather than illuminating God's ways to Man, the *Tales* comment on institutions such as marriage and the position of women in society, or the current political situation at the English Court. So when the Wife of Bath, for example, characterises herself for the benefit of her listeners, she is able to do so in five succinct lines of astrological allusion:

> For certes, I am all Venerian
> In feeling, and mine heart is Martian.
> Venus gave me my lust, my lecherousness,
> And Mars gave me my sturdy hardiness.
> My ascendant was Taurus, and Mars [was] therein. [*Prologue to her tale*, 609–13]. [3]

Mars, then, makes her bold, Venus sensual, and the position of Mars in Taurus perhaps indicates she was deaf in her left ear. What is more, since Taurus is the latest sign in Lent, a period of sobriety and chastity, neither of which can be said to belong to the Wife of Bath, the extent of her rebellion against both, and against the expectations of Church and secular society with respect to orthodox behaviour on the one hand, and traditional male-female relations on the other, is made clear. Again, the *Merchant's Tale*, a black comedy, tells the story of January, a knight from Pavia, who waits until he is sixty before marrying a young girl, May. Not long afterwards, January's young squire, Damian, falls in love with May, and there ensues a tale of lechery, futility, adultery, and blindness which seems to take a sidelong glance at the relationship of the aged King Edward III and Alice Perrers. After the death of his wife in 1369 the King, then aged fifty-seven, fell under the ambitious influence of a woman who had already been his mistress, but quietly, for some five years. Once the Queen's hand was removed, however, Alice started to accumulate wealth and power on a notable scale as Edward slipped into a long and dangerous dotage. This lethargy of the King enabled Alice to exercise influence through a number of men who formed her clientele or coterie, one of whom was Chaucer himself who probably owed his position as Comptroller of the Custom to Alice's intimacy with the King. She and Chaucer were about the same age. This means that when she began her liaison with Edward in 1366 she was about twenty-five, and thus the disparity between January and May in Chaucer's tale mirrored, mutatis mutandis, real life as Chaucer saw it at Edward's Court.

Once decided upon marriage, January forwards the wedding and enjoys the wedding night, labouring until dawn and then sleeping late. Eventually he rises, 'but fresh May/ held to her chamber until the fourth day', by which time the moon had changed its place in the zodiac:

> The moon which was at noon that day
> That January had wedded fresh May
> In the second degree of Taurus, had glided into Cancer. (*Merchant's Tale*, 1859–60, 1885–7)

This piece of information, incidentally, allows us to date the tale to 1388, and this new celestial influence therefore now favours May's young would-be lover, Damian. As the story progresses and May gains ascendancy over January, (that is, the month of May leaves January further behind as it advances to June), the heavens change once again in her favour:

> Bright was the day and blue the firmament;
> Phoebus has sent down his streams of gold
> To gladden every flower with his warmness.
> He was at that time in Gemini, as I guess,
> Not far from his declination
> Of Cancer, Jupiter's exaltation. (*Ibid.*, 2219–24).

What are we being told astrologically? 'May' is dominated by Gemini and Cancer, the former associated with Mercury, a volatile planet indicating quickness of mind, fluency of speech, changeability of disposition; the latter associated with the moon, also indicating an impressionable and changeable nature. 'January', on the other hand, is ruled by Capricorn and Aquarius, both under the rule of Saturn, the aged planet of depression, rigidity, and sense of responsibility. Clearly a match between these two 'months' is probably doomed from the start. Chaucer thus uses astrology in this tale to forward the reader's understanding of the progress of his actors, to outline the basic traits of their characters as they are likely to unfold in the story, and to pass sardonic and detailed comment on the English political situation in the 1370s. Moreover, the marriage of January and May, as Brown and Butcher point out:

> is above all a perversion of the true state of holy matrimony ... [and] by extension this marriage may be applied metaphorically to the kingdom as a whole. Servile obsession has deprived the kingdom of royal authority; the creature that brought about the King's fall couples with the devil in the garden; and the mistress and the trusted servant betray the kingdom while continuing to exploit to their profit the favour of Edward III.

Chaucer was lucky to get away with it, for his politically charged astrology would have been understood at once by anyone who heard it.

How early they began to learn may be indicated by Chaucer's treatise on the astrolabe, written in *c*.1391 for 'Little Lowis', a boy aged ten. It was never finished, probably because its intended audience, Lewis, died, and was written in English perhaps because a boy of ten would not yet have sufficient Latin to be able to cope with a technical subject, perhaps because Chaucer was hoping to aim at a wider public. The essay's style is simple and repetitive, entirely suitable for such a readership, and its content unoriginal, largely a version of Māshā'allāh's work on the same subject, as Chaucer himself makes clear. 'Consider well that I do not claim to have produced this work from my own labour or my own cleverness. I am but an ignorant compiler of the labour of old astrologers and have translated it into English only for your instruction.' (*Prologue* 48–51). Part I describes the different working parts of the astrolabe and the signs of the zodiac, and when it comes to the latter, it is noticeable that Chaucer is careful to give a series of explanations of their names, so that Lewis may appreciate both the complexity and the subtlety of the science, even in its simplest aspects:

> In the zodiac there are the twelve signs which have the names of beasts; or else when the sun enters into any of these signs, he takes [on] the properties of such beasts; or else because the stars which are fixed there are disposed in signs of beasts or shaped like beasts; or else when the planets are under those signs they produce in us, by their influence, behaviour and effects like those of beasts. And understand also that when a hot planet comes into a hot sign, then its heat increases. And if a planet is cold, then its coldness diminishes because of the hot sign. (Part I, 338–48). [4]

Part II, which is incomplete, sets out to describe how to operate the astrolabe, breaking off at the point where Chaucer is telling Lewis 'how to know at what hour of the day or of the night shall be flood or ebb'. The remaining three promised Parts were either never written or have been lost altogether. They would have included, as we know from Chaucer's remarks at the very beginning of the whole work, an explanation of the movements of the heavenly bodies and the motion of the moon every hour of every day.

Does the *Treatise* give any indication of what was Chaucer's personal view of astrology, since those expressed in the Canterbury Tales (as in his other poems) are either those of his fictional characters, or are manipulated for essentially artistic ends? Theodore Wedel was of the opinion that Chaucer was fascinated by the subject of destiny, returning to it over and over again:

> For in the stars, clearer than is glass,
> Is written, God knows, whoever can read it,
> The death of every man, without fear. (*Man of Law's tale*, 96–8).

Yet, in spite of his apparent acceptance of astral determinism in his poetic works, when he came to what Wedel calls 'cold prose', he felt obliged overtly to repudiate this notion, presumably to avoid any clash with the Church's teaching on the matter. 'The ascendant, truly, in all nativities [*genethliacal horoscopes*] as well as in questions and elections of times is a thing these [ancient] astrologers greatly observe.' (*Treatise on the Astrolabe* 2.475–77). The ascendant and the lord of the ascendant, they say, may be fortunate or unfortunate as, for example, when no ill-favoured planet such as Saturn or Mars is in the house of the ascendant. 'But these are the observances of judicial [astrology] and pagan rites in which my spirit has no faith or knowledge of her horoscope.' (*Ibid.*, 517–19). Evidently the fate of Cecco d'Ascoli a generation earlier had not gone unnoticed. [5]

Both Dante and Chaucer, then, used astrology for artistic as well as larger purposes, confident that their allusions would not be lost, but rather resonate with their similar audiences who were clearly sufficiently acquainted with the astrological lore to be addressed in this kind of way. Lesser poets, on the other hand, might use their craft simply to deliver a sermon. Thus John Barbour (*c*.1330–1395), Archdeacon of Aberdeen, interrupted his narrative of the Wars of Independence fought by King Robert I to express conventional doubts about astrology's reliability as a science:

> Many people are so curious and greedy to know things that through their great knowledge or else through their devilry, they make an attempt to have knowledge of things to come in these two ways: one of them is astrology whereby learned men who know how to do so may know planetary conjunctions, and whether the planets' orbit places them in a favourable or a hostile house; and how the arrangement of the sky as a whole can have an influence on things down here on localities or on climates, [an influence] which does not have the same effect everywhere, but is less in some places and greater in others according to whether its rays are extended evenly or unevenly. But I think it would show great mastery [of his art] for any astrologer to say, 'This will happen in this place and on this day.' For although a man spends his whole life studying astrology with the result that he cracks his head on the stars, the wise man says he could not make three [such] reliable days in the whole of his life and he would always have doubts until he saw how it turned out in the end. So there is no reliable judgement [in astrology]. Or if those who wish to study the craft of astrology were to know the details of every person's birth, and knew the constellation which gives them their natural dispositions which incline them to good or bad, so that through the knowledge of learned men or through their mastery of astrology they could tell what danger was coming to those who are naturally disposed to it, I believe they would fail to let them know what might happen to them. For whether a person is inclined to virtue or to wickedness, he can perfectly well hold his will in check, either because he has been brought up that way, or through an exercise of his reason, and turn himself completely in the opposite direction. (*The Brus* 4.688–734).

Scepticism or opposition or both are often found in writers of the fourteenth century. The historian Giovanni Villani, for example, wrote that no constellation could subjugate human free will or the intentions of God, and his brother Matteo, that astrology was a vice inherited from the Romans. But consistency does not necessarily go hand in hand with condemnation. Petrarch (1304–74), for instance, is well known as someone who had no time at all for many professional astrologers whose charlatanry was a byword, despite their constant employment by royal and noble patrons. In a long letter, now famous, to Boccaccio, written on 7 September 1363, he gave vent to his deep dislike of their foolish pretensions:

> Amid these evils [of plague and war], you have heard what the astrologers are dreaming … They maintain that Mars and Saturn are coming together somewhere among the stars, and that that 'conjunction' (to use their word) after the end of the year will last for a full two years … *We* do not know what is happening on the heavens, but, with rashness and impudence, *they* claim to know … Theirs is not only ignorance, but blindness and total madness, which many times in the past was plain to everyone, but never more clearly than during this present plague … When they prate about human affairs and vicissitudes, things known only to God, they ought to be spurned as fabricators of dismal lies and refused the society not only of scholars but of all good men.

Having delivered himself of this general diatribe, Petrarch continues with anecdotes intended to illustrate his point. Before making an assault on Pavia, Galeazzo Visconti, who subsequently became ruler of the city, delayed his attack on the advice of astrologers because the propitious time for such an action had not yet arrived. Up till then the weather had been hot and dry, but the moment the astrologers declared the auspicious hour had finally come, the skies opened and a torrential downpour began, which lasted for several days and put an end to the immediate expedition. Petrarch later quizzed the principal astrologer – possibly Maino de Maineri, the Court physician – responsible for giving Visconti the advice to delay:

> Why had his judgement about this important matter so declined that he did not see such a dangerous, and such a precipitate change in the weather? He answered that it was very difficult to foresee the winds and the rains and the other so-called 'impressions of the air'.

Petrarch was scathing. So it was easier to foretell what would happen to someone years in advance than it was to forecast an almost immediate change in the weather!

Not satisfied with this victory, and in spite of his claim that he rather liked the man, however, Petrarch does not hesitate to bring up an incident from seven years previously. In 1354 Galeazzo Visconti and his two brothers were being invested with the sovereignty of Milan, and Petrarch was delivering a panegyric when the astrologer suddenly interrupted him 'to say that the hour [of installation] had come, which could not be allowed to slip by without grave danger'. Petrarch thereupon yielded the floor, only to be told that the moment had actually not *quite* arrived, and would he carry on with his speech? Petrarch icily replied he had nothing left to say, so the astrologer was left looking foolish and embarrassed until he decided to announce the auspicious moment and give to each brother the sceptre symbolising authority within the city. But this he did so slowly and with so many prolix congratulations and words of encouragement that, says Petrarch, the auspicious moment must have passed for at least one of the brothers – as indeed turned out to be the

SIGNS OF THE ZODIAC

ARIES	♈	LIBRA	♎
TAURUS	♉	SCORPIO	♏
GEMINI	♊	SAGITTARIUS	♐
CANCER	♋	CAPRICORN	♑
LEO	♌	AQUARIUS	♒
VIRGO	♍	PISCES	♓

PLANETS

SUN	☉	MOON	☽
SATURN	♄	VENUS	♀
JUPITER	♃	MARS	♂
MERCURY	☿		

1. Signs of the zodiac and the planets.

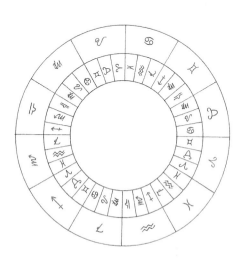

2. The decans.

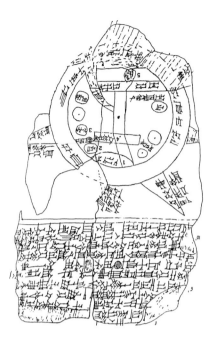

3. The Babylonian cosmos: clay tablet, *c.* seventh century BC.

4. Symbols of the deities as astronomical signs.

5. Aristotle as master astonomer-astrologer with the sign Leo.

6. A denarius of AD 74 showing the crescent moon and the seven planets.

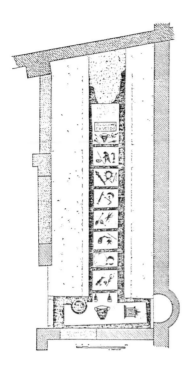

7. Mithraism. Mosaic showing the seven grades of the cult.
Felicissimus Mithraeum, Ostia.

8. Averroes.

9. Al-Kindi.

10. Statue of Alfonso X, cloister of Burgos
Cathedral.

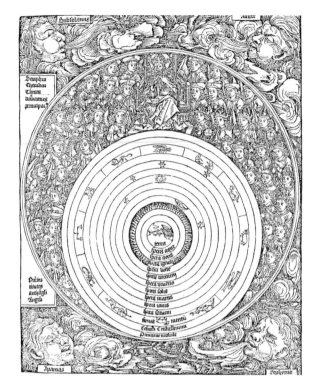

11. The universe, from the
Nuremburg Chronicle, 1493.

12. Cardinal Pierre D'Ailly.

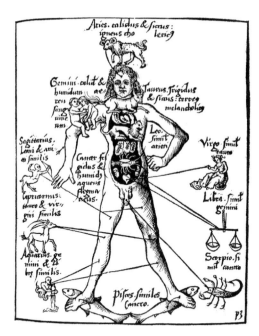

Above left: 13. Roger Bacon.

Above right: 14. The human body distributed among the signs of the zodiac. Gregor Reisch, *Margarita Philosophica*, Freiburg 1503.

Right: 15. Astrological signs related to the palm.

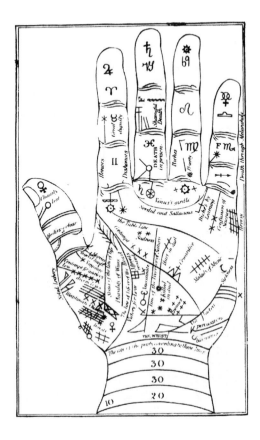

Left: 16. The onset of syphilis, explained by the conjunction of Saturn and Jupiter in Scorpio. After Albrecht Dürer, woodcut, 1496.

Below left: 17. Edward Kelley's horoscope. E. Ashmole, *Theatrum Chemicum Britannicum*, p.479.

Below right: 18. John Dee, *Monas Hieroglyphica*.

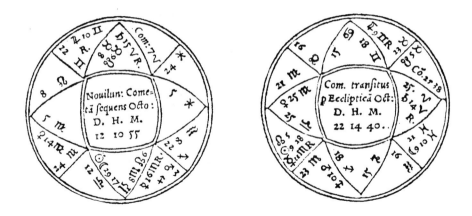

19. Horoscopes of the 1585 comet, drawn up by Tycho Brahe in *De cometa seu stella crinita rotunda*, 1586.

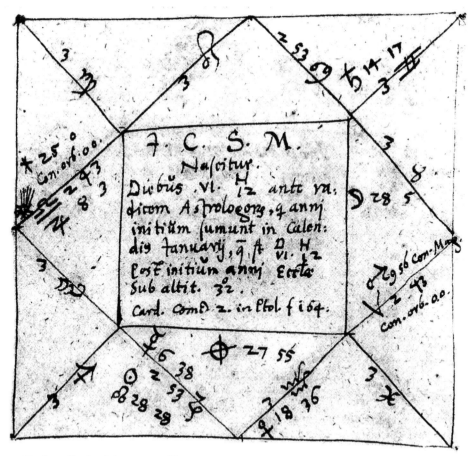

20. Girolamo Cardano's horoscope of Jesus.

21. Scheme of the vault paintings in the garden loggia of the Villa Farnesina.

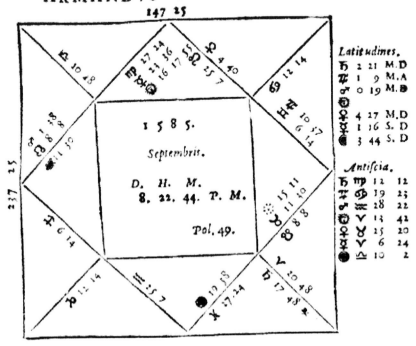

22. Horoscope of Cardinal Richelieu drawn up by Andrea Argoli, later changed by Jean-Baptiste Morin.

Nativitas Joan. Armandi Du Plessis Cardinalis Richelii.

23° 58.

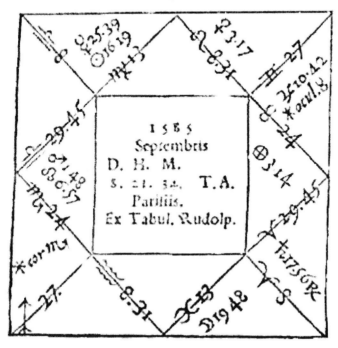

Latitudines

♄	2. 47.	M.
♃	0. 6	M.
♂	0. 29.	M.
♀	4. 7.	M.
☿	0. 50.	S.
☽	3. 45.	S.

23. Morin's version of Richelieu's chart.

24. Sagittarius, from *A Persian Book of Stars and Constellations*, 1630.

25. *The Shepherd's Kalendar*, 1631.

26. Jupiter, Saturn, the sun and moon from Michael Maier's *Viatorium, hoc est de montibus planetarum septem, seu metallorum*, 1651.

XVIII

LA·LUNE

27. An early Tarot card showing the moon.

28. Francis Barrett. Frontispiece of 1801 edition of
The Magus.

The Moon in ♈ at Birth. Their fortunate day is **Tuesday.**	The Moon in ♉ at Birth. Their fortunate day is **Friday.**
The Moon in ♊ at Birth. Their fortunate day is **Wednesday.**	The Moon in ♋ at Birth. Their fortunate day is **Monday.**
The Moon in ♌ at Birth. Their fortunate day is **Sunday.**	The Moon in ♍ at Birth. Their fortunate day is **Friday.**
The Moon in ♎ at Birth. Their fortunate day is **Saturday.**	The Moon in ♏ at Birth. Their fortunate day is **Tuesday.**
The Moon in ♐ at Birth. Their fortunate day is **Thursday.**	The Moon in ♑ at Birth. Their fortunate day is **Monday.**
The Moon in ♒ at Birth. Their fortunate day is **Wednesday.**	The Moon in ♓ at Birth. Their fortunate day is **Saturday.**

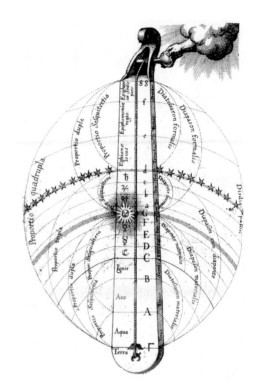

Above left: 29. The fortunate days of the week according to a nineteenth-century almanac.

Above right: 30. The divine monochord. Robert Fludd, *Utriusque cosmi maioris scilicet et minoris metaphysica, physica atque technica historia, Pars Prima*, Oppenheim 1617, p.90.

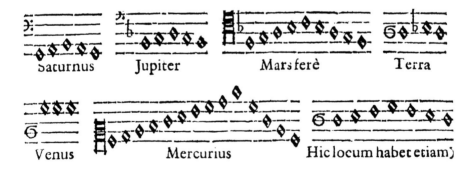

31. Planetary scales. Johannes Kepler, *Harmonices Mundi*, Linz 1619, p.207.

case. Still, irritated though he had been by the interruption to his speech, Petrarch calmed down sufficiently to seek to excuse the astrologer's faux pas – 'His age and his dire need to raise a large family, which sometimes bends even great talents to unworthy expedients, make me hold him a little less to blame' – and says the astrologer actually acknowledged that Petrarch's suspicions were correct. 'Dear friend,' Petrarch reports him as saying, 'I feel exactly as you do in this matter, but this is how I have to live.'

Nevertheless, if Petrarch was willing to make allowances for this particular man, he shows no such restraint for astrologers in general, and after these two anecdotes returns to his wider condemnation. 'Astrologers trumpet with the greatest insolence whenever one or two things prove true by chance, [but] find excuses for constantly lying, and fly into a rage at whoever questions the basis for their prediction.' Indeed, what he detests most of all, says Petrarch, is their mendacity, and since books refuting their errors seem to do no good in suppressing astrologers' nonsensical claims, 'what is needed are blows and the full rigour of the law'. In sum, he advises Boccaccio to avoid astrologers and trust God to deal with natural catastrophes as He sees fit. If plague occurs as a result of corrupted air or an unknown disposition of certain stars, it will end when the corruption is burned off by the sun or dispersed by the wind; and when that will take place, no 'sky-watcher' knows, only God Himself, or perhaps some devout individual to whom He reveals it. It certainly has nothing to do with Mars or Saturn. Astrology, in fact, is nothing more than subservience to the stars – a wretched, slave-like condition, at once ridiculous and impious – and those who practise it are committing a brazen, not to mention blasphemous outrage in pursuit of money, for which they deserve the strongest condemnation.

Boccaccio, then, can have been left in no doubt about Petrarch's contempt and distaste for the science; and yet the sound and fury conceal a degree of unease which Petrarch cannot quite shake off. In case of plague, he says in the same letter, 'I would not rule out a certain amount of human precaution', by which he means a change of residence, 'so that we leave behind for a time the places where the pestilential star has raged more violently'; and when he turned sixty-three, (one of the significant climacteric years according to astrological medicine), even though he wrote to Boccaccio dismissing the notion of climacterics as puerile, twelve months later he wrote to him again to say that 'the security I expressed in my former letter sprang, not so much from a feeling of scorn for the threats of the astrologers, as from a desire to continue my meditations on the necessity of death and the folly of fearing it' – an explanation which gives the impression that someone was whistling in the dark.

Boccaccio himself (1313–75) was not so vehement. He spent his years between the ages of fourteen and twenty-eight in Naples where he studied law at the university, had access to the library of Robert of Anjou, a ruler particularly interested in medicine and astrology, and studied arithmetic, geometry and astrology under the famous Paolo Dagomari da Prato – also known as Paolo dell'Abbaco, because he taught the use of the abacus, and Paolo Astrologo, because of his prowess in that science – and Andalo di Negro, author of an *Introductorius ad iudicia astrologie* which makes use of works by several Islamic astrologers, whom Boccaccio especially praised as his teacher of astronomy-astrology. The fruits of this instruction can be seen scattered through Boccaccio's literary works. In his

Genealogy of the Pagan Gods, for example, which he began in *c.*1350 and continued to revise until his death, one can see the lessons of the schoolroom regurgitated:

> What we call 'cupid' is a passion of the mind inflicted by exterior things ushered in via the phys-
> ical senses, and rendered acceptable by the special quality of their intrinsic powers, for which
> the supracelestial bodies are responsible. For according to the interpretation of astrologers,
> as my respected friend Andalo [di Negro] used to maintain, when it turns out in someone's
> horoscope that Mars is in the house of Venus, in Taurus, or in Libra, and is the signifier of the
> horoscope … the person born at that time will be lustful, a fornicator, someone who will take
> advantage of lecherous people, a wicked person in relation to such things. In connection with
> this, in his commentary on Ptolemy's *Tetrabiblos*, the scholar known as Haly [*'Ali ibn Ahmad*
> *al-Imrani*] said that whenever Venus and Mars are found together in someone's natal chart,
> one must attribute to him or her a disposition inclined to acts of promiscuity, fornication, and
> lust. He is driven by a specific inclination, with the result that as often as such a man sees a
> woman whose outward appearance delights him, the fact that she has pleased him immedi-
> ately transports him in the direction of his inward sensory potentialities. First of all it comes
> to the imagination, and from there it is transmitted to consideration, and from these sensory
> locations it is carried to that kind of capability which is the more noble among the apprehensi-
> ble potentialities: that is, to the potential mind. This is the receptacle of types, as Aristotle says
> in his *De Anima*. Once there, if the sufferer's willing disposition which controls his freedom to
> reject an impression or to retain it if it be approved recognises and understands the impression,
> his memory confirms that this is something of which he approves, and the strong feeling, now
> called 'love' or 'lust', takes up its position in his sensory appetite; and various agencies work
> upon it there and sometimes cause it to become so great and powerful that it forces Jupiter to
> leave Olympus and take the shape of a bull. (Book 9, chapter 4). [6]

But when he wrote his epic poem *Teseida* some ten years earlier, he used astrology as a framework within which the narrative of the loves and adventures of two Theban knights, Arcita and Palemon, is set. As was considered proper for such a work, *Teseida* is divided into twelve Books, each of which correlates with a sign of the zodiac. [7] Thus, Book 1 which deals with a military victory and Theseus's marriage in the Temple of Venus relates to Pisces, the house of Jupiter, the sign containing the exaltation of Venus; Book 2 is about war and ends with a thanksgiving in the Temple of Mars, so it is matched with Aries, the house of Mars; Book 6 has Leo for its sign, correlating the knightly tournament described in the narrative with the sign for knights, armed men, and kings; Book 10 contains frequent references to Jupiter, which align the narrative with Sagittarius; and the other Books can be correlated in similar fashion with the rest of the zodiacal signs. It will be noted that Boccaccio has here ignored the usual sequence of the signs – which begins with Aries and ends with Aquarius – precisely because he wanted to fit them to the unfolding events of his story as he conceived them. So, he completes his epic with Capricorn and Aquarius, both houses of Saturn, not because Saturn was the planet of harm and despondency, (its usual associations), but because Classical tradition described him as the ruler of the Golden Age, and Book 12 ends with a marriage and the promise of hope and happiness for the future.

In addition to providing a framework for the epic, however, astrology also provides reference points for specific events in the story and comments upon action and character, just as it does in the *Commedia* and *Canterbury Tales*. When, for example, Arcita and Palemon, the two heroes, first see the Princess Emilia with whom they both fall in love, and whom Palemon will wed in the end, we are told:

Phoebus, ascending with his horses,
Holds the humble animal of heaven
Which carried Europa, without a space between them,
There where his name dwells at this moment;
And together with him, dwelling places pleasing to the eye.
Venus shines as she makes her way upwards
Because the whole sky smiled
At Amun [*Jupiter*] who meanwhile dwelt in Pisces. (3.5).

In other words, Venus and the sun are rising together in Taurus which is the house of Venus, and Jupiter is in his house of Pisces, and thus the three planets are in their most favourable aspects. Therefore, as Boccaccio explains in the next verse:

From this happy aspect of the stars,
The earth takes pleasing effects,
And re-clothes its lovely places
With fresh grass and beautiful flowers.

Every aspect, then, bodes well for the three humans concerned, except that Palemon and Arcita are opposites, mirror-images of one another, and in consequence we find that in Book 7, for example, before each fights the other in a joust for Emilia's hand, Arcita prays to Mars *as the lover of Venus* for victory in battle, while Palemon prays to her *as the lover of Adonis* to let him win Emilia. This linking of Mars and Venus symbolises adulterous passion and lust, as Boccaccio himself explains elsewhere, and it is only because there are two possible Venuses, one of concupiscence and the other of chaste or married love, and that the presence of Jupiter tempers the baleful influence of Mars – Mars with Venus makes people lustful and depraved, whereas Jupiter with Venus makes them temperate and pure in love, as Ptolemy said – that everything turns out well in the end, with the lawful Venus triumphing through the marriage of Palemon and Emilia. [8]

Now, the fourteenth century was one of extraordinary wretchedness for great numbers of people throughout Western Europe in particular. Severe and widespread famine between 1315 and 1322 left behind a vivid consciousness of hunger, warfare, and disease; the Black Death raged between 1347 and 1351; and 1337–1453 saw the intermittent terrors of the Hundred Years' War. Circumstances began to improve somewhat during the fifteenth century, but even then there were ten worse than usual outbreaks of plague between 1400 and 1485, bringing to a sad kind of conclusion a century and a half which saw the population of Europe reduced by some 30 per cent, with the survivors acutely aware of the fragility of earthly existence and the chaos attendant upon it. Under such conditions, the need to find that behind the confusion and incoherence lay an unassailable order and certainty gave astrology a relevance and importance to everyone in society, not merely those who studied it professionally. Cosmic order, maintained by divine sanction, provided reassurance that the confusion of terrestrial life was not replicated elsewhere in the universe or in the states of being beyond the material, and the stars and planets were comforting signs of this otherworldly stability. At the very least, astrology furnished an explanation of how things were and a promise of better modes of existence when this earthly one had been left behind. Even the notion of astral determinism, though frowned on by the Church, could offer a kind of contentment, in as much as it relieved the individual of responsibility for his or her character and actions, and thus lifted the sense of blame which often torments those who are deeply traumatised by a violent tragedy. Little wonder, then, that if literature expresses, among its other preoccupations, certain themes important to the society of its day, astrology can be seen to play a not insignificant role in both polite and popular works of the later Middle Ages.

It can also be found in many of the drawings, paintings, mosaics and sculptures of the period. Illustrations with astrological themes or references in books and manuscripts, for example, tend to fall into four broad categories: religion, natural philosophy, medicine, and social comment. Thus the prayer book, *Les Tres Riches Heures du duc de Berry* (1410–16) contains one picture showing lords and ladies conversing and gathering flowers in the countryside under a domed sky containing both stars and the two zodiacal figures of Aries and Taurus, thus telling us that we are in the month of April, and reminding us that there is an intimate connection between life upon earth and God's order as expressed in the heavens. We see this again in the same volume in a picture of 'zodiacal man', the figure of a human being with signs of the zodiac placed over those parts of the body they were supposed to affect or govern – Aries on the head, Leo and the sun over the heart, Pisces next to the feet, and so on – the whole being contained in an oval with the degrees of each sign marked in a sequence of fives. Outside this, the zodiacal signs appear anti-clockwise, and outside these again the degrees of each sign are marked out as before, this orbit of signs again reinforcing the message that human beings live under the dominance of the stars. Indicating the passage of the seasons and the activities appropriate to each is regularly done by use of an astrological figure. Thus, in the *Grandes Heures de Rohan* (*c.*1400–50), we see a peasant and wild boar in a wood under the sign of Sagittarius, because gathering wood for winter fuel and hunting the boar were proper to the period over which the Archer rules, November and the beginning of December. [9]

These pictures come from works of religious devotion. Others, quite similar, are to be found in textbooks discussing the nature and working of the universe: the fourteenth-century *Losbuch in deutschen Reimpaaren* which shows a variety of men under a circular heaven of seven planets from which stream rays, depicted as straight lines, connecting each planet with the humans below; or the various illustrations in *De Sphaera* (fifteenth century), some extraordinarily elaborate, such as that showing Saturn as an aged semi-naked cripple leaning on a crutch, with bandaged legs and a medical patch on one thigh.

He holds a sickle in his left hand and is surrounded by stars and blue and red and yellow circles representing the heavens of water and fire above the earth. Next to his legs stand Aquarius and Capricorn, the two houses with which he is closely associated. Below this representation of the celestial realm are buildings, and men engaged in various activities such as playing chess. The notion that human life is subject to the highs and lows of good and bad fortune is underlined by the ground on which they stand – a flooring of alternate red and white squares stretching from the foreground to a castle or prison in the distance. Brilliant colouring, however, is not necessarily a requisite for such illustrations, for engravers were equally able to convey their astrological messages, as in pictures by The Master of the Housebook whose 'Planet Moon and her Children' (c.1480) shows a female on horseback – the moon – accompanied by Cancer (her zodiacal house), riding in the sky over a terrestrial scene of diverse activities including hunting, (a reference to the moon as the Classical goddess Artemis/Diana, patron of the hunt), fishing, (because the moon rules over the tides), and conjuring tricks, (associated with Classical Hekate, the goddess of magic, especially the darker sort).

Medicine, of course, as one might expect, provided astrological pictures, but these tended to be produced for practical ends. Variations upon 'zodiac man' are common, and there is an example from c.1399 which is contained in a folding almanac, whose figure is almost obscured by the signs painted over it. Illustrators were not always skilled, and so their depictions of the signs might be slightly peculiar, as in a fifteenth-century German example in which Cancer looks like a lobster, Scorpio like a snail with a tail, Capricorn like a stag, and Gemini like two disgruntled women having an argument over Leo. Another useful device for the travelling physician or surgeon was the volvelle, an instrument consisting of one or more revolving discs, (the central one with a pointer), rotating within a fixed matrix. They showed the months of the year, the signs of the zodiac, and the degrees of each sign. The pointer represents the index of the sun, enabling the physician or surgeon to discover accurately the sign and degree of the zodiac through which the sun was passing on the day and at the time in which he was interested. A separate index of the moon would let him know her sign and degree of influence at the same time. Hence he could see whether the moment for an operation or bloodletting he wished to carry out would be favourable or not.

Sometimes an illustrator recorded the astrologer as a figure of some importance. Hence we find a miniature of c.1327 showing a king with a physician on one side and an astrologer on the other, the former waiting for the latter to tell him whether the time was auspicious for bloodletting or not; and in another from *Tabulae Astronomicae* (c.1457), we see Giovanni Bianchini offering astrological tables to Emperor Frederick III. Every so often, however, a picture is not so complimentary, and there is a miniature of c.1350 which shows an astrologer at his desk, consulting a star map and at the same time summoning a demon. The spirit – humanoid, black, hairy and bat-winged – is enclosed in his own sphere. The astrologer's left hand is partly in, partly out of that sphere, indicating contact between the two worlds, and the demon's feet are balanced upon the rim of his sphere, showing that he is about to leave the spirit-world and enter the terrestrial. We are thus reminded that astrology could be and was used for magical purposes as well as others more legitimate.

But if engravings, line drawings, and small paintings were largely confined to books or pamphlets designed for the noble or the professional, the big canvasses, mosaics and sculptures of churches and palaces were seen by a very much wider and diverse public. Some pictures commemorated specific events, such as the painting of the night sky as it was on the date of the consecration of the high altar in the Old Sacristy of the Church of San Lorenzo in Florence, 8–9 July 1422; others relate to an individual, such as the horoscope of the banker Agostino Chigi (1466–1520) on the vault of the Sala di Galatea in the Palazzo Farnesina, painted by Baldassare Peruzzi, which takes the form of panels showing the constellation of Leo at the north end, Aquarius in the south, and the Wain, Pegasus, and Perseus in the middle. A line drawn between them gives the approximate time of Chigi's birth. More famous still is the astrological cycle belonging to the Palazzo della Ragione in Padua. Originally painted by Giotto, it was destroyed by a fire in 1420 and repainted by Niccolò Miretto and Stefano da Ferrara a few years later. Running round the four walls of the room, the panels show the constellations, the planets and their influences, the signs of the zodiac and their influences, and the months of the year. Each of these months has an Apostle, the appropriate zodiac sign, a personification of the month, its associated planet, the influences which may be expected to flow therefrom, and further constellations not included in the zodiac. The onlooker is thus presented with a virtual textbook on astrology and reminded, if a reminder were needed, that the stars have effects on everything below them. Is it implied, however, that the stars produce *necessary* effects, and are frescoes such as these lessons in astral determinism? That is much more difficult to gauge because their context is missing. We cannot stop and ask their owners and onlookers the questions needed to produce definitive answers, and therefore we are left, to a great extent, admiring the pictures as art, which was not the main purpose of their being created in the first place.

Even more public than the palaces of the rich and noble were, of course, churches whose naves were thronged daily both during times of Mass and at other hours during the day. The crowds who came to San Miniato al Monte in Florence, for example, would have walked on a representation of the zodiac in the pavement of the nave, set there in 1207 at the building of the church. This zodiac has the usual twelve signs, but at its centre is not a picture or symbol of the earth, as one might expect from a pre-Copernican vision of the universe, but a bright circle with petal-like rays emanating from it – clearly a representation of the sun. Such a heliocentric cosmos, however, is no precursor of later discoveries, but a *mundus* with Christ at its centre, reminding us that Christ and the sun were frequently identified, and because of its relationship with the other astrological symbols in the church, Fred Gettings has referred to it as 'much more than a complex foundation chart, and more than merely the spiritual hub of a sophisticated wheel of symbols'. For the church contains a richness of symbols and images relating to the stars which are linked to one another, the zodiac providing both an initial, or initiatory resting-point and a focus for the rest of the symbolism.

But zodiacs are not the only astrological symbols used in public buildings. The outer walls of the Palazzo Ducale in Venice bear sculpted images of the planets, dating from the mid-fourteenth century, and a chapel in the Tempio Malatestiano in Rimini has figures of the planets done in relief by Agostino di Duccio a century later. Inside and out, then, these buildings presented for public viewing a variety of astronomical-astrological images which served as constant mementoes of a relationship between earth and other levels of being, humankind and spiritual entities, whether angelic or demonic, which widened people's horizons beyond the purely material and confirmed their particular role in the universal scheme of things, devised and maintained by God. Nor, one must remember, were these images and their relationships the produce solely of learned minds, for these edifices were constructed and their decorative details set in place by skilled artisans who may have lacked the extensive book-learning of those who commissioned their work, but certainly understood the complexity and significance of the images they fashioned and painted. Experience of astrology was therefore not limited to relatively small groups of people in Mediaeval society, but was available to all, enshrined indeed for the majority in the heart of that institution which expressed most suspicion of it and sought, often diligently, to condemn and excise those parts of it which she considered especially dangerous to the health of the soul. [10]

II

Astrologers at Work c.1500–c.1600: The Stars in an Age of Reform

Paint and stone, however, were not the only media through which astrology could impinge on people's consciousness. Until the mid-fifteenth century in the West, written learned culture was scribal, which meant that books were relatively few, open to serious corruption as mistakes were incorporated into a text which was copied and re-copied in different places at different times by people whose individual levels of comprehension, health, attention to the task in hand, or dependence on the intelligibility of the person dictating from a copy perhaps itself corrupt, were bound to be variable. 'Publication' of such books was therefore slow and indeed the word 'publication' itself under such circumstances implied that the text was read aloud and heard rather than being perused in silence by an individual using his or her eyes to look at a written text. But between 1436 and 1440, Johann Gutenberg had established a press of moveable letters, and in 1452 produced a copy of the Bible, printed not written, and so initiated an extraordinary change in the way literature might be made available and an explosion in the number of items, long and short, weighty and ephemeral, which, because of this greater number, stood a better chance of surviving and thus transmitting their contents to a literate public. These contents, too, were likely to be marred by fewer mistakes as the resulting book depended upon one master copy rather than versions from multiple hands; and while printed books obviously benefited the *literati*, (that is, those who could read and understand Latin), they also provided an impetus to compose and publish in the vernacular – translations from Latin works, for example – for the benefit, not so much of those who had no Latin at all, but of those who would welcome immediate acquaintance with the volume's subject matter. Pictures and drawings, too, which would otherwise have taken a long time to produce were now, by this new process, easily copied and, with the addition, let us say, of a few verses, could provide an illustrated book appealing to scholars and non-scholars alike. Blockbooks, such as the *Biblia pauperum praedicatorum* ('A Bible for Poor Preachers') were popular between c.1430 and 1470 among those with responsibilities but not enough learning; and a compilation such as Guy de Marchant's *Le Compost et Kalendrier des Bergiers* ('A Confection and Calendar for Shepherds') contained a calendar, elements of popular astrology, recipes derived from folk medicine, didactic verses on vices and virtues, a vision of Hell, and prayers, mostly in French with a few pieces in Latin, items in verse and prose, and many illustrations, and was clearly aimed at a readership which had scarcely existed before the advent of printing presses opened it to the novel pleasures of this combination of diverse elements. [1]

Another big change, actually pre-dating the printing press by several decades but with equally important implications for the history of astrology, was the invention of the mechanical clock. Time before this had been measured by the position of the sun or moon or stars, by the sounding of church bells, or by devices such as the water-clock or marked candle. All these, however, give the impression that time is intimately connected with human relationships rather than governed by impersonal numbers, that it operates within the discretion of individuals rather than moving of its own accord, regularly, ineluctably, without necessary reference to human beings. Time, indeed, was rather a puzzle. As St Augustine said, 'I know perfectly well what it is, provided no one asks me, but if I am asked what it is, and try to explain, I am in a quandary.' But by the late fourteenth century a word for 'clock' had entered various European languages, and large public devices with striking mechanisms, such as the astrological clocks of Münster and Prague were on show, the former in 1408, the latter in 1410. [2] A mid-fourteenth-century clock in St Albans was designed specifically to help astrologers by calculating for them the movements of the sun and moon, the changing position of the planets, and the advent of eclipses. Richard of Wallingford who designed it wrote a detailed essay on its construction, *Tractatus Horologii Astronomici*, which makes clear its astronomic-astrological purpose:

> Proposition 7: Given that a planet traverses a definite part of the zodiac in an integral [number of days] or even [that it covers] the whole of the zodiac and some additional parts, to find the number of rational parts in which a wheel should be divided up into teeth, so that it may carry the planet over the circle of signs in accordance with its mean motus, doing so by means of another wheel divided according to times.

So, too, the clock designed for the Ducal Library in Pavia in 1381, which housed the seven dials of the Primum Mobile, the moon, and the other five planets apart from the sun, along with a dial for the fixed feast days of the Church and another for her moveable feasts. The effects of these and so many other similar time-telling devices which quickly became fashionable accessories in civic and aristocratic buildings all over Europe were to sharpen people's awareness of time by dividing it visibly into regular segments, some long, some short, and thus gradually divorce both day and night from their relationship with liturgical hours. One might say that this was a secularisation of time which suggested that, time being mechanised and made regular independent of divine or human institutions, the movements of the stars and planets were also mechanical, like those of a clock, and therefore *accurately* predictable. This was a possible riposte to the old complaint that astrologers' calculations were not dependable; and to imply that, if the universe worked according to strict, measurable movements, the influences of both stars and planets were equally fixed and predictable – a nod, at least, in the direction of astral determinism. For the astrologer, the clocks' practical use was to save a great deal of time he would otherwise have spent in calculation – as John North puts it, 'An astrologer who had ears to hear the striking of a tower clock, or who had access to a clock, preferably with a dial, no longer had any need to make an observation of the heavens to fix the time of birth' – while for the populace in general, the sight of these often highly elaborate structures acted as a reminder, subliminally perceived no doubt, that every activity here on earth was governed by the stars and planets who, it seemed, regulated time in the most orderly and now noticeable fashion. The prestige of astrology, therefore, as the available interpreter of these movements, regulations, and influences was likely to be enhanced rather than diminished in public consciousness. [3]

At least, so one might have thought; but in fact the quarrels, disagreements, and hostilities between supporters and opponents of astrology continued more or less unabated as the fifteenth century slipped into the sixteenth, and the wave of Classically-inspired 'modernisation' known now as the Renaissance gained purchase and momentum. Part of the perceived problem with astrology was its long-standing association with magic. At the end of the fourteenth century, for example, a learned Italian physician, Antonio de Monte Ulmi, (floruit 1384–90), produced a book entitled *Liber Intelligentiarum* ('Book of [Angelic Entities called] Intelligences'), although he himself preferred to call it *De occultis et manifestis* ('Hidden and Plainly Apprehensible Things'). The book deals with Intelligences and their constellations, the twelve hierarchies of angels related to the signs of the zodiac, and the ways in which both Intelligences and angels affect human beings, some Intelligences specialising in temptations to sin, and all subordinate Intelligences connecting themselves with newborn children at the behest of the chief Intelligence of the sign in the ascendant at each individual birth. Antonio then explains that these Intelligences are, in fact, fallen angels and the zodiacal spirits, good angels, before going on to discuss the astrological conditions appropriate to the appearance and summoning of spirits. Here, of course, we have entered the realm of magic, and Antonio raises both theoretical and practical questions to which he provides answers for the magician. Are the spirits likely to be furious at being summoned? (Yes). Why do they appear visibly to some people and not to others? (Because the spirits decide to arrange it so). How do they appear? (By preference in water and highly polished surfaces undisturbed or clouded by rain or wind). Next, after discussing the different fumigations proper to divers types of spirits, Antonio talks about images, the construction of which according to astrological principles we have noted earlier. A successful magician, he says, is born under the constellation proper to his science, from which set of influences he will derive his gift, his firm faith and will, and a knowledge of the tricks and deceptions commonly used by spirits to elude or frighten their invoker.

Antonio's work must not be taken as mere theory. His book contains images of the twelve signs of the zodiac, which he says he himself tested at Bologna and Padua – that is, in the making of magical talismans – and found them wonderfully effective; and as far as we can tell, his career as physician-astrologer-magician suffered no check or danger from the authorities. Such apparent tolerance, (and he may have been known to the Holy Roman Emperor and the rulers of Mantua and Padua, none of whom would have put up for long with any suspicious or dubious character), depended on the good will of Church and state, and upon the astrologer in question not stepping over the mark. In July 1441, however, two English clerics, Richard Bolingbroke and Thomas Southwell, were accused of doing just that. They had cast a nativity (birth horoscope) of King Henry VI – not the only one, for others from the same period exist – and were arrested, along with the Duchess of Gloucester and a witch, on charges of conspiring to bring about the King's death. Astrology and magic here go hand in hand, as is made clear in an account of Bolingbroke's execution:

> A certain cleric, one of the most notorious in the whole world in astronomy-astrology and the art of necromancy, Master Richard Bolingbroke, was arrested and publicly, in the cemetery of Saint Paul's, with his magic vestments and waxen images, and a very large number of other pieces of magical apparatus, he sat in a tall, high-backed chair so that what he had done could be seen by everyone. Afterwards he was hanged, drawn and quartered, and his head placed on London Bridge. This Master Roger was one of the most remarkable clerics in the whole world … and after his death many people mourned him very much indeed [4]

That last comment is noteworthy. Astrology-cum-magic, it seems, was by no means unpopular, even if its practice might, on occasion, turn out to be dangerous. But treading the line was difficult and would almost always evoke opposition from some quarter, as can be seen in the case of Marsilio Ficino (1433–99). Ficino – a man self-conscious about his lack of height – 'Lofty as you are,' he wrote to Cardinal Jacopo of Pavia, 'yet you from afar seen Marsilio, so near the ground and insignificant', (*Letters* 2.54) – was one of the principal Italian scholars of the day, a renown which caused Cosimo de' Medici, effective ruler of Florence, to appoint him to lead his re-founded 'Platonic Academy', a learned society for the discussion and propagation of new ideas, and to commission him to translate into Latin manuscripts of the entire surviving works of Plato, which would thus be made fully available to the West for the first time. In *c.*1460, however, a copy of the *Corpus Hermeticum* was brought to Florence by a monk from Macedonia, and Cosimo was so excited at the prospect of being able to read works by Hermes Trismegistus, a sage, it was said, older even than Moses, that in *c.*1462 he told Ficino to stop work on Plato and translate the *Corpus* instead, a task the young man performed in only a few months. His success had been foreseen, said John of Hungary in a letter to Ficino, by two astrologers who claimed, 'that you were going to revive the ancient philosophical teaching in accordance with a particular configuration of the heavens'. (*Letters* 7.18). Ficino himself would probably have been sceptical, since he had no time for judicial astrology or for certain types of astrologer. 'I am composing a book,' he wrote in 1477, 'on the providence of God and the freedom of human will, in which I refute, to the best of my ability, those pronouncements of the astrologers, which remove providence and freedom.' (*Letters* 3.20). [5] Still, he conceded there could be such persons as true astrologers, but they had to be good, not wicked men (*Letters* 4.10), and in a letter to one of the great opponents of astrology, Giovanni Pico della Mirandola, Ficino had no difficulty in recording a reply he made to a question from Lorenzo de' Medici about the reasons for greatness in human beings. Had he (Ficino) found any hidden cause for it?

> A configuration or harmony of the heavenly bodies which portends a safe and easy life is so different from one which promises glory and pre-eminence in virtue that very rarely can they coincide, if ever. Furthermore, there are daemons, like secondary stars, in the

airy region of the heaven which is closest to us. Of these daemons, it is the higher that are like stars, and there are also lower ones. Both are guardians of human beings: the higher for those who are outstanding, and the lower for those who are ordinary. Now the lower daemons, like humans, are moved by human emotions but are especially affected by pride and envy. So they are aggrieved that the people entrusted to the more exalted daemons are openly acknowledged to be of higher worth than those entrusted to themselves. For this reason they do not want outstanding people to rule, to prosper, or to live. Therefore they stir up a great many of their own crowd everywhere against them and, what is more, they put beasts and even the elements in their way. (*Letters* 7.62). [6]

The mention of *daemones* here by no means implies 'demons' or evil spirits, as can be seen by their being divided into higher and lower types. Nevertheless, Ficino's use of the term carries with it a certain ambiguity because while in Neoplatonic philosophy a *daemon* could be regarded as good until it was proved bad, in Christianity a *daemon*/demon was irredeemably bad, and it is by the simple, though not entirely consistent device of variation in spelling that Ficino sought to differentiate between the two. Thus, in his *De vita libri tres* ('Three Books About Life'), composed originally as three separate treatises between 1450 and 1489, *daemon* appears seventy-two times, on most occasions favourably as mediators between humankind and the spirits of the stars and planets. Book 1, *De vita sana* ('The Healthy Life'), deals with melancholia or depression, and how to treat it pharmaceutically; Book 2, *De vita longa* ('Long Life'), describes how one should go about living for many healthy years; Book 3, *De vita coelitus comparanda* ('Obtaining Life from the Heavens'), is quite different and deals with astrological magic, the creation of talismans, and various other magical operations. Now, the order of these books, as Remo Catani suggests, may well have been carefully calculated to mislead readers into thinking that the third one flowed naturally and harmlessly from the first and second; but of course it does not, and Ficino quickly found himself the subject of a complaint to Pope Innocent VIII, which it took him nine months of intensive lobbying to counter successfully. Book 3, then, discusses how human nature attracts 'gifts from the celestials', absorbing the spirit of the universe through the rays of the sun and Jupiter; the relationship between our characters and bodies and the signs and stars, and how these last may be used via medicine to our benefit; how to acquire celestial power through the use of images, again making use of stellar rays, and how to recognise what sort of character is influenced by which particular planet:

Astrologers are of the opinion that images intended to attract the favour of the gods have a power through which they change, in some fashion, the nature and behaviour of the person who wears them. They restore him (they think) for the better, so that he transcends [circumstances] as though he were someone else, or at least keep him in good health for a very long time. But harmful images (they say), have against their wearer the power of [a dose of] hellebore which has been taken over and above what medicine prescribes and the patient can withstand – that is to say, a power which is poisonous and deadly. But they say that images which have been fabricated and directed against another person, aiming to ruin him, have the power of a bronze concave mirror so accurately situated that, once it has gathered together and reflected rays directly back at him, they reduce him to ashes if he is close by, and if he is at a distance their force dazzles him and makes him blind and dizzy. Hence has arisen the story or belief which thinks that people, animals, and plants can be paralysed by the action of the planets, or waste away to nothing because of the devices of astrologers and acts of poisonous magic by magicians. For my part, I do not really understand how images exert power upon any object which is not close to them, but I imagine they have some on the person who is wearing them. In my opinion, however, they do not have the kind of power many people claim they do – and it arises from the material which is used to make them rather than the figure depicted on them – and (as I have said before) I very much prefer medicine to images …

Now, some people regard the spirits of the stars are wonderful powers belonging to celestial objects; others regard them as inferior but god-like entities [*daemones*] who are servants to this or that star. So they think that whatever the spirits of the stars may be, they are grafted on to statues and images in just the same way as when demons [*daemones*] sometimes take over human bodies and use them to speak, move, move other things, and perform marvels. They believe that the entities [*daemones*] who inhabit the cosmic fire are inserted into our bodies via fiery humours or humours which have been set on fire, and likewise via ardent dispositions [*spiritus*] and emotional states of this kind. Likewise, they think that the spirits of the stars can be inserted into images made of materials compatible with those spirits by means of rays caught at the right moment, suffumigations, lights, and vigorous chanting, and can work wonders upon the person wearing them or standing near them. I think this can indeed be done through the agency of demons [*daemones*], not so much because they have been confined in a particular material as because they take pleasure in being worshipped.

The Arabs record that when we fabricate images in the correct ritual way, if our spirit has been concentrating fully upon the work and the stars through our imagination and emotional state, it is conjoined with the cosmic spirit itself and with the rays of the stars, through which the cosmic spirit acts; and when it has been conjoined in this way, it is also [conjoined] in the motive [for creating the image], with the result that the particular spirit of any star – that is, a power full of vital force, especially one which is compatible with the spirit of the operator at that moment – is poured into the image by the cosmic spirit through the rays. (3.20).

That Ficino was rather nervous about the way this book might be received is shown by the defence of it (*Apologia Quaedam*) he tacked on to the end, addressed to three of his friends. 'Someone will say: Marsilio is a priest, isn't he? Indeed he is. What business then do priests have with medicine or, again, with astrology? Another will say, What does a Christian have to do with magic or images?' Ficino's answers are scarcely convincing. To the first, he says that Chaldaean, Persian and Egyptian priests were physicians and astronomer-astrologers, and to the second that when he spoke of magic and images, he was not approving them but merely recording them during an interpretation of Plotinus. As a defence it is rather feeble and, to judge by the trouble he was in afterwards, it clearly did not work.

In gauging Ficino's theories and his subsequent retreats, however, we need to be aware of the context in which he was writing. The second half of the fifteenth century was awash with astrological predictions, many of them from Churchmen, dealing not only with what one may call the usual foresights of war, famine, eclipses, and disease, but, much more controversially, with the date of Jesus' birth and the nature of the sudden darkness which attended His crucifixion. [7] Thus in 1465 Johann Müller (1436–76), later known as 'Regiomontanus', who gave astrologers a new and elaborate set of houses and auxiliary tables which were considered to be more accurate than those hitherto in use, was asked by Jakob von Speyer, Court astrologer to Federico d'Urbano, to calculate the year of Christ's birth from 'a conjunction of the superior bodies by the laws of the stars' which was taken to signal the imminence of a great event. Giovanni Pico della Mirandola (1463–94), a fierce critic of astrology, referred in 1494 to:

tall stories which these silly presagers tell about the birth of Jesus Himself, saying that He was born while the first aspect (which is what they call the decans) of Virgo was in the ascendant. Albumasar [Abū Ma'shar] writes that in this [decan] there is a beautiful virgin holding two ears of corn in her hand and suckling a child, and that a certain tribe calls him 'Jesus'. In consequence, they think the miracle of the incarnate Word is confirmed by the science of astrology which has discovered the Virgin and Jesus among images in the sky. As far as I am concerned, I do not feel all that much resentment towards them on the grounds that they usually support their teachings with 'evidence' such as this, thinking we shall readily accept it in order to corroborate *our* teachings. The truth of Christianity, next to which even the important things [said] by philosophers are virtually fables, does not need these exercises in imagination.' (*Disputationes* 5.14).

Pico was close to the Dominican religious reformer and self-proclaimed prophet Girolamo Savonarola (1452–98) whose opposition to astrology was savage. He viewed it as heretical on the one hand and Satanically inspired on the other, and denounced virtually the whole science in a 'Treatise Against Astrology' published in 1497. The only part of it he was prepared to allow was that part we now call 'astronomy':

So observational astrology is a real branch of knowledge because it seeks to recognise effects from real causes such as eclipses, the conjunctions of planets, and similar effects which always necessarily follow from their causes. Likewise, one can call 'art' or 'branch of knowledge' the astrology which seeks to recognise certain natural effects which more or less always proceed from how far or how near the sun is to us, or the conjunction, opposition, and movements of the moon. But divinatory astrology which rests entirely on effects which proceed indifferently from their causes, especially in human affairs which proceed from free will and only on rare occasions proceed from their causes, is completely worthless and cannot be called either an art or a branch of knowledge.' (Part 2, chap.3).

Savonarola's hostility was, perhaps, only to be expected, given the fierce determination of his mission to reform society and the Church, and his view that astrology trespassed unwarrantedly upon the province of the divinely-inspired prophet by claiming to see into the future with the help of mere observation of the position and movement of heavenly bodies rather than as the result of a special grace conferred by God. But while Savonarola had a deeply personal influence on Pico, Pico's dismissal of astrology sprang from his own, not Savonarola's convictions, and one of those convictions was one he expressed more than once – that astrology was no more than a figment of astrologers' imaginations:

> The arrangement [of stars] the astrologer observes is not celestial but one which he him-self has constructed in the sky according to worthless, imaginary rules based not on Nature but upon the opinion of astrologers. God, the father of human beings and of the gods, did not make images in the sky, nor signs, divisions, *antiscia, dodecatemonia*, houses, and other things of this kind used by astrologers. The astrologer, however, deceiver of humankind and defamer of the gods, has fabricated them in the sky, and so it is no wonder if this art can have no sure foreknowledge of anything.' (*Disputationes* 3.19).

The implications of these and other attacks for university curricula, decision-making by political or sometimes religious authorities, and half the procedure of medical diagnosis were potentially serious. Part of the problem, as we can see from the above passage from Savonarola's treatise, was the increasing divergence in many learned quarters between 'astronomy' and 'astrology', or at least those parts of astrology such as the 'judicial' discipline which claimed to make specific predictions in relation to particular events, and which were now labelled 'superstitious' in consequence. Jean Calvin, for example, while willing, like Savonarola, to allow a very limited value to certain aspects of astrology, treated the rest of it with contempt – notice his emphasis on astrology as a 'superstition', an appeal to his Protestant readers to associate astrology with Catholicism which was regularly having the word 'superstition' thrown at it in polemical literature – although it is interesting to see how he sometimes exaggerates and makes mistakes in his keenness to make his points:

> From ancient times, people's minds have been invaded by something like a wasting, con-tagious disease – the silly eagerness to predict from the position of the sky and the stars what is going to happen to someone and what will be each person's inborn fate. In what follows, I shall prove (with God's help) that this is a Satanic superstition. Undoubtedly there is universal agreement that it is deadly to the human race, and that it was rejected and repudiated for a long time. But now it is being revived in such a way that many people who think themselves cleverer than anyone else hold it in great esteem and are almost bewitched by this superstition … This is what happens when people resort to it. Some are so depressed and so ill that they devote all their energy and effort to what is a ludicrous fraud, and torture themselves with immense labour and immense misery for no reward at all. I know that some titles give a false appearance of respectability to this ridiculous superstition. No one will say that the art of astrology is not noble in its principles and that it is not worthy of the highest honour. So they call themselves 'mathematicians', wrapping themselves up in this title as though it were a tunic, and by this label imply they are prac-titioners of the liberal arts …
>
> All earthly bodies and (let me speak in general terms) all inferior bodies have some affinity with the course of the stars and hence derive some kind of distinguishing charac-

teristic ... Natural astrology will show that these inferior bodies are affected by the moon. Oysters and shellfish grow and shrink with the moon and, similarly, bone marrow is governed by phases of the moon. From this authentic art of astrology, doctors judge when it is opportune to draw blood, and prescribe medicines and pills, and other things of that sort. Therefore it must be said that the condition of human bodies has some affinity with the stars. All this comes under the heading of 'natural astrology'. But certain imposters, under the cloak of this art, have been willing to go further and have devised another type of astrology which they call 'judicial'. This is based on two things in particular: first, a thorough knowledge and understanding of people's natures and physical appearance; and secondly, investigating what is going to happen to each individual and what each is going to do or suffer during his life ... Let us posit two men with entirely different natures, whose wives are equally different. Each conceives at exactly the same moment. We shall see what is the result. The children are affected more by their heredity than they are by the influence of the stars, in spite of the fact that each was subject to the same influence ... Lest I be longwinded in running after every possible example, let me mention just this one. Sixty thousand men are killed in a single battle. I am not looking for any bigger disasters. This one has enough deaths in it, so this one will do. My question is, did all those men conjoined in one and the same loss of life have the same horoscope? (*Advertissement contre l'astrologie judiciaire*).

Little of what Calvin was saying here is original, of course. St Augustine for example, had drawn attention to the astrological problem of twins centuries before. But in addition to hostile scholars' raking over and renewing old arguments, and pursuing others more subtle and more mathematically-based, there was also the unhappy experience of Simon de Phares for professional astrologers and their supporters to consider. Simon was Court astrologer and physician to the French King, Charles VIII, and had, according to his own account, travelled widely in Europe and Egypt in pursuit of knowledge. This may or may not have been true, but by 1488 he had settled in Lyons where he acquired both a great reputation as an astrologer and the patronage of the new King of France. Public and royal acclaim, however, did not necessarily offer him immunity from criticism or official hostility. In 1491 he was forbidden by the Archbishop of Lyons to practise astrology – a condemnation which need not have been personally inspired, as some have suggested, for astrology was suffering a theological backlash whose effects we have seen already. Unable to work in Lyons, Simon transferred himself and his working library to Paris where he hoped the Parlement would resolve the situation. But the Parlement delayed and dithered and submitted his case to the theological faculty of the Sorbonne for consideration and advice. It took the theologians there a good ten months (1493–4) to deliberate and produce their decision, which was that while 'astronomy' might be permitted, and certain predictions based on planetary conjunctions (such as those of Jupiter and Saturn) might be legitimate, divinatory astrology (such as genethliacal or judicial) was entirely to be condemned, and that eleven of Simon's books should be burned, as containing objectionable matter.

On the basis of this report, the Parlement refused to entertain Simon's request to be allowed to practise either as an astrologer or as a physician – the two, indeed, went together, so he could hardly have been permitted the one profession and forbidden the other – and, on the further basis of exaggerated and somewhat curious interpretation of his career in Lyons, ordered him to be arrested in April 1494. The wording of the Parlement's condemnation makes it sound as though Simon was a relapsed heretic, a very serious matter, and since Charles VIII had openly and, indeed, officially supported his petition to live and work in Paris, the Parlement could not escape criticism (did it wish to?) that in condemning Simon, it also condemned the King. Perhaps fortunately for the Parlementaires, Charles VIII was absent in Italy on a military expedition, and in the meantime Simon managed to weather the storm and emerge in 1498 victorious from the struggle. Simon's arrest, however, had had effects. It had been a warning-shot over the bows of practising astrologers, and those with somewhat unorthodox views, such as Giovanni Pico della Mirandola and Marsilio Ficino, found themselves obliged to retreat and retract. Ficino, for example, in spite of his defence of astrology, (mingled, as we have seen, with astral magic), published a curious work, *Apologia*, in 1498, addressed to the College of Cardinals, in which he used astrology to prove that Savonarola was not a divinely-inspired prophet but a man possessed by a devil. He expresses himself in such a way that he gives the impression that, even if he had not actually given up his belief in astrology, he was now prepared to be extremely circumspect in his public pronouncements and seem, at least, to have rejected his former opinions. It is notable, too, that the teaching of astrology in Paris was badly affected for twenty years after Simon's condemnation, in spite of the defences of the science composed in the 1490s by Giovan Battista Abioso and Gabriele Pirovano. Both were acutely aware of the criticisms offered by Pico in his *Disputationes* and both sought to defend the integrity of the science against charges that astrology was essentially blasphemous, and that the inaccuracies of its data, particularly in the hands of unlearned practitioners, made it both worthless and ridiculous. There was also strong support for the use of astrology in medicine by a Spanish physician, Jerónimo Torrella, whose book *De motu caelorum* ('The Movement of the Heavens'), published in 1496, was addressed 'not only to medical but also to educated men', and took the fight for respectability to the critics' camp, although to be sure on grounds which virtually everyone was prepared to agree were valid.[8]

Religious controversy as well as a more general scepticism about its claims and the quality of its observations and calculations, however, continued to dog astrology as the sixteenth century produced a series of upheavals usually termed the 'reformation'. But the new Protestants were as divided in their opinions of the science as ever Catholic theologians had been and were. Luther, for example, dismissed it more or less out of hand. During a conversation in 1543 he gave four reasons for disbelieving its validity: (i) astrologers' predictions about the weather never agree; (ii) if a child is said to be affected by astral rays, why is it that only those belonging to stars above the horizon at his or her birth produce effects, and not all stars equally? (iii) why are astral effects said to happen only when the child has come out of the womb? Why not in the womb as well? (iv) The twins Esau and Jacob were born under one star, so why were their natures so different? This last, derived from St Augustine, had become something of a chestnut in astrological controversy. Indeed, Luther's objections to the science were not in the least novel, although they may have been sharpened to some extent by his friendship with Philip Schwarzerd ('Melanchthon') who, while being a Protestant theologian, saw no necessary conflict between religion and astrology. 'I don't care a fig about your astrology,' Luther told him on one occasion and on another, remarked to one of his students in Wittenberg, who had spoken in praise of astrology:

> Astrology is not a science because it has no principles and proofs. On the contrary, astrologers judge everything by the outcome and by individual cases and say, 'This happened once and twice, and therefore it will always happen so.' They base their judgement on the results which suit them and prudently don't talk about those which don't. [He observed in 1537] I regret that Philip Melanchthon adheres so strongly to astrology. He's very much deluded, for he's easily affected by signs in the sky and he's deceived by his own thoughts. He has often been mistaken, but he can't be dissuaded.

Melanchthon, however, was perfectly willing to put into print his views on astrology, which were as conventional in their advocacy of the science as were those of Luther in opposition to it:

> It is true that temperaments are governed and made various by the position of the stars ... Moreover, there is a power in the stars to awaken inclinations, which cannot be adequately attributed to the temperament. But let us not argue this with over-much subtlety. Let us say what is indeed the fact of the matter, that often the basic causes of chance events are temperament and the position of the stars ... Most of the noteworthy qualities in the temperament are both good and bad and have their origin in the stars. Take the case of children, who inherit physical characteristics from their parents and therefore look somewhat like them; and yet some have strong, healthy bodies and are full of life, while others are listless and unlikely to live long. Most notable causes of this kind of dissimilarity are to be found in the stars. Consequently, the stars are often the fundamental causes of chance events. John Albert, Archbishop of Magdeburg, has the moon in Aries in the sixth house. This is a sign of ill health. The moon is flanked by Mars which is also in Aries, and by Saturn which is in Taurus, and the sun and moon are in opposition. These are clear signs of unremitting, severe bouts of illness.
>   There are not only clear signs of ill health in the stars, but of fortunate or unfortunate tendencies in the arts, too, or in other activities which are an intimate part of people's natures in their pursuit of the highest honours, engagement in battle, and the dangers of life. Musicians become melodious, poets become charming, public speakers dazzling, when the sun, the moon, Venus and Mercury are fortunately placed for them. On the other hand, those who are hindered by Saturn and Mars become ghastly and uninspired ... So both bitter and happy natures are rightly attributed to the stars, and many events agree with their natures. But some of the extraordinary things which happen in the case of princes should be attributed rather to God who, since He sustains or changes empires, often guards princes in a particular way which cannot be attributed to the stars ... Nature governs a great deal, but not everything. One must not remove God from astrological

governance, but declare that God moderates many tendencies which originate with the stars, and pray that He help those which are good and suppress those which are bad. (*Initia doctrinae physicae*, Book 2).

Notice the emphasis on the supreme controlling hand of God: as Erasmus Reinhold, Rector of the University, expressed it, 'He decorated the sky with wonderful writing.' While this is entirely to be expected – it would be foolhardy for anyone at this period overtly to suggest that the cosmos and its governance was divorced from God's dominion – there was a particular reason for Melanchthon's underlining the religious dimension of astrology, namely, that the University of Wittenberg, so closely associated with both Luther and Melanchthon and so much a centre of reformist theology, was also at this time a magnet for scholars and students of astrology. There were at least forty-six of them, ('almost without number', as one disgruntled critic of astrology exaggerated), and while their opinions on the science itself differed, they were generally agreed that astrology was a valid and important method of interpreting the will of God as exhibited through His celestial writing, and that, in order to secure it against the attacks of critics such as Pico della Mirandola who denied it was a science at all, its principles and methods should be based on those of natural philosophy, empiricism, and logic. It was an ambitious programme, and went far beyond Melanchthon's personal attempts to emphasise the importance of free will and of a much more precise observation of stellar and planetary movements in relation to events in the sublunary world. Caspar Peucer, for example, Melanchthon's son-in-law and Professor of Mathematics at Wittenberg, proposed that casting the horoscopes of famous people of the past, whose subsequent actions, health and character were now well-known, could be used to correct the methods of horoscopic interpretation currently in use, and so provide not only a better understanding of famous individuals, but also a more refined and accurate instrument for future interpretation. Nor would this be all. The more astrology could be given a universal validity by tying it to accurate observation of extraordinary natural phenomena, the more likely it was that at least some powers or signs then regarded as 'occult', (that is, hidden or not presently explicable), could be understood when the connection between astral causes and terrestrial effects was more plainly comprehended:

Every age has recognised particular or decisive days as indicators of exceptional weather, and of fertility or sterility – not in a heedless, haphazard or superstitious way, but because it would have been recognised that the signs they exhibited were consistent with one another, even if the causes were not understood, [causes] which consensus of opinion agrees come from the sky. Moreover, any divination of this kind is is devoid of superstition and sanctioned by experience. It has sprung from things which have happened consistently over very many years and have been produced by material causes … [and] although not everyone has a sight of them, and although not everyone understands them even after they have been investigated, and although they may not give rise to similar effects in any given year, nevertheless they derive from the power of the constellations (*siderum*) and an effectiveness and combined action which is amazing and almost divine.

The stars (*astra*), he also acknowledged, acted upon and caused changes in the fundamental elements of which everything is made, but when it came to things manufactured by human beings, the stars had no effect.

Catholic defenders of astrology, or at least judicious commentators on it, were equally careful to distinguish between what might be considered valid and what invalid. The Jesuit Martín Del Rio (1558–1608), for example, divided astrology into four: *Revolutions*, dealing with the prospects for war and peace, food and want, or disease; *Nativities*, which relate to a person's expectations through life; *Elections*, answering specific questions about an immediate activity – travel, business, and so on; and *Making Images*, connected with the manufacture of talismans. This last he condemned out of hand, so that left him with the first three and with regard to these he came to the following conclusions:

1. The astrologer who does not depart from general principles and those guiding premises which are immediately relevant can, in accordance with the canons of his art, predict with accuracy general events many years, perhaps, before they happen unless either his calculations or his instruments deceive him.
2. The first type of astrology is not superstitious if it merely expresses an opinion together with a fear that the opposite may also be true.
3. Astrology which goes further than these three types and predicts that something is bound to happen is definitely illicit and superstitious. All divination of this kind is uncertain and useless and unworthy to be called an 'art'.
4. Those physicians who make diagnoses according to the position of the moon and the other planets in the signs of the zodiac, (e.g. which sickness will happen to someone, and which arrangement of stars will enable a cure to be found), even if they are not superstitious are certainly harmful to the patients. So are surgeons who examine wounds in the same way and take into account the day on which the wound was made and the stars which preside over them … and thus pronounce the wound either mortal or curable.
5. The kind of divination which inquires particularly into secret matters [*occulta*] such as thefts, treasure, virginity, etc. is pernicious and plainly forbidden under any kind of law.

It is noteworthy that in general terms the Jesuit and the Calvinist are in agreement. Some aspects of astrology – those close to astronomy and meteorology – may be allowable, but those which attempt to predict the future are at best uncertain, and those belonging to the craft of medicine and surgery or magic are beyond the pale. Little wonder, then, if proponents of two religious extremes could find themselves in broad harmony on this question, thereby summarising in their own persons several tendencies which had been gathering speed for many years past, so that an unorthodox scholar such as Ficino should have been compelled to retract his favourable attitude towards astral magic and preach against it.

Two questions, however, preoccupied people perhaps more than any others: what was the relationship between human free will and determinism; and could future events genuinely be predicted with some degree of accuracy? The latter lay behind the constant use of astrologers by rulers, both ecclesiastical and secular, and their officials; the former intrigued theologians in particular. Let us take this first question first. Do people behave the way they do because they decide to, or because they are under some kind of compulsion? (These days we might re-phrase the question to ask how far people's behaviour is or is not genetically programmed). The Italian Humanist, Giovanni Pontano (1429–1503), raised the Emperor Nero's supposed bloodthirstiness as a topic for this kind of discussion:

> Nero Augustus was renowned for his singular cruelty. But who will refuse to acknowledge the sensible notion that during Nero's procreation the temperature of the semen and the humours from which the foetus was formed was to a high degree malign, and that the stars made a very real contribution to that situation, with the result that Nero was inclined and excited to savagery by his very own nature? Therefore the causes of this situation were (a) Nature herself which gave rise to Nero, because she had been badly leavened; and (b) the evil condition of the stars and their unnatural configuration, which either followed the humour – that [malign] humour indeed! – which had been affected contrary to the proper order of things, or affected him by its own malignity and distortion.

Nevertheless, he concludes, Nero acted cruelly because he wished to do so, not because of any astral influence or intrinsic corruption of character. So does this principle apply across all cases? Bishop Luca Gaurico (1476–1558), a skilled and eminent astrologer, opined that a combination of Venus and Mars in the twelfth house made Francesco Filelfo burn 'with every kind of lust for virgins, and especially boys', ('boys' meaning males between the ages of fourteen and twenty-two). Likewise, the French physician Antoine Mizauld (1510–78) apparently suggested in one of his poems that bitchy queens were 'made' by being born under the rising of the Pleiades:

> Those who are born under the rising of the Pleiades bring back the following behaviour. They follow Bacchus and Venus. They will always be conscious of the way they look and their elegant expression. Extravagance and allurements please them, and a golden pin secures their curly hair. In addition, their remarkable, gentle good looks shine with rosy mouths. His [sic] attire is like that of a girl and his chest is fragrant with Assyrian myrrh. Wines, amusing jokes, and impudent language please him. They always love caustic witticisms and words dipped in poison, and anxiety awakens new fires. But lust reigns victorious in his heart. He is no less ambitious and struggles for honours; but they quickly regret the kind [of person they are] very much indeed. Consequently, they want to make themselves look like a woman, to polish their hairy arms and legs with hollow pumice stones. It is never enough for them to love; they want to be seen to love.

Pontano agreed. If Saturn and Mars were in opposition in a man's horoscope, he said, that determined – i.e. issued a judicial decision or decree – that the man would be a *cinaedus*, a sexually passive male, and would acquire a bad reputation as a result. At first glance, then, it appears that these astrologers are arguing the case for astral determinism in a debate which almost mirrored the contemporary theological arguments about whether some of humankind were predestined by God to be saved and some to be damned, or not. But in

fact the astrologers were consciously looking back, not forward. Pontano's astrology owed
much to Firmicus Maternus, an important manuscript of whose complete *Mathesis* had
been found by Poggio Bracciolini in 1429 at Monte Cassino, and that of Antoine Mizauld
to Manilius's *Astronomica*. Moreover, there was a tendency among astrologers – and we
have seen this in Peucer's work – to look first at a person's character and habits, and
then read those back into a horoscope. Girolamo Cardano (1501–76) who compiled two
books of such examples drawn for past and present individuals – *Liber de exemplis centum
geniturarum* and *Liber duodecim geniturarum* – may have been the best known exponent
of this practice, but Luca Gaurico was even more explicitly interested in improving future
astrological interpretation by re-reading the past, and five of the six books of his *Tractatus
Astrologicus* (1552) are devoted to nativities of famous persons, mainly past but a few present,
including Popes, cardinals, bishops, secular rulers, scholars, musicians, and artists, the aim
of this study being, in the words of the book's extensive title, to provide 'similar examples
whereby each person who casts a horoscope dealing with everyday affairs will be able to
predict the future, in as much as experience has created the technique through various
occurrences, and an example points the way [to interpretation]'. It was an endeavour surely
destined to failure for, as I have observed elsewhere:

> Hamstrung to a certain extent by its dependence on antique models and commentators,
> early modern astrology fell back on stereotypes, injecting a kind of pseudo-life into them
> by the occasional reference to its own period, but interpreting the genethliacal horoscope
> in very much the same way as its *fons et origo*, Claudius Ptolemy, had done before. [9]

Meanwhile theologians debated the nature of free will and tried to disentangle those
aspects of the occult sciences which might be regarded as legitimate from those which
were either 'superstitious' (to use the jargon of the time) or illicit and condemnable.
Nothing was left out of account. Even medicine, as we have seen, came under attack from
some authorities for its use of and reliance on astrological calculation and interpretation.
But while everyone agreed that astronomy-meteorology was acceptable and astral magic
was not, and although quite a number of people were willing to put trust in genethliacal
horoscopes, judicial astrology bore the brunt of extensive and frequent criticism, since
this branch of the science intruded most evidently upon the vexed no-man's-land of
predestination and free will. How ironic, therefore, that the rulers of the Church as well as
of the state should be willing to make use of it, or at least to accept and treat as valid its
predictions and conclusions in matters relating to themselves or their personal interests.
Antonio Campanezzo, for example, addressed Pope Julius II with a prediction that the
Pope's reign would be long and successful, while admitting that it was not actually legally
permitted to cast the Pope's horoscope. He need not have feared, however, because Julius
was happy to seek the advice of astrologers anent a favourable moment for his coronation,
the foundation of the castle of Galliera, and the erection of his own statue at Bologna.
His successor to the See of St Peter, Leo X, heeded Gaurico's advice and had his palm
read over the course of three days by the Prior of the Convent of San Francesco, and was
so taken by the abilities of the astrologer Franciscus Priulus, (who wrote a book on the

Pope's nativity and therein revealed, from his study of the stars, a large number of secrets Leo thought no one else knew), that he remarked that astrology, once extinct, had been revived in this extraordinary man. Nor did writers hesitate to address Leo with astrological terminology. 'Under your auspices, o Leo,' wrote Girolamo Fracastoro in his medical poem *Syphilis*, 'the malign influences of the stars have vanished, and Jupiter has not poured upon us any but the propitious fires of his purest rays.' No wonder, then, if Pope Leo founded a chair of astrology at the Sapienza, the University of Rome. A decade later, Pope Paul III, whose accession to the Papal See had been predicted twice by Gaurico, in 1529 and 1532, called Gaurico to the Papal Court and made him Bishop of Giffoni, although Gaurico was not the only astrologer to receive the Pope's encouragement and patronage. Then in 1543 he was consulted by Paul anent the most favourable moment to lay the corner stone of a new building, and three years after that dedicated to him a lengthy work dealing with astrological medicine, *Super diebus decretoriis axiomata* ('Axioms on Critical Days'). Paul attracted similar works from others and was praised fulsomely by Vincentius Franciscucius Abstemius for restoring the reputation of astrology which had lain for so long in the darkness and barbarism of past centuries.

But Popes were by no means the only rulers to live in a whirl of astrology and benefit from its predictions. As Claudia Brosseder notes, 'Obsessively commissioned analyses of enemies were the order of the day', and secular princes of all kinds and religious fealties either had astrologers attached to their Courts or consulted individual practitioners *ad hoc* in an effort to gain advantage over rivals and enemies by catching a glimpse of the future. Even a prince hostile to astrology for most of his life, Johann Friedrich of Saxony, finding himself by ill fortune incarcerated in Innsbruck, felt driven to ask an astrologer when and whether he would eventually be released. The Emperors Maximilian I, Ferdinand I, Charles V, and Maximilian II all had Court astrologers, as did Johann, Margrave of Küstin, who consulted his, an otherwise little-known pupil of Peucer, Petrus Hosmann, on the eve of his taking part in a tournament against Prince Elector August of Saxonia. Indeed, so trusting in the accuracy of astrological prediction was the Margrave that he did not reserve his consultations for minor matters, but even planned his contribution to an Imperial campaign against the French King, Henri II, according to the advice he received from Hosmann. Imperial, royal, princely, and noble betrothals, weddings, and coronations, not to mention births and medical treatments, were arranged to coincide with favourable aspects of stars and planets. The astrologer Jean-Baptise Morin discreetly concealed himself in the chamber of Queen Anne of Austria so that he could record the precise moment when the Dauphin (later Louis XIV) was born and so be able to cast the young prince's nativity; and we have a very full account of the progress of the fatal illness of the Duke of Milan in 1494, recorded in the letters of several of his close relatives who expressed themselves in astrological terms:

> [The doctors] have not yet ordered that he be given the medicine, because they are waiting for Nature to take its course. So far this has been very successful. [They also want] to let the present conjunction pass because, as the moon is in conjunction with Mars, this would have a negative effect upon the medicine.

Even the most trivial details were not necessarily too small for astrological consideration. Leonora of Aragon refused to pray until her astrologer told her to imitate the kings of Greece, who always obtained their desires when they prayed during a conjunction of Jupiter and the moon; and every day Leonello d'Este would choose what to wear by choosing a colour which would draw down favourable influences from the planets.

But astrologers were not confined to Papal, royal, or noble Courts. The municipality of Basel employed its own astrologers, and astronomer-astrologer-mathematicians were appointed to Chairs in more or less every university from whose studies and cloisters the war against and the struggle for astrology was waged unrelentingly throughout the sixteenth century, never more avidly, perhaps, than during the early decades when argument and counter-argument raged about whether a conjunction of all the planets in Pisces, forecast for February 1524, would or would not result in a devastating and destructive deluge. 'No' was the opinion of Agostino Nifo, Professor of Mathematics at Padua, and Michael de Petrasancta, Professor of Metaphysics at Rome; 'Yes' was that of Johann Carion, Court astrologer to the Elector of Brandenburg, and a Dominican, Sebastiano Constantini of Taormina, a Professor of Sacred Theology and a mathematician; 'Yes and no' was that of Pedro Cirvelo, Professor of Theology at the University of Alcalá. In fact, Cirvelo was the nearest to being right, as 1524 started by having an unusually dry February, the time of the conjunction, before developing heavy rains in March, which lasted until November, a long succession of wet weather which caused clergy and people to unite in prayers for a break to save their grain and crops.

In spite of these and other scholarly wrangles, however, it is evident that astrology was a vibrant science and one which was valued highly by Church and state, high and low, alike. Theologians might fulminate and astronomer-mathematicians criticise or dismiss, but there were as many defenders as critics among all these disciplines and astrology was by no means inclined to surrender its outstanding role as the science which both underpinned and explained the visible universe. Nor was the growing gap between its astronomical and astrological sides sufficiently wide to cause the majority of people adhering to the primary importance of the former to dismiss the latter as altogether worthless. 'What powers do the heavens possess?' asked Pietro Angelo Manzoli, an Italian poet, in c.1534. 'The stars rule the world and change everything. The stars create and govern everything on earth. The astronomer teaches this, and it is commonly held opinion.' (*Zodiacus Vitae* 11.428–31). Manzoli was quite right. It was.[10]

12

Questioning the Macrocosm
c.1600–c.1700:
The Pursuit of a 'Sane' Astrology

Francis Bacon wrote in his *Proficience and Advancement of Learning* (1605):

> The ancient opinion that man was Microcosmus, an abstract or model of the world hath
> been fantastically strained by Paracelsus and the alchemists, as if there were to be found in
> man's body certain correspondences and parallels, which should have respect to all varie-
> ties of things, as stars, planets, minerals, which are extant in the great world.

Bacon may have objected that the analogy was false, but almost any physician, of whom
Paracelsus was merely a notorious and unorthodox example, would have told him
otherwise. For the effects, real and supposed, of constellations and planets upon the entire
physical universe in even its tiniest atom provided a sine qua non for medicine, which even
the most major realignments of the astrologers' cosmos had not been able to displace.

The primary such realignment was, of course, that of the Polish astronomer, Mikolaj
Kopernik (1473–1543) whose *De revolutionibus orbium caelestium* ('The Revolutions of
Heavenly Bodies') was ready in manuscript by late 1529 or early 1530. Copernicus did not
originally intend to publish it, for fear of being ridiculed by other scholars, but its thesis
leaked out and slowly spread through Europe, being discussed, for example, at the Papal
Court in 1533, until finally, after much urging, Copernicus allowed it to go to a printer in
Nuremberg in 1542. The book was dedicated to Pope Paul III whose interest in astronomy-
astrology was well known, and Copernicus reassured the Holy Father that he had taken the
trouble 'to read again all the works of philosophers accessible to me to find out whether any
of them did not by chance express an opinion on the motion of the spheres different from
the hypotheses accepted by professors of mathematical [*i.e. astrological*] science'. Needless
to say, they did. Cicero, Philolaos, Herakleides of Pontos, and Ekphantos, for example, all
thought the earth was not stationary, but moved, and hence he began to reject Ptolemy's
argument for its being immobile and to question the reasoning of those who agreed with
him:

> That is why I wish Your Holiness to know that, in turning my thoughts to another prin-
> ciple for calculating the motions of the spheres, I was prompted by nothing other than
> the observation that in their studies of them the mathematicians [*astrologers*] are not in
> agreement with one another. Above all, they have so many doubts as to the motion of

the sun and the moon that they are unable even to determine and calculate the constant magnitude of the tropical year. Next, when determining the motions both of those two and of the other five planets they do not use the same assumptions and premises … [They adopted] a great many assumptions which are obviously inconsistent with the fundamental principles of uniformity of motion. Nor did they discover (or they failed to deduce) the most important thing, namely, the system of the universe and the established order of its parts.

With this as preface, then, Copernicus proceeds to his principal propositions: the centre of the earth is not the centre of the universe; the centre of the universe is the sun around which all other spheres, including the earth, revolve; and the apparent motion of bodies in the sky is actually produced by the movement of the earth:

> In the middle of everything dwells the sun. For who would put this lamp in another or better place in this most beautiful place of worship, from where it can illuminate the whole at one and the same time? At any rate, certainly people not inappropriately call it 'the lantern of the world', others 'the mind', others 'the governor'. Trismegistus [calls it] a visible god.

It had taken Copernicus a long time to come to these conclusions – from at least 1514 when he refused the invitation of Pope Leo X to reform the calendar, because he had not completed his computations of the movements of the sun and moon, although he had actually set down his main propositions a decade earlier in an essay, *Commentariolus*, not printed but probably circulated in manuscript. Copernicus's work was revolutionary, of course, (in more senses than one), but he had built it on the endeavours, not merely of those Greek and Roman authors whom he cites in his preface, but of Mediaeval Islamic astronomer-astrologers, and Europeans such as Nicolas Oresme (*c*.1323–82) who debated whether the earth could move or not before deciding it probably did not, and perhaps also Celio Calcagnini (1479–1539) who came to the opposite conclusion. Indeed, the idea of a rotating earth and a stationary heaven seems to have been current in the fourteenth century, since Jean Buridan (1295–1358), in his *Quaestiones super libris quattuor de caelo et mundo* ('Questions on four Books about the Sky and the World'), remarked that many people thought it possible the earth moved on its axis while the sphere of the stars remained motionless. Copernicus's conclusions were therefore the latest in a lengthy line of argumentation and any controversy they generated also had a long history behind it. Nor did Copernicus entirely overturn Aristotle's cosmology; rather, he reapplied its categories, as J.D. North has pointed out, by retaining the notion that, while the earth was displaced from the centre of the universe, its motion was still constant and circular, like that of the other planets:

> For my own part, I think that gravity is nothing but a certain natural striving implanted in the parts by the divine providence of the Maker of all things, so that they may come together in the form of a globe, in unity and wholeness. It is believable that this striving

is present also in the sun, the moon, and the other bright planets, so that they keep the resultant round shape which they show, even though they make their circular movements in many different ways. [1]

One consequence emerging from the publication of Copernicus's theory was a desire – not new, for we have seen signs of it already – to separate the observational aspects of astronomy-astrology from the interpretational and predictive, and one of those most keen to forward such a disjunction was Georg Joachim von Lauchen ('Rheticus'), Professor of Mathematics at Wittenberg and one of Melanchthon's circle, whose enthusiasm for the theory had stimulated Copernicus into submitting his manuscript for printing. Rheticus and Erasmus Reinhold, a colleague of his from Wittenberg, did much to propagate Copernicus's ideas through their own publications, although one should note that neither of them altogether threw over astrology in the course of their eagerness for the new system. Rheticus, for example, still asserted in 1557 that the stars were threatening the Turks with ruin because a watery triplicity of planets was about to yield to a fiery, and Reinhold, while puffing *De revolutionibus* in 1542, maintained the traditional astrological notion that eclipses and conjunctions foretell great political change. Moreover, we should not run away with the idea that Copernicus had proposed cosmological theories which were unanswerable. The Jesuit Christoph Clavius (1538–1612), a mathematician and an astronomer, and the person responsible for the reform of the calendar adopted by Pope Gregory XIII, which is now in general use, rejected heliocentrism and suggested a cosmology which kept earth at the centre of the universe while making adjustments to the Ptolemaic system, including the speculation:

Beyond this world, or rather beyond the empyrean heaven, no further body exists, but there is a kind of infinite space, so to speak, in the whole of which God exists in His essence – as the theologians affirm – and in which He could make an infinite number of worlds, better even than this one, if He wanted.

Others, of course, were not so subtle or scholarly, but dismissed the idea out of hand:

We find among us frantic minds which are always losing their way with abstruse opinions and, forgers of monsters, cannot row on the calm waves of a sea we all share. Such, in my opinion, are these writers who think it isn't the heavens or the stars which dance round the earth, but the earth which each natural day makes a perfect orbit. (Du Bartas 1578)

The whole earth stays in one spot, immobile, leaning upon itself. It doesn't run off upwards in a straight line, or to the right or to the left, and neither does it sink downwards ... [But] imagine that the sky is standing still, its structure unmoving, its flames inactive, and that the earth is rotating in a circle, its perpetual orbit enveloped in 3 x 8 hours of shadows and light ... The earth would veer first west, then east, and at the same time with vast uproar it would shake all the churches, houses, and cities along with their wretched citizens, and unexpected destruction wrought by sudden collapse would overwhelm them. (George Buchanan 1591)

But if Copernicus presented astrologers with major alterations to their picture of the cosmos – alterations they noted but tended either to ignore in favour of retaining the Ptolemaic system, or to adapt to the needs of their science – Galileo Galilei (1564–1642) changed the picture still further, principally through his *Nuncius Sidereus* ('Starry Messenger'), published in 1610, in which he proffered to his readers the results of his observations with his telescope – the existence of four moons belonging to Jupiter, and the phases of Venus, which supported heliocentric theory since these phases appeared to indicate that Venus moved round the sun. Naturally, the Church took an interest. In fact, Christoph Clavius was asked to let the astronomers of the Roman College look at Galileo's work and confirm his observations if they could. Clavius's own reaction turned out to be ambiguous, not necessarily because he intended it to be so, but because there is disagreement among modern historians about how to interpret his most opaque sentence: 'Since things are thus, astronomers ought to consider how the celestial orbs may be arranged in order to save these phenomena.' Was he calling for an adoption of Galileo's (not to mention Copernicus's) discoveries and propositions, or merely for a tweaking of the Ptolemaic system? In fact, by mid 1611 both Clavius and the Roman Jesuits accepted what Galileo had told them, and so the astronomical part of the science was set to diverge quite noticeably from the astrological unless the astrological found a way of accommodating these new and future observations.

This divergence, however, was not altogether obvious to everyone during Galileo's lifetime. One Jesuit called him 'the lynx-eyed astrologer', and Galileo himself practised astrology both for himself and his daughters as well as wealthy clients such as Christina of Lorraine, Grand Duchess of Tuscany, who asked him to review her sick husband's horoscope, and he was happy enough, in the fashion of the time, to employ astrological language, incorporating recent discoveries, in the dedication of his *Nuncius Sidereus* to Cosimo II of Tuscany:

> Indeed it appears that the Maker of the stars Himself, by clear arguments, admonished me to call these new planets by the illustrious name of Your Highness before all others. For as these stars, like offspring worthy of Jupiter, never depart from his side except for the smallest distance, so who does not know the clemency, the gentleness of spirit, the agreeableness of manners, the splendour of the royal blood, the majesty in actions, and the breadth of authority and rule over others, all of which qualities find a domicile and exalta-tion for themselves in Your Highness? Who, I say, does not know that all these emanate from the most benign star of Jupiter, after God the source of all good? It was Jupiter, I say, who at Your Highness's birth, having already passed through the murky vapours of the horizon, and occupying the mid-heaven and illuminating the eastern angle from his royal house, looked down from that sublime throne upon your most fortunate birth and poured out all his splendour and grandeur into the most pure air, so that with its first breath your tender little body and your soul, already adorned by God with noble ornaments, could drink in this universal power and authority.

Galileo also taught astrology to medical students at the University of Padua, and indeed in 1604 was denounced to the Inquisition in Padua for drawing up nativities which seemed to specify a determined rather than a possible outcome. None of this, of course, suggests that Galileo sought to cloak his observational discoveries with the pretence that they were somehow astrological rather than astronomical. It merely means that he was a man of his time, excited by and slightly in awe of the possibility that Aristotle and Ptolemy had not been infallible and that the astronomical-astrological science taught in universities might stand in need of radical revision. Nor does Galileo's use of astrological language in his work for noble patrons necessarily imply he accepted every item of astrological theory. Clearly he did not. But the fact that he and so many others in his position were prepared to employ that language in their dedications and poetry does show that it was more or less ubiquitous, and suggests that it constituted less a literary fashion and more a mode of intercourse, one to be treated with some degree of seriousness because it was allied to a science which constantly pushed at the boundaries of knowledge. [2]

But how radical was the problem posed for consideration and debate by post-Copernican and subsequently post-Galilean intellectuals? For the medical students to whom Galileo was teaching the elements of an astrological craft essential to their future expertise as physicians, there was apparently no radical change at all; and similarly it may seem that Galileo did not to hesitate to use standard astrological language and images, courtier-fashion, in his dedications and addresses to useful and important patrons, until one realises that, as we have just seen, not only was he actually incorporating the discoveries he made with his telescope into his flattery of the Medici family by relating Jupiter to Cosimo and its 'new' moons to Cosimo's children, but that he also used up-to-date observational techniques to improve his interpretation of Cosimo's horoscope. When it comes to medicine, however, these incorporations did not on the whole take place, although improvement in the mathematical bases of the science inevitable filtered through in course of time. Not that the practice of medicine entirely escaped waves of criticism directed with increasing frequency at its astrological foundation, even from doctors themselves. During the 1530s, the German astrologer Johann Pfarrer (de Indagine) observed:

The stupid herd of doctors we see these days, growing proud and imposing their exalted status on us, are aware of the precept they have read in their medical authors, that no one should be treated according to astrological advice. But actually, the person who is ignorant of astrology is so far removed from medicine that he ought not to be called a doctor but an imposter. Nowadays, indeed, it has come to the point when you will find scarcely one or two in a hundred who really know how to judge the right time to prescribe any sort of medicine. Still, perhaps this is not surprising. Which would be quicker for them – to occupy themselves in astrology, or read their Galen and Hippocrates? (*Chiromantia*, Book 4, preface)

So, too, François Rabelais (*c.*1495–1553), himself an expert astrologer, criticised the abuses of the science – 'Go on and learn the rest, also the rules of astronomy. But leave divinatory astrology and Lully's art alone I beg you, for they are frauds and vanities' – but asserted that the wonderful network of cosmic influences enveloping the human body not only enabled doctors to know when they should let blood and administer certain medicines, but helped to explain the origins and workings of intangibles such as imagination, reason, judgement, and so forth. Indeed, he published a series of almanacs between 1533 and 1541 designed to provide physicians with just this kind of practical and theoretical knowledge. Criticism, (and in Rabelais's case, mockery), therefore had its place but also its limits. At more or less the same time, Heinrich Cornelius Agrippa published his *De occulta philosophia* (1531) in which he reviewed the importance of astrology to understanding how the planets and zodiacal signs govern and influence the human body and character, while an essay circulated under the name of Paracelsus (1493–1541), entitled *Of the Mysteries of the Signs of the Zodiac: being the magnetical and sympathetical cure of diseases as they are appropriated under the twelve signs ruling the parts of the body*. [3] This is, in effect, a book of astral magic describing and illustrating talismans to be made and worn in cases such as headaches, epilepsy, palsy, gallstones, gout, 'leprosy', cramp, and so on; and whether it is a genuine work by Paracelsus or not, it illustrates very well that willingness to unite medicine, magic, and astrology, which was common enough among sixteenth-century doctors. Why should such a marriage work? Because, as the writer explains in his preface:

> Characters, letters, and signs have several virtues and operations wherewith also the nature of metals, the condition of heaven, and the influence of the planets with their operations, and the significations and properties of characters, signs and letters, and the observation of the times, do concur and agree together. Who can object that these signs and seals have not their virtue and operations, one for infirmities in the head, being prepared in his time, another for the sight, another for gravel in the reins and stone, etc; but every one is to be prepared in his own proper time, and helpeth such and such infirmities, and no other, as drink is to be taken within the body and not otherwise. But all this is to be done by means, by the help and assistance of the Father of all medicines, our Lord Jesus Christ, our only Saviour. (94–5) [4]

Obeisance to God in these circumstances was, of course, essential, but it was also a heartfelt acknowledgement of perceived realities. For astrology posed, after its own fashion, questions which preoccupied the sixteenth and early seventeenth centuries: what is the cosmos like, how does it work, what exactly is humankind's place in it, what is the relationship between the physical universe and other potential universes, physical and non-physical, how far is it permissible or desirable, under God, to investigate these questions, and are there dangers, damaging or lethal to humankind, in undertaking speculations and investigations of this sort? Research of this kind sped those who undertook it into new and exciting, but strange and potentially perilous territories, an intellectual activity which mirrored, in its way, the journeys of exploration which were being ventured by small numbers of hardy (and perhaps foolhardy) individuals cooped up in tiny ships upon vast, largely uncharted seas, many of whom died on the way or later in unfamiliar regions inhabited by strange beings whom their exploration had uncovered; and while astrology might be likened on the one hand to merchant boats plying a welcome trade along well-known routes, on the other it might be compared to those ships of searching curiosity some of whose endeavours opened sights and experiences hitherto unknown or only guessed at by land-locked theoreticians.

Medical astrology was perhaps more like the former than the latter kind of craft. This is partly because it was tied to medical theory – itself a tradition which was fossilised in the shape of Hippocrates and Galen, even though some extraordinary changes, not least in anatomy, were under way during the sixteenth century – and partly because the association of plants, minerals, and the human body with stars and planets was by its nature a fixed and limited system. If the association is real, one has said virtually all there is to say about it by making and expounding the connection. Room for changing or expanding one's interpretation is more or less circumscribed. Hence Johann Kepler, a mathematician and astronomer rather than a doctor, was able to say:

> Because it concerns diseases, doctors know this universal truth – when the air is disturbed, our bodies are disturbed as well. Therefore, when there are indications that winter is going to be changeable, it means there will be a lot of illness, especially at the beginning of the following March and May. But when the summer seems to be turbulent, the following autumn will be somewhat rotten because of the conjunction of Saturn and Mars, and in some places there will be plague, borne by a poisonous wind. I have particularly noted any days which are harmful because of frequent [*astrological*] aspects. These stir up diseases in suitable subjects and are more difficult for those already sick. When someone is already ill in bed, or when defective humours are already seething in his body, then one should certainly no longer disregard the configurations of the moon with the planets, and especially with the sun, as I have done up till now. For, to be more specific, they displace and move the humours, as that great Chaos of humours, the Ocean, bears witness; and I should not deny that it is useful to consider the stars while one is making up some medicine. The doctor spares someone seriously weakened by illness from further harm, if he can, when the moon is revolving in a powerful aspect. For any aspect is, in itself, a natural purgative, and if anyone needs to use strong purgatives, let him choose to do so during powerful configurations, so that each may affect the other. What is more, the whole business of climacterics [*critical periods during which some great change takes place*] depends on the return of the moon and its configuration with the planets, and it is in vain that one seeks an explanation for them anywhere else. (*De fundamentis astrologiae certioribus*, chap.67)

Interestingly enough, the sixteenth-century English herbalist and surgeon, John Gerard, made no reference to either stars or planets when composing his *Herball* (1597), whereas Nicolas Culpeper in the seventeenth took particular note of them,[5] but the difference is that Gerard's book is a catalogue of plants in the herb garden belonging to the College of Physicians in London, of which Gerard was Curator. It offers descriptions and illustrations of plants, along with what we should call botanical details, and their 'virtues', which is to say the inner power they possessed to cure illnesses or indispositions. None of these, however, is linked to astral influence. Culpeper, on the other hand, is a physician writing with other physicians in mind, and therefore the planetary connection of the plants he is describing is of major importance. Occasionally, there were physicians who had their doubts. François Repard, a physician from Bruges, for example, published a book in 1551 in which he maintained that times for bleeding and purging and bathing should not be determined by the stars. But his scepticism was rebutted the following year by Pierre Haschard, a physician from Brussels, with particular reference to the wonderful remedies invented by Paracelsus; and in 1584 Giovanni Paolo Gallucio defended the bases of astrological medicine in his *Four Books on Getting to Know and then Curing Diseases from [knowledge of] the Position of Heavenly Bodies*, a work which he followed in 1588 with *The Theatre of the Universe and of Time, in which their most important parts are described, the reason for measuring them given, [and] the principles of astrology pertaining to medicine determined* – a title which sufficiently explains the contents. By slight contrast, a glimpse of the effect new astronomical discoveries might have on medicine can be seen in Cornelius Gemma's *Two Books on the Divine Characteristics of Nature, and the Rare and Extraordinary Sights, Causes, Signs, and Properties of Things in every Part of the Universe* (1574). Herein, while issuing a condemnation of judicial astrology in particular, Gemma defends astrological medicine and notes that the large number of *lusus naturae* to be found both in Europe and in newly-discovered islands are, according to physicians, attributable at least in part to the influence of the stars; and it is worth remarking that Gemma was inspired to seek explanations for these and similar phenomena by the discovery of a 'new star', a supernova which burst out in the Milky Way at the beginning of November 1572. Lines of communication between astronomy and astrology were thus kept open, as in the case of Giovanni Magini, Professor of Mathematics at Bologna, who wrote a treatise on the proper use of astrology in medicine – *The Astrological Explanation for and Use of Critical or Decisive Days, and in particular How to Recognise and Cure Illnesses from a Recognition of the Heavenly Bodies* (1607) – and was both a very competent astronomer, (publishing in 1588 a book entitled *New Theories of the Celestial Spheres*, in which he took a post-Copernican stance), and, by their invitation, an astrologer to the leading men of his university town.

Paracelsus, whose medical theories and practice were defended by Pierre Haschard, came from a medical family and had accumulated a great deal of practical experience in both herbal lore and surgery during extensive travels all over Europe and Russia between 1517 and 1524. These experiences engendered in him a desire to reform medicine in such a way that it would combine academic theory with actual practice of treating sick people – the two were usually split in late Mediaeval Europe, physicians rarely tainting their hands by putting them on a patient, and surgeons knowing little of the theory of medicine – but when Paracelsus settled in Basel and tried to put his ideas into practice, the University was outraged and saw to it that he stayed in the city for scarcely more than ten months. Combining theory with practice, however, was only one of Paracelsus's innovations. He saw astronomy-astrology as one of the four pillars of medicine, along with philosophy, alchemy, and virtue, and in a series of books, *Paragranum* (1529–30), *Opus Paramirum* (1531), and *Astronomica Magna* (1537–8), he argued that each celestial body contains an invisible power which he called 'astrum', and that since every created being or thing has both a material and an 'astral' component, the greater whole (macrocosm) affects and is affected by the individual part which mirrors it (microcosm). Hence, illness and health alike are governed by astral influences, and the purpose of any medical remedy is to restore equilibrium between the 'astral' part of the human being and the 'astrum' which is most relevant to the case in hand. Therefore a physician must, along with all his other expertise, be a skilled astrologer so that he can find out and understand the cause of an illness and thus know how to treat it. This may sound familiar, but Paracelsus's concept of 'astrum' was actually new and the notion that it must be balanced by other sources and receptors of power is equally peculiar to him. His insistence upon the necessity for astrology in the theory and practice of medicine thus differed in kind as well as in intention from that of his more traditional contemporaries.

Doctors, then, were not necessarily stuck in the rut of an intractable tradition, although tradition was more the norm than innovation. Nevertheless, the Paracelsian philosophy of medicine seeped into medical practice in spite of the suspicions and anathemata of many in positions of influence, as may be seen in the case of Simon Forman (1552–1611), a somewhat louche individual who practised medicine in London and promoted Paracelsus's ideas in his many writings, and ran foul of the College of Physicians more than once for practising without a licence. Like Paracelsus, Forman relied on experience to advance his career as a doctor – he first learned about drugs while apprentice to a grocer, and learned astronomy-astrology while earning his living as a schoolmaster – and, like Paracelsus, was openly and deliberately dismissive of other physicians who did not agree with and follow his way of diagnosing illness and treating a patient. Unlike Paracelsus, however, he himself developed no new theories or techniques as a result of that experience, and when he was examined by the College of Physicians in c.1596, it was recorded that '[he was] found very ignorant …. He then acknowledged … that he only practised physic by his skill in astrology, in which art being again examined, he was found not to understand the common principles of it'. One notes, then, as did Barbara Traister, that the College criticised him, not because he was an astrologer, but because he was, in its eyes, an incompetent astrologer – as well the College might, in its own estimation, since doctors regularly used astrology to determine the appropriate days for blood-letting and so on, and, less regularly, to help them in diagnosis. If Forman was an inadequate astrologer, it followed he must be an inadequate physician and thus a constant danger to his patients. In spite of this, however, Forman managed to build up a thriving medical and astrological practice, and between 1596 and 1603 was consulted as an astrologer more than 8,000 times, mainly on medical matters.

In contrast to the College of Physicians, the seventeenth-century astrologer, William Lilly, held Forman's abilities in high esteem and remarked that 'had Forman lived to methodise his own papers, I doubt not but he would have advanced the iatromathematical [*medical-astrological*] part thereof very completely'. Forman himself was quite clear that astrology was central to the practice of medicine:

No man ought to study *physicus* except he be well sene [*versed*] in astrology. For it is impossible to give a just judgement of the state of a disease only by seeing the urine, or by feeling the pulse or sidge [*stool*], by the sight of any urine or seeing the sick. For a man by astrology will say more by a question demanded for the state of the sick for his sickness and disease, and touching life and death, or curing of the party hurt or sick, than ten physicians that shall see the urine or speak with the sick body. For many are sick that know not their own disease, nor the cause nor deepness thereof; and by astrology it is to be known and by no means else, because the bodies of men are subject to diseases according to the influence of the heavens.

Forman's way of proceeding with patients illustrates the central part played by astrology in his medical treatment. First, he asked the patient his or her name and current address; next he drew a horoscope, (and since this was to be directed towards a specific question at a specific time, he was clearly practising a form of judicial astrology, just the type which attracted most criticism from reforming practitioners and sceptics alike). Thirdly, he read the chart, diagnosing from it the disease in point and foretelling the outcome, before finally prescribing appropriate medicines and treatments, and presenting his bill for immediate payment. We can see a general outline of the later stages of this procedure in a letter he sent to his pupil, Richard Napier. In it he answers Napier's query about how to treat certain patients who were troubled in mind:

> The way to help them is to purge the arteries, for they are spiritual diseases and proceed from the heart and brain. Therefore, after you have purged the body first of gross humours with feralogodon 2 or 3 [times], then must you purge the blood in the arteries when the moon is in Libra, Gemini, Aquarius, going to Capricorn, and in ascendance. But these parties [*patients*] in my opinion will have no remedy till [a] fortnight after Easter next, or thereabouts. They have overpassed their time.

Forman also treated a number of patients, not merely by bleeding and herbal or mineral remedies, but by the long-established creation of astral talismans whose efficacy owed more to magic than to medicine. He advocated the use of electrum, for example, (a mixture of two or more metals with apotropaic powers), to make a ring to help in cases of cramp and epilepsy and to ward off impending illness, and noted that an amulet containing St John's wort should be worn round the neck as an apotropaic against ghosts and madness. He designed many sigils – symbols of planets or zodiacal signs accompanied by words of power such as the names of angels or demons – which were intended to be worn, or engraved on precious metal such as gold to form a lamen which would then be carried about the person. He himself possessed one, and once thought he had lost it until he found it had slipped from the front to the back of his doublet; and we can see his designs for several of these sigils in the various manuscripts which streamed from his pen throughout his working life. They were not necessarily cheap; a gold lamen he designed for Jean Sherly in 1610 took four days to make and cost £4 13s 0d. If we wish to have some idea of what this means, we can look at the *Calendar of Patent Rolls* and see there that in 1590 one gunner was allotted pay of 12d per day and another half that. So the cost of Forman's lamen amounted to 93 days' pay for one gunner and 186 for the second. This use of magic, as we have seen, was by no means unusual and Forman had been studying the subject since the mid-1570s. He owned a number of magical texts and went beyond medicine in trying to evoke spirits in the manner of a ritual magician, although he noted he had no success therein despite his continual efforts until the summer of 1594 when he had a dream that Christ had shown him some magical diagrams. This seems to have opened his abilities, for thereafter he began to see spirits and communicate with angels; he recorded a conversation with the angel Raziel, for example, during which the angel told him that mistletoe 'belongeth to Jupiter especially, and Venus hath a part therein, and it ought to be gathered and administered in the hour of Jupiter, between the first quarter and the full moon, and best in May. It is good against the dropsy, being rubbed thereon; and after, rub the place with a red cloth'. [6]

Such divagations into magic were, of course, potentially dangerous in more ways than one. Heinrich Cornelius Agrippa (1486–1535) provides an interesting parallel with Forman. Not long after 1520 he became principal physician of Freiburg, even though he had no university training and continued to pursue a medical career – sometimes in the highest circles: he was at one point Court physician to the Queen Mother of France – in spite of hostility from various medical bodies. At the same time, he practised alchemy and divination in the form of geomancy (on which he wrote a treatise), as well as astrology which he both praised and demeaned in his letters to friends and clients. 'I predict these things to you,' he wrote to one, 'not by doubtful methods of conjecture, nor acting under the influence of mental perturbation contrary to true reason, but from true arts of vaticination, oracles, prediction, and foreknowledge.' To a Dominican who had asked him for an astrological opinion he remarked with notable acerbity:

> Judicial astrology is nothing more than the fallacious guess of superstitious men who have founded a science on uncertain things and are deceived by it. So think nearly all the wise; as such it is ridiculed by some most noble philosophers; Christian theologians reject it, and it is condemned by sacred Councils of the Church. Yet you, whose office it is to dissuade others from these vanities, oppressed, or rather blinded by I know not what distress of mind, flee to this as to a sacred augur, and as if there were no God in Israel ... [However,] lest you think me but denying you, and by a subterfuge avoiding trouble for a friend, I shall do all you ask me, to the best of my ability, having thus warned you first not to put more faith in these judgements than befits a Christian.

To another correspondent he was less forthright, but still condemned the science on the practice of which much of his income depended:

> Why do we trouble ourselves to know whether man's life and fortune depend on the stars? To God who made them and the heavens, and who cannot err, neither do wrong, may we not leave these things, content, since we are men, to attain what is within our compass, that is to say, human knowledge? But since we are also Christians and believe in Christ, let us trust to God our Father hours and moments which are in His hand; and if these things depend not on the stars, astrologers indeed run a vain course. But the race of man, so timorous, is readier to hear fables of ghosts and believe in things that are not, than in things that are. Therefore, too eager in their blindness, they hurry to learn secrets of the future, and that which is least possible (as the return of the Deluge) they believe the most. So also, what is least likely they believe most readily of astrologers, as that the destinies of things

are to be changed by planning from the judgements of astrology – a faith which, beyond doubt, serves to keep those practitioners from hunger.

When reading these semi-private thoughts of his, however, we should remember that they were written while Agrippa was fighting for recognition and patronage at the French Court, during which time he was clearly in grave difficulties, since his Protestant sympathies did not recommend him to the Queen Mother. He found it next to impossible to get the Royal Treasurer to pay his salary, and injudicious phrases from a letter to a supposed friend – 'using those astrological superstitions by which the Queen shows herself so greedy to be helped … [The Queen] should no longer abuse my talent by condemning it to such unworthy craft, nor force me any more to stumble through this idle work' – phrases the Queen saw, since the 'friend' was foolish or conniving enough to give her the letter to read, meant that initial royal favour quickly turned into royal displeasure. Court astrology therefore brought Agrippa little but trouble, and it is clear he despised many of his noble clients whom he regarded as both superstitious and frivolous. By September 1526 he had completed, but not published, an important work, *De incertitudine et vanitate scientiarum et artium atque excellentia verbi Dei* ('The Uncertainty and Emptiness of the Various Branches of Knowledge and the Arts, and the Excellence of the Word of God') in which he seemed to repudiate the occult sciences, arguing that they, and indeed virtually all human knowledge, are nothing in comparison with the excellence of God's word. This last, and this last alone, provides a sure and trustworthy foundation for learning and experience, and while we are permitted to philosophise, speculate, and debate on all manner of things, we should not put our faith in any conclusions drawn therefrom. Only divine matters are worth our trust and hope. So his repudiation of the occult sciences was not wholesale but partial, and *De incertitudine* turns out to be, in fact, a Protestant cry for a return to simple faith in the Bible, unencumbered by the intellectual subtleties of academic theologians. By 1528, Agrippa's personal circumstances had taken a turn for the better and, in the following year he published a number of theological pieces, a venture into print which may have encouraged him to publish *De incertitudine* in 1530. In harmony with its contention that study of the occult sciences was allowable, however, he went on to publish the first volume of his best-known work, *De occulta philosophia*, in 1531, (it received its final version two years later), and herein we find the extent of his long years of study in magic, divination, and astrology, studies which, unluckily for him, quickly generated accusations that he was a practising magician and a heretic, and lost him his lucrative position at the Court of Queen Margaret of Austria.

The *De occulta philosophia* devotes a great deal of space to planetary and astral connections with people and material objects or places: with the four basic elements (1.8), with the human body (1.22), and a broad range of these and other things (1.23–32, 48). They signify character (1.52); numerical tables akin to magic squares are assigned to them (2.22), and the distance between them is mirrored in musical scales (2.26). Close observation of celestial bodies is essential for working magic, especially when it comes to astrological talismans (2.29–52), and it is impossible to practise any kind of divination successfully without astrology (2.53). One must also know the names of the planetary governors (2.59) and of the spirits ruling over the zodiacal signs, the corners of the sky, and the elements (3.24); and one can discover these names from the disposition of celestial bodies (3.26) and by using the traditional methods of Kabbalists (3.27, 30).

Such overt and apparently enthusiastic revelation of the theory and techniques of magic inevitably garnered a wide readership at the same time as it incurred the anger of theologians. Debt, the death of his wife, hostility from both Court and Church, and his own undiplomatic responses to criticism ended with a spell in prison, and had it not been for the intercessions of Cardinal Campeggio and Bishop Everard of Liège with the Holy Roman Emperor (who had taken violently against him), he might well have suffered a far graver penalty. As it was, after yet more struggles with Church and state, he ended his life in exile from Germany, living on a pension from the Archbishop of Köln. Typical of the way his reputation was subsequently modelled and reported is a notice by André Thevet in *Portraits et Vies des Hommes Illustres* (1584):

At last, having betaken himself to Lyons, very wretched and deprived of his faculties, he tried all the means that he could to live, waving, as dextrously as he could, the end of his stick, and yet gained so little that he died in a miserable inn, disgraced and abhorred before all the world which detested him as an accursed and execrable magician because he always carried about with him as his companion a devil in the figure of a dog, from whose neck, when he felt death approaching, he removed the collar, figured all over with magic characters, and afterwards, being in a half-mad state, he drove it from him with these words: 'Go, vile beast, by whom I am brought utterly to perdition.' And afterwards this dog, which had been so familiar with him and had been his assiduous companion in his travels, was no more seen, because after the command Agrippa gave him, he began to run towards the Saône, where he leaped in and never came out thence.

Equally unfortunate, and for many of the same reasons, was the English scholar John Dee (1527–1609). At one period during his life he enjoyed equal fame abroad and notoriety at home, being employed by Elizabeth Tudor as an unofficial Court astrologer and having his extensive library destroyed by a hostile mob during one of his absences in Poland and Bohemia. Like Agrippa, he suffered from his enthusiasm for the occult sciences which, in his case, was taken to serious practical lengths. If it was his interest in alchemy which got him invited to the Court of Emperor Rudolf II at Prague, it was his extended series of conversations with non-human entities, seen and reported by his partner Edward Kelley, which turned him, in both official and popular eyes, into a magician; and underpinning both his alchemy and his attempts to understand the cosmos more clearly and more personally, (part of which attempts resulted in those 'angelic' conversations), was astrology, a science whose techniques he exercised with skill.

One can see in his diary how easily these came to him, as indeed they did to so many others of his generation and time. On 22 October 1580, he wrote that while he was pleading his own case in a law-suit he suffered 'a marvellous hoarseness and in manner speechlessness', which he explained by 'favourable ascension in Taurus. Mars in opposition to the sun and the moon in Taurus; and Taurus was in the sixth house of the radix, up to where Saturn makes a quartile aspect and now reflects very brightly on both sides'. While in Taurus, Mars and the moon influenced the throat and Saturn the chest – hence Dee's hoarseness and inability to articulate properly. In January 1582 he recorded that his three-year-old son Arthur and a little girl, Mary Herbert, were pretending to be married and calling each other husband and wife. 'I note this,' he said, 'because of Jupiter coming to the cusp of [*blank in ms.*] for seven hours, and Jupiter and the moon being in conjunction there the other day.' The birth of his son Michael in Prague on 22 February 1585 took place at 3.28 p.m. with Mars in the ascendant. Place = the sun. Pisces 3° 32' 39" while that of Theodore on 28 February three years later had 'Mercury ascending in his horoscope'; and when Elizabeth Tudor summoned him to Richmond Palace in November 1590, he was careful to mark the planetary positions on that occasion – Jupiter in trine of his radix, Venus almost in trine of the sun's radix, Mercury and Jupiter on the cusp ascending. Illnesses and accidents, too, were marked by astrology. On 1 January 1588, his son Michael tripped and fell while carrying a candle stuck on top of a stick, and the sharp end of the stick went through his eyelid next to his nose. The eye was treated with St John's wort and the boy slept well. 'The moon was separating [*from its aspect*], opposition of Mars radix which was Jupiter and Mars himself already almost in opposition of his radix in house 7. It would have caused a great deal of harm if Jupiter had not ascended to the very cusp.' In order to have produced these comments, Dee must have drawn a horoscope soon after the event, and applied horary astrology to find out why the accident had happened and what the outcome was likely to be – just the kind of astrology practised by Simon Forman for the benefit of his patients, and a good illustration of how normal it was for educated people, at least, to turn to astrology at a moment's notice, even for a domestic mishap. Similarly, when Michael became later 'became distempered in his head and back and arms', Dee drew attention to 'the planet Mars. Saturn, Mars, Venus beginning to cross the horoscope [*horizon*]'; and when Katharine, his daughter, had a serious nose-bleed occasioned by a hard blow on her ear, delivered by her mother, Dee diagnosed arterial blood, 'the moon being at the heart and in quartile the sun, applying to a square of Saturn'.

For Dee, however, the most important aspect of astrology was its association with magic. As early as 1555 he was imprisoned for over two months, charged with 'lewd, vain practices of calculating and conjuring' to enchant Queen Mary, and although the accusation was false and malicious, it served as a reminder that the combination of astrology with magic, particularly in relation to royalty, might prove dangerous for the practitioner. The basis for Dee's belief that the power of astral magic was genuine was traditional enough. He wrote in his *Mathematical Preface* (1570):

Astrology [is] an act mathematical which reasonably demonstrateth the operations and effects of the natural beams of light, and secret influence of the stars and planets in every element and elemental body at all times in any horizon assigned … [and] we also daily perceive that Man's body and all other elemental bodies are altered, disposed, ordered, pleasured, and displeasured by the influential working of the sun, moon, and other stars and planets.

But in investigating further the causes and workings of these influences, Dee became convinced that there was a hidden mode of being in Nature, which manifested itself in rays which filled the cosmos, the strength of each ray's power being determined by the kind of body from which it was emitted or through which it passed, and by the effects it produced; and since each ray was different, together they produced an extraordinary variety of harmonies and dissonances, sympathies and antipathies throughout the universe. This remarkable diversity was then 'perceived' by human senses and its outpourings coalesced 'within our image-sensing spirit, as though in a mirror, where they show themselves to us and work wonders in us'. (*Propaedeumata Aphoristica* 13 and 14)

Dee created a symbol both to embody this concept and to act magically upon anyone who chose to contemplate it and understand its significance. It is composed of a crescent moon piercing the disk of the sun which stands upon a cross representing the four elements, the whole being supported by two connecting half-circles, the sign of Aries. The complexities of this symbol, however, are enormous, as Dee himself tried to explain in his essay on it, *Monas Hieroglyphica* (1564), although he also offered a summary in a single sentence which can be read on the left of the printed version: 'There is in this monad whatever wise people seek.'

Dee's erudition, daring speculations, international reputation, and royal favour, however, did him little good in the end. The wardenship of a collegiate church in Manchester brought him only increasing poverty and strife with the College Fellows, and when James VI and I succeeded Elizabeth Tudor, Dee was battling once more, as he had been in his youth, with accusations of being 'a conjuror or caller or invocator of devils or damned spirits'. An appeal to the King to have him tried and so give him an opportunity to clear his name came to nothing, and in March 1609 he died in a poverty and obscurity brought about, at least in major part, by his lifelong adherence to the notion that astrology and magic could uncover a little more of the mind of God as revealed in the secret workings of His creation. [7]

Equally famous, and one much less fortunate in his end, if Dee's end can be called 'fortunate', were the Dominicans Giordano Bruno (1548–1600) and Tommaso Campanella (1569–1639). Bruno had an extraordinary imagination which enabled him to envisage many more universes than the one visible to us, and to make a number of daring proposals: that the stars are actually suns like our own; that the infinite universe is filled with a kind of pure air, (a demonstration, in his own terms, that Nature abhors a vacuum); and that because God is infinite, 'He excludes Himself from every limit, and every one of His attributes is one and infinite', a notion he extends by saying that 'God is *totally* infinite because His totality is in all the world, and in every part of it, infinitely and totally' – which comes close to saying that God is immanent rather than transcendent, a proposition theologically unacceptable. Bruno's astrological ideas were no less bold. If the universe is a physically homogeneous whole, he said, the sublunar world cannot be a reflection of the divine world – a flat contradiction of established astrological theory – and he was prepared to provide astronomical, as opposed to astrological, explanations for comets and the appearance of 'new' stars. The combative tone he often adopted in propagating these notions can be gauged from one of his best-known dialogues, *Spaccio della bestia trionfante* ('Overthrow of the Triumphant Beast'), published in 1584, in which he has Jupiter calling for a thorough-going reform of planetary associations:

> Let us remove from the heaven of our minds the Ursa of deformity, the Sagitta of detrac-tion, the Equus of levity, the Canis of murmuring, the Canis Minor of flattery. Let us banish the Hercules of violence, the Lyra of conspiracy, the Trigonus of impiety, the Boötes of inconstancy, and Cepheus of cruelty. May the Draco of envy be far from us, and the Cygnus of imprudence, the Cassiopeia of vanity, the Andromeda of laziness, the Perseus of vain anxiety. Let us chase away the Ophiucus of evil speaking, the Eagle of arrogance, the Delphinus of lust, the Equus of impatience, the Hydra of concupiscence. Let us put far from us the Cetus of gluttony, the Orion of ferocity, the Flumen of superfluities, the Gorgon of ignorance, the Lepus of timidity. Let us no longer carry in our breast the Argo of avarice, the Scyphus of insobriety, the Libra of iniquity, the Cancer of slowness, the Capricorn of deception. Let not the Scorpio of fraud come near us, nor the Centaur of animal affection, the Altare of superstition, the Corona of pride, the Pisces of unworthy silence. May the Gemini of indecent familiarity fall with them, and the Taurus of concern for mean things, the Aries of inconsiderateness, the Leo of tyranny, the Aquarius of dis-soluteness, the Virgo of fruitless conversation, and the Sagittarius of detraction.

Nevertheless, Bruno did not suggest any disappearance of or diminution in planetary and stellar influences. Far from it. His developed views on astrology are expressed in *De rerum principiis et elementis et causis* ('The Basic Principles, Elements, and Causes of Things'), and endorsed the traditional view that such influences do indeed exercise dominion over all created things and beings although, true to style and consonant with much of the criticism of his period, he objected to those techniques of astrology, such as aspects and configurations, which were actually essential to astrological (as opposed to astronomical) interpretation of the observed sky. 'Superstitious manipulations' he called them, again employing a favourite adjective of contemporary critics; and yet he was prepared to support the belief in causal links between celestial bodies and everything else when it came to medicine. He expressed this at his trial before the Venetian Inquisition:

> [Astrology] could be well handled by a God-fearing man, who is able to judge from which principles proceed the right and forbidden effects, and in which guise they are imple-mented by virtue of the forces of the celestial dispositions and the efficacy of images and characters, and to judge whether they are executed by wise men or by demons, who do not differ as to the effecting of marvellous works by respecting signs and hours and treating the inferior matter with ceremony, that is, works which either damage or benefit mankind. I never had any intention of propagating that science, since I did not like that practice, except for that part pertaining to medicine, which this science greatly contributes to, as claimed on several occasions by Hippocrates and Galen.

But while it was obviously prudent not to draw attention to his acceptance of the validity of magic, certain of his writings make it clear he included this in his attempted synthesis of human experience. 'There is no physical, medical, or magical action which does not contemplate divine action in relation to things below' [*i.e. in the sublunar world*], he wrote in *De principiis*; and in *De magia mathematica* ('Astrological Magic'):

> God flows into angels, angels into the heavenly bodies, the heavenly bodies into the elements, the elements into composite beings, composite beings into the senses, the senses into consciousness, and consciousness into the living creature. The living creature ascends via consciousness to the senses, through the senses into composite things, through composite things into the elements, through the elements into the heavens, through these into *daemons* or angels, and through these into God or divine operations.

These flowings and re-flowings between realms of being constituted what Bruno thought of as a 'ladder of Nature', and to explain this re-working of the older theologically-inspired hierarchy of creation, he introduced the notion, (not his own, but one adapted from much earlier speculative thought), of 'bonds' (*vincula*) which tied everything together to make one homogenous whole. In *De magia* he calls them 'multifarious' and notes twenty, ranging from the first which has three aspects – physical, astrological, and metaphysical – through the governors of the four cardinal points of the universe, the souls of the stars, the *daemones* presiding over times, days, weather, and the elements, names of God, written characters and sigils, the power of the elemental, celestial, and intellectual worlds, and religious observations, to [magical] rings and the modes of casting spells. Bruno's concept of magic owes more to Kabbalah than to popular belief in teeming spirits, although childhood experience of such spirits' mischievous behaviour did linger with him and cause him to acknowledge their reality:

> Certainly in the interior regions of this [earth] there are living creatures of more subtle body, lively, not terribly rational, which have little in common with us; and [in the night air] there are *daemons*, neither particularly friendly to human beings nor particularly unfriendly, but nevertheless mockers and liars. They may have no more wit than we, but they excel in this: because their bodies are as ductile as the bodies of clouds, they can fuse and contract themselves into various shapes, and enter into our dreams, and announce things to us which they have seen more rapidly than we. Hence they are thought to see the future, when in fact they are a good deal less discerning than we. (*De immenso et innumerabilibus*)

We find, therefore, that by and large Bruno recasts the universe in such a way as to render the old version of celestial relationships within it impossible to accept as before, and yet still manages to adhere to several aspects of that old version, (albeit re-thought), which enable him to propose a working of magic, and in particular astral magic, which differs little in *practical* terms from that employed or described by magical theorists and practitioners both in his own day and before it. As Eugenio Garin points out, Bruno's model for astronomy was Copernicus, and yet the Hermetic magic of Agrippa had left its mark – hardly surprising, since Bruno transcribed whole pages of his work. But it may be seen as significant that

Bruno's last published treatise, *De imaginum, signorum, et idearum compositione* ('The Construction of Images, Sigils, and Illusory Appearances'), which appeared in 1591, deals with the way the sixteenth century conceived and then used images. The 'images, signs, and appearances' to which Bruno refers are those of the Greek and Roman deities aligned with the planets and the attributes and astral influences traditionally associated with them. (So one may wonder whether at this point he was retreating somewhat from the position he had advocated in his *Overthrow of the Triumphant Beast*.) Mythology thus links arms with magic in pursuit of a system designed to alert the person who masters it not only to the immense diversity of things, but also to the possibility that all this diversity may construct within him a sense of the oneness of everything. Magical images awaken his imagination which transfers what it 'sees' to the mirror of the soul, and by doing so transmits those images' individual influences in such as way that the soul is steered towards virtue and a heightened sense of divinity.

The end of such astral magic, then, was conceived as a kind of devotion and almost a prayer. But whether Bruno had these lofty motives for his magic or not, he ended his life accused and found guilty of heresy, although it should be said that this owed more to his heterodox religious ideas than his astronomical-astrological speculations. Nevertheless, the court which tried him was much disturbed by his notion of a possible infinity of universes beyond this one and by his alleged denial of articles central to the Catholic faith, and because he refused to recant – contemporaries remarked that he died because he was a Lutheran – he was sentenced to death and executed in 1600. Thus, astrology and magic, while not bringing him directly to the stake, did nothing to keep him from it. [8]

Tommaso Campanella was equally unorthodox, although his fate was far less grim. He was a precocious child and became a Dominican early, taking his religious name from St Thomas Aquinas. The course of his life took place in fits and starts, punctuated by appearances in court and periods of imprisonment, brought about partly because of his unacceptable ideas and partly because of his unacceptable actions. Following his defence in 1592 of the propositions of Bernardino Telesio who said that human experience should be the basis of philosophy, Campanella was arrested in Naples and put in gaol. Released from there, he went to Padua where he was accused of sodomy and, fortunately for him, since sodomy could well be a capital charge, found innocent. A year later, however, in 1594, he was accused of debating Christianity with a 'Judaiser', a Jewish convert to Catholicism, and sent to Rome where, in 1596, he managed with difficulty to persuade the authorities to let him enter under the control of a Roman friary – a form of house arrest, in effect – whence, in 1597, he made his way to Calabria and became involved in a plot to overthrow Spanish rule there. Inevitable arrest and trial followed, and he would have been sentenced to death had he not feigned insanity. As it was, he was condemned to life imprisonment and actually served a period of twenty-seven years before being given his freedom in 1626 through the intervention of Pope Urban VIII who valued his astrological expertise and kept him in Rome to serve as his personal adviser. A final brush with sedition in 1634, however, sent him fleeing into exile, to the Court of Louis XIII, where he was welcomed by Cardinal Richelieu and the King, and managed to live out the rest of his days in safety and comfort, though banished from his native land.

Far from being a danger or a hindrance, then, astrology proved to be Campanella's passport, first to freedom, then to royal favour. He published several treatises on the subject, the burden of which is entirely traditional – a collection of *Six Books on Astrology* and *How to Avoid Astral Destiny*, all of which were sent to a Lyonnais printer in 1629 and published without his permission. The stars he discusses behave, with a few exceptions, according to the rules laid down by Claudius Ptolemy and human affairs are governed almost entirely by those same stars, subject only to the independence of human will, although even here it is possible for the astrologer to make predictions, provided he and his client realise that such predictions are not infallible. All-embracing though the influence of the stars seems to be, however, specific, malign instances of that influence can be avoided with the help of planetary magic, and after describing ways to escape such calamities as illness, the anger of a prince, wounds and violence, poison, heavy objects falling on one's head, shipwreck, loss of income, and (somewhat ironically), imprisonment, Campanella turns to what he calls 'more secret' remedies:

> There are stones, metals, plants, colours, smells, and other things which acquire in their own particular fashion the power of the planets, and these protect us against malign happenings when they are brought into play under the operation of specific constellations.

He gives one or two examples before adding, significantly, 'and many other things which natural magic suggests are desirable'. Natural magic did not employ demons as its agents; hence Campanella felt able to say, 'magic is the flower of all branches of knowledge', and his method for avoiding the dire effects of an eclipse sprang from personal experience of just such 'natural' magic in which, without daemonic help, the participants in an apotropaic ritual tried to enlist the beneficent influences of well-aspected planets to protect them both before the eclipse began and during its ominous shadow. It happened in 1628, when Urban VIII was particularly nervous because a number of his enemies had prophesied that an eclipse would cause his death, and the Holy Father agreed to take part in just such a ritual with the help of Campanella and members of the Papal Court. Campanella later used this magic for his own benefit, too, in 1639 because he feared that the consequences of an eclipse would otherwise prove fatal to him:

> First take every pain to live temperately, according to reason and as closely to God as possible, by dedicating yourself to Him by means of prayer and holy rituals. Secondly, close up your house entirely so that no one else's air may enter therein. Sprinkle the house with rose-flavoured vinegar and waft it with aromatic odours. Make a fire and burn thereon laurel, myrtle, rosemary, cypress and other aromatic woods. There is nothing more powerful than this for dissipating the poisonous operations of the sky, even if these are administered by the Devil. Thirdly, decorate the house with white silk cloths and branches of fern. Fourthly, burn two lights and five torches to represent the planets, so that their places may be filled on earth at the time they are absent from the sky, just as one sets up a lantern at night to supply the place of the Sun when he departs at night, so that there may be no lack of light when daylight has been removed. Make representation of the planets from a mixture of aromatic substances, and once you have made copies of the twelve signs of the zodiac

(according to the principles of philosophy and not of superstition as the common people believe), you may proceed. Fifthly, have with you friends and associates whose horoscopes have not been subject to the evil of an eclipse. Apotropaic procedure does a lot of good, as does procedure which imitates the desired outcome. The former drives away the event you do not want and the latter invites the even you do want. Sixthly, have people play music belonging to Jupiter and Venus in the room, so that it can break up the evil character of the air; and let symbols of beneficent things exclude the power of maleficent stars. Seventhly, since the symbols of each star are found in stones, plants, colours, odours, music and movements … provide those which attract the power of beneficent stars and which put to flight that of maleficent stars. Liquors distilled under planetary influences should be drunk, as they have a great deal of power. You should do all this for three hours before the start of the eclipse and for three hours after it, until such time as the beneficent stars have arrived at the angles and absorbed their strength.

Creating an alternative favourable cosmos here on earth to counter the malign state of the actual cosmos above expressed Campanella's heterodoxy rather well. His best-known work, *La città del Sole* ('The City of the Sun'), envisaged an ideal state, the city being divided into seven circular divisions representing the stations and orbits of the seven planets, with an enormous temple on top of a central hill. In the temple is an altar dedicated to the sun, bearing a huge map displaying heaven and earth, and seven lamps, always lit, representing the seven planets. Above the altar stretches a dome on which are painted the principal stars, along with their names, qualities, and powers – representations repeated on the curtains and outer walls of the temple. The rest of the city is meant to remind its citizens of the immense variety and wealth of natural creation and the ingenuity of certain gifted beings – Moses, Osiris, Jupiter, Mercury, and many others – whose statues line the outer part of the outermost city-wall. Clearly, therefore, with an astral temple at its heart, the city of sun was an image of the idealised commonwealth governed by the stars and planets, whose natural magic Campanella envisaged maintaining, or helping to maintain, the stability and happiness enjoyed by its citizens; and the temporary astral environment of the ritual to ward off the effects of an eclipse created something very similar, and shows just how profoundly astrological symbolism in its magical aspect had penetrated Campanella's thinking. [9]

Both Bruno and Campanella, then, were indebted to the astral magic of Marsilio Ficino, and in consequence both glided dangerously far over the boundaries set by orthodox theology. Their magic was natural, not demonic, although it could not be said that it was not 'daemonic', since both posited spirits acting as intermediaries between the natural and preternatural worlds. But Bruno envisaged influences travelling up and down his 'ladder of Nature', whereas Campanella tried (not always successfully) to keep separate the different planes of being, the divine from the created, and the action of the magician from that of a demon or daemon. In the end, however, Campanella's ambiguity landed him in prison just as did Bruno's more plainly expressed unorthodoxy, and it was mere luck which allowed Campanella to end his days as a pensioner of the King of France rather than as a condemned man at the stake in the manner of Bruno. Astrology and magic were frequently bed-fellows, and their suspicious proximity, although often taken for granted, (like the contemporary sleeping arrangements of travellers or apprentices who were liable to share a bed with one or more others), might well, quite without warning, (like the accusations of sodomy sometimes brought against those same travellers or apprentices), end unhappily in imprisonment or death. The fates of Campanella and Bruno might therefore serve as warnings to admonish and restrain the rest. Meanwhile in England it was remarked on 20 November 1601:

> Mr John Chamber, one of the prebendaries of the Chapel of Windsor and Fellow of Eton College hath written a learned treatise against judicial astrology. Noteth it as a gross and hea-thenish superstition, condemned by the Church in all ages. 'Witchcraft,' quoth he, 'because it toucheth our hogs and cattle sometime, findeth now and then some hard entertainment, as it well deserveth. But this damnable superstition [*of astrology*] which dishonoureth God, polluteth heaven, deceiveth and seduceth men, goeth without touch or check, the astrologer 'scaping while the witch is punished.' Moreover of late some even of the practizers have gone about to reform it, setting out reformed almanacs wherein they have not meddled at all with wind, weather, dismal days, purges, and such like, but only with changes of the moon, festival days, and such like.

Chamber, a clergyman, was inveighing against not only that aspect of astrology which claimed to predict future events, but also against that which dealt with medicine and meteorology. His may have been a somewhat extreme view, but the need for or desirability of reform was widely agreed – hence Bacon's call for a 'sane' astrology – and there were many and varied attempts to make astrology a more exact and reliable science, from the computational changes brought by Regiomontanus in the second half of the fifteenth century, to the constant checking of horoscopes cast for figures in the past, measured against the known courses of their lives, a method favoured by Peucer and continued throughout the sixteenth century. Now, what these reforming measures, and the defences thrown up against critics of astrology, the constant use of astrologers by everyone, high and low, in Church and state, and the frequent dangers to health, livelihood, and limb, which injudicious or unlucky practitioners of the science encountered, all had in common was an acknowledgement that astrology was a serious business and so worthy of being treated seriously. Medicine and surgery were unable to function effectively without it; lives lived in the midst of ever-present perils and catastrophes – epidemics, floods, fires, sterility of persons, animals or crops, famine, the uncertainties of war – found a kind of comfort in the possibilities of a science which could predict the future and explain causes, and thus allow people to cast the burden of their precariousness upon the stars; the great changes of history were explained by the astrology of stellar conjunctions; and excesses in the character of individuals, sexual proclivity, and good fortune enjoyed beyond the usual measure, could be ascribed to planetary influence upon the new-born child or, according to some theories, the newly-conceived foetus in the womb. Astrology permeated literature, whether this was domestic, (such as the plays of Shakespeare), or ephemeral, (such as the abundance of pamphlets predicting disaster, which flooded the sixteenth century), or artistic, (such as Dürer's star charts). Ephemera were especially influential in keeping astrology before the eyes of the general populace, whether as religious aids, (e.g. Lorenz Faust's allegorical picture of the prophet Daniel, with symbols of the planets, elements, and seasons); teaching aids, (e.g. Hector Schöffler's table for learning the planetary hours, useful for medical students, or Dietmar Helmer Klant's planetarium); or calendars with pictures of the planets and Zodiac Man, (e.g. those by Melchior Sachse the Younger, Nicolaus Knorr, Joachim Heller, or that by Leonhard Straub the Elder with the monitory verses: 'Never expose a part of the body to danger when the moon is in its sign. This is confirmed by all physicians').

Astrology, in short, was everywhere, in the high reaches of academe where it was the subject of intense research, speculation, and debate, as well as being a standard and required discipline in the university curriculum; in the Courts of Kings, princes, nobles, and Popes, where it might be consulted and vilified in almost equal measure; and in city streets and private houses where the questions asked of it were simple and practical, and its prognostications equally helpful and straightforward. Criticism and objection, it seemed, served only to strengthen its hold on the minds and lives of its multifarious clients. [10]

13

Prophets & Sceptics c.1700–c.1800: Astrology Fighting Decline

The crucial role played by astrology in treating the sick can be seen with particular clarity in the work of Richard Napier (1559–1634), a physician who recorded his notes about medicine, astrology, alchemy, magic, and religion, sixty volumes of which, collected and bound by Elias Ashmole, are now kept in the Ashmolean Museum. His special fascination with astrology was piqued and then developed by Simon Forman whom he consulted first on a matter involving stolen property, after which the two became instructor and student, with Napier learning how to apply astrology to a wide range of both medical, social, and personal problems. It was the application of medical astrology, however, which interested him most and in 1597 he began to treat patients, a service in which he was so successful that by 1607 he was treating up to 2,000 people a year.

He would begin a consultation with questions similar to those asked by Forman: who is the patient? Where does he or she live? What is the patient's age? Then he noted the time and date of the inquiry and began to draw up the relevant chart, under which he recorded information about the disease or problem in point. But unlike Forman, Napier rarely prescribed a magical remedy. His answers to problems tended to be more reliant on purges, bleedings, and medicines than on lamina or exorcisms, and this was true even in cases of mental or emotional disorder rather than physical. When Daniel Georg complained of light-headedness because he had been studying too hard, or Mistress Mathew that she was troubled in spirit because her husband was unkind to her, for example, Napier prescribed purges, emetics, and bleeding, a reliance upon purely physical answers to psychological problems which may seem surprising at first – one might think that these were just the kind of cases which might benefit from recourse to magic in one or more of its forms – except that it is clear from Napier's case-notes that he never attributed his patients' mental or emotional disturbances to the movements of celestial bodies alone. He assumed, along with most other people at the time, that body and mind, matter and non-matter, were interlinked and that therefore a disturbance in the one was liable to produce disturbance in the other – hence the use of physical remedies to mitigate the effects of non-physical distress.

In this, however, Napier was actually somewhat unusual. In a period when illness of any kind could easily be attributed to divine anger or demonic malevolence as readily as to unfortunate astral configurations or straightforward physical causes, people were as likely to turn to prayer or magic as to conventional medicine in their pursuit of a cure or easement. Consequently, even Napier from time to time provided his patients with talismans or astral sigils to stamp upon their medicines before taking them, and it seems that in his later years – again just as in Forman's case – he consulted angelic spirits to assist him in diagnosing an illness. In 1619, for example, he asked the Archangel Raphael about a number of his patients and was told that five of them were bewitched but that two of them would recover. Nevertheless, he did not altogether trust the information he received by these means, noting on one occasion that Raphael's prediction was wrong – he had said a female patient would escape her bewitchment and live to marry, whereas in fact she died of consumption. Napier's notes therefore not only let us see how he used hindsight to correct both his divinatory and his astrological attempts to diagnose illness and prescribe effective relief, but also his awareness, not so much of the limitations of these approaches as of their reliability, and his willingness to learn from experience how to apply them with greater efficacy.

So, as the child is father of the man, so did sixteenth-century astrology produce that of the seventeenth which then proceeded to develop in its own way, but always in harmony with those familial ties which bound it to the past. Thus, when the future Louis XIV was born, it was recorded:

The Dauphin's constellation [is] composed of nine stars, the nine Muses according to astrologers, surrounded by the Eagle (great genius), Pegasus (excellent horseman), Sagittarius (infantry), Aquarius (naval power), the Swan (poets, historians, orators who will sing his praises). The Dauphin touches the Equator (justice). Born on Sunday, the day of the sun. Equal to the sun, he will bless France with his heat and light, and be a Dauphin friendly to France. Already he suckles [from] a new nurse. Everyone runs away because he pulls hard on their breasts.

Identifying a monarch's life, or that of his heir, with the sun was, of course, a cliché of such predictions. It had been said of Louis XIII, as well, and even in non-royal cases the sun played a crucial role in guaranteeing a long and healthy life. Cardano, for example, said so of his father. 'Because the sun was the ruler of his life, along with Jupiter and Venus in Leo, he had a robust, healthy life. He lived until the sun in quartile with Mars arrived in Libra where both fell in the bounds of Saturn. Having completed seventy-nine years, he died on 28 August 1524.' (*Liber XII geniturarum*, p.519)

But while the stars, naturally, could not guarantee long life, they could indicate the end of it and when Senelles, a physician, cast Louis XIII's horoscope and from it predicted that the King would die in September 1631, he quickly found himself in the Bastille, condemned to serve in the galleys, his property confiscated to the state. Similarly, and just over a year earlier in May 1630, Orazio Morandi (1570–1630), Abbot of the Monastery of Santa Prassede, decided to advance his career by predicting the imminent death of Pope Urban VIII, a man who, as we have seen, was particularly sensitive when it came to the stars and his own person. Having engaged Tommaso Campanella and the Papal Court to assist in an elaborate piece of astral magic calculated to ward off the double threat of a solar followed by a lunar eclipse that very year, the Holy Father was incensed to find that Campanella had given a detailed description of the ceremony, (though without mentioning names), in his treatise *Astrologicorum libri VII*; and so when Morandi interpreted the Pope's nativity and found that his death was imminent because of the baleful influence of a solar eclipse on the horoscope, allied to the information that in 1630 Urban would attain his sixty-third year, in medico-astrological terms a 'grand climacteric' and therefore a significant and not very fortunate age, the Pope ordered his arrest. 'The Abbot,' says the contemporary record, 'was apprehended, along with his associates, [and] after interrogation at the palace of the Governor of Rome, they were sent to prison.'

Morandi had not acted on a sudden impulse, nor was his attempt to gain further prestige for himself by using astrology out of character. By the time he became Abbot of the San Prassede monastery he had already occupied himself in the occult sciences, but it may have been the supernova of 1604 and the great swirl of interest it generated which drew his attention to astrology in particular. Armed with this enthusiasm, he acquired the patronage of the Medici family, principally via Antonio de' Medici who turned his house into an informal academy for the study of the occult sciences, and Giovanni who kept a complete alchemical laboratory in his house and stocked his library with large numbers of prohibited books. This latter example may have stirred Morandi to build up the monastery's library in a similar fashion and also, perhaps, to adopt a remarkably liberal attitude to people borrowing from it, readers, as we know from its lending-list in the 1620s, encompassing priests and lay people, (including women), writers and students. Among the books available to them were standard astronomical texts, ancient and modern, and a very large set of astrological works ranging from Ptolemy and Firmicus Maternus to contemporary treatises such as Lindhout's *Speculum Astrologiae* (1608) and Goclenius's *Uraniae divinatricis quoad astrologiae generalis libri duo* (1614). This predominance of astronomical-astrological tomes mirrored the interest of learned and polite society as well as Morandi's personal predeliction. Astrology was still a university subject, and indeed would continue to be so in certain places such as Salamanca until the eighteenth century. The expectation of the arrival of a New Age in the history of humankind was also prevalent and was governed, of course, by astrological interpretation of significant celestial configurations. Thus, 1524 had seen the conjunction of Mars, Jupiter and Saturn in Pisces; 1584 a conjunction of nearly all the planets in Aries, an eclipse of the sun in Taurus, and a comet; and 1623 a conjunction of Saturn and Jupiter in the fiery trigon. These, and the appearance of major 'new' stars in 1572, 1602 and 1604, and notable comets in 1577, 1585, 1593, 1596, 1607, and 1618 meant that prophetic speculation was almost at fever pitch. Hence, at least in part, the keen interest a wide range of readers showed in the San Prassede library, including some from the highest ranks within the Church.

In the face of all this legitimate curiosity, the monks decided to follow the well-trodden path of astrological reform and re-establish the science with more accurate and more reliable techniques. This they did by having recourse not only to their own burgeoning library, but to skilled individuals outwith the monastery itself, such as Ottavio Marini who provided information on astrological matters and Giambattista di Giuliano, an expert on astronomy. But astronomy-astrology being what it was, the monks soon included study in other fields, too: astrological medicine allied with sympathetic magic, and astral magic allied with divination and magical Kabbalah. No wonder, then, that Brendan Dooley can tell us, 'By the time Morandi went to jail, Santa Prassede had become the astrological Mecca not only for the neighbourhood, but for a significant portion of the ecclesiastical aristocracy as well.' The seriousness of the monks' quest, however, was only one aspect of the immense interest in astrology which was noted at the time. Equally resurgent were hawkers and other dubious characters who did a good trade among the streets and alleys of Rome. Mercantonio Conti remarked during Morandi's trial:

> The whole of Rome is filled with these charlatans, and I am amazed the Pope has not given sufficient provision against these imposters. Among them is a knife-seller whose name I don't know, and a certain Battelli, and certain Spaniards who go round selling their opinions about nativities, as I have heard.

Buoyed by the belief that he was on the respectable side of all this activity, and noting that contemporaries such as Galileo Galilei (whom he knew through personal correspondence) gained lustre and advancement through their courting of powerful figures in the Church and state, Morandi set his sights on the grandest patron of all, the Holy Father, with, however, results we have already noted. His prediction that Pope Urban was fated to die in 1630 proved badly mistaken, since the Pope lived until 1644. Morandi himself, on the other hand, did die that year, and in 1631 the law of unintended consequences came into force as Urban published the most severe Bull to date against astrologers. Tommaso Campanella later attempted a reply, disguised as censure of those who objected to it:

> This Bull pursues astrologers with much more hostility than heretics and schismatics. It even excommunicates them, removes all their property, and punishes astrologers right from the start with a fine and a sentence of death … Astrologers are lumped together with diviners and augurers when they go beyond the bounds of the science of Nature, just as happens to doctors who are classed with the workers of maleficent magic when they give their patients superstitious medicines and useless amulets which do not have the power they promise. (*Disputatio contra murmurantes citra et ultra montes in Bullas SS. Pontificum Sixti V et Urbani VIII adversus judiciarios*, Paris 1636, pp.255–6) [1]

Going beyond the bounds of the science of Nature was, of course, something astrologers were almost certain to do, given the character of their science and its extension into other types of knowledge. Still, one can understand Pope Urban's nervousness of it, and his ultimate wish to distance the Church and her Christian faith from it, when one looks at some of the by-ways into which astrological speculation was prone to stray. Consider, for example, the case of Jacques Gaffarel (1601–81), a priest and astrologer. He acquired a wide knowledge of several Oriental languages – Hebrew, Arabic, Syriac, Persian – and developed an interest in Kabbalah whose 'mysteries' he defended against criticism in several books, but it was his *Curiositez inouyes sur la sculpture talismanique des Persans, horoscope des Patriarches, et lecture des estoiles* ('Unheard of Curiosities concerning the Engraving of Talismanic Images by the Persians, horoscope of the Patriarchs, and Reading of the Stars'), published first in 1629, which brought him to the favourable attention of Cardinal Richelieu who appointed him his librarian and sent him abroad to look for and purchase rare books on his behalf. In *Curiositez* Gaffarel discusses the history of astrology, maintaining (contrary to the usual theory) that the ancients did not actually worship the stars and that, in consequence, ancient astrology was not idolatrous. He also argues that astrological images are natural, not diabolically inspired, and that astral talismans or images are not without power, although many historical instances of them – such as the Israelites' golden calf or the bronze serpent of Moses – had been misinterpreted and were not talismanic at all. Other images, however, (and here Gaffarel seems to have had in mind principally those engraved for medical use), might certainly be influential, although it was superstitious to think that their use had to be accompanied by certain (i.e. magical) words.

It is when he comes to 'reading the heavens like a book', as Melanchthon had envisaged astrology, that Gaffarel shows himself at once individual and deviant. Here he describes how the stars are actually arranged in the form of Hebrew letters which may therefore be read and understood:

> [We may] be able to give a reason of that which hath hitherto been unknown to us: as when the astrologers affirm that when Caput Algol, or Medusa's Head, was vertical to Greece, the stars did foreshow the calamities which afterwards happened unto it by reason of the tyranny of the Mahometans, without giving us any reason why: no more than they do of their confidence in assuring us that the same constellation, which will in a short time be vertical to Italy also, foreshows a strange desolation that is to fall upon this pleasant and fertile country. Now all these disasters, though, according as they are foretold, so do they certainly come to pass; yet nevertheless is the foreseeing of them grounded merely upon experience, neither can the authors of these predictions for the most part give any other reason of them. But now, according to this doctrine of the celestial writing, we know that these mutations shall happen on the earth because we see they are written in the heavens. And this is the reason that Rabbi Chomer affirms that the aforesaid Medusa's Head, or the stars that compose it, did foretell the lamentable desolation of Greece, because that five of the principal vertical stars did for a good while together make up this word, *Charab*, which in the second conjugation signifies 'to be desolate', understanding this particularly of Greece over which these stars shone because that the number of its letters, which are *jod, vau, nun*, and which being put together make up *Javan*, that is to say, 'Greece', do yield the same number that Charab doth, as you may see here: 'Charab' = 2+2+8 = 12, 'Javan' = 5+6+1 = 12. According to these principles, any man may foresee, by the putting together the stars of the same constellation, the disasters that Italy is threatened with. However it be, Junctin, an Italian priest and a very excellent astrologer, is bold to utter these words: 'That,' (saith he, speaking of this Medusa's Head), 'is now vertical over Toleto, Apulia, and the Kingdom of Naples. It will soon invade Italy. That it is going to bring its destruction to these is very much to be feared.' Now how long beforehand these celestial letters do foreshow the changes that are to happen, no one author that I know of hath precisely determined. They say only that before they are vertical, they do foreshow this change and whatsoever is going to happen, God being willing thus to prepare us for the evils which

are to befall us. After that they are precisely vertical, if our repentance hath yet found any place in His mercies, He then causeth some new star to appear, and by its intervening to show … a quite contrary thing to what was before signified. (Translated by Edmund Chilmead London 1650, 415–18)

Little wonder, perhaps, that the book as a whole was condemned by the Theological Faculty of the Sorbonne almost as soon as it appeared, and that Gaffarel was obliged to retract his opinions, although he seems to have argued that the propositions in the book were not his own teachings, but merely a collection of ideas culled from Arab and Hebrew writers. Whether the doctors of the Sorbonne were satisfied by this apparent compliance with their demands that he condemn and reject his own book is not clear, and it is even less clear whether Gaffarel's retraction was serious or not, especially as he continued to allow printing and subsequent editions without altering his expressed views on astral and talismanic magic.

But if Gaffarel was unusual, it was in comparison with contemporaries whose clientele was concerned with questions more immediate than the exact nature of star-groupings and the history of astral talismans. We have already looked at physicians, but they were by no means the only people to derive a partial living from astrology. Indeed, if we consider William Lilly (1602–81), 'England's prophetical Merlin', to use the title of one of his books, we find that combination of everyday assistance and politico-religious prediction fairly typical of the better-reputed astrologers of his day. Lilly's family was too poor to afford him a university education, so he made his way via trade and a large inheritance from his second wife. He learned his astrology, along with the rudiments of magic – mainly the evocation of spirits – from a cunning-man, John Evans, and while his experimentation with magic did not last long, his astrological career burgeoned. So, as he recorded in his autobiography, 'perceiving there was money to be got in London, and thinking myself to be as sufficiently enabled in astrology as any I could meet with, I made it my business to repair thither'. In London during the 1640s he found the atmosphere febrile as the two kingdoms of Scotland and England gradually worked themselves up into the derangement of civil wars. Lilly himself supported the English Parliament and, because his religious views tended to Puritanism, work partly as a medical astrologer, but more especially as a prognosticator of war successful to the parliamentarian side, quickly came his way; and in April 1644 he published the first of his almanacs, *Merlinus Anglicus Junior* ('The Younger English Merlin'), which sold out within a week, to some extent because an influential MP whom he had treated in his role of astrological physician was seen carrying a copy in the House of Commons, a friendly puff which ensured that others made haste to buy their copies, too.

Why was it so popular? There were many almanacs on the market – most of their authors lived in London and the south-east of England – so he had plenty of competition, and a breakdown of printing controls during the 1640s meant that officially approved almanacs were often outnumbered by illegal and counterfeit imitations, often railing against astrology and astrologers. These were frequently near-illiterate, and partisan in both politics and religion, not to mention libellous because of personal quarrels between their rogue authors. But almanacs, official or not, fulfilled a variety of perceived needs by supplying information such as weather forecasts, tables of weights and measures, the dates of fairs, astrological advice to country folk on the best time to plough, sow, harvest, fell timber and so on, and the most favourable times to let blood or take medicine. Extravagant prophecies anent politics or religion also lent spice to the publication, so it is not surprising to find that the most popular almanacs sold in very large numbers. John Booker, for example, had a print order of 12,000 for his 1640 edition; Seth Partridge sold 18,500 copies in 1648; and by 1659 Lilly himself was said to be selling 30,000 per year. The scale of Lilly's popularity argues that there was something about his almanacs which made them more attractive than those of his competitors, and we can attribute this partly to their being less silly and better written, partly to his ability to match his tone with fair accuracy to the popular mood of the day, and partly, of course, to his having influential connections in high places. But we must also take into account certain of his predictions which were believed to be remarkably accurate, such as that of 1645 which appeared to predict the outcome of the battle of Naseby. Lilly actually made this in answer to a prediction by the astrologer George Wharton, a royalist supporter, who foretold a major victory for King Charles at the same battle. In coming to the contrary conclusion, Lilly, in his own words:

> made use of the King's nativity, and finding that his ascendant was approaching the quadrature of Mars, about June 1645, I have this unlucky judgement: 'If now we [*i.e. the parliamentarians*] fight, a victory stealeth upon us;' and so it did in June 1645, at Naseby, the most fatal overthrow he ever had.

This stroke of luck (or accurate calculation) made Lilly famous especially, perhaps, as he published Wharton's prediction along with his own so that everyone could see which astrologer was the superior; and thus he set in train a remarkable career as a semi-official astrologer and publicist of the parliamentary cause.

In addition to his almanacs, Lilly also published pamphlets whose tenor may be gauged from their titles: *A Prophecy of the White King's Dreadfull Deadman Explained* (1644), *England's Propheticall Merline* (1644), *The Starry Messenger* (1645). But in 1647 came his most substantial work, *Christian Astrology*, a remarkable study of the science based, as one may tell from its accompanying bibliography, on his reading of more than 200 earlier treatises on the subject, most in Latin translation, but several in English, including a very recent publication, John Booker's *Of the Conjunction of Saturn and Mars* (1646), and the hostile *Against Judicial Astrology* by John Chambers (1601). At the very start of his preface Lilly explains the circumstances during which he had written his book, and apologises for any errors which may have crept therein:

> I have oft in my former works hinted the many fears I had of that danger I was naturally like to be in in the year 1647, as any may read, either in my *Epistle before the Conjunction of Saturn and Jupiter*, printed [in] 1644, or in page 108 thereof, or in the *Epistle of Anglicus 1645* where you shall find these words: 'I have run over more days than fifteen thousand, five hundred, fifty and nine. Before I am sixteen thousand, four hundred, twenty two days

old I shall be in great hazard of my life. But that year which afflicts me will stagger a monarch and kingdom,' etc. What concerns myself hath almost in full measure proved true in 1647, having in this untoward year been molested with palpitation of the heart, with hypocondry melancholy, a disaffected spleen, the scurvy, etc. and now at this present (viz. August 1647) when I had almost concluded this treatise, I am shut up of the plague, (having the fourth of August buried one servant thereof, and on the 28 of the same month another), myself and remainder of my family enforced to leave my proper seat and betake myself to change of air: so that if either my present epistles or the latter part of the book itself being anything defective, as well they may, being written when my family and self were in such abundant sorrow and perplexity, I desire the reader to be so civil as to pass over those slight imperfections (if any be) with a candid censure.

Lilly's textbook, because this is what *Christian Astrology* was and was meant to be, retained its popularity and usefulness for a very long time. Like Gaul, it is divided into three parts. The first Book, *An Introduction to Astrology*, deals with the elementary grammar of astrology – 'the number of planets, signs, aspects, with their several names and characters; the use of the ephemeris, how to erect a figure of heaven by the ephemeris and table of houses', – everything being explained as simply and directly as possible:

The Querent is he or she that propounds the question and desires resolution: the Quesited is he or she or the thing sought and inquired after. The significator is no more than that planet which rules the house that signifies the thing demanded: as if Aries is ascending, Mars being Lord of Aries shall be the significator of the Querent, viz. the sign ascending shall in part signify his corporature, body, or stature, the Lord of the Ascendant, the moon and planet in the ascendant, or that the moon or Lord of the Ascendant are in aspect with, shall show his quality or conditions equally mixed together; so that let any sign ascend, what planet is Lord of that sign shall be called Lord of the House, or significator of the person inquiring, etc. So that in the first place therefore, when any question is propounded, the sign ascending and his Lord are always given to him or her that asks the question. (Book 1 chap.20)

The second Book, *The Resolution of all Manner of Questions and Demands*, is directed towards horary astrology and concentrates on the significations of the twelve houses and how to read these for a client. Lilly often accompanies these expository chapters with illustrative horoscopes as, for example, in the case dated 2.15 p.m., Thursday 4 March 1632 of a querent asking six questions:

(1) If he were like to live long, yea or not; (2) to what part of the world he were best direct his course of life; (3) what part of his life was in probability like to be most fortunate; (4) he desired I would relate (if possible by a figure) some of the general accidents that had happened to him already; (5) what accidents in future he might expect, good or evil; (6) the time when' – [meaning, when any of these future incidents might happen].

To the first Lilly replied that the chart indicated a man 'of a middle stature, strongly compacted, neither fat nor fleshy, but comely, with a disposition exceeding valiant, choleric, high minded, and of great spirit'. So, considering the sun was above the earth and that Jupiter and Venus were angular and more potent than Saturn or Mars, 'I concluded that according to natural causes, he might live many years, and that Nature was strong, and he subject to few diseases.' This, Lilly observed, proved to be an accurate reading, 'he being yet alive this present, March 1646'. Anent the second question, Lilly advised him to go to Ireland because 'the moon applied so strongly to the trine of Jupiter, and he and Venus were in Taurus, and [that] sign signifies Ireland'. Apparently this was good advice because 'the querent did go into Ireland and there performed good service and obtained a notable victory against the rebels'. Lilly went on to say that he judged the querent's younger years – meaning his mid twenties – would actually be his best, and in answer to the querent's test question about his past, (evidently designed to find out whether Lilly was competent or not), said he had been involved in some quarrel about money, that he and his wife had been at loggerheads, she being 'a virago, or gallantly spirited woman, and not willing to be curbed or else to submit', and that some important lawyer or courtier had tried to resolve the differences between them. In each point, Lilly adds, his reading of the chart was perfectly correct. Thence to the future: the querent was going to travel abroad, settle the education of his children, and that after several years of comfortable living, he would find himself in danger of losing everything – 'life, goods, lands, and fortune'. Yes, and so it proved, says Lilly, adding:

> Very little of this judgement had already failed. [One cannot help admiring the disclaim-
> er of complete infallibility]. I have been herein somewhat large because young students
> might hereby benefit the more and if my judgements do vary from the common rules of
> the ancients, let the candid reader excuse me, since he may still follow their principles, if he
> please; and he must know that from my conversation in their writings [*my familiarity with
> the ancients' works*] I have attained the method I follow. (Book 2, chap.26)

Book 3, *An Easie and Plaine Method teaching how to judge upon Nativities*, goes through the twelve houses, describing the techniques of reading this type of horoscope, both those he himself had read about and those he and his contemporaries used in their practices:

> Some have delivered a way to find out the hour of conception, but I hold it a matter too
> nice fully at this time to be handled, nor give I any credit to it: yet it's thus. You must
> take the right ascension of the sun for the noon of the day of conception, deduced from
> Capricorn, in what sign soever the sun is. You must take the oblique ascension at the day
> of birth, of the moon under the elevation of the Pole where the birth is. Subtract the sun,
> his right ascension, from the oblique of the moon. What remains, convert into time, and
> those hours show the time of conception. Or thus: take the time from noon in the table of
> houses, adhering to the 10th house, over against the degrees of the sun in the sign he is in
> at the conception. Take the time from noon over against the place of the moon in the birth
> under the ascendant. Subtract the hours corresponding to the place of the sun in the 10th

house from those answering to the place of the moon in the ascendant by adding 24 hours, if need be. What remains is supposed to be the time of the hour of conception. (Book 3, chap.98)

The Book also contains tables – right ascensions, oblique ascensions, directions of the ascendant, mid-heaven, the sun and moon, and the parts of fortune, all of which were designed to help the practitioner in his mathematical calculations – and finally, predictions for the years between 1644 and 1667 relating to someone aged twenty-nine to fifty, along with specimen charts for each of these years.

Taken as a whole, then, *Christian Astrology* provided readers with a straightforward, clearly-written guide to the technicalities of the science and showed itself remarkably free from that obscurity of jargon which sometimes marred similar publications – its being in English rather than Latin also helped – and also of the silliness which was all too characteristic of many of the almanacs of the day. In one way, it sealed Lilly's reputation as an astrologer and enabled him to continue his career with a success rivalling that of Simon Forman a generation earlier. According to his notebooks, nearly 2,000 clients a year consulted him between 1644 and 1666, men as well as women, aristocrats as well as servants; from 1649 to 1658 he was a leading figure in the Society of Astrologers, attended by George Wharton whom he had bested in the predictions anent Naseby, Elias Ashmole, Nicolas Culpeper, and several others, whose aim it was to revive and protect astrology which, they said, 'was hardly known to this (herein unhappy) segment of the terrestrial globe or (if at all) but lodged in the retired bosoms of some few'; defenders and critics of the two English universities praised him by name on account of his 'unwearied pains for the resuscitation and promotion of this noble science'; and one anonymous pamphlet even went so far as to complain that people put more confidence in Lilly than they did in God. Indeed, it is worth noting that in 1654 one of Lilly's fervent admirers, John Webster, author of *Academiarum Examen* ('An Investigation of the Universities'), having praised Lilly, Culpeper, and several others, recommended that divinity be abolished from the university curriculum and replaced by astrology and other occult sciences. Lilly also, as I mentioned earlier, fulfilled the unspoken and unofficial function of astrologer to the Cromwellian government, and his yearly almanacs supported ever more openly the alliance between the republic and King Carl X Gustaf of Sweden, with propaganda very thinly disguised as prediction:

[1658], several negotiations on foot to reconcile the Swedish King with Denmark, which people too late may repent their treacherous taking up of arms against so firm an ally of the English Lord Protectors, and against a person so full of honour as Charles Gustavus, King of Sweden, both whose fortunes are not to be counterpoised by any single king, prince, people or nation of this world at present.

It was an adventure into international politics which brought Lilly further esteem and the gift of a gold chain and medal from the Swedish monarch.

Nevertheless, things were not wholly well. While it is true that Lilly's career in the 1640s and 1650s had coincided with a revival of interest in astrology in England, the 1660s saw a decline in Lilly's astrological practice and, indeed, a certain danger to his person, the result of his having predicted in *Monarchy or No Monarchy* (1652) both the plague and the fire of London. Two of its pictures show three corpses laid upon the earth while two grave-diggers open the ground to receive two coffins, and two further 'hieroglyphs', as Lilly called these illustrations, show a city in flames beside a broad river, and men throwing water on a fire into which is falling the zodiacal sign Gemini, the sign which signifies or 'rules' the city of London. In his own copy of the pamphlet, Lilly had written, 'death about 1665' under the woodcut of the plague, and under that of the fire, 'you may expect this in 1693 or sooner – perhaps 1666 or 1667'. So serious was the fire that conspiracy theories about its origins began almost immediately, and in October 1666 Lilly was summoned before a committee investigating the causes of the fire and was obliged to convince its members that he had not actually started it himself, (presumably to verify his own prediction), or foreseen its outbreak with any particular accuracy; and here we must remember that the dates he recorded were in his personal copy, not the one seen by the committee. Had they seen '1666 or 1667', he would probably have been in grave danger for, as *The London Gazette* for 29 April 1666 had reported anent a treasonous conspiracy involving eight former soldiers:

> The better to effect this hellish design, the city was to have been fired and the portcullis let down to keep out all assistance; and the Horse Guard to have been surprised at the Inns where they were quartered, several ostlers having been gained for that purpose … The third of September was pitched on for the attempt, as being found by Lilly's almanack, and a scheme [*astrological chart*] erected for that purpose, to be a lucky day, a planet then ruling which prognosticated the downfall of monarchy.

All eight were tried, found guilty, and executed. Hence Lilly's interrogation. His fame was therefore uncomfortable, and from this time until his death in 1681 Lilly turned his attention to the practice of medicine in which his astrology would bring his patients benefit and himself considerably less disquiet. But his career had never been without its critics. On 24 October 1660, for example, Samuel Pepys recorded a sour comment by one John Booker that Lilly was 'writing to please his friends and to keep in with the times (*as he formerly did to his own dishonour*), and not according to the rules of art, by which he could not well err, *as he had done*', (my italics), and on 14 June 1667, 'At dinner we discoursed of Tom of the Wood, a fellow that lives like a hermit near Woolwich, who as they say … foretells the burning of the city, and now says that a greater desolation is at hand. Thence we read and laughed at Lilly's prophecies this month in his almanac this year.' Samuel Butler may have parodied him as a quack astrologer and cunning-man, Sidrophel, in Part 2, canto 3 of his satire *Hudibras* – an attack on Cromwellians and the presbyterian establishment. This Butler chose to do partly because the presbyterian establishment had become closely associated with astrology, and opponents of that establishment saw astrology as a major contributor to the fissiparous condition of reformed religion in England during the 1650s, as well as a source or error, crime, and irrationality among the people. Astrology, they said, was condemned by Scripture, undermined free will by subjecting the individual to the tyranny of astral determinism, created endless opportunities for charlatans to deceive and fleece the gullible and ignored those astronomical discoveries which placed the whole basis of astrological theory in question. Butler's Sidrophel personifies all these negative aspects alleged of astrology, and does so in lively, vivid terms which render the satire particularly incisive, especially in the mouth of Hudibras himself, the presbyterian 'hero' of the mock epic:

> He had been long t'wards mathematics,
> Opticks, philosophy, and staticks,
> Magick, horoscopy, astrology,
> And was old dog at physiology:
> But, as a dog that turns the spit,
> Bestirs himself, and plies his feet
> To climb the wheel, but all in vain,
> His own weight brings him down again;
> And still he's in the self-same place,
> Where at his setting out he was:
> So, in the circle of the arts,
> Did he advance his nat'ral parts:
> Till falling back still, for retreat,
> He fell to juggle, cant, and cheat:
> For as those fowls that live in water
> Are never wet, he did but smatter:
> Whate'er he labour'd to appear,
> His understanding still was clear …

> Do not our great reformers use
> This Sidrophel, to forebode news?
> To write of victories next year,
> And castles taken yet i'th'air?
> Of battles fought at sea, and ships
> Sunk, two years hence, the last eclipse?
> A total o'er throw giv'n the King
> In Cornwall, horse and foot, next spring?
> And has he not point-blank foretold
> Whatso'er the Close Committee would?
> Made Mars and Saturn for the cause,
> The moon for fundamental laws;
> The Ram, the Bull, the Goat, declare
> Against the Book of Common Prayer;
> The Scorpion take the Protestation,
> And Bear engage for reformation;
> Made all the royal stars recant,
> Compound, and take the covenant.

Further criticism came from John Dryden, (who was himself a skilled astrologer and had correctly predicted the death by drowning of his son Charles), threw in a sarcastic aside during his play, *An Evening's Love, or, The Mock Astrologer* (performed in 1688), when one character advises another anent astrological predictions:

> If at any time thou ventur'st at particulars, have an evasion ready, like Lilly: as thus, 'It will infallibly happen – if our sins hinder not.' I would undertake with one of his almanacs to give very good content to all Christendom, and 'what good luck fell not out in one kingdom should in another'. (Act 2, scene 1)

Even as far away as New England his name was not safe, with the Protestant minister, Increase Mather, in his history of comets (*Kometographia*, 1683), making a particular assault on 'that blind but insolent buzzard, William Lilly'. [2]

Lilly, in fact, had both the good fortune and the misfortune to live at a time when astrology was simultaneously popular in many quarters and under increasingly heavy attack from others. Pierre Bayle (1647–1706), for example, dismissed it as at once ridiculous and dangerous. 'There has never been anything more impertinent or more chimerical than astrology,' he wrote in his *Pensées diverses sur la comète* in 1682, 'nothing more ignominious in human nature to whose shame it will always be true to say that there have been men treacherous enough to deceive others under the pretext of knowing heavenly things, and men stupid enough to give credence to them.' Claude Pithoys (1587–1676), originally a friar before turning Protestant, concentrated his fire on judicial astrology which he called a 'diabolical invention', and declared his intention to make war on judicial astrologers and their science, 'this crew of evil spirits, this infernal spirit of vengeance, this mother of insolence, impiety and blasphemy', which he wanted to press 'so hard that it will be forced to take itself back to Hell'. Jacques-Bénigne Bossuet (1627–1704), Bishop of Meaux, was somewhat less forthright, though no less condemnatory:

> These malign and fraudulent spirits dupe and deceive curious, and in consequence credulous souls by means of a thousand illusions. One of their secrets is astrology and other kinds of divination, which sometimes succeed, depending on whether God thinks it just to deliver an insane curiosity to error or simply to torture.

As for astrology's role in medicine, Claude Saumaise (1588–1653), a Classical scholar, brushed it on one side. The notion of climacteric years, for example, he said was 'a mistake by popular astrologers', and he positively sneered at the notion astrology was needed to interpret someone's character from his or her physical appearance:

> Even without consulting the stars, a physiognomist can certainly work out someone's character. What is more, the common people lay claim to a little of this skill when they tell each other that tall men are vain and stupid, that short men are proud and irritable, and when they state as a fact that those who are blind in one eye, or lame or hunch-backed are malign and wicked. They have no less hesitation in judging a person's character from the colour of his hair. Experience has taught people all this without knowledge of the stars!

Yet the prospect of medicine-with-astrology was still capable of exerting a hold, even over the roundest of sceptics. Marin Mersenne (1588–1648), for example, a brother of the Order of Minimi, rejected the notion of astrological houses altogether and condemned astrology more or less out of hand in at least two of his published works, *Quaestiones in Genesim* (1623) and *La Vérité des Sciences* (1625). But in the latter, he also maintained that a physician must know the phases of the moon, the courses of the stars and planets and their effects, while on wider questions he was inclined to agree that the stars might be signs of events with natural causes, such as the weather or disease, and that comets might indeed signal the death of monarchs. Clearly, then, scepticism about one type of astrology did not necessarily embrace every other type, and it is perhaps notable that even those who devoted much of their intellectual energy to the exploration of the astronomical side of celestial observation, such as Tycho Brahe (1546–1601) and Johannes Kepler (1571–1630), were by no means prepared to throw over its sister science. 'To deny the power and influence of the stars is to detract from divine wisdom and influence,' said Brahe in a lecture to the University of Copenhagen in 1574:

> What more prejudiced or what sillier thought could one have about God than that He had made the most enormous and extraordinary of all heavens and a theatre of so many shining stars in vain and to no useful purpose, when no human being does even the most worthless task except for a particular purpose?

Kepler, who seems to have been prepared to jettison the zodiac along with much of the traditional furniture of astrology, was still willing to advise physicians to 'refrain from treating a seriously weakened patient when the moon is in a powerful aspect', and apparently could not help writing to a friend in 1602 that 'Mars never crosses my path without involving me in disputes and putting me in a quarrelsome mood'. Less distinguished astronomers can be seen to follow a similar pattern. Thus, Ilario Altobelli not only wrote on the 'new' star of 1604, sent a letter to Galileo about the satellites of Saturn in 1610, and published a treatise on the occultation of Mars in 1615, but also defended the Ptolemaic system of houses against that of Regiomontanus, and issued an astrological prediction of the fate of Venice, which he considered dire because of most unusual movements within the heavenly bodies; and Giovanni Giuffi's apparently astronomical treatise, *Tractatus de eclipsibus* (1623), while certainly discussing how eclipses may be predicted and how long they are likely to last, is actually cast in an astrological mould, since the reader is told how to discover the lord (i.e. spirit governor) of the eclipse, what the eclipse signifies in each sign of the zodiac, and what its effects will be in each sign and house.

All these – and indeed many more – examples illustrate the very slow disentanglement of astronomy from astrology, and actually Kepler's throw-away remark about how Mars made him bad-tempered and quarrelsome shows how deeply ingrained astrology was in the early modern psyche, regardless of the many and increasing astronomical discoveries which were undermining the traditional Ptolemaic cosmos. We can see another example of the same thing in the astrological diary kept by Samuel Jeake (1652–99), a provincial merchant from the port of Rye in Sussex, a nonconformist in religion, described by Michael Hunter and Annabel Gregory as 'an earnest, self-preoccupied figure, conscientious, hard-working, and ever keen to better himself'. His diary has been called 'astrological' because it includes thirty-six horoscopes which Jeake himself drew up, relating to important incidents in his life. One, for instance, obviously drawn some time after the event, bears upon his first day at school, others upon the days he began to learn astrology, geometry, arithmetic, and logic, interestingly enough, in that order, showing that he started astrology before the other disciplines, on 25 June 1667 when he was aged fifteen. Many of his horoscopes note the arrival of illness – smallpox on 18 July 1666; tertian fever on 1 April the following year; quartan ague on 31 August 1670, and two further occasions in 1672 and 1693 – or a providential escape from some accident which would otherwise have proved serious: a cart could have broken his foot (9 January 1669), a fall into a dark cellar might have drowned him or cracked open his head (16 June 1670), a tumble downstairs was avoided (8 January 1686), he nearly hit his head on an open door in the street (16 January 1688), his horse did not actually throw him into a stream or trample him in the dark of night (30 September 1693). Several of these are accompanied by a pious acknowledgement – 'through the good providence of God', 'by a merciful Providence', 'the good hand of God directed me' – but the more interesting point is that, in spite of the relative mundanity of the near-accident, Jeake chose to undertake the laborious process of constructing a horoscope so that he could understand both why the danger had threatened and how he had been able to avoid it. In the last of those cases, for example, he records that Saturn and the moon were on the cusp of the house of death, Jupiter and Mars were in conjunction in a watery sign, as were the moon and Venus. Had he been sitting at home, noted Jeake, the accident would not have happened. But because he was out of doors at a particular place (passing the stream) at that particular moment, the rays of the badly aspected planets subjected him to their maleficent influence. But Jeake records cheerful moments, too – a pleasant journey to London on 11 May 1687 and another back on 23rd, with two horoscopes for the latter, one timed at 8.15 a.m. and the other at 9 a.m.; his proposal of marriage (14 June 1680) and the marriage itself (1 March 1681); and the laying of the foundation-stone for a new warehouse (13 June 1689). Out of all these incidents, only one is not domestic or entirely personal, and that is the landing of French soldiers in Rye on 6 July 1690, anent which he drew up a horoscope for the time he first learned the news, 6 a.m. while he was still in bed.

Now, one of the most important features of the astrology in this record of forty-two years is that it shows us: first, that a relatively ordinary individual living most of his life outwith the metropolis and nowhere near the intellectual centres of Oxford and Cambridge took a detailed astrological interest in those events of his life which were important for or significant to him personally; secondly, that he was equipped from his early years to cope with the intricacies of drawing up a horoscope and interpreting it afterwards; thirdly, that in spite of his very frequent invocations of Providence and the kindness of God in connection with his escape from various accidents, Jeake chose to explain both accident and escape by referring to the configurations of the stars; and fourthly, his interest in and use of astrology were governed by a sense that the course of the events he described with astrological commentary was an entirely natural phenomenon, one which could be calculated, recognised, and predicted in much the same way as the reoccurrence of comets could be foretold by the careful, rigorous, and objective appliance of mathematics.

In this, Jeake was managing to illustrate, both in his inclination to the science and his use of it in everyday life, the way the seventeenth century was discovering and refining that 'sane astrology' for which Francis Bacon had called, a reform of traditional practices and attitudes most clearly set out in the work of the French physician and astrologer, Jean-Baptiste Morin (1583–1656), whose principal work, *Astrologia Gallica* (1661), Jeake had begun to read on 3 April 1684. Morin had published several works on astrology before *Astrologia Gallica*, all dedicated to improving the techniques of the science with a view to making its conclusions more accurate and therefore more trustworthy. *Letters to Southern and Northern Astrologers, with a view to having astrology revived* (1628) and *Astronomy now Restored without Fault or Error from its Foundations* (1634) are two examples which give the flavour of his intentions and approach. The 'foundations' to which he referred in *Astronomia Restituta* are those of Ptolemy, and *Astrologia Gallica* sets out and defends at enormous length the basic principles of Hellenistic astrology shorn of Islamic accretions (which Morin describes as 'false, fraudulent, and diabolical'), and those of later Mediaeval revivalists, while at the same time Morin take the opportunity to confute certain contemporaries such as the Italian astrologer Placido de Titis, Descartes, and Pierre Gassendi (1592–1655). Gassendi had profound doubts whether anything could be predicted with certainty from reading the stars, and positively denied that either comets or planets had any influence on individuals at all – conclusions which were published post mortem in his *Syntagma Philosophicum* (1658). Morin, however, vigorously defended the traditional theory of influences, with certain slight modifications, and the significations of the zodiacal houses, again with slight modifications, including changes in the rulerships of the triplicities, his principal gifts as an expounder of astrological theory being his ability to construct rational arguments for his preservation, adaptation, or rejection of traditional ideas, and his strong foundation in mathematics, the latter because he was Royal Professor of Mathematics at the Collège Royale, and one of the earliest people to try to solve the problem of longitude, for which efforts Cardinal Mazarin granted him a pension in 1645.

It is thus easy to see why he would have appealed to Samuel Jeake, for whom the more astronomical-meteorological aspects of astrology held a particular attraction, just as Jeake's interest in and common use of astrology helps to show that contemporary attacks on the science had limited effect, especially on ordinary folk. Physicians, however, had picked up the more cautious note sounded by the latest theorists who were keen to promote accuracy in their astrology, as can be seen from a monitory preface to Richard Saunders's *Astrological Judgement and Practice of Physick* (1677):

> The one thing I would request from the sons of art, that before such time as long experience, (which is the *lapis Lydius* to try the truth from falsehood), hath established their opinion in the predictions following, that they never presume to give any judgement or sentence of this art, except the time of the day or night be exactly known, when the sick person, or else some other in his behalf, doth consult with thee concerning his disease, or the time he bringeth or sendeth his urine to thee be assuredly known, that thereby the

ascendant, and the angles of the figure may be exactly taken, as also the cusp of the eighth house, that the lords of the ascendant, fourth and eighth house, be no ways mistaken: for upon these and their several habitudes and configurations all our whole scope dependeth. Another thing also is to be diligently observed, that there be no error committed in the calculation of the planets, so that the true degree (of their longitude at least) may be perfectly had, the which by way of caveat I thought good to remember, lest this art and myself should be both unjustly accused, or blamed without dessert; and especially be careful in the motions of Mars and Mercury, for there are calculations now extant that have erred in the retrocedation of Mars above 2°, and in the slow motion, and especially in the retrogradation of Mercury, it is usual at sometimes to miss 3 or 4, if not 7 or 8°, which intolerable error is more than the semidiameter of his beams.

But far more serious for seventeenth-century astrologers was the increasing divorce between the macrocosm and the microcosm. For centuries the two had been linked, humankind being looked upon as an image in miniature of the greater cosmos; but now that the picture of the cosmos was being altered, matched by parallel changes in the way people conceived the human body and its working as dissection of it turned from a barely tolerated practice to a popular theatrical spectacle, the two were drifting apart so far that re-linking them would be extremely difficult. Ryan Stark makes this point in reaction to William Harvey's work on the circulation of the blood:

> By grounding the impetus of circulation within the body itself, Harvey, in one swift blow, shatters Renaissance conceptions of physic, including magical and astrological thinking based upon macrocosm to microcosm correspondences, where objects like the stars and the planets are thought to influence the body's and society's agency through occult verisimilitudes.

Moreover, astrology's close relationship with magic, astral or demonic, was bound to affect it when intellectual credence in magic began to falter. By the late seventeenth and early eighteenth century, intellectual trends were beginning to ask the old questions about humanity's place in the universe – its relationship with the universe's separate parts, and how best to survive and flourish here on earth in the face of Nature's uncertainty and human greed or cruelty or indifference to the suffering of others – by pointing those questions in other than the traditional directions. A deep-seated materialism was beginning to seize the ancient citadel of the human heart and offer explanations and solutions based largely on an egocentricity which in the fullness of time would replace an animated, spiritual cosmos in which humanity had its special, though not central place, with an almost unimaginably vast mechanism in which humanity had nothing but itself and surrounding matter to which it could cling for any sense of meaning or worth or direction.

At the beginning of this process, however, attacks on astrology were often disguised as attacks on astrologers, and astrology in many ways stood for more deeply-seated contemporary targets. Two years in the seventeenth century, 1652 and 1654, for example, saw two eclipses of the sun which were visible all over Western Europe. Between them they spawned an extraordinary outburst of Messianic and mystical pamphleteering and sermonising, both of which were assisted by the relatively new form of publicising events and comments, the newspaper, and in the atmosphere of panic, (not too strong a word for people's reactions to these phenomena), there flourished a degree of charlatanism and superstition which neither religion nor astronomy seemed able to combat with much success. (To catch something of the more extreme oddities thrown up by such an atmosphere, it may be worth recalling the arrival of the comet Hale-Bopp in 1997 and the conviction of a religious group, Heaven's Gate, which was persuaded that a spaceship was coming in the comet's wake; and to escape disaster on earth and save their souls, thirty-eight members of the cult, along with its leader, committed suicide by poison).

In spite of the peculiarly frenetic ambience, however, opinion-formers such as scholars from the universities were divided on the subject of astrology. Some opposed it, others defended it. But slowly, as the seventeenth century began to settle after the destructive and emotive wars which had disfigured so many of its decades, the opponents' arguments in favour of a mechanical rather than an animate universe began to win hearts and minds among the political classes for whom the fervours and spasms of war and the frangibility of religious confessions no longer offered routes to power in the same way they had done. To a certain extent, too, we must bear in mind the attraction for opinion-formers and their audience of the intellectual cachet attached to the New and the Revolutionary. To feel oneself at the forefront of discovery, embracing the future and rejecting the past, provides various types of satisfaction, including that of separating oneself from those who do not share one's radicalism – the conservative, the uneducated, the ignorant. But breaking with the past and abandoning ancient sciences would not be easy. As Jesus warned, 'No man putteth a piece of new cloth unto an old garment ... neither do men put new wine into old bottles, else the bottles break and the wine runneth out, and the bottles perish,' (*Matthew* 9.16–17); or, perhaps, as a mid-seventeenth-century proverb expressed it, 'What is new cannot be true.' The separation of macrocosm from microcosm was being mirrored (paradoxically enough) by the flight of the intellectual and ruling classes from the rest of society and, with the emergence of rapidly evolving technology as a major force in the lives of almost everyone in the nineteenth and twentieth centuries, it would be interesting to see whether the new would indeed prove to be true, as its supporters would insist, or not, as the adherents to older ways would hope and believe. [3]

14

New Planets, Esotericism & Almanacs
c.1800–c.1900:
Astrology in the Post-Industrial World

The expansion of horizons which came with the discovery of 'new' stars, new religious confessions, and more intimate knowledge of the workings of the human body was accompanied by a succession of revelations that the world was larger and more diverse than had previously been realised, and here too astrology played a significant role. Anyone who went on a long journey by sea was likely to have consulted an astrologer about the likely outcome, and Francis Crow who lambasted the science in his book *The Vanity and Impiety of Judicial Astrology* (1690) noted that sailors rarely set forth without seeking assurance from astrology that their voyage would take place under fortunate celestial aspects and influences.

Some of the countries they visited already had astrological traditions of their own. China, for example, unlike the ancient Middle East or Europe, concentrated its astrological attention on those circumpolar constellations which never rise or set, but remain visible every night. These were divided into twenty-eight houses or 'mansions', each associated with one of the feudal states of ancient China, and in consequence were significant for rulers rather than ordinary individuals, a characteristic they shared, of course, with their Mesopotamian-Babylonian counterparts:

> When Mercury appears in company with Venus to the east, and when they are both red and shoot forth rays, then foreign kingdoms will be vanquished and the soldiers of China will be victorious … The Hanging Tongue [*six stars in the constellation Perseus*] governs rumours. If Mars stands near by it, there will be rebellions among the people. The Prince will be injured by rumours, and robbers will arise.

Predictions such as these were based on observations of the moon, the sun, the five planets – Mercury, Venus, Mars, Jupiter and Saturn, as in the West – their risings and settings and conjunctions with each other, and on constellations which were different from those recognised by Babylonian or Greek astronomer-astrologers, and while the methods of obtaining those predictions were mostly similar to those employed by the West, they seem to have evolved independently in China before contact with Iranian, Indian, and later Islamic astrology opened channels of intercourse and cultural influence. [1] Horary, judicial, or genethliacal astrology which concern themselves with the individual, his or her character and prospects, or his or her immediate preoccupations, did not really develop in

China until the first century AD, but thereafter they flourished and by the eighth century the astrologer Chang Kuo had produced an enormous encyclopaedia on the subject, *Hsing Tsung* ('The Company of the Stars'), and the astronomer Chhüthan Hsia-Ta, a compendium of astronomy and astrology, *Khai-Yuan Chan Ching* ('The Khai-Yuan reign-period Treatise on Astrology').

Influences in Chinese astrology, however, were not considered to flow only in one direction. It was important for human beings, especially the Emperor and his administrators, to perform their rituals consistently and correctly, otherwise Nature would suffer adverse reactions as a result of disturbances in heaven:

> Someone asked whether a sage could make divination. [Yang Hsiung] replied that a sage could certainly make divination about heaven and earth. 'If that is so,' continued the questioner, 'what is the difference between the sage and the astrologer?' [Yang Hsiung] replied, 'The astrologer foretells what the effects of heavenly phenomena will be on man; the sage foretells what the effects of man's actions will be on the heavens.' (Yang Hsiung, *Model Discourses*, chap. 6)

The Emperor, indeed, played a key role in astronomy-astrology by personally observing the pole star and the sun, and so fixing the four cardinal points. He also appointed the Imperial Astrologer, (an hereditary office), whose job is described in chapter 6 of the second-century BC *Chou Li* ('Record of the Rites of Chou'):

> He concerns himself with the stars in the heavens, keeping a record of the changes and movements of the planets, the sun and the moon, in order to examine the movements of the terrestrial world, with the object of distinguishing [*prognosticating*] good and bad fortune. He divides the territories of the nine regions of the Empire in accordance with their dependence on particular celestial bodies. All the fiefs and principalities are connected with distinct stars, and from this their prosperity or misfortune can be ascertained. He makes prognostications according to the twelve years [*of the Jupiter cycle*], of good and evil in the terrestrial world. From the colours of the five kinds of clouds he determines the coming of floods or drought, abundance or famine. From the twelve winds he draws conclusions about the state of harmony of heaven and earth, and takes note of the good or bad signs which result from their accord or disaccord. In general he concerns himself with the five kinds of phenomena, so as to warn the Emperor to come to the aid of the government, and to allow for variations in the ceremonies according to the circumstances.

But, as in the West, astronomy and astrology seem to have been bed-fellows. In a memorial to the Emperor in AD 1092, Su Sung noted that those who made astronomical observations with instruments provided the state not only with correct calendars, but also with predictions about future good and bad luck for the country, and if we believe in the authenticity of Marco Polo's account of his travels and accept that one of the chapters in one of his texts is genuine, we have evidence that in the thirteenth century the Great Khan supported no fewer than 5,000 astrologers who used astrolabes and ephemerides to assist in their prognostications which they produced not merely for the Khan but for large numbers of other people, too. Fascination for this state-sponsored astrology seems to have remained strong, even as late as the seventeenth century, as we can gauge from the somewhat dismissive account of Nicholas Trigault in his *De Christiana Expeditione* (1615):

> They have some knowledge also of astrology and the mathematics: in arithmetic and geometry anciently more excellent, but in learning and teaching confused. They reckon four hundred stars more than our astrologers have mentioned, numbering certain smaller which do not always appear. Of the heavenly appearances they have no rules. They are much busied about foretelling eclipses and the courses of the planets, but therein very erroneous; and all their skill of stars is in a manner which we call 'judicial astrology', imagining these things below to depend on the stars. Somewhat they have received of the western Saracens, [*i.e. Islamic astronomer-astrologers*], but they confirm nothing by demonstration, only have left to them tables by which they reckon the eclipses and motions.
>
> The first of this royal family [*the Ming dynasty*] forbade any to learn this judicial astrology but those which by hereditary right are thereto designed, to prevent innovations. But he which now reigneth maintaineth divers mathematicians [*astronomer-astrologers*], both eunuchs within the palace and magistrates without, of which there are in Peking two tribunals, one of Chinese which follow their own authors, another of Saracens which reform the same by *their* rules and by conference together. Both have in a small hill a plain for contemplation, where are huge mathematical instruments of brass ... One of the college nightly watcheth thereon ... That of Nanking exceeds this of Peking, as being then the seat royal. When the Peking astrologers foretell eclipses, the magistrates and idol ministers are commanded to assemble in their officiary habits to help the labouring planets, which they think to do with beating brazen bells and often kneelings all the time that they think the eclipse lasteth, lest they should then be devoured (as I have heard) by I know not what serpent.

The general impression one has of Chinese astrology, then, is that while its observational information was the same as, in and many respects superior to that of Western astronomer-astrologers, [2] its employment first by the state and later by private individuals – and here perhaps one should note the development of a technique of using astrology in company with the classical divinatory system, *I Ching*, during the Ming dynasty, i.e. fourteenth to eighteenth centuries AD – followed much the same path as its Western counterpart. But here somewhat different stars, constellations, and divisions of the sky were used to provide the basis for interpretation and prediction, and in consequence Chinese astrology (as opposed to astronomy) had no direct contribution to make to the history of that science in the West.

Likewise, India had her own traditions which, however, were open to Middle Eastern influence, particularly in the sixth century BC when the Persian King Darius invaded the Indus Valley, and then to Greek after the incursion of Alexander the Great. Hindu astrology is properly known as *jyotish*, referring to a candle-flame, light as a divine principle of life, and hence 'the science of light' or 'the wisdom of the heavens'. The planets are the seven known to ancient Western astrology, but the zodiac is different in as much as while the Western (tropical) zodiac shows the earth's relationship to the sun, the Hindu (sidereal) zodiac is concerned with the moon's relationship with the stars. Thus, the position of the moon and its passage through the *nakshatras*, (divisions of the ecliptic which measure the distance the moon travels in one solar day), which are associated with particular stars in successive constellations as well as particular deities, are of fundamental importance to the Hindu astrologer. They are referred to in the oldest Hindu writings, the *Vedas* – 'Seeking favour of the twenty-eight-fold wondrous ones, shining in the sky together, ever-moving, hasting in the creation, I worship with songs the days, the firmament' – but in spite of this ancient pedigree may owe something to Middle Eastern influence, as there are striking similarities between a list of *nakshatras* and a Babylonian star-list of seventeen constellations in the path of the moon.

Still, cross-cultural fertilisation could just as easily have gone the other way and it is the similarities between Hindu and Iranian astrology which are worth noting, rather than arguments over their respective origins.[3] The *nakshatra* system did not remain static. At first a record of the moon's daily location among the stars, it later became a way of recording the positions of the planets against the sidereal background, and when the Western zodiac was introduced into India during the second century AD, with the names of the twelve signs translated into Sanskrit, impetus was given to the development of Indian mathematics and to astronomical observation, both of which resulted in a definition of the zodiac somewhat different from that of the Babylonians. One of the key elements in bringing about the difference was the *yuga* system, the notion that there is a Great Year during which every planet returns to its point of departure in the zodiac, a series of successive revolutions which, according to the fifth-century reforming astronomer-astrologer Aryabhata, takes 4,320,000 years to complete. This is obviously similar to the Greek concept of a Great Year, outlined in Plato's *Timaeus*, and variations in the length of such a year are numerous. But there did emerge an agreed method among Indians and Iranians for calculating such a year: from the arrival of the planets at the first degree of Aries until their arrival at the last degree of Pisces. Thus, starting with a grand conjunction of the planets at 0° Aries, an astrologer can follow the cycles of the planets in their revolutions of the zodiac and so determine the mean sidereal period of each planet, based on the assumption that such a grand conjunction took place in 3,101 [BC].

As we saw earlier, Indian astrology, having been influenced by Iran and Greece, in its turn influenced Islamic astrology, partly through the presence of Indian astrologers at Muslim Courts, partly through translated texts and the writings of such scholars as Abū Ma'shar who, for example, noted that 'the Indians thought the Beginning happened on a Sunday, with the sun in the ascendant; and between them, (that is, between that day and the day of the Flood), there are 720,634,442,715 days'. Māshā'allāh, however, describes something peculiarly Indian, the theory of *navamsas*. A *navamsa* is a one-ninth division of each sign of the zodiac, each such segment coming under the influence of a zodiac sign – first *navamsa* of Aries ruled by Aries, the second by Taurus, and so on in order – thereby producing a system of signs within signs and rulerships within rulerships. These in turn, of course, signal passages, periods of transition, and therefore the creation of new relationships involving not only the celestial bodies themselves, but also human beings whose lives are in a constant flux which forms a process of alteration mirroring (or being reflected by) that of the stars and planets above them. The more refined the calculation of *navamsas*, then, the more subtle and more accurate the predictive interpretation of the horoscope by a skilled astrologer. [4]

From east and south, we should now turn north to Russia where knowledge of astrology was heavily influenced, as one might expect, by Byzantine traditions, and since these traditions were largely brought first by Christian missionaries, then via Biblical texts and commentaries, we find almost from the start a sharp division between ecclesiastical condemnation of the science and toleration of or interest in it by the state. Thus, the Trullan Council of 692 condemned it and the Russian Church followed, reiterating the tenor of its censure as late as 1551 when a Council held in Moscow at the instance of Tsar Ivan IV (1530–84) strongly recommended that the Tsar punish all works describing astronomy, signs of the zodiac, almanacs, and the pseudo-Aristotelian *Gates of Aristotle*, while a penitential listed belief in stars, horoscopes, and astrology in general among 'Hellenic' practices the Church considered undesirable. In spite of this, however, interest did exist and after the fall of Constantinople in 1453 texts dealing with the occult sciences began to spread in Russia via clerical refugees, and thus stimulated interest even further.

One sign of this is that during the fifteenth century, the Grand Dukes of Moscow started to hire physicians from Western Europe, and this meant that Western astrology came into Russia with them as, for example, in the case of Nicolas 'the German' who introduced a new medical text, *Hortus Sanitatis* ('The Garden of Health'), which turned out to be very popular, contained information about astrological medicine and, in its Russian translation, parts of pseudo-Aristotle's 'Secret of Secrets', a compilation which strongly advocated the use of both astrology and magic. [5] Nevertheless, as William Ryan observes, 'In Mediaeval Russia there was little more than hearsay knowledge of astrology.' It was really not until the advent of Western influences during the sixteenth and seventeenth centuries, along with a late advance in the mathematical skills necessary to draw up a horoscope, that astrology became prominent enough for the state to take any interest in it, and even then the state tended to follow the Church in condemning it. The trouble was that astrology was seen as a Western, and therefore Catholic, import – hence one reason for the Russian Church's hostility – and that astrology seemed to be closely associated with magic, not to mention the Jews, several of whose astronomical, calendrical, and astrological texts were translated into Russian as early as the thirteenth century and remained popular until at least the eighteenth. Almanacs, another Western import, also captured public attention, mainly because they contained such useful information as the signs of the zodiac, dates of eclipses, favourable times for blood-letting, and so forth, although Muscovy rumour in the sixteenth century said that Tsar Ivan IV bought every almanac which entered the city, for fear the people would learn more than was good for them.

As elsewhere, however, individual rulers and nobles took a personal interest in the science. Tsar Alexei Mikhailovich (1645–76) had a zodiac room in the Kremlin and an astronomical-astrological ceiling in his palace at Kolomenskoe, while Prince Golitsyn had the ceiling of

his dining room painted with the zodiac and that of his bedroom with the planets – signs
that Western, perhaps especially Italian Renaissance influence had permeated the Russian
Court before the advent of the Russians' great westerniser, Tsar Peter the Great. But as far
as the majority of Russians were concerned, astrology was best ingested in simpler guise.
During the 1780s short divinatory texts were popular, particularly in the form of illustrated
dream-books – two such, both published in St Petersburg in 1784, for example, include an
astrological guide to the influence of the planets in addition to a table of unlucky days, a
description of the four humours, and explanations of dreams – and during the 1790s these
relatively short publications were incorporated in much larger compendia which included
a mish-mash of information vaguely or directly connected with fortune-telling. These
in turn passed out of fashion by 1830, having been supplanted during the early 1800s by
books claiming to be less astrologically, more astronomically based, but which were in fact
unable to make up their minds whether they were 'scientific' in content or merely the old
dream-books dressed in the latest mode. Astrology, however, had never really established a
firm foothold in the Russian consciousness since the Mediaeval Church condemned it, and
perhaps also because it was regarded as somehow foreign and undesirable. Hence, outwith
the charmed circle of the Imperial Court and that educated élite which was keen to be
considered 'advanced' and therefore embraced rather than rejected foreign ideas, Russia
did not develop a particular interest in nor find a widespread use for astrology, in which it
differed considerably from the West its élite was eager to imitate. [6]

But if we now turn our attention west, we find an altogether different picture. Traffic
between the British Isles, the West Indies, and the American colonies, for example, was
imbued with astrological prediction, and traders and colonists exported their interest
in and reliance upon the science of the stars to those parts of the world in which they
settled or with which they did business. A good example of how astrology came into New
England can be seen in the library of John Winthrop, Junior (1606–76). He was born in
England, but followed his father over the Atlantic and eventually became Governor of
Connecticut in 1658 and then again in 1659, holding the post thereafter until his death.
He made the journey between New England and the old country more than once, in 1634
and again in 1641. His library shows he had a particular interest in what we should now
call the 'sciences' – an enthusiasm which led to his being elected a member of the newly-
formed Royal Society of London in 1662 – but these included alchemy (for which he had
a special penchant), witchcraft, and astrology, this last being represented by two volumes,
Astrologia Aphoristica Ptolemaei Hermetica (Ulm 1641) and *A Table of the Twelve Astrological
Houses of Heaven* (London 1654) written 'by one V.B, a well-willer to the mathematicks'.
The *Table* includes a number of blank diagrams and others which have been filled in, such
as one for an Alice Wilkins, dated 11 January 1656. The handwriting, however, is not that
of Winthrop and it seems he was sent the book from London, a testimony both to his
interest and to the trade which sent such things overseas.

Indeed, library lists from late seventeenth- and early eighteenth-century Virginia show
that large numbers of people in the American colonies owned books dealing with one or
more of the occult sciences: *Urania Practica* (1649) deals with astrology and astronomy, as
does *A Tutor to Astronomie* (1659); *The Art How to Know Men* (1670) explains the art of

using astrology, chiromancy, and metoposcopy to predict the future; and *Medicina Practica* (1692) contains dozens of astrologically based cures for illness. These last two were owned by an Anglican clergyman, Thomas Teackle, who, one is perhaps not surprised to learn, was accused in 1662 of teaching false doctrine, although the complaint came to nothing and he continued to serve his parish until 1696. Some people clearly used the books they acquired to practical effect, as in the case of a rich woman from New England, Katharine Harrison, who told fortunes, basing her expertise, (as she herself said), on her reading of 'Mr Lilly's book', presumably his *Christian Astrology*, and that of Charles Morton, a Harvard tutor, who wrote a textbook for students in the natural sciences, *Compendium Physicae*, in which he referred to and encouraged the use of astrology in medicine. This situation was not quick to change, and in 1764 we find Nathaniel Ames giving expression to his view and that of many others:

> Astrology has a philosophical foundation. The celestial powers that can and do agitate and move the whole ocean have also force and ability to change and alter the fluids and solids of the human body, and that which can alter and change the fluids and solids of the human body must also greatly affect and influence the mind: and that which can and does affect the mind has a great share and influence in the actions of men.

But if learned books were for the few, almanacs were for the many, and while the amount of their astrological content varied, that which did appear was seriously directed towards informing and educating its readers – it was via almanacs, for example, that knowledge of astronomy and astronomical discoveries was spread among the general public – and Ames's references to the human body remind us that many of the almanacs contained material helpful to the practice of astrological medicine. One such was the *Kalendarium Pennsilvaniense, or, America's Messenger* (1685) by Samuel Atkins who described himself as 'a student of the Mathematics and Astrology', and others published by Daniel Leeds in 1694–9, 1713, and 1715 contained a section on 'The most apt times to gather herbs, when the planets that govern them are dignified'. Some producers of almanacs, of course, railed against astrology altogether, (in 1746 Jacob Taylor called it 'a mere cheat, a brat of Babylon, brought forth in Chaldaea, a place famous for idolatry'), but this was the exception. Slowly but determinedly, almanacs increased the public's awareness of judicial astrology in particular, that branch of the science so much maligned by critics, and over a period of about forty years, under the influence of a number of New England printers almanacs containing judicial astrology became very popular. (Those by Nathaniel Ames, for example, sold between 50,000 and 60,000 copies each year). So in spite of the apparent wish of many almanac-publishers to play down the 'occult' content of their books and pamphlets, it was actually just this content which appealed most to their readership [7] – hence, for example, the constant appearance in them of 'Occult Man', the human figure surrounded by signs of the zodiac relating to the body's different parts, as may be seen from Nathaniel Ames's almanac of 1729 – and so popular did these almanacs become that in 1743 one Jacob Taylor complained bitterly that in moments of crisis families turned to them rather than to the Bible for a solution.

One can see what he means from the example of Daniel Leeds, an almanac-publisher, who in the last years of the seventeenth century and opening decades of the eighteenth promoted astrology and other occult philosophies in his publications, treated astrology as though it were theology, and maintained that the proliferation of sects within Christianity pointed to a corruption of true religion which was to be found in humanity's relationship with the stars. Leeds had been a Quaker before that confession expelled him, and it looks as though the Quakers suffered more than once from a similar deviation from their orthodoxy, since in 1695 Philip Roman, Junior, and his brother Robert were threatened with expulsion for, among other things, 'professing the art of astrology [and undertaking] thereby to give answers and astrological judgements concerning persons and things'. Philip caved in, Robert did not and was pursued by charges that he used astrology, geomancy, and occult [*i.e. magical*] means 'to take the wife of Henry Hastings away from her husband and children'.

Needless to say, not everyone took the occult sciences seriously. There were many sceptics in the pre-independent United States, as elsewhere, and those who were prepared to mock when confronted by practitioners. In 1744, a traveller from Maryland, Alexander Hamilton, described a chance meeting in New Jersey:

> A solemn old fellow lighted at the door. He was in a homely rustic dress, and I under-stood his name was Morgan. 'Look ye here,' says the landlord to me, 'here comes a famous philosopher.' 'Your servant, Mr Morgan, how d'ye?' The old fellow had not setted himself long upon his seat before he entered upon a learned discourse concerning astrology and the influence of the stars, in which he seemed to put a great deal more confidence than I thought was requisite. From that he made a transition to the causes of the tides, the shape and dimension of the earth, the laws of gravitation, and 50 other physical subjects in which he seemed to me not to talk so much out of the way as he did upon the subject of judicial astrology ... I found him very deficient in his knowledge that way, though a great pretender. All this chat passed while the old fellow drank half a pint of wine, which done, the old don took to his horse and rode off in very slow solemn pace, seemingly well satis-fied with his own learning and knowledge.

Nevertheless, as in parts of Europe, the various churches, unhappy at the hold over their congregations exercised by such perceived ignoramuses (not to mention frauds), continued to condemn what Jacob Taylor called the 'filthy superstition of heathens', especially when they found disconcerting evidence that clergymen themselves were not necessarily immune from dabbling in it, as happened in New Jersey when the presbyterian Synod of Philadelphia received a complaint in 1728 that one of its ministers had been practising judicial astrology. Church discipline, however, did not always work and as late as 1810 *The Clergyman's Almanac* for that year included the signs of the zodiac, as did *The Christian Almanac* for 1821, both without comment or censure. But the clergy could not, and did not bring themselves to ignore entirely celestial and meteorological signs of God's providence or displeasure. In 1684, for example, the Trustees of Harvard College moved the date of graduation when they found out that there would be a solar eclipse on 2 July, and although the ceremony passed without incident on 1st, the College President died on 2nd, just as the eclipse was beginning its final stage. Increase Mather, the new President, was a minister who took these signs seriously, having just published *An Essay for the Recording of Illustrious Providence*, a book which was based on three years' worth of reports from clergy throughout Massachusetts, wherein they sent to Mather their accounts of 'Divine judgements, tempests, floods, earthquakes, thunders as are unusual, strange apparitions, or whatever else shall happen that is prodigious, witchcrafts, diabolical possessions, remarkable judgements upon noted sinners, eminent deliverances, and answers of prayer'.

Outwith what one may call the regular versions of Christianity, however, astrology positively flourished in early Mormonism. The family of Joseph Smith (1805–44), founder of the Latter Day Saints, is said to have possessed a dagger inscribed with the astrological symbol of Mars and the sigil of the planet's ruling spirit, and parchments on which were written the signs of the planets and the zodiac; seventeen of Smith's marriages were celebrated on astrologically significant days; and even his physical appearance and tendency to disorder of the legs conformed to the expected types of those born under Jupiter in Capricorn. Smith himself also possessed a silver talisman engraved on one side with Jupiter, the seal and sigil of the planet's ruler, and (in poor Latin) 'I give assurance, o most powerful god', while on the other side appeared the magic square of Jupiter and the Hebrew names *Abba*, *Jophiel*, and *El Ab*. That all these were considered to be significant at the time can be gauged from the remark by Brigham Young, one of Smith's successors as leader of the new Church, that 'the only thing the Prophet believed in was astrology' – an exaggeration, perhaps, but a signal of the importance Smith attached to the science.

The influence of the writings of the English astrologer Ebenezer Sibley (1752–c.1799), many times reprinted, also seem to have been important to Smith in his construction of magical lamina and parchments which were distributed among his extensive family. So it is not surprising to find that astrology in particular continued to play a part in Mormon psychology long after its foundation as a movement in 1830. In public, Smith himself gave the impression of disapproving of astrology, but his private practice, as we have seen, was rather different, and in fact even important days in the early history of Mormonism happened at astrologically significant moments to an extent which it is difficult to accept was entirely coincidental. Thus, for example, Joseph Smith went through the movement's endowment ceremony in 1842 on a Thursday, the day of Jupiter, when the moon was in Pisces, over whose sign Jupiter is also the ruler; and when Joseph was anointed prophet, king, priest, and ruler over Israel on earth in 1844, the ceremony took place on another Thursday when Saturn was in conjunction with the moon. In 1853 a number of Mormons held meetings to study astrology and their group nearly turned into a regular School of Astrology in 1855, but petered out in the face of opposition from others. Astrology, then, was strong among Mormon pioneers in spite of hostility and condemnation from others within the fledgling confession, and the 1860s and 1870s saw it flourish – significantly enough with the help of almanacs which were still proving to be popular. Indeed, there is plenty of evidence to show that many Mormons were actively interested in astrology well into the twentieth century, although by that time differences in education and access to a wide range of technologies of communication naturally had an effect on the readiness of newer generations of Mormons to accept the occult science as cordially as their recent forebears had done. [8]

But change affected everyone, not just small groups of religious innovators, and one of the biggest challenges to traditional astrology came on 13 March 1781 when Sir William Herschel observed through a telescope set up in his garden a 'curious either nebulous star or perhaps a comet' which consensus among astronomers and interested parties to whom he communicated his observation finally agreed was actually a new planet. This presented an immediate practical problem. 'Some of our astronomers here,' wrote Sir Joseph Banks in a letter to Herschel dated 15 November 1781, 'incline to the opinion that it is a planet and not a comet, [and] if you are of that opinion, it should forthwith be provided with a name and our nimble neighbours, the French, will certainly save us the trouble of baptising it.' Herschel took the hint and decided to call his discovery *Georgium Sidus* ('George's Star') after his patron, King George III, with a flimsy reference to the Roman poet Horace's equally cloying *Julium sidus* ('Julius's Star') providing literary, as well as political precedent. Fortunately the Prussian astronomer Johann Bode produced something better and more acceptable outwith the confines of England. Since the new planet lay beyond Saturn, and it had been the custom hitherto to use Classical mythology as a source for celestial names, Saturn's father seemed to offer an appropriate nomenclature: and so 'Uranus' was adopted. The French, however, did manage to contribute after all, for Jérôme Lalande wrote to Herschel on 7 April 1784 to say that 'we have had a new sign engraved for your planet. It is a globe surmounted by the first letter of your name, [so] there you are, associated in spite of yourself with all the divinities of antiquity'. The sign in question was the astrological, not the astronomical symbol of the planet. How far Herschel was pleased or not he did not commit to paper.

Uranus, however, had to be accommodated astrologically. Modern astrologers associate it with freedom, originality, and unexpected change because it lies beyond the traditional boundary marking the last of the seven planets, and because it was discovered at a time of invention and discovery and new ways of doing old-established things. Hence its indication in a horoscope of a person's impulse to venture into the unconventional or novel. That Uranus might indicate unforeseen accidents was sufficiently proved to the satisfaction of the painter John Varley (1778–1842) who practised astrology and was fascinated by the new planet:

Varley spent much time inserting Uranus in his own and other people's charts, watching carefully to see what kinds of events it provoked when it came into conjunction or aspect with other planets – also when affected radically by other planets. He had evidently come to the conclusion that if Uranus was excited by Mars, there would be sudden or unexpected eruptions. One particular morning he announced to his family that he would stay at home, as something very serious was going to happen and he must be present when it occurred. At noon, part of the house caught fire. Not one bucket of water did Varley carry, but he sat down to write notes on the effect of Uranus. Let me quote his son Albert who tells the story: 'He was so delighted at having discovered what the astrological significance of Uranus was, that he sat down while his house was burning, knowing though he did, that he was not insured for a penny, to write an account of his discovery ... Although he lost everything in the fire, he regarded that as a small matter compared with his discovery of the new planet's potential.'

The astrologer Thomas White also included Uranus in a horoscope he drew for King Louis XVI of France, dated January 1793 and published in *The Conjuror's* (later *Astrologer's*) *Magazine* that same year. The chart was produced so quickly that it contained a number of mistakes, (probably the printer's rather than White's), but it does show Uranus in opposition to the ascendant, thereby intimating violence and destruction to the King, a fate which came to pass, as the King was guillotined in January that year. Nevertheless, something of the uncertainty attendant on Uranus's absorption into the astrological system persisted as late as 1881 when 'Zadkiel', (a popular pseudonym for astrological authors who wished to remain anonymous, or add an exotic mysteriousness to their publications), produced *An Introduction to Astrology by William Lilly, with Numerous Emendations, adapted to the Improved State of the Science in the Present Day*. For although 'Zadkiel' notes the qualities of unexpectedness and novelty attached to the planet, he does not call it 'Uranus' but 'Herschel':

> This is the most distant planet from the sun. His motion is very slow, as he takes 83 years 151 days to go through the twelve signs. The nature of H[erschel] is extremely evil. If he ascend or be with the chief significator in any figure, he denotes an eccentric person, far from fortunate, always abrupt, and often violent in his manners. If well aspected, he gives sudden and unexpected benefits; and if afflicted, he will cause remarkable and unlooked-for losses and misfortunes. He is not so powerful as Saturn or Mars, yet can do much evil. Persons under his influence are partial to antiquity, astrology, etc., and all uncommon studies, especially if Mercury and the moon be in aspect to him. They are likely to strike out novelties, and to be remarkable for an inventive faculty. They are generally unfortunate in marriage, especially if he afflict Venus, the moon, or the seventh house, either in nativities or questions.

Partly because of such continuing additions to the heavens, astrology came under increasing attack during the eighteenth century. In England, for example, it was strictly speaking illegal, since the Witchcraft Act of 1736 had outlawed practice of the science, and both before it and after, astrologers were subject to waves of contempt and mockery from a variety of sources. In a famous incident from 1707 Jonathan Swift took up his pen against John Partridge, an astrologer and publisher of the somewhat clumsily-written almanac, *Merlinus Liberatus*. Pro-Nonconformist and anti-Anglican, Partridge's attacks on the established Church, coupled with a predilection for boasting about his astrological abilities, made him a prime target for Swift's brand of satire; and so in 1707 Swift produced *Predictions for the Year 1708, wherein the month and day of the month are set down, the persons named, and the great actions and events of next year particularly related as they will come to pass: written to prevent the people of England from being further imposed on by vulgar almanack-makers. By Isaac Bickerstaffe, Esq*. The pamphlet begins, 'I have long considered the gross abuse of astrology in this kingdom, and upon debating the matter with myself, I could not possibly lay the fault upon the art, but upon those gross imposters who set up to be the artists.' After this Swift launches into a condemnation of those gross imposters who 'do not so much as understand common grammar and syntax, that they are not able to spell any word out of the usual road, nor even in their prefaces to write common sense or intelligible English' – a direct hit at Partridge. Next he gives instances of predictions so vaguely worded that they must be true of someone somewhere at some time: 'This month a great person will be threatened with death or sickness'; 'this month an eminent clergyman will be preferred'; 'such a planet is such a house shews great machinations, plots and conspiracies that may, in time, be brought to light'. Swift/ Bickerstaffe now proposes to make a series of very precise predictions, and begins his list with the acme of this piece of satire:

> My first prediction is but a trifle, yet I will mention it to shew how ignorant those sottish pretenders to astrology are in their own concerns. It relates to Partridge, the almanac-maker. I have consulted the star of his nativity by my own rules and find he will infallibly die upon the 29th day of March next, about eleven at night, of a raging fever. Therefore I advise him to consider of it, and settle his affairs in time.

Partridge, of course, did not die as predicted, and must have been highly perplexed when an elegy on his supposed death, and an epitaph, made their appearance in print along with a new pamphlet purporting to describe the circumstances of his death, along with a death-bed confession:

> Well, 'tis as Bickerstaffe has guessed,
> Though we all took it as a jest:
> Partridge is dead; nay more, he died
> Ere he could prove the good 'squire lied.
> Strange, an astrologer should die
> Without one wonder in the sky!
> Not one of all his crony stars
> To pay their duty at his hearse ….
> The sun has rose and gone to bed
> Just as if Partridge were not dead. (*Elegy* 1–8, 11–12)

> Here, five foot deep, lies on his back
> A cobbler, starmonger, and quack,
> Who to the stars in pure good-will
> Does to his best look upward still. (*Epitaph* 1–4)

I told him his discourse surprised me, and I would be glad he were in a state of health to tell me what reason he had to be convinced of Mr Bickerstaffe's ignorance. He replied, 'I am a poor fellow, bred to a mean trade, yet I have sense enough to know that all pretences of foretelling by astrology are deceits, for this manifest reason, because the wise and the learned, who can only judge whether there be any truth in this science, do all unanimously agree to laugh at and despise it, and none but the poor ignorant vulgar give it any credit, and that only upon the word of such silly wretches as I and my fellows who can hardly write or read.' I then asked him why he had not calculated his own nativity to see whether it agreed with Bickerstaffe's prediction; at which he shook his head and said, 'Oh sir, this is no time for jesting, but for repenting those fooleries, as I do now from the bottom of my heart.' 'By what I can gather from you,' said I, 'the observations and predictions you printed with your almanacs were mere impositions on the people.' He replied, 'If it were otherwise, I should have the less to answer for.' (*An Account of Partridge's Death*)

The satire struck home and Partridge found himself a laughing-stock, especially as Swift continued the joke with further pamphleteering which simply added to Partridge's discomfiture. But the sting proved painful even if it did not quite kill, for the Company of Stationers struck Partridge off its list of approved publishers and sought itself to take over publication of his almanacs. In a word, Partridge was ruined, and it was not until 1714 that he was able to recover sufficiently to go into print again, which he did with an almanac entitled *Mercurius Redivivus*. (To be fair, however, one should point out that it was not only the learned who played practical jokes on the less intellectually deft astrologer. In 1752 John Collier, for example, decided to raise a laugh at the expense of George Clegg, a cunning-man and astrologer, by commissioning him to draw up his daughter's horoscope and then arranging to meet him to discuss the result. The place chosen was a rented room and the plan was to put a pound of gunpowder under the chair in which Clegg would be sitting, and to pour lavatory filth on his head from the safety of the room above. At the insistence of the landlord, water was substituted for the muck, and on the appointed day Clegg turned up with many pages of a lengthy prediction for Collier's daughter. After listening to him for a while, Collier then ignited the gunpowder, accomplices let loose the water from above, and Clegg was left soaked, dazed, and humiliated).

So Church, *bien pensants* and the professional classes – Collier was an author and a teacher – had the law on their side and were able to do damage not only to astrologers' livelihoods but also their reputations, and thus it continued into the nineteenth century. In 1807 Middlesex magistrates sent an astrologer to Bridewell Prison as a rogue and a vagabond; in 1813 Thomas White who had cast the horoscope relating to Louis XVI was arrested and imprisoned, and died in Winchester gaol the following year; and in 1823 a woman was tried at Stafford for claiming she could 'rule the planets, restore stolen goods, and get in [*recover*] bad debts'.

Some astrologers, on the other hand, did not help themselves or their fellows. Richard Walton, a servant before he turned professional cunning-man and astrologer, claimed to have taught himself astrology but also confessed to deceiving his clients, selling his remedies at too high a price and making up his astrological predictions, although he seems to have done so, not out of cynicism as laziness. But the climate was cold even towards well-meaning attempts to provide instruction for practitioners of magic and astrology, as can be seen from the case of Francis Barrett (floruit 1780–1814), a synthesiser of texts, magical, alchemical, astrological, rather than an astrologer himself. His book *The Magus*, published in 1801, should have contained sufficient astrological material to make it useful as a work of reference, especially in those long sections devoted to the relationship of the planets and magical images; but Barrett was dismissed by his contemporaries and *The Magus* failed to gain much of an audience until 1875 when it was reprinted during the revival of interest in the occult sciences in nineteenth-century London and Paris. More fortunate in his public was Ebenezer Sibley (or Sibly) (1751–*c*.1799) who published much more extensively, his principal work being his *New and Complete Illustration of the Celestial Science of Astrology* which went through twelve editions between its first appearance in 1784 and the revised version under the 'New and Complete' title in 1817. Sibley was trained as a physician, although his theory was not altogether orthodox, being influenced by vitalistic conceptions of the Deity, alchemy, atomism, astrology, magic, and Mesmerism. Not that he was unaware of the recent and contemporary natural scientists – he agreed, for example, with the interpretation of the aurora borealis offered by John Canton and Benjamin Franklin, that it was caused by the presence of positive and negative electricity in the atmosphere, and he was fully cognisant of the work of the chemists Joseph Priestly and Antoine Lavoisier – but he preferred to interpret Nature, using the instruments of alchemy and astrology, according to the lights of older wisdom. Allen Debus has summarised this approach as Sibley expressed it in his *Complete Illustration*:

> For Sibly, the concept of the grand unity of nature and its connection with divinity was in danger of being lost. To be sure, all agreed that God had framed this world in terms of number, weight, and measure, but this had been accepted by philosophers other than the mechanists. It was necessary to accept first the fact that our world is based upon a perfect plan, one that operates harmoniously and sympathetically throughout its far reaches. Here superiors rule inferiors so that celestial bodies act on and influence all earthly substances by a regular inherent cause that was implanted at the Creation by God. If a model were needed, it should be that of the wheel. There are wheels within wheels in a divinely inspired motion that is perpetual. Here is to be found the path of communication from the celestial regions to our earth for life, spirit, power, virtue, magnetism, sympathy and antipathy, and attraction and repulsion.

Sibley was therefore convinced that disease was caused by astral influences and, after many years of study and experiment, he produced two basic medicines, a solar tincture for men and a lunar tincture for women, which, as he explained in his *Key to Physic and the Occult Sciences* (1794), 'can never be affected by change of weather or climate, nor by heat or cold; nor will they suffer any diminution of their strength or virtue by remaining open or uncorked'. These medicines he prescribed for a remarkably wide range of infirmities, including night emissions and hydrophobia, and proceeded to sell to the general public with a patter worthy of the most accomplished purveyor of snake-oil.

He included many horoscopes in his *Complete Illustration* covering such eminent figures as Alexander the Great, Henry VIII of England, Philip II of Spain, Erasmus, Luther, Melanchthon, and William Lilly, but they were mostly lifted (as he himself acknowledges) from the works of John Gadbury (1627–1704), William Lilly's principal rival, although Gadbury's versions are awash with careless mistakes. Still, if Sibley did not contribute anything new to the development of astrology – and it is notable that he did not include the new planet Uranus in his calculations – he should not be censured too heavily for his omissions. For his significance lies, perhaps, in his whole work, not just one strand of it. The eighteenth century in the West was engaged in the latest stage of that debate which had preoccupied the sixteenth and early seventeenth centuries: what is the universe, how does it work, what is the relationship between the universe and God, and what are humanity's place and role within this system? The mechanists were beginning their march to what the twentieth century would present as ultimate victory, but their theories and explanations would not go without challenge, and Sibley was only one among very many who were willing to reformulate an alternative, mystical view and assert it with some force. [9]

The mechanists' voice can be heard in the *Encyclopédie ou Dictionnaire Raisonnée des Sciences, des Arts, et des Métiers*, complied by Diderot and D'Alembert and published in 1751. (Notice the 'raisonée': the mechanists and their disciples were and are fond of laying claim to 'reason' and implying that those who think differently are 'unreasoning' and hence 'unreasonable'). There is no entry for astrology or, indeed, astronomy: simply *stars*, labelled 'mythology', followed by a short, dismissive paragraph:

> The pagans worshipped the stars. They believed they were immortal and animate because they used to see them move with a continuous motion and shine without any altera-tion. The influences the sun clearly has on everything produced on our earth led them to attribute similar [influences] to the moon and, by generalising this notion, to all the other celestial bodies. It is worthy of remark that here superstition meets physical astrology.

But while the learned mocked and dismissed, the rising middle class to which most of them belonged was by no means entirely ready to join the chorus of condemnation and surrender those insights into the future which could comfort or forewarn the present. Sibley's approach to the occult sciences, for example, preserving what was best in the old while accommodating and making use of the new, made exactly the right appeal to the mentality of his own time and that of the coming century.

A good instance of this can be found in Johann Pfaff (1774–1835), from 1804 until 1809 Professor of Mathematics and Astronomy at the reopened University of Dorpat in Estonia. Well-known as an astronomer, in 1816 he published a book entitled *Astrologie* which consisted of twelve chapters, each headed by a sign of the zodiac, expounding the history of astrology and explaining its principal theories. His apparent conversion to astrology irritated many contemporary academics and in a letter to one of them, Bernhard von Lindenau, Pfaff recounted what an effect his reading of Ptolemy and Kepler had had on him. His extensive researches into the subject, he said, had convinced him that in spite of the mistakes which could be found in parts of it, the astrological tradition, long-standing as it was, deserved a better hearing than it had received recently or was getting at the moment, and that his own book was an attempt to provide a new and more accurate picture of what astrology was and meant. His apologia did no good. Two colleagues, in correspondence with each other, dismissed his book as frivolous, the science itself as superstition, and astrologers as 'crass'. But Pfaff was not to be put off and continued to publish: a book on conjunctions and the star of Bethlehem (1821) and, under the title *Astrological Pocket*

Book, a translation of Books 1 and 2 of Ptolemy's *Tetrabiblos* (1822) which was still being reprinted as late as 1950. More followed, including a translation of *Tetrabiblos* Books 3 and 4, but, in accord with the approach to astrology we noted in Sibley, Pfaff also spent time and effort on trying to extend Kepler's attempts to harmonise planetary movements with events on earth, so as to include Uranus and the discovery between 1800 and 1807 of the major asteroids (called 'planets' until 1848) Ceres, Pallas, Juno, and Vesta. But it is a measure of academic hostility to or dismissal of astrology at this period that a perfectly competent astronomer and mathematician such as Pfaff could be ridiculed (and even called 'mad') simply because he showed an interest in astrology, did not conceal it, and published his thoughts on the subject.

So the learned sneered and the middle classes skittered between wanting to appear up-to-date and quietly consulting the stars, one way or another, to determine their future actions or explain the unexpected. One can see what one might call the 'official' nineteenth-century attitude to the occult sciences in Sir Walter Scott who claimed to have no doubt that astrology was discredited nonsense. In his *Letters on Demonology and Witchcraft* (1830), he gives a brief résumé of its history, couched in dismissive terms: 'the road most flattering to human vanity while ... at the same time most seductive to human credulity'; 'the natural consequence of the degraded character of [its] professors was the degradation of the art itself'; [anent astrologers of the seventeenth century], 'there was no province of fraud which they did not practise'; 'this dishonoured science'; and he draws attention to what he sees as the wide gulf between the credulous of earlier times and the rational of his own. '[Astrology] was little pursued by those who, faithful in their remarks and reports, must soon have discovered its delusive vanity ... the calm and disinterested pursuers of truth'. Consequently, when Scott makes use of astrology in his novels, he employs it as a sign either of want of rationality in the character who practises it, or of the superstitious credulousness of an earlier society. In *Guy Mannering* (1815), subtitled *The Astrologer*, for example, he has the eponymous student of the science tell the fortune of a newly born baby, to the evident contempt of one of his auditors:

> [Mannering said], 'I shall calculate his nativity according to the rule of the triplicities, as recommended by Pythagoras, Hippocrates, Diocles, and Avicenna. Or I shall begin *ab hora questionis*, as Haly, Messahala, Ganivetus, and Guido Bonatus have recommended ...' [Sampson] turned a gaunt and ghastly stare upon the youthful astrologer, and seemed to doubt if he had rightly understood ...
>
> 'I am afraid, sir,' said Mannering, turning towards him, 'you may be one of those unhappy persons, whose dim eyes being unable to penetrate the starry spheres, and to discern therein the decrees of heaven at a distance, have their hearts barred against conviction by prejudice and misprision.'
>
> 'Truly,' said Sampson, 'I opine with Sir Isaac Newton, Knight, and erstwhile master of his majesty's mint, that the (pretended) science of astrology is altogether vain, frivolous, and unsatisfactory.' And here he reposed his oracular jaws.
>
> 'Really,' resumed [Mannering], 'I am sorry to see a gentleman of your learning and gravity labouring under such strange blindness and delusion. Will you place the brief,

the modern, and, as I may say, the vernacular name of Isaac Newton in opposition to the grave and sonorous authorities of Dariot, Bonatus, Ptolemy, Haly, Etzler, Dieterick, Naibod, Hasfurt, Zael, Tanstettor, Agrippa, Duretus, Maginus, Origan, and Argol? Do not Christians and heathens, and Jews and gentiles, and poets and philosophers unite in allowing the starry influences?'

　'*Communis error* – it is a general mistake,' answered the inflexible Dominie Sampson.

　'Not so,' replied [Mannering], 'it is a general and well-grounded belief.'

　'It is the resource of cheaters, knaves, and cozeners,' said Sampson.

But the introduction of astrology to this narrative is actually done merely to create suspense to see whether Mannering's predictions anent the baby's future will come true or not, and when Scott decides to use astrology in some of his other novels – *Kenilworth, Quentin Durward, The Talisman* – it is significant that he not only shifts it further and further back in terms of historical chronology, but also presents it as a craft used by charlatans or lunatics, an attitude consistent with that he presumed belonged to his principal audience. [10]

Nevertheless, not everyone belonging to that audience was quite as sceptical as he or she may have wanted to appear, and in addition to the learned and the middle class, there was a third group ('the rest') which quietly persisted in its traditional practice of reading almanacs, going to fortune-tellers, and having its horoscope cast as though nothing essential had changed in the human picture of the universe. 'Popular enthusiasm,' as James Sharpe puts it, 'for eclipses, comets and other astronomical phenomena lived on, as did the taste for prediction, prophecy, and fortune-telling.' Still, the onset of the nineteenth century saw difficulties for astrology in various quarters. In England and Wales, for example, astrologers were classed as undesirables by the *Act for the Punishment of Idle and Disorderly Persons, Rogues and Vagabonds* (1824), whose provisions, interestingly enough, were not extended to Scotland until 1871. Then in 1846 a new planet and an attendant moon were discovered, thereby throwing the astrological map of the sky into more of that uncertainty which had followed the sighting of Uranus. First noted and drawn by Galileo in December 1612 and again in January 1613, Neptune disappeared from ken, (largely because Galileo mistook it for a fixed star rather than a planet), until its existence was posited mathematically in 1821 and its observation in Berlin on 23 September 1846 by Johann Galle who also saw its largest moon, Titan, not long after. The usual flurry of suggestions for the planet's name ensued; Galle himself proposed 'Janus', the English astronomer James Challe favoured 'Oceanus', but the French astronomer Urbain-Jean-Joseph Le Verrier successfully persuaded everyone to call it after Jupiter's brother the god of the sea, the bluish tinge of the planet when seen through a telescope lens making 'Neptune' an appropriate choice. But if incorporating Uranus into the astrological scheme of things had been difficult, Neptune was a step too far, and nineteenth-century astrologers tended to leave it out of their calculations.

Yet in the face of these various obstacles, 'popular enthusiasm' continued. Its published expression, the almanac, sold well during the nineteenth century, as it had during the seventeenth, principally perhaps because of the efforts of two men, 'Raphael' and 'Zadkiel', to tap into the underground stream of popular eagerness for the kind of information the almanac purveyed. 'Raphael' was the pseudonym of Robert Cross Smith (1795–1832), a journalist living in London, who in 1824 put together, from already failed ventures, *The Astrologer of the Nineteenth Century*, a publication containing all kinds of astrological material, from the horoscopes of famous historical figures such as Napoleon, to predictions based on contemporary readings of the planets' movements and instruction in astrology for beginners. After this too collapsed, Cross's next venture, *Urania* (1825), also failed; but his third attempt, *The Prophetic Messenger*, changed the formula by including forecasts of events for every day of the coming year and this proved to be a most successful format, so much so, indeed, that *The Prophetic Messenger* is still in publication under the title *Raphael's Almanac*. Raphael's colleague and rival, 'Zadkiel' (Richard Morrison, 1795–1874), a naval officer before he became a professional astrologer and journalist, was an enthusiast for astrology, much more so than Raphael, and not only published several books on the subject, as well as *The Herald of Astrology*, later known as *Zadkiel's Almanac*, but also conducted a long and fierce campaign to free himself and his fellow-astrologers from the dangers presented by the Vagrancy Act by getting it repealed. After much sustained effort, he managed to persuade two Members of Parliament in 1852 to present a private Member's Bill which would have had the effect he wanted, but the Bill fell foul of the Parliamentary time-table and that was that.

In 1861, however, he did have one notorious success. His almanac for that year, published in the autumn of 1860, noted:

> The stationary position of Saturn in the third degree of Virgo in May, following upon [the full moon in March], will be very evil for all persons born on or near the 26th August; among the sufferers I regret to see the worthy Prince Consort of these realms. Let such persons pay scrupulous attention to health.

Prince Albert died after a short illness on 14 December, and although at first Zadkiel's monitory prediction went more or less unremarked at first, once the newspapers got hold of it there was a storm and an outrage, with cries for retribution against the unfortunate prognosticator. The *Daily Telegraph* commented:

> We should rejoice to hear that the police had routed out the 'cunning' men who lurk in garrets in poor neighbourhoods, and delude inexperienced girls and frivolous young married women. 'But, at the same time, we claim an equal need of justice to be applied to an imposter quite as impudent and thrice as mischievous as the beggar, the gypsy, or the 'cunning man'. There is a fellow who calls himself ZADKIEL, and who for thirty-two years, it seems, has been suffered to publish annually a farrago of wretched trash which he calls an almanac, and in which, pretending to interpret the 'voice of the stars', he gives vent to a mass of predictions on public affairs. Once in every five years or so, one of Zadkiel's prophecies, which are generally the stupidest jumping at probable eventualities, may by an accident come true; whereupon the seer goes into raptures of the 'Right again!' description, and sells his almanac, we are sorry to learn, by thousands. Very recently the public were scandalised to hear that a London alderman, in the very performance of his magisterial functions, had so little respect for the dignity of the Bench as to call the attention

of newspaper reporters to one of Zadkiel's predictions for 1861 which had a kind of hazy coincidence with the death of the Prince Consort. The Almanac has gone up prodigiously in the market, we are told, since Alderman HUMPHREY's ill-advised escapade; but it now becomes the duty of the press to apply a corrective to aldermanic folly, and to expose this Zadkiel in his true colours … We might pass this rubbishing pamphlet by with contempt; but this publicity it has recently attained demands that it and its author, whoever he may be, should be exposed and denounced. The one is a sham, the other is a swindler … Who is this Zadkiel, and are there no means of ferreting him out, and hauling him up to Bow Street under the statute as a rogue and a vagabond?

If the Vagabond Act were not repealed, the *Daily Telegraph* might indeed succeed in achieving its desire: hence Zadkiel's earnest campaign to see it go. As it was, however, a few months later, the *Telegraph* published a letter from Rear Admiral Sir Edward Belcher, accusing Zadkiel by his proper name of falsely giving the impression he was still a naval officer, and of hoodwinking the public not only via his almanac but also through the use of a crystal ball for prediction. Zadkiel was incensed and sued Sir Edward for libel. The resulting trial in June 1863 saw Zadkiel questioned very closely about his astrological and divinatory activities, but in spite of the successful attempts by defending counsel to make him look a fool and in spite of the judge's partial and prejudiced remarks upon astrology during his summing up, the jury returned a verdict in Zadkiel's favour. Thus they found Sir Edward indeed guilty of libel, but they awarded Zadkiel damages of only twenty shillings – a paltry sum and one which reflected their contempt for the man and his means of earning a livelihood.

But it was not only in England and the United States that almanacs were popular reading matter. France also catered for a wide public. The *Almanach du Cultivateur* for 1834, for example, published prognostications largely related to the weather, while the *Almanach du Bon Cultivateur* of a few years earlier – one notes from their titles the principal intended audience for these publications – observed among other pieces of folk wisdom that 'it is quite certain that if there is a new moon before the rising of the Pleiades, it is very dangerous for the fruits', and, 'sowing should take place when the moon is in one of the moving lines, such as Aries, Cancer, Libra, and Capricorn, or when it is in trine or sextile with Saturn, mainly if this planet is in a favourable aspect'. Did farmers understand these technical terms? If not, the advice would be somewhat useless and one might ask why they would buy an almanac, intended to offer them practical advice, if at least some of that advice was being expressed in impenetrable language. If, on the other hand, they were sufficiently conversant with it to know what they were being advised to do, it argues that at least basic astrology was familiar to the rural classes. But if these French almanacs preserved and disseminated a variety of occult subject matter to a potentially very big readership, Alphonse Louis Constant, better known by his pen-name, Eliphas Lévi (1810–75), addressed himself to a narrower, more learned audience and revived the long-standing connection between astrology and magic. In a series of books including *Dogme et Rituel de la Haute Magie* (1855) and *La Clef des Grands Mystères* (1861), Lévi promoted magical, alchemical, and Kabbalistic systems of theory and operation appealing to the emerging esotericism of the mid-nineteenth century. This was partly a development from the Romanticism of the eighteenth century, partly a reaction against the materialism of the nineteenth, and partly a frame of mind stimulated by such phenomena as the table-rappings of the Fox sisters in 1848 which were to lead to Spiritualism and the search for evidence of life after death. Lévi's particular interests lay in occult sciences other than astrology, but he did give a brief comment on it in his *Dogme et Rituel*, published under the title *Transcendental Magic*.

'True' astrology, he said, was derived from the Kabbalah but was profaned by the later Greeks and Romans who changed the names of planetary angels into those of pagan deities, and by astrological practitioners during late antiquity and the Middle Ages. What was now needful was to restore astrology to its earliest purity. Lévi then refers to 'astral light', a difficult concept to define, but one which Lévi himself defined elsewhere as follows:

> There exists a force which is far more powerful than steam, by means of which a single man, who can master it, and knows how to direct it, might throw the world into confusion and transform its face. It is diffused throughout infinity; it is the substance of heaven and earth. When it produces radiance, it is called light. It is substance and motion at one and the same time; it is a fluid and perpetual vibration. In infinite space, it is ether, or etherised light; it becomes astral light in the stars which it magnetises, while in organised beings it becomes magnetic light or fluid. The will of intelligent beings acts directly on this light, and by means thereof, upon all nature, which is made subject to the modifications of intelligence.

'The signs,' he went on, 'imprinted in the astral light by the reflection and attraction of the stars are reproduced on all bodies which are formed by the co-operation of that light.' Hence human beings too bear the imprint of the stars, and those imprints may be read as both character and destiny.

> The planets preside over collective existences and modify the destinies of mankind in the aggregate; the fixed stars, more remote and more feeble in their action, attract individuals and determine their tendencies. Sometimes a group of stars may combine to influence the destinies of a single man, while often a great number of souls is drawn by the distant rays of the same sun. When we die, our interior light in departing follows the attraction of its star, and thus is it that we live in other universes, where the soul makes for itself a new garment, analogous to the development or diminution of its beauty.

Astral light also made it possible for magical adepts to travel to the planets – not physically, of course, nor to the actual planets themselves, but in spirit to the planets' psychic energies. This, for example, is what Annie Horniman and Frederick Leigh Gardner, two members of the Hermetic Order of the Golden Dawn, set out to do over a period of several weeks in 1898. First they created individual talismans for each planet, then they performed rituals intended to clear their working-space of unwanted non-human entities and thus protect themselves, and immediately entered a state of spirit vision, or something similar, in which they visited their chosen planet. Saturn, their first port of call, was approached via an indigo-white ray. Once arrived on a barren mountain, they summoned a guide who proceeded to inform them about the planet. It was, apparently, a dying world with a declining civilisation, its inhabitants easily frightened even though, out of consideration for their nervousness, Horniman and Gardner rendered themselves invisible for part of their visit. Jupiter, by contrast, was inhabited by a dignified, well-ordered society which, thought the visitors, made a sad contrast with the wretched state of things on earth.

The Golden Dawn, however, in spite of its broad curriculum drawn from the occult sciences and its inclusion of making talismans as part of its magical training, did not devote as much attention to astrology as perhaps one might expect. Its ceremonies and teachings concentrated more on ritual magic, the Kabbalah, and alchemy. But it did require newly-initiated members to learn some of the very basic terms of astrology – names of the planets, astrological symbols, houses in the zodiac, and so forth – and certain features of its instruments or later ceremonies involved at least an awareness of astrological symbolism. Thus, the lotus-tipped wand which formed part of the equipment of the individual magician required him or her to hold it in a particular way, according to the work being done.

> In working on the plane of the zodiac, hold the wand by the portion you refer to between the thumb and two fingers. If a planetary working be required, hold the wand by the portion representing the day or night-house of the planet, or else by the sign in which the planet is at the time.

Planet	Day-House	Night-House
Saturn	Capricorn	Aquarius
Jupiter	Sagittarius	Pisces
Mars	Aries	Scorpio
Venus	Libra	Taurus
Mercury	Gemini	Virgo
Sun	Leo only	
Moon		Cancer only

> Should the action be with the elements, one of the signs of the triplicity of that element should be held according to the nature of the elements intended to be invoked.

Members were also informed about the magical images attached to each of the decans – 1st decan Aries: Mars: a tall dark man clothed in white with a red cloak; 2nd decan Aries: the sun: a woman in green with one leg uncovered from knee to ankle; 3rd decan Aries: Venus: a man dressed in scarlet, and gold bracelets, and so forth – and were taught the figures of geomancy which were classified under the heads of the elements, the signs of the zodiac, and the planets; and the names and attributions of the Tarot trumps and minor arcana. There was also a lecture for members of the Order, in which the twelve tribes of Israel are aligned with the twelve signs of the zodiac, and the blessings of Jacob upon them are worked out astrologically:

> Of Gad (Aries), Jacob says, 'Gad, a troop shall overcome him, but he shall overcome at the last.' Moses says, 'blessed be he that enlargeth Gad: he dwelleth as a lion, and teareth the arm with the crown of the head, and he provideth the first part for himself because there, in a portion of the law-giver, was he sealed; and he came with the heads of the people, he executed the justice of the Lord, and his judgements with Israel'. The armorial bearings of Gad are, white, a troop of cavalry. All this coincides well with the martial and dominant nature of Aries, the only one of the twelve signs in which the superior planets alone bear sway, for it is the house of Mars, exaltation of the sun and triplicity of the sun and Jupiter. The symbolism of the lion is also proper to Aries on account of its solar, fiery and martial nature.

These points, however, summed up the Order's overt emphasis on astrology, although individual members, of course, were free to follow and develop their particular interests, as did Annie Horniman and Frederick Gardner. Aleister Crowley, too, was a more expert astrologer than many in the Order and wrote a treatise on the subject, *Liber 536*, while he was in the United States of America in 1917–18. It arose out of conversations he had with Evangeline Smith Adams (1868–1932), one of the most famous astrologers of her day, and one who successfully survived a legal action taken against her as a 'fortune teller', her defence being – and here, according to the newspapers, the judge agreed with her – that she had raised astrology to the dignity of an exact science. At first the work was to have been a collaboration, but relations between the two soon broke down and the book remained as it then stood. It opens with a preface of typically Crowleyan sarcasm, an apparent diatribe against both the science and its practitioners, ending with the supposed plan of 'a wise and patriotic statesman' to engineer prosecutions of astrologers in such a way that they will never be able to win:

> If this plan has sometimes failed to work as it should, it is because the Astrologer is too often impervious to all reason and good sense, as well as to manners and good taste. He may even exclaim, malicious as a dog cornered by a gang of street urchins, that on the whole he would rather go to prison. 'It is not very creditable, perhaps, to be at large in a country with such rulers.' So deplorable a temper is indicative of incorrigible vice, a perversity of the soul plainly Satanic. Such people are dangerous to a state; they may perhaps hit back. Perhaps our sterner forefathers were wiser after all; perhaps we should go after the dollars of the Common People in some other way, and deal with the Astrologer by reviving the methods of the inevitable Matthew Hopkins [*witch-hunter*]. Unless we can do so, and there is indeed some danger that those contemptible creatures, the Common People, might not readily acquiesce, it is to be feared that we shall see the ruin of Civilisation with its greatest glory, our unique political system, and become impotent witnesses of that catastrophe, the Triumph of Astrology.

Thereafter his treatise is straightforward enough, although he also includes two substantial chapters on Uranus and Neptune, noting by way of preliminary to his interpretation of their significances that they 'represent those parts of ourselves which apprehend these vaster mirrors of the All-One', a remark which betrays the influence of the relatively new discipline of psychology, one which was to play an increasingly important role as the twentieth century loomed and proceeded. [11]

The Golden Dawn, however, was not the only esoteric society to offer a mixture of occultism, spiritual adventure and exploration, and psychic experimentation to its members. The Theosophical Society, founded in 1875 in New York by a group of men and women with just such sympathies and interests, and led by a Russian emigrée, Helena Blavatsky (1831–91), was not a university of magic like the Golden Dawn, but an organisation devoted to revealing what it saw as the true nature of the cosmos, refuting materialist science and providing in its place a more soundly-based explanation of the workings of the universe and humanity's place and role therein. Complex these may appear, said Blavatsky, but at basis they are very simple. The universe is spiritual, materiality an illusion; cosmic evolution causes spirit to condense into matter and then matter to revert to spirit; and this whole cyclical process relates to a single passage through the zodiac. Astrology was therefore important because it provided a key to unravelling the mysterious synchromesh of the various cosmic forces. This interesting mixture of spiritual and scientific approaches is well illustrated – if in a somewhat unusual fashion – by one of the Society's early members, an astrologer calling himself 'W. Gorn Old', although his middle name was actually 'Richard'. Best known by his pen-name 'Sepharial', he used to spend his nights travelling in his astral body and his days engaging his attention and energies in developing a system of astrological forecasting for the Stock Market and the Turf.

One of his friends, and a close associate of the London Theosophists, was Alan Leo (1860–1917), an astrologer who was convinced that in astrology lay the salvation of humankind. Leo changed his name from William Allen in c.1888 to reflect the preponderance of planets in that zodiacal sign when he was born. He joined the Theosophical Society in 1890 and earned his living partly by commercial travelling and lecturing, partly by editing and publishing a new periodical, *The Astrologer's Magazine*. To encourage interest and tacitly to invite personal business, Leo also sent out free horoscope readings to new subscribers. These, though popular, did not get him very far commercially until he realised that people would actually pay, and pay well, for detailed readings. So he began to charge and was gratified by the result. (Others had already heard the penny drop. In 1890 some Somerset newspapers carried the following advertisement: 'Astrology – Love, Marriage, Success, 1s 7d. Future Prospects, 1s 1d; Three Years' Events, 2s 7d. Send sex, birth-time, Signor DASMAIL, Connaught Road, Walthamstow'). The *Magazine*, however, did not make money, nor did it spread the Theosophical message to Leo's satisfaction, and in consequence in July 1875 he began a new venture, *Modern Astrology*, followed in January 1896 by a new organisation, the Astrological Society. But even after giving up his other commercial activities and working at astrology full time, Leo still found himself exhausted from the sheer labour of calculating the enormous number of horoscopes constantly demanded of him, and it was not until 1898 that he hit upon a solution to his self-created behemoth – production-line horoscopes. One sheet calculated for the sun's sign, another for the moon's, along with the ascendant planet and its ruler, and so forth, would give increasingly detailed but still generalised readings. The more detail – that is, the more sheets – an inquirer wanted, the higher the price, and as these sheets did not need much by way of calculation, they could be mimeographed to clients with a fraction of his previous trouble. Indeed, they did not need Leo himself to do the work at all, and soon he was employing several people to run off these generalised horoscopes as though they were hands in a factory. Meanwhile Leo was able to use the profits generated by this assembly line to subsidise his books: fourteen pocket manuals and seven more comprehensive volumes, including *Astrology for All* (1901), *The Horoscope and How to Read it* (1902), *Practical Astrology* (1902), and his final book, *Esoteric Astrology* (1913).

Things therefore at last seemed to be going well, but lurking in the background was the Vagrancy Act. Leo's success and its attendant publicity had given birth to dozens of more or less unscrupulous imitators who were likely to serve as a collective brush with which the authorities could tar him; and sure enough in 1914 he was summoned to appear in court to answer charges of unlawfully pretending to tell fortunes and so deceiving and imposing upon Hugh McLean, a police officer, contrary to statute. McLean had, in fact, tried to entrap Leo by asking through the post for a complete horoscope and supplying him with a false name and false date of birth. In the event, the case was dismissed, quite possibly because it was seen to be entrapment, but Leo was not awarded costs and this should, perhaps, have served as a reminder that his zeal for astrology was not shared by everyone. Indeed, three years later, in September 1917, he was summoned to court again on similar charges under that same Vagrancy Act, and this time he was found guilty and fined £5 with £25 costs. In a way he was fortunate. He could have been sent to prison for three months, with hard labour.

Leo is notable for trying to simplify the complexities of astrology, so making it more accessible to students, and for his attempts to psychologise the science by explaining planetary influences as indications of character rather than arbitrators of future events. This came about partly because he made the sun central to his analysis of character, and partly because he reinterpreted the zodiacal signs in ways quite different from those of historical tradition. Thus Aries, he wrote:

> represents undifferentiated consciousness. It is a chaotic and unorganised sign in which impulse, spontaneity, and instinctiveness are marked features. Its vibrations are the keenest and most rapid, but without what may be called definite purpose, except towards impulsiveness and disruption. It signifies explosiveness, extravagance and all kinds of excess. Its influence is more directly connected with the animal kingdom, in which life is full and without the directive power of fully awakened self-consciousness.

Here Leo quite clearly shows the effect of Theosophy on his thinking, and if we take this into account and the influence of Hindu philosophy and astrology derived from two trips he made to India in 1909 and 1911, we can find threads to guide us through the otherwise somewhat piecemeal material contained in his final book, *Esoteric Astrology*, 'The significance of caste and social distinctions', (the title of one of its chapters), not being quite the topic one expects to find in a book on astrology.

Leo's legacy, then, was one of a marriage, or at least a partnership, between a simplified sun-based astrology and elements of nineteenth-century occultism with a dash, as in Crowley's case, of nineteenth-century psychology. It was a way of treating astrology which may not have been immediately popular, but its effects were permanent., and twentieth-century astrology in the West owes much to Leo and those who adopted his essentially unhistorical approach. [12]

15

Plus ça Change c.1900–2000:
Facing the Future

The First World War saw a further burgeoning of interest in occult subjects, especially those which might give some clue about life after death and the way events here on earth were likely to turn. It was at just this time that Leo achieved his maturity as an astrologer and that he was prosecuted as a rogue, and while he conducted his astrological business, principally through his articles and contributions to *Modern Astrology*, with a seriousness and dignity, it took him time to provide an answer to the most obvious initial question of the hour, why had the War broken out?

> In the solstitial map (21 June 1914) for the sun's entry into Cancer, Mars is rising in the ascending sign of Leo, with Jupiter in opposition, thus densifying the war clouds. This unfortunate map is followed by the eclipse of the sun on 21 August, which falls exactly on the place of Mars in the solstitial map. In the east of Europe, Mars was rising and Jupiter setting. Both the June and August maps are very evil indeed … and over the whole of Europe Saturn is rising; it denotes downfall and disaster for monarchs.

Work was also done on the horoscopes of the principal actors in the tragedy – the Kaiser, the Tsar, the British King – but here British interpretation tended to differ from that of German astrologers, understandably enough in the heat of the immediate conflict, and so partisanship overcame disinterested interpretation.

One mentions German astrologers, but in fact Germany at this time did not have the popular interest in astrology it would manifest in the 1920s, although this is not to say there was no interest at all. Hamburg, for example, provided a stage and then an intellectual centre for some radical thinking on the subject, of which Alfred Witte (1878–1941) and Friedrich Siegrünn (1877–1951) were the principal movers. Witte was a surveyor by profession, but had a particular fascination with astrology, and Siegrünn was the chairman of the Hamburg Kepler Circle and provided Witte with his first astrological platform by inviting him to address the society. (It was this Circle which the two of them later turned into a school of astrology, the *Astrologische Studiengemeinschaft Hamburger Schule*, in August 1948). Witte followed the trend which wanted to see astrology treated as a science like any other, and in pursuit of this aim revised certain technical details and rearranged the rulerships of the zodiacal signs, such as giving Uranus to Sagittarius and Neptune to Scorpio, his stimulus for doing so being the existence of new planetary bodies he claimed to have detected beyond the orbit of Neptune: Cupido, Hades, Zeus, and Kronos, as he named them. Siegrünn added four more, and thus the theoretical increase in astral influences to be calculated and interpreted in any given horoscope became considerably more complex and required the kind of adjustment Witte suggested.

While the First World War was running its course and Witte was taking his first steps towards developing these distinctive theories, Gustav Holst (1874–1934) was working on *Seven Pieces for a Large Orchestra* (1914–16) which he later renamed *The Planets*. Holst was fascinated by astrology, having been encouraged to develop his interest in it by his musical mentor, Clifford Bax, while he and Holst were holidaying with others on Majorca in the spring of 1913. His daughter wrote:

> It was not so much the fortune-telling part of it that appealed to him, nor had he any use for psychical research in any shape or form. But he had always felt a keen interest in other people, and he found that horoscopes threw an astonishing light on the strength and weakness of some of his friends. It was fascinating to puzzle over contradictory aspects and try to decide why one friend never made a success of anything in spite of inheriting unusual talents, and why another, who always seemed to be heading straight for disaster, should manage to get on so remarkably well. There were very few people with whom he could discuss astrology, and he seldom mentioned it for fear of embarrassing his listeners.

The idea of *The Planets* was suggested to him by Bax, but after this initial seeding, astrology does not seem to have played an overt part in the gestation and writing of the music. But it is worth noting that he did not take any notice of the proper order of the planets in their orbits round the sun, a rearrangement done in accord with his musical aim of composing a series of mood pictures which would act as foils to one another, and one which exploited the astrological associations of each planet to suggest the mood he wanted to evoke. In this regard, it is worth bearing in mind that Holst was familiar with Theosophist teachings partly through his stepmother who was a keen adherent of the movement, partly through a friend of his, the Classical and Sanskrit scholar, George Mead, a leading figure in the Theosophist Society, and partly through Alan Leo, one of whose books – *How to Judge a Nativity* – he bought and read. According to Holst himself, he began to consider *The Planets* two years before actually starting work on it, and this takes us back to 1912 when Leo published *The Art of Synthesis*, a book containing chapters on each of the planets, describing their special qualities and characteristics; and here, thinks Raymond Head, is the treatment which inspired the way Holst conceived *The Planets*. A combination of Theosophy and astrology, then, lies behind Holst's most famous work, although Holst was always cagey about acknowledging these influences – the programme notes to the first performance in 1919, for example, said, 'The composer wishes his work to be judged as music [although] the poetical basis is concerned with the study of the planets' – and we should bear in mind that Leo had not long been prosecuted under the Vagrancy Act, and so any public flaunting of astrology might attract unwanted official attention. 'The study of the planets' might be explained away as astronomy; 'seven influences of destiny and constituents of our spirit', as he privately described the work in 1927, could not. Holst, then, should be added to the number of other artists of the period – W.B. Yeats, Wassily Kandinsky, Piet Mondrian, André Breton – whose works reflect, to a greater or lesser extent, Theosophy or astrology in ways which both preserved the traditional science and also modified it in accordance with the occultist preoccupations of the period.

By contrast, Sigmund Freud (1856–1939) was not in the least happy at the increase of interest in all the occult sciences which he noted were resurgent all over Europe, especially in the wake of the First World War. He complained:

> Occultists will be hailed as liberators from the burden of intellectual bondage, they will be joyfully acclaimed by all the credulity lying to hand since the infancy of the human race and the childhood of the individual. There may follow a fearful collapse of critical thought, of determinist standard and of mechanistic science.

Perhaps Freud had not noticed that bondage, determinism, and mechanism were precisely those theoretical aspects of astrology which had attracted criticism since the days of Rome and Hellenistic Greece, and it is certainly ironic that, after investigating one particular German astrologer much in demand by people of the highest rank in Bavarian society, he sought to rationalise her apparently successful predictions as 'thought-transference', a theory as remote from the workings of mechanistic science as astrology itself, but one he chose to prefer as the explanation of the astrologer's ability. There can be little doubt, actually, that Freud was emotionally disturbed by any manifestation of the occult sciences or people's interest in them, even though he could not stop himself from being curious about them and investigating some of them. An exchange between himself and his younger colleague, Carl Jung (1875–1961), recorded by Jung in his autobiographical writing, illustrates this nervousness. Freud asked Jung never to abandon his (Freud's) sexual theory because it was vital it become 'an unshakeable bulwark'. 'Bulwark against what?' asked Jung. 'Against the black tide of mud,' answered Freud adding, after a moment's hesitation, 'of occultism'. Still, he capitulated in the end, to some extent at least. 'In matters of occultism I have grown humble,' he wrote to Jung after a visit to a medium. 'I promise to believe anything that can be made to look reasonable. I shall not do so gladly, that you know. But my hubris has been shattered.'

Jung, however, had been more favourably inclined towards astrology from the very start of his career, casting horoscopes of his patients to help him in analysis. He wrote to Freud in June 1911:

> My evenings are taken up very largely with astrology. I make horoscope calculations in order to find a clue to the psychological truth. Some remarkable things have turned up which will certainly seem incredible to you … I dare say that one day we shall find in astrology a good deal of knowledge that has been intuitively projected into the heavens. For instance, it appears that the signs of the zodiac are character pictures.

This really sums up Jung's belief in the value of astrology – that it provides an extraordinary storehouse of accumulated insight into human character. He developed his views in a letter to an Indian astrologer in 1947:

As I am a psychologist, I am chiefly interested in the particular light the horoscope sheds on certain complications in the character. In cases of difficult psychological diagnosis, I usually get a horoscope in order to have a further point of view from an entirely different angle. I must say I have often found that the astrological data elucidated certain points which I would otherwise have been unable to understand. From such experiences I formed an opinion that astrology is of particular interest to the psychologist, since it contains a sort of psychological experience which we call 'projected' – this means that we find the psychological facts as it were in the constellations. This originally gave rise to the idea that these factors derive from the stars, whereas they are merely in a relation of synchronicity with them. I admit that this is a very curious fact which throws a peculiar light on the structure of the human mind.

Having suffered a notable decline in status and popularity during the nineteenth century, astrology thus invented a new vocabulary for the expression of its interpretive (as opposed to predictive) side. But in February 1930 it had to cope with the discovery of yet another planet beyond furthermost Neptune – an observable, not a theoretical planet such as those of Witte and Sieggrün. 'Pluto' had been predicted by the American astronomer Percival Lowell, but it was first seen by one of his younger colleagues on 18 February, and named (at the suggestion of an English schoolgirl) after the brother of Jupiter and Neptune, a god who was hidden in darkness and therefore invisible unless encountered face to face. In astrology, Pluto's influence brings hidden truth to light and is regarded as transformative, creative, and regenerative. But soon after its discovery, the German astrologer, Fritz Brunhübner, was of the immediate opinion that Pluto could be called 'the cosmic aspect originating the Third Reich', and the planet's functions may indeed be regarded as essentially those of Mars, much magnified and negative. In fact, an early symbol used by the astrologer Isabelle Pagan (who followed a French colleague, Charles Nicoullaud, in intuiting Pluto's existence before it was officially observed), was that of an inverted Mars. [1]

In that same year 1930, however, Evangeline Smith Adams became the first astrologer to host a wireless show, broadcasting three times a week and through it receiving more requests for horoscopic readings that she could possibly cope with. Newspapers were not to be left behind, and the first regular astrology column in Britain was published in the *Sunday Express* on 24 August 1930, beginning with that of the infant Princess Margaret, born only three days before; and so successful did this prove, (commercially speaking), that other newspapers quickly followed suit both in Britain and the United States of America. Occasional spectacular fulfilments of their predictions fed the popularity of their astrologers' columns. In October 1930, for example, the *Express*'s astrologer, Richard Naylor, predicted that British aircraft would soon be in danger, and that very day the British airship R-101 crashed in France. 'Whenever the new moon or full moon falls at a certain angle to the planet Uranus,' Taylor wrote in the next week's edition, 'aircraft accidents, electrical storms, and sometimes earthquakes follow' – an interesting indication that Uranus had now fully come into its own as one of the major astrological planets; and in 1936 *The People*'s astrologer, Edward Lyndoe, accurately predicted the death of George V, and the short reign and abdication of Edward VIII.

Meanwhile in Germany popular interest in astrology had also burgeoned, coupled, as in Britain, with the spread of Theosophy. Hugo Vollrath (1877–post 1937), for example, had been secretary to a prominent Theosophist, Franz Hartmann, and in 1907 or 1908 settled in Leipzig where, amid local recriminations and difficulties, he founded a Theosophical publishing house which rapidly became notable for its astrological books and magazines. They sold well and by 1923 his 'Astrological Library' series numbered nearly twenty titles. Alfred Witte, of course, had continued his researches and speculations throughout the Twenties, setting out his distinctive theories in *Regelwerk für Planetenbilder* ('Rulebook for Planetary Pictures') in 1928, although once the Nazi Party had come to power the book was banned, copies burned, and Witte forbidden to work any further. In the early Twenties, too, the astrologer Elsbeth Ebertin (1880–1944) gained a considerable reputation, partly for writing on astrological matters in a straightforward fashion which appealed to her many readers, and partly because of one particular horoscope she drew and upon which she commented in the 1924 edition of her yearbook, *Ein Blick in die Zukunft* ('A Glance into the Future') which was actually on sale by the end of 1923. An enthusiastic supporter of Adolf Hitler sent her the date of his birth – although not the hour, which she could scarcely have been expected to know – and asked what Elsbeth made of his horoscope. Elsbeth wrote:

> A man of action born on 20 April 1889, with the sun in 29° Aries at the time of his birth, can expose himself to personal danger by excessively incautious action and could very likely trigger off an uncontrollable crisis. His constellations show that this man is to be taken very seriously indeed. He is destined to play a 'Führer role' in future battles. It seems that the man I have in mind, with this strong Aries influence, is destined to sacrifice himself for the German nation, also to face up to all circumstances with audacity and courage, even when it is a matter of life and death, and to give an impulse, which will burst forth quite suddenly, to the German Freedom Movement. But I shall not anticipate Destiny. Time will show.

It did not take any remarkable insight, even in 1923, to realise that such a request from Munich might well involve Hitler, as Elsbeth's use of the phrase 'Führer role' suggests, even though at the time she denied any knowledge of National Socialists or their movement. But the putsch which followed in November, regardless of its immediate lack of success, meant that the Party now took an interest in her, even if Hitler himself did not. 'What on earth have women and the stars got to do with me?' he said dismissively when shown her comments on his horoscope. Nevertheless, Elsbeth's reputation soared and other German astrologers quickly stepped forward to enjoy the unusual light. Inevitably, therefore, jealousies, wrangling, quarrels, and personal attacks in print began to convulse the astrological community as its members struggled to formulate their reactions to the new and increasingly dangerous political situation of the state in which they lived. Some individuals stuck out. Hubert Korsch (1883–1942), for example, was yet another reformer who wanted to purge astrology of its incompetents, charlatans, and esotericists, and establish it as a 'proper' science, to which end he founded a new astrological magazine, *Der*

Zenit ('The Zenith') in January 1930 and fought, without eventual success, to dominate the German astrological establishment. Wilhelm Wulff (1893–c.1984), a painter and sculptor as well as an astrologer, lived and worked in Hamburg where, through some of his clients, he came to know Felix Kersten, Himmler's masseur, and thence eventually Himmler himself. Wulff's astrological practice appealed to Nazi ideology more than the usual kind because he based himself on ancient Indian astrological texts, (having studied Sanskrit in order to do so), and this made his astrology more 'accurate', in as much as it was derived from the actual positions of the planets and stars as seen against the ecliptic, as opposed to the traditional positions used by conventional Western astrologers: and because his system was that of ancient India, it was seen as Aryan and hence respectable. Not that this prevented his being arrested and detained in a concentration camp in May 1941. His release after only a few months came as a result of his being known to Himmler, and from then until the end of the war he seems, according to his own account in his memoir, *Zodiac and Swastika*, to have drawn horoscopes for Himmler and one or two other SS leaders. Many of the predictions these contained, in the opinion of Walter Schessenberg, one of Himmler's principal cronies, were remarkably accurate: Hitler would survive a great danger on 20 July 1944; Hitler would be ill in November that year; Hitler would die a mysterious death before 7 May 1945. Himmler was impressed and, according to Schessenberg, from 1941 he 'seldom took any steps without first consulting his horoscope'.

At least Wulff seems to have survived his wartime experiences. Karl Krafft (1900–45), a statistician as well as an astrologer, did not. For a decade after he graduated from university, he worked on a thesis which tried to use the statistical analysis of a large number of horoscopes to show that astrology might be able to provide data beyond the norms of mathematical probability, and after processing the birth data of 2,800 musicians born since 1820 and analysing thousands of observations derived therefrom, he came to the conclusion that there was indeed a relationship between the birth constellation and musical ability. Pushing his statistics further, he was also convinced that 'the birth constellation determines, once and for all, an individual's physical constitution as well as his predispositions and immunities'. But this apparent success of his methods led him into difficulties with his father who insisted he get a proper job, for which purpose he was sent to Zurich – his sojourn there may account for his often being described as Swiss rather than German – but his stay ended in humiliation when directors refused to elect him to the board of 'Globus', the department store to which he had been despatched, and it was only the death of his father in 1933 which relieved him of a degree of financial embarrassment.

Throughout the Thirties he continued to work on astrology, but by 1939 he was living in Germany and had become entirely sympathetic to Nazi ideology – not that this was entirely unusual, for many German astrologers joined the Party in or after 1933, some cases at least perhaps because they thought membership might offer them a degree of protection against growing official hostility to the science. Then on 2 November 1939 Krafft's fortunes took a notable turn. He wrote to a friend that Hitler's life would be in danger 'by the use of explosive material' between 7th and 10th of the month, and when a bomb went off in the Bürgerbräu beer hall in Munich on 9th only a few minutes after

Hitler and a number of Party officials had left, Krafft was eager to draw attention to his accurate prediction and eagerly got in touch with Rudolf Hess. As a result, his stock began to rise, (once it was realised that his foreknowledge of the explosion did not actually come from his being personally involved in the plot), and in January 1940 he was employed by Joseph Goebbels to help decipher the meaning of Nostradamus's prophetic quatrains in such a way as to make them favourable to the present German cause. (There was nothing especially new about this, of course. Only twenty years earlier a German postal official, Carl Loog, living in Berlin had published *Die Weissagungen des Nostradamus*, ('The Prophecies of Nostradamus') in which he claimed to have discovered the key to interpreting the quatrains and thereby a prophecy regarding constitutional crises in Britain and Poland in 1939. Goebbels wanted to use him to work on Nostradamus for the Propaganda Ministry, but Loog refused and Krafft got the job instead).

Krafft's interpretations were quickly developed into pamphlets which were then printed in large numbers for widespread distribution. Krafft himself was not responsible for these travesties which emanated entirely from hacks in the Ministry, because his interest lay in preparing a facsimile edition of the *Prophéties* with his own commentaries; but by Spring 1941 he was told to stop all such activity and then rapidly found himself caught up in the flurry of arrests which followed Hess's flight to Scotland. Astrologers and occultists in general – 'swindlers', as Martin Bormann's decree indiscriminately labelled them – were netted during the trawl for suspects and potential opponents of the régime, and found to their chagrin and fright that being a Party member helped not at all. The Gestapo subjected each individual to rigorous interrogation, and Ellic Howe has provided, from a document used by the Secret Police in Munich, examples of the kind of questions they might be asked:

1. For how long have you been interested in astrology and how did you come to the subject? Were you self-taught or did you receive instruction?
2. State the names of any well-known persons for whom you have cast horoscopes.
3. Are you a member of an astrological society? Have you any personal connections with leading personalities in the Reich and the Party? What astrological literature have you read? What books do you own yourself?
4. Do you subscribe to any astrological periodicals? Have you actively practised astrology?
5. Have you lectured on astrology or given instruction to anyone? What systems do you use?
6. With what astrological circles are you regularly in touch, and how frequently?
7. Have you attended any astrological congresses, either in Germany or abroad?
8. What are the names of the astrologers of your acquaintance and with which of them are you in touch?
9. Do you believe that you can substantiate the validity of astrological interpretations?
10. In your opinion do planetary constellations determine human fate, and how do you account for free will and hereditary factors?
11. Should members of different races (Aryans, Jews, Chinese, and Negroes) born at the same place under identical constellations expect the same astrological interpretations?

If yes, then do you not admit the racial requirements of fate?
12. Are you connected with occult or spiritualist organisations and have you participated in séances?
13. Have you been identified with other occult sciences?
14. What do you feel about clairvoyance and fortune telling?

These are, of course, the obvious questions to ask, apart from no. 11 which relates specifically to Nazi ideology, and are reminiscent of the kind of questions asked in earlier centuries of witches and similar practitioners of various occult sciences. They begin with the assumption that the person being interrogated is indeed an astrologer of some kind, professional or amateur, and then seek to widen the net to make sure no one has escaped arrest and investigation, and to find out whether there are any subversive organisations underpinning the suspect's activities. The big difference between these arrests and those of witches is that in the case of witches the questioning was largely motivated by concerns over theology, whereas in that of astrologers the informing motive was political. The danger for those concerned in both cases, however, was just as real.

But why was the German government so interested in astrologers at this juncture and willing to spend a lot of time and effort on them? The answer must be that, in part at least, astrology had been one of the factors in Hess's decision to undertake his extraordinary journey. He was persuaded to do so by various astrologers, one of whom pointed out in January 1941 that an unusual planetary conjunction consisting of six planets in Taurus would take place on 10 May. This did not in itself actually amount to a recommendation that Hess choose 10 May for his flight – indeed the astrologer in question, Ernst Schulte-Strathaus, flatly denied that Hess chose the day in accordance with his or any other astrologer's advice; but a wink is as good as a nod, and Ellic Howe records testimony which clearly suggests that astrology, if not the activating force behind Hess's ill-fated scheme, undoubtedly gave his resolve a hefty push:

> Hess's astrological foible strengthened his own conviction that everything possible must be done and hazarded in order to end hostilities without delay, because at the end of April and beginning of May 1941 Hitler's astrological aspects were unusually malefic. Hess interpreted these aspects to mean that he, personally, must take the dangers that threatened the Führer upon his own shoulders in order to save Hitler and restore peace to Germany. Time and again Hess's astrological 'adviser' had told him that Anglo-German relations were threatened by a deep-seated crisis of confidence … Indeed, at this time there were very dangerous [planetary] oppositions in Hitler's horoscope.

Krafft, in spite of his influential connections, did not escape the purge which followed. He was arrested and spent twelve months in prison, after which he was again set to work on drawing up horoscopes, this time of leading Allied generals and admirals. But the physical conditions of his employment were not good – they amounted to house-arrest in the Propaganda Ministry building – and Krafft's emotional and mental state rapidly deteriorated. An unwise (if later accurate) prediction early in 1943 that British bombs would fall on the Ministry and destroy it caused him to be arrested again, and this time he was held in an overcrowded prison where he caught typhus. Perhaps in its way this was a small blessing, because arrangements had been made to transfer him to a new prison, Buchenwald, and he died before it could reach it. [2]

As I mentioned earlier, one of Krafft's astrological innovations was to gather enormous quantities of astrological data and analyse them for statistical anomalies which might prove to be significant, a type of investigation pursued earlier by Paul Choisnard (1867–1930) and Léon Lasson (1901–89), and he was followed by two French scholars, Michel Gauquelin (1928–91) and his wife, Françoise, who undertook even more extensive collection and analysis. At first, Michel was favourably impressed by their endeavours, but when he tested their work, disappointment quickly set in. He wrote in his book *Neo-Astrology*:

> When I saw Choisnard's claims disappear one after the other under the weight of my painstaking calculations I resented him for being the cause of my fruitless efforts and of the hopes I had entertained …
>
> I confess to having once – it was a long time ago, though – promised myself to dedicate my first essays to the memory of the great Karl Ernst Krafft. Today I shudder at the thought … Armed with an immense desire to understand, and some statistical knowledge just acquired at university, to my great disappointment I found myself compelled to topple my idol from his pedestal. His evidence, as it became clear, was based on erroneous reasoning, from the statistical point of view …
>
> Lasson's neglect, or ignorance, of the roles of astronomical and demographic factors is even more serious. This error clearly explains some of the results he published …
>
> The only merit of Choisnard, Krafft, and Lasson is that they ensured a sort of continuity in astrological research.

Choisnard had claimed that sun-Mars aspects seemed to be prominent in the horoscopes of those who suffered violent death, moon-Mercury aspects in those of philosophers, and sun-moon aspects in those of actors. The Gauquelins' researches and analyses, however, produced a number of somewhat different results which Michel published, with varying detail, in several books. By working their way through the birth certificates of thousands of individuals, he and his wife came to the conclusion that when Mars was rising or predominant in a horoscope, it favoured the development of sporting champions or military leaders; Jupiter in the same position appeared most often in the horoscopes of future actors and politicians; and members of the Académie des Sciences had Saturn dominant in their charts. Objections to these claims broke out at once and continued to dog Gauquelin for the rest of his career. Michel himself pointed out one problem of which he was well aware and which he had taken into account. Until the end of the Second World War or thereabout, midwives had seldom interfered with the process of natural birth. After the 1940s, however, obstetrics took more and more frequently to intervention in one way or another, and thus interrupted or changed the relationship between the planets and the growing foetus, with disastrous astrological results. 'All planetary effects on heredity disappeared', in fact. There was also a difficulty in using birth certificates as sources of information. They did not record the exact moment of birth, only an approximation – a half-hour to an hour either way – and in consequence the Gauquelins' data were likely to be faulty. This, too, the Gauquelins took into account, but their efforts to put astrology on a statistically sound basis received little but hostility from the scientific community whose members seemed determined not to listen to any argument or test any evidence relating to astrology, a subject they had already dismissed as superstition and poppycock. Indeed, one said baldly, 'If statistics prove astrology, then I shall cease to believe in statistics.'[3]

With this note we seem to be entering the realm of faith rather than investigative science, and it may therefore be appropriate to note some of the reactions to astrology by a number of modern religious confessions. The *New Catholic Encyclopaedia* (second edition 2003) is uncompromising: 'As a pseudo-science, astrology survives only among the uneducated and the credulous, while the influence of the heavenly bodies upon Earth and man has become the subject of various strictly scientific studies without occult implication.' Evangelical opinion can be equally negative, too, pointing out, (as Christian criticism has long done), that the practice of astrology is prohibited by various Biblical texts; that many modern astrologers have occultist beliefs incompatible with orthodox Christianity; that Church Fathers and many Protestant reformers rejected astrology on the grounds that it was idolatrous and conflicted with the sovereignty of God; and that it is in any case irrational, superstitious, and inconsistent with modern astronomical cosmology. Add the more general objections that astrology does not work, that its practitioners publicise their occasional successes and ignore those which prove wrong, and that any acknowledgement of the validity of the science involves a surrender of the notion of free will, and we can see that criticisms of astrology have actually remained more or less the same since Hellenistic times.

In spite of this, however, astrology continues to flourish, more in some environments than others. Many newspapers and magazines remain wedded to their astrological columns, faulty and indeed works of imagination though these tend to be, in the composition of which the effect of the nineteenth century can be seen in their descriptions of character and psychological motivation as well as their highly generalised predictions of future events, since those events are often attributed to a particular type of character or set of characteristics. Television has followed suit – subject to its fashion of creating 'personalities' – with the predictions of its astrologers embodying on screen the generality and vagueness of the newspaper and magazine column. It is a style which is pure nineteenth century, in spite of its technological trappings. The increased accuracy of calculation which was the goal of so many pre-twentieth century would-be reformers is now available through computers which not only enable the mathematics of astrology to be done at remarkable speed, but also allow incorporation of hypothetical planets if desired – Witte and Siegrünn would be pleased – and movement between different systems, such as those using the tropical or (like India) the sidereal zodiac. The drawbacks, of course, are the increased complexity of the techniques available and hence the increasing retreat of the science into a specialised jargon which makes it less rather than more accessible to the student.

But if these are aspects of astrology in the West, elsewhere the picture is somewhat different. In India, for example, astrologers professional and amateur are far more frequently found and have often influenced politics in a way not common in the West. Many members of Jawaharlal Nehru's cabinet employed astrologers who used to travel with them to provide instant consultation; the prime ministers Morarji Desai and Narasimha Rao suffered both ridicule and criticism for their belief in astrology; and in 1984 articles by astrologers appeared in several newspapers, warning Indira Gandhi of personal danger to her in the November of that year, predictions which were virtually accurate, as she was murdered by her Sikh bodyguards on 31 October. The reaction of her son Rajiv who succeeded her as Prime Minister was to have a law passed in 1987, which was clearly aimed especially at astrologers. It provided that action would be taken against anyone who, as it said, 'predicts, prophesies, or pronounces, or otherwise expresses in such a manner as to incite, advise, suggest, or prompt the killing or destruction of any person bound by oath under the constitution', with the *minimum* penalty, for anyone charged and found guilty, of seven years' imprisonment. The Act may have been intended to gag astrologers, but in fact it did not do so, at least not for long, and from August 1990 astrologers were once again publishing admonitions in newspapers, including *The Times of India*, saying that the assassination of a major political figure – clearly Rajiv Gandhi himself – was to be expected before the elections of 1991. The astrologers were proved right. Rajiv was killed by a bomb on 21 May.

Making political predictions, of course, always carries with it an element of risk, as Chandrasiri Bandara, a Sri Lankan astrologer, found out very recently. Bandara was one of the best-known astrologers in the country, with a weekly television show and a political column in one of the pro-opposition newspapers. This obviously means that his prediction may have been influenced by his personal opinions, (although we are not entitled to assume that it *must* have been), but whether it was or not, his prediction said that in June 2009 the Sri Lankan President, Mahinda Rajapaksa, would soon be removed from office. Police officers were thereupon dispatched to his home where he was arrested and disappeared from public view. This is significant because it illustrates not only how popular Bandara was in Sri Lanka – an obscure practitioner would scarcely have attracted Government attention – but also how seriously Sri Lankan society takes astrology itself. Indeed, after the event, the President felt obliged to issue a statement saying that he was a devoted believer in it, and telling foreign reporters that he often consulted a favoured astrologer for advice on what time to make speeches or to leave for trips at home or abroad.

The political role of astrologers, however, is not confined to eastern governments, for it is well known that the American President, Ronald Reagan, and his wife Nancy were constant clients of more than one astrologer both before and after they entered the White House. The moment for Reagan's inauguration as Governor of California, for example – sixteen minutes past midnight on 1 January 1967 – seem to have been chosen by his current astrologer, Carol Richter, while another, Joan Quigley, made sure the President neither said nor did anything anent the Iran-Contra crisis for nearly four months, presumably because the stars were unfavourable to him during that period. Nor did politico-astrological comment cease with Reagan, for from the Russian astrologer, Pavel Globa, comes the prediction that President Obama will be assassinated in 2011 and that a third World War will follow, a dire warning with which the Moscow astrologer, Pavel Sviridov, agrees. [4]

Assassination and war, however, are dour notes upon which to end this survey of one of the most alluring of the occult sciences, and we should perhaps look for something more positive. Arthur Versluis has lamented what he calls the 'objectification' of modern Western intellectual, emotional, and physical life during the past 200 years or so:

> The rise of the sciences, technology, and industrialisation are all linked by their adher-ents' objectification of the cosmos … Astrology and astronomy … exemplify this shift. Astrology is founded in the relationships between and meanings of the planets or stars and the natural and human realms and cycles, but astronomy is based exclusively in quan-tification or measurement and identification. Meaning, in the senses found in astrology, is almost completely jettisoned from modern astronomy, and out of this absence in turn springs the profound antipathy that many – perhaps almost all – astronomers have had for astrology. Whereas in astrology a planet links together a whole constellation of meanings in the human and natural realms, in astronomy the planet is defined exclusively in terms of its size, density, trajectory, mineral deposits, and so forth.

Mike Harding, however, sees the glass half full rather than half empty. 'In astrology,' he says, 'we have a unique form of speaking about the world, in which mathematics and poetry co-exist.' If we take up this notion of co-existence between astronomy and astrology, we may be led to contemplate one of the more ancient concepts to span what the modern world sees as an unbridgeable gulf separating them, the idea of a *musica universalis*, a music of the spheres. The Greek mathematician Pythagoras is usually credited with originating this concept – that intervals in the spacing of the seven planets are comparable to musical intervals, and that the movements of the planets thus produce distinctive notes. Saturn, being the outermost planet, orbits more slowly round the earth than the others and so emits the lowest note of all, while the moon, which travels the fastest, produces the highest, all seven notes sounding in perfect harmony. Many people found the idea both attractive and convincing, and some, such as Plato, allowed their imaginations to elaborate: 'On each circle [of the cosmos] stood a Siren who was carried round with its movements, and uttered the concords of a single scale.' (*Republic* 10, 617b). Needless to say, Aristotle dismissed the notion in his *De Caelo*, with a somewhat clunking appeal to literalism – we cannot hear the sounds, therefore they do not exist – and his dismissal influenced a number of Mediaeval scholars, such as Vincent de Beauvais and Roger Bacon, who said either that this music must be understood metaphorically, in case the idea of a *musica universalis* encouraged astrologers, or that it was an idea popular among the uneducated and had no basis in fact. Defenders of the thesis, however, drew attention to the enormous distances separating the earth from the planets, which would render the notes too faint to be heard by human ears, while other scholars ignored the objections altogether and concentrated on employing ever more sophisticated mathematics to determine the exact pitches which made up the cosmic harmony. [5]

But the concept did not stop there, and an anonymous twelfth-century poet, noting the hierarchy inherent in the planetary scale, extended it to include the nine orders of angels in an elaboration of correspondences which was followed and made more complex by succeeding generations of musical theorists, astrologers, and philosophers both natural and Hermetic. Giorgio Anselmi, for example, included the fixed stars and elements, Ramis de Pareja changed the angelic orders to the nine Muses, Guy Lefèvre de La Boderie restored the angels and added Hebrew names of God, the ten sephiroth of the Kabbalistic tree of life, and eight virtuous faculties, (knowledge, fear of God, intellect, and so on), while Robert Fludd stretched the whole system to cover three octaves embracing the supercelestial, celestial, and elemental worlds. In case this seems to be straying too far into the realm of imagination, however, let us call to mind the work of Johannes Kepler, an astronomer (in the modern sense) and mathematician, as well as an astrologer. Of his labours Max Caspar has observed:

> If a work presents science with such a valuable contribution as the third planet law, (not to mention the mathematical and musical fruits), then a critic must seek the lack in himself if he does not achieve an understanding of the manner of contemplating nature out of which the work has arisen. This lack consists in the thinking being stuck fast in a rut of a one-sided contemplation of nature. It has been forgotten that that which is visible is a symbol of that which is invisible Therefore, the poet, the artist, brings us closer to nature and can convey more and profounder and better things about it … That was the case with Kepler. [6]

Pythagoras's original notion, we should recall, was based upon mathematical measurement and assessment of proportion, quite in the 'scientific' style. The musical ratios Kepler found in the motions of the planets were based on his calculation of how they would appear from the sun – a novel approach, taking into account Copernican theory, whereas earlier work on the subject had focussed upon the earth as the intended recipient of this harmony – and while he agreed with Aristotle that the planets did not actually emit sounds, (because they have no air), he did not abandon earlier conjectures and theories. On the contrary, he embraced and developed them, and the consequence is that these musical consonances, the accuracy of whose computation by Kepler stands up to modern scrutiny, with very little need for change, form the basis of his entire cosmology, and paradoxically produce in the vast silence of space a type of polyphonic hymn to God the Creator. In Kepler's work, then, science and imagination join hands, and their betrothal provides a peaceable co-existence in which astronomy and astrology, for nearly three centuries forced into opposition, may sing once more in harmonious amity.

Appendix:
Horoscopes of Christ

One of the more daring exercises in astrology was casting Christ's horoscope in an effort to penetrate more deeply into the Christian faith and discover well-springs of Truth which might better inform not only the higher reaches of theology, but also the daily practice of prayer and devotion. Motivated by reverence as much as by curiosity, establishing such a horoscope was nevertheless an endeavour which could easily go astray and bring down anger and punishment on the practitioner. If one of astrology's perennial difficulties was that of providing accurate data on which to base its interpretations, how much more essential was it in this case to verify and re-verify one's calculations, for mistakes could lead to error upon error of interpretation, and that, unless realised and corrected, (or suppressed), spelled potential danger for the souls of the astrologer and his trusting readers. When was Jesus born presented the first difficulty, which year, which day, at what time? Without decisions on these crucial points, no nativity could be drawn and hence the attempt would founder before it had even started.

One assistance to help pinpoint the year could be found in the theory of 'Great Conjunctions'. It had been discussed at length by the Islamic astrologer Māshā'allāh in his *Kitāb fī al-qiranat wa al-adyān wa al-milil* ('Book on Conjunctions, Faiths, and Religions'), in which the periodical conjunction of Saturn and Jupiter is said to mark a significant stage in human history. This conjunction happens about once every 20 years and, since it takes about 1,000 years (actually *c.*960) for these conjunctions to work their way through the twelve signs of the zodiac, the end and beginning of each such 'millennium', when the series of conjunctions returns, as it were, to its starting-point, must be regarded as especially ominous. The Gospel narratives narrowed the search for the year of Christ's birth, of course, but even so, did not give it exactly, and so astrologers were obliged to rely on other astrologically meaningful data to guide them in their researches. Māshā'allāh's treatise is lost, but parts of it can be read in a summary by a ninth-century Christian astrologer, Ibn Hibintā, and here we find two different years given for the birth: 12 [BC] and 2 [BC]. Abū Ma'shar, however, provided another clue when he said that in the first decan of Virgo was a beautiful, pure young woman seated on a high-backed chair and looking after a child whom 'some people call "Jesus"'. Abū Ma'shar's text was translated into Latin during the twelfth century and was thus available to Hermann of Carinthia who quoted from it in his *De essentiis* (1143), and St Albertus Magnus who, in chapter 12 of his *Speculum astronomiae* (post 1260), also commented on this passage, making it clear that although Jesus *had* been born while Virgo was ascending, this was not because He was compelled to this moment by any configuration of stars, but 'because it was a sign, or rather, as is more true than the truth, He Himself was the cause whereby the manner of His miraculous birth was signified via the heavens'.

A connection between the conjunctions of Saturn and Jupiter and the sign of Virgo was then made by St Albertus's near-contemporary, pseudo-Ovid, in his De Vetula ('The Elderly Woman'):

> The 'masters of the stars' say that every twenty years Jupiter and his father [*Saturn*] are conjoined, and when they have been conjoined twelve or thirteen times in the sign of one triplicity, as happens every so often, at length their conjunction is changed to the next triplicity ... In the signs which are described by Indian, Chaldaean, and Babylonian savants, in the writings of the ancients, it is said that there ascends in the first decan of Virgo 'a pure virgin with long hair, a great spirit, great seemliness, and even more rectitude ... She feeds a boy, giving him permission to eat; and a certain race calls this boy 'Jesus'.

Further investigation of the star of the Magi – what was it and when did it make its appearance? – provided more astronomical-astrological evidence which could help pinpoint the date of Christ's birth, and so we find that in spite of the danger inherent in trying to cast His horoscope, the enterprise was sufficiently intriguing to send several well-known astrologers to their tables and papers in an effort to draw up an accurate nativity. As a preliminary exercise, Pietro d'Abano may have attempted the horoscope, not of Christ but of the Saturn-Jupiter conjunction most likely to have heralded His birth, and Cecco d'Ascoli may actually have drawn a nativity for Him – if so, it has not survived – but he certainly did hold the view that Christ's life and death would have been readable from His horoscope, an assertion which carries with it the implication that His life and death would have been determined by the stars. This last was a proposition undoubtedly made by Agostino Nifo who, however, tried to avoid blasphemy by suggesting it was only Christ's physical constitution which was liable to such influences. Pierre d'Ailly denied that Christianity itself was under any kind of astral governance, and made certain important alterations to Abū Ma'shar's conclusion, (supported by Roger Bacon), that Christ's birth had occurred while Virgo was ascending. D'Ailly thought it took place in Libra, and that the conjunction signalling the advent of Christianity occurred in Cancer rather than in Taurus. This, of course, affected the nativity he constructed for Christ whose birth he set for 24 December 1 [BC] – it contains some errors, but that was one of the hazards attendant on drawing up any horoscope, let alone one which referred to an event over 1,400 years previously – and shows the sun in 1° of Capricorn, the moon in 4° of Taurus, Mercury in 27° of Capricorn, Venus in 19° of Aquarius, Mars in 10° of Aries, Jupiter in 9° of Libra, and Saturn in 15° of Gemini.

Interestingly enough, however, D'Ailly did not offer a reading of this horoscope beyond saying:

Christ, our law-giver, received from His nativity a very good character by nature, [and] it is therefore not contrary to the Faith and it is in accord with natural reason that He should be born under the good celestial disposition of His constellation, from which the goodness of His character naturally derives.

This is entirely bland – hardly surprising from a Christian and a cardinal – but in any case, D'Ailly's intention in drawing up the horoscope was simply to provide an illustration of the technical points to which he objected in Bacon's essay. His caution and intentions were followed by others, and in fact it is not until we come to Girolamo Cardano (1501–76) that we find an astrologer willing to undertake the potentially perilous task of reading a character from these astrological data. Cardano was a physician, mathematician, and astrologer with a great thirst for self-publicity. He pursued fame from an early age and quickly proved that there was genuine talent behind the promotion, and although modern interest in him may choose to concentrate on his contribution to the development of algebra and his invention of a useful piece of technology, the universal joint, to his contemporaries he was best-known as an astrologer who produced several short essays and lengthy tomes on the science. He himself saw astrology as a science of the highest importance:

Astrology is the most lofty of the branches of knowledge because it deals with celestial things and with the future, knowledge of which is not only divine but also very useful. (*Aphorismorum astronomicorum segmenta* VII.5.30)

If there is any skill which human beings need to use, any beneficial discipline, any study which gives delight, any divine wisdom, astrology is without doubt not only such an art but is of all other arts or sciences which deserve a share of these praises the most pre-eminent. For it alone, and more than all the others, has instructed us about the courses of the stars and their dignities and their seasons, and so about the gods themselves … Therefore astrology must be more beneficial and more divine than any other branch of study. Who can doubt it will prove more useful, too, since it tells us how to find out whether the future will be successful or not, and how to avoid it or bear it with equanimity? Whoever has knowledge of such things well in advance will bear them more easily, even if he does not know how to mitigate their effects. (*Encomium astrologiae* 5.727–8)

Cardano was also keen to promote greater accuracy in technical skill and interpretation by casting the nativities of famous people of both the past and present to see how the known facts of their lives, appearances, and characters complied with the indications promised by the individual horoscope. Thus, in *De iudiciis geniturarum* ('Interpreting Nativities'), he discusses the relationship between heavenly bodies and their influences in producing a wide range of behavioural characteristics and a series of events to be enjoyed or endured by the individual concerned. These he illustrates every so often by means of a horoscope which he then interprets.

Please understand, an astrologer will never be master of his craft unless he compares what the stars predict with the actual situation … In my case, in 1529 it happened that the

sun underwent an eclipse in the vicinity of the ascendant, that is, in the eighth degree of
Taurus. Venus, too, at that time was the mistress of my ascendant in opposition to Saturn.
Three quarters of the sun was obscured in the ninth house, and astrologers decided that
this was threatening I should die soon. Yet six years have gone by and I am still alive.
Indeed, I have never felt better, and if you say that provided the moon is not ascending,
she signifies life to me, why have I not suffered so much as any physical ailment? (pp.440,
450)

Not that Cardano himself was infallible. His most notorious mistake was to produce a
nativity for the young English King, Edward VI, in which he noted that Edward would live
more or less the usual life span, reign for many years, and also take a wife. Since Edward
died in 1553, aged not quite sixteen, Cardano was forced to admit his error, although he
did so with a number of excusatory remarks intended to show that if he had not been
right about Edward's fate, he had not been as wrong as his prediction might suggest, an
explanation along the lines of 'I was completely incorrect on that occasion, but had I used
different data, I should simply have been incorrect as opposed to completely incorrect'. This
horoscope appeared in his *Liber XII geniturarum* ('A Book of Twelve Nativities'), which
was a kind of supplement to his *De exemplis centum geniturarum* ('A Hundred Examples
of Nativities'), itself intended to instruct its readers in the art of interpreting horoscopes,
and to take advantage of the growing market for such reading matter. The book's range
is wide and intriguing. It includes three Popes (Paul III, Leo X, Julius II), several secular
rulers (Charles V, five Dukes of Milan, and Cosimo de' Medici of Florence, among others),
Luther and Erasmus, the Emperor Nero, members of his own family, events such as the
building of Venice and the foundation of Milan, generalised groups such as 'effeminates'
and 'deformed births', and curiosities such as 'damage to an eye' and 'a parricide'. The
former of these two referred to a fourteen-year-old who was staying in Cardano's house:

> I predicted that he would shortly either lose his left eye or that it would be much endan-
> gered. Within eighteen months his left eyelid became so inflamed that he was in danger
> of losing the eye. The reason I predicted this was that the moon was unfortunate in the
> seventh [*house*], in quartile with Saturn which was exalted.

The parricide had killed his father while his father was telling him off, and this happened,
says Cardano, because Mars was in an unfortunate aspect with Saturn and so was Jupiter
with the sun. Both signifiers of 'father' were thus unfortunately aspected, and in addition
the sun and Jupiter were accompanied by three stars, 'all with the same character as Mars'.
What is more, the head and heart of Scorpio, and the rays of Saturn and Mars, badly
affected the ascendant and so signified wicked behaviour and a violent death.

In light of these multiple endeavours to cast and then publish a wide range of activities,
it is not surprising that Cardano should have turned his attention to the well-established
problem of providing a horoscope for Christ. He did so in *c*.1532, adding an interpretation
some four or seven years afterwards. Presuming that the time and date of Christ's birth
were midnight on 25 December [1BC], Cardano worked out that the sun was in 2° of

Capricorn, the moon in 28° of Aries, Mercury in 6° of Capricorn, Venus in 18° of Aquarius, Mars in 9° of Aries, Jupiter in 8° of Libra, and Saturn in 14° of Gemini. (This date, and in consequence these calculations, he changed in a second version of the horoscope he published later). Cardano also noted a comet crossing the ascendant line in Libra, which he took to be the star of the Magi, and above the comet an eight-pointed star called *Spica* which had long been associated with Christ in the lap of the Virgin. Another star, Castor, in Gemini shared the nature of Mars and thus signified that Christ's life would be marked by violence, while the position of the sun near the lowest point of the chart foretold a death which would be both public and scandalous. Saturn in the ascendant 'because it had height and a trigonal boundary there, made Him sad and taciturn … He seemed older than His age, for a sad spirit dries out the bones … [Saturn] together with Venus made Him spotted in the face [*i.e. freckled*] … Soundness of body, and beauty, fell to Him through the trigonal rays on the horoscope of the lords of the horoscope, Saturn and Venus, and the presence of Jupiter in it'. The retrograde position of Saturn in the ninth house also indicated that Jesus would be eager to overturn the Jewish Law into which He was born, and the presence of the moon near the Pleiades signified unrest and rioting among the common people.

Cardano ends his lengthy analysis of the horoscope – and Wayne Shumaker reckons it would have taken Cardano a solid two weeks' work to check and re-check his calculations and interpret from them – by observing that in drawing up this nativity he had followed the principles laid down by Claudius Ptolemy, and if following these rules had produced such an accurate prediction of Christ's character and life, how could anyone now doubt that astrology was a true and valid science? He felt obliged (or genuinely wished), however, to add a caveat. 'I do not want you to understand me to say that either the divinity in Christ, or His miracles, or the sanctity of His life, or His promulgation of the [new] Law depends on the stars'; on the contrary, it was God who 'embellished His horoscope with the best and most wonderful disposition of the stars'. Such a caveat notwithstanding, Cardano's enterprise was not without risk, for the very notion that Christ may have been susceptible to planetary influences was potentially heretical, and indeed Cardano was arrested and imprisoned on charges of heresy. But since this horoscope was made public in *c.*1557 and Cardano did not fall foul of the Inquisition until 1570, it seems unlikely that its publication was a direct cause of his arrest, although it will scarcely have done him any good when his beliefs and opinions were questioned.

Why did Cardano draw up this horoscope? For more or less the same reason he undertook the laborious task of casting so many others and interpreting them, first for his own benefit, then through publication for the edification of a wider audience. One of the effects of the religious reformations of the sixteenth century had been the impetus these changes gave to self-examination – not so much the navel-gazing solipsism of the twentieth century as a quest to understand better the relationship of the individual human with his or her wider world: the community, the state, the Church, the cosmos and its indwelling entities, and God. By exploring empirically a wide variety of horoscopes, Cardano clearly hoped to illuminate both these large questions and, paradoxically, the smaller, more detailed challenges relating to the minutiae of an individual's life and character. Can the perpetually changing positions of stars and planets present doctor and patient with a continuous map of illness, mental or physical? How can one express more and more accurately the character traits revealed in these heavenly movements? If a reading proves to be incorrect, is this a fault in the astrologer, in his technique, or could it be an intimation that the heavens hold secrets, (such as the 'new' moons of Jupiter), of which the astrologer is unaware, and whose effects necessarily throw awry his calculations? The increasing boldness of the sixteenth-century astronomer-astrologer in venturing so far into fields more commonly dominated by theology or philosophy aroused the unease and suspicion – as surely it must be expected it would do – of those whose interest and expertise lay precisely in those two disciplines, and so it is not surprising to find Papal condemnation of the science forcibly and lengthily expressed. Pope Sixtus V issued a Bull, *Coeli et Terrae*, in 1586, whose tenor cannot be misunderstood:

> There are no true arts or branches of study which seek foreknowledge of future events and chance happenings. Future events, with some exceptions, come about necessarily or at least frequently from natural causes which owe nothing to divination. Such arts are deceptive and false, established by human cunning and demonic fraud, and it is from the operation, counsel and assistance of evil spirits that all divination spreads, either because they are invoked expressly to reveal the future or because they, with their personal depravity and hatred towards humanity, secretly push themselves forward and before a person is aware of it, thrust in front of him questions about the future. The result is that people's minds become entangled with deadly vanities and deceptive announcements about the things which fall to their lot, and they are corrupted by every type of impiousness … Some people do not pay attention to these things faithfully and devoutly, as they should, but run after curiosities and so gravely offend God. They err and bring others into error. Prime examples of this are astrologers (or 'mathematicians', 'casters of horoscopes', and 'planetaries' as they used to be called). They employ an idle, false knowledge of the planets and stars, and with the utmost audacity busy themselves now with anticipating a revelation of God's arrangement of things. They use the movements of the planets and the course of the stars to give a lying account of people's nativities or horoscopes, and make judgements about the future or even about what is hidden in the present and the past. They take the moment a child was conceived, or its birthday, or some other ridiculous observation and note of times and circumstances, and from this rashly presume to foretell, judge and pronounce upon each person's rank and situation, how his life will proceed, his honours, riches, offspring, health, death, travels, struggles, enmities, imprisonments, murders, various crises and other fortunate or unfortunate events which may come his way …
>
> We, therefore, by reason of Our pastoral duty, must keep inviolate the integrity of the Faith and look to the salvation of souls, and with the aid of God's grace, We are determined, from the bowels of Our fatherly love, to perform this task. Therefore We condemn and reject all types of divination which, springing as they do from the Devil, are accustomed to deceive the faithful by means of the aforesaid curiosities or morally depraved human beings. Moreover We desire, as is reasonable, to preserve unimpaired and incorrupt from all taint of error the holy simplicity of the Christian religion, especially where it concerns the supreme power, wisdom and providence of God the Creator. We wish also

to deal with the aforesaid false credulity, the detestable study of unlawful divinations and superstitions, and hateful scandals and impurities of this kind, so that it can be said of Christians as it was written of God's people in ancient times, 'There is no taking of omens in Jacob, nor divinations in Israel.' Therefore by this decree, which will be for ever valid, and by Our Apostolic authority, We decree and declare against astrologers, 'mathematici', and any others who practise the art of what is called 'judicial astrology' (with the exception of those who make predictions in relation to agriculture, the art of sailing, and medicine); also against those who dare to cast and interpret people's birth-horoscopes with a view to foretelling future events – be these contingent, successive, or fortuitous – or actions dependent on human will, even if the astrologer maintains or testifies that he is not saying anything for certain; also against others of either sex who practise, advertise, teach or learn the aforesaid damned, idle, fallacious, pernicious arts or sciences of divination: or who make unlawful divinations, cast lots, practise superstitions, make poisonous charms or incantations, or utter forth detestable villainies and sins of this kind.

That, as far as the Church was concerned, made the position clear enough. Astrologers and their clients or supporters, however, were just as clearly not so sure, and when John Milton came to write *Paradise Regained*, (ready for the press in 1665 but not actually published until 1667), he was perfectly prepared to envisage Satan as an astrologer speaking to Christ and reading His horoscope almost as though He had come for a consultation:

> Now, contrary – if I read aught in heaven,
> Or heaven write aught of fate – by what the stars
> Voluminous, or single characters
> In their conjunction met, give me to spell,
> Sorrows and labours, opposition, hate,
> Attends thee; scorns, reproaches, injuries,
> Violence and stripes, and, lastly, cruel death.
> A kingdom they portend thee, but what kingdom,
> Real or allegoric, I discern not;
> Nor when: eternal sure, as without end,
> Without beginning; for no date prefixed
> Directs me in the starry rubric set. (4.382–93).

Thomas Newton in 1752 read this as a satirical comment on Cardano, a notion which is somewhat unlikely given the context in which it occurs, the identity of the speaker, and that of the person he is addressing. Acceptance of and belief in astrology more or less regardless of its type – natural, judicial, horary, and so forth – reached one of their high points in the middle decades of the seventeenth century in England, and at this time, in the words of David Gay, 'astrology was both a synchronic feature of Restoration discourse and, like monarchy itself, a diachronic paradigm in the English mind'. In *Paradise Lost* Milton had already associated Satan with astrology, eclipses, and portents, using the language and symbols of astrology to map Satan's rise and fall, and at the same time draw certain parallels between real events of the 1650s in England and the developing stages of his epic narrative. Astrology also attended the restoration of Charles II to his English throne, with poets and pamphleteers vying to outdo one another in their extravagant ebullitions, as in John Gadbury's *Britain's Royal Star, or An Astrological Demonstration of England's Future Felicity, deduced from the position of the heavens as they beheld the earth in the meridian of London, at the first proclaiming of his sacred Majesty, King Charles the Second, on May 8, 19h. 57m. am, 1660* – a title which says it all. Milton, of course, was having none of this, not because he rejected astrology as such – astrology was popular among members of the Puritan establishment during the Commonwealth – but because he objected to the alliance made by so many between astrology and a theology which served the purposes of monarchy. An astrology which served the purposes of Milton's theology was different, and in *Paradise Regained* he makes Satan an astrologer only partly competent because of his blinkered vision. In Jesus' horoscope Satan sees no further than His suffering and death, a failure which Jesus corrects by reference to prophetical Scripture wherein His greater destiny is revealed; and so in Milton's hands Christ's nativity becomes a peg upon which to hang a particular theological and political discourse. Nothing further from Cardano's intentions, or those of his predecessors, could be imagined. [1]

Notes

1. The Land Between the Rivers *c*.800 BC–*c*.600 BC: Interpreting Portents

1. Koch-Westenholz, *Mesopotamian Astrology*, 59-72, 128. Swerdlow, *The Babylonian Theory of Planets*, 14, 100, 104-8, 109. Campion, *The Dawn of Astrology*, 72-3. Baigent, *From the Omens of Babylon*, 53-5. Oppenheim, 'Divination and celestial observation', 114-20. De Lubac, *The Drama of Atheistic Humanism*, San Francisco: Ignatius Press 1995, 22-3. Campion, *op.cit.*, 48. Cf. 'The entire enterprise was entirely rational. And by rational, I do not rely on the word's modern colloquial sense of "based on scientific evidence", but on the more accurate sense of the product of reason, of a coherently thought-out set of ideas about how the world works, and the means of managing such a world for the common good.' *Ibid.*, 42.
2. Horowitz, *Mesopotamian Cosmic Geography*, 8-15, 243-67. Rochberg, *The Heavenly Writing*, 44-9. Quotations: *op.cit.*, 45, 289. Oppenheim, 'A Babylonian diviner's manual', 203.
3. Ben-Dov, *Head of the Years*, 207. Baigent, *From the Omens of Babylon*, 61, 62-3, 73-4. Campion, *The Dawn of Astrology*, 69: quotation, 82.
4. Bottéro, *Religion in Ancient Mesopotamia*, 176-7: quotation, 130. Reiner, *Astral Magic in Babylonia*, 61-79: quotation, 69. Rochberg, *The Heavenly Writing*, 82. Cryer, *Divination in Ancient Israel*, 145-8, 257-9, 168-80.
5. See further, L.W. King, *Babylonian Magic and Sorcery*, Montana: Kessinger Publishing 2003, 118-29.
6. Parploa, *Letters from Assyrian Scholars*, nos. 60 & 61. See Oppenheim, 'A Babylonian diviner's manual', 2-3-5. I have adapted his translation in an effort to make it clearer at certain points.
7. The Babylonian zodiac was a fairly late formulation – about fifth century BC – and is of a type known as 'sidereal', that is to say, it is defined in relation to the stars which appear within it. The tropical zodiac favoured by later Greek astrologers depends on the movement of the sun and presents both astronomers and astrologers with a different frame of reference for their work.
8. Powell, *History of the Zodiac*, 151-94, (a reconstruction of the Babylonian star catalogue). Rochberg, The Heavenly Writing, 6-7. Baigent, *From the Omens of Babylon*, 159-66. Rochberg, 'Lunar data in Babylonian horoscopes', 32-45. For a case study, relating to 15 March 669 BC, see Koch-Westerholz, *Mesopotamian Astrology*, 140-9. Campion, *The Dawn of Astrology*, 70-1. Koch-Westerholz, *op.cit.*, 50-1.
9. Reiner, *Astral Magic in Babylonia*, 50-3, 102, 58-60, 97. Leibovici, 'Sur l'astrologie médicale néo-babylonienne', 278-9. Magic, on the other hand, tended to cling to the planet-deity connection, as can be seen, for example, in a prayer to the sun god, stressing the necessity of having him be present in benign forms of magic. 'Without you, the diviner cannot make the proper arrangements. Without you, the exorcist cannot lay his hand on a sick person. Without you, the exorcist, the ecstatic, the snake charmer cannot go about the streets to do their work.' Rochberg, *op.cit.*, 94.

2. Greece & Rome c.600 BC–50 BC: The Religious Zodiac

1. Panchenko, 'Who found the zodiac?', 32-44. Brack-Bensen & Hunger, 'The Babylonian zodiac', 280 (quotation). Powell comes down firmly on the side of a Babylonian origin, *History of the Zodiac*, 6-7. On the various zodiacs, see *Ibid.*, 11-15. See also Tester, *A History of Western Astrology*, 14-15.

2. It is also worth remembering that the fourth century BC in particular debated the question of whether the earth was indeed unmoving or whether, as Aristarchus of Samos argued, it both rotates and orbits the sun. See further, T.L. North, *Aristarchus of Samos* Oxford: Clarendon Press 1913, 301-6. D. Panchenko, 'On Copernicus's success and Aristarchus's failure', *Antike Naturwissenschaft und ihre Rezeption* 10 (2000), 97-105.

3. Campion, *The Dawn of Astrology*, 128, 131, 133, 139-47. My discussion of Plato and Aristotle is based partly on Campion's chapter 10. The quotation comes from p.164. See also Barton, *Ancient Astrology*, 32-7. Ness, *Written in the Stars*, 84-6. Wright, *Cosmology in Antiquity*, 28, 109-16. S. Leggatt (ed.), *Aristotle on the Heavens, I and II*, Warminster: Aris & Phillips 1995, 6-13, 32-7.

4. *Orientis*, which refers to rising above the horizon, or coming into existence, or being born. It leaves unresolved the old question of whether celestial influences begin at the moment of someone's conception or at the moment of birth.

5. It is worth noting the different Latin words for 'astrologer'. *Chaldaeus* preserves the historical link with Babylonia-Assyria. *Astrologus* is borrowed from Greek and refers to someone who knows how to hear the stars speak. *Mathematicus* draws attention to the considerable and increasingly complex mathematical skill needed to calculate the position of the planets in the sky and their relationships with one another at a particular moment, and for many centuries 'mathematician' continued to imply skill in astrology.

6. Cicero, *De divinatione* 1.2; 2.89. Ennius, quoted in Cicero, *op.cit.*, 1.132. Cato, *De agricultura* 1.5.4. Juvenal, *Saturae* 6.553-4, 562, 569-81. Panaetius in Cicero, *op.cit.*, 2.94-6. St Augustine, *De civitate Dei* 5.3. St Augustine's vocabulary at one point is ambiguous, probably intentionally: 'the marks he had contrived', *signa quae fixerat*. The verb seems to indicate that Nigidius had stabbed the whirling clay with a pen dipped in ink and thus made two nicks more easily visible because of the black of the ink. But *fingo* also means 'fabricate, invent, misrepresent' with an implication of cheating which is hard to miss as one reads the sentence, and one's suspicion that St Augustine intends us to pick up on this jeu de mots is strengthened by the opening of his next sentence. 'This contrivance (*figmentum*) is more flimsy than the vessels which are fashioned (*finguntur*) during that rotation'. *Figmentum* and *finguntur*, like *fixerat*, are derived from or are part of that same verb *fingo*, and their appearance at the start of St Augustine's dismissal of Nigidius's explanation seem to be more deliberate than coincidental. On Nigidius, see further G. Wissow & W. Kroll (eds.), *Pauly Real-Encyclopädie des classischen Altertumswissenschaft* Vol. 17, Stuttgart: J.B. Metzlersche Verlagsbuchhandlung 1936, cols. 200-12. Aemilius Paulus: Plutarch, *Aemilius Paulus* 17.1-6. There could be a small play on words in the adjective 'deaf' which may also mean 'ignorant', but since we have just been told about the uproar created by the soldiers, 'deaf' is perhaps the more appropriate translation here. Cicero, *De re publica* 1.15.23. Cramer, *Astrology in Roman Law and Politics*, 44-50, 69-74. André le Boeuffle suggests that for a long time astrology acted as an instrument of opposition to official Roman religion and politics, *Le ciel des romains*, 57.

7. Cumont, 'Expulsion of astrologers', 14-17. Valerius Maximus, *Facta et Dicta Memorabilia* 1.3.3. See also the commentary by D. Wardle, *Valerius Maximus*, Oxford: Clarendon Press 1998, 148-51. Cicero, *De divinatione* 2.98. Diodorus Siculus, *Bibliotheca Historica* 36.5.2-3. Cicero, *op.cit.*, 1.125. The 'something real' which is born from intertwined causes is *res* which may mean a fact, a deed, or a situation. Campion, *The Dawn of Astrology*, 197-8. Cramer, *Astrology in Roman Law and Politics*, 61-2.

8. Beck, 'The mysteries of Mithras', 121-2; *Planetary Gods*, 85-90. F. Coarelli, 'Carta topografia del mitraismo a Ostia' in Bianchi, *Mysteria Mithrae*, 81-3 and map. K. Riger, 'Les sanctuaires

publics à Ostie de la République jusqu'au Haut Empire' in J-P. Descoeudres (ed.), *Ostia: Port et porte de la Rome antique*, Geneva: Musées d'art et d'histoire 2001, 259-61. Beck, 'Mithraism since Franz Cumont', 2022-6. An Iranian origin for the cult has long been brought into question. See for example, Swerdlow's review article 'On the cosmical mysteries of Mithras', 49-50. Gasparro, 'Il mitraismo nell'ambito della fenomenologia misterica', 319. Beck, *Planetary Gods*, 4-11, 34-42. Barton, *Ancient Astrology*, 198-210. Small, 'The raven: an iconographic adaptation of the planet Mercury' in Bianchi, *op.cit.*, 531-49. David Ulansky's suggestion that the religion began in response to the second-century BC Hipparchus's discovery of the precession of the equinoxes has not found universal favour. See further Ulansky, *The Origins of the Mithraic Mysteries*, 76-87. Swerdlow, *op.cit.*, 52-61.

9. Campion, *The Dawn of Astrology*, 99-108. See also Waterfield, 'The evidence of astrology in Classical Greece', 3-15. For planetary and astral religion among the Romans, see Le Boeuffle, *Le ciel des romains*, 129-35. Celsus quoted in Origen, *Contra Celsum* 6.22 (ed. & trans. H. Chadwick, Cambridge: Cambridge University Press 1954, 334). Origen wrote his polemic in 248 AD, about 70 or 80 years after the treatise of Celsus which he is quoting here. Beck, *Planetary Gods*, 73-84. Gordon, *Image and Value in the Graeco-Roman World*, 126-30, (diagram, 127), 140-2: quotations, 142, 146. See also Heilen, 'Astrological remarks', 135.

3. Hellenistic & Roman Egypt 50 BC–*c*.AD 100: Personal Horoscopes

1. Campion, *The Dawn of Astrology*, 66, 90, 108. Berossus: Vitruvius: *De architectura* 9.2.1. Quotation on fire and flood: Seneca, *Naturales Quaestiones* 3.29.1. It is interesting that Berossus (or his source) designates Cancer as the planetary meeting-place for conflagration, since Cancer is a water sign, ruled by the moon. Capricorn is an earth sign, ruled by Saturn.

2. Pingree, 'Pseudo-Petosiris', 546-9. Quotation: Hephaestio of Thebes, *Apotelesmatica* 1.21.12. *Catalogus Codicum Astrologorum Graecorum* Vol. 7, Brussels: Henri Martin 1908, 132 = *Excerpta Moncensia*. On catarchic astrology, see Tester, *A History of Western Astrology*, 88-9. Barton, *Ancient Astrology*, 175-7. On the transmission of Dorotheus's text, see Pingree's translation of the *Carmen*, x-xi. Quotation: *Ibid.*, 267-8.

3. Anoubion: *Oxyrhynchus Papyri*, Vol. 66 (1999), no. 4503, back fr. 2. Cf. *Ibid.*, no. 4504, col.ii.

4. Dorotheus quotations, *op.cit.* supra, 172, 180, 197, 204, 210-11, 220, 206, 263, 272, 283, 285, 302-3, 305. Pseudo-Aristotle, *Physiognomica* 6 [812a]. Adamantius, *Physiognomica* = R. Förster (ed.), *Scriptores Physiognomici Graeci et Latini* 2 vols., Leipzig: Teubner 1893, 1.394. Plautus, *Pseudolus* 1218-19. Martial, *Epigrammata* 12.54. Anon, *De physiognomia* 14 = Förster, op.cit. 2.22. M. Delcourt, *Pyrrhos et Pyrrha*: *Recherches sur les valeurs du feu dans les légendes hélleniques*, Paris: Les Belles Lettres 1965, 13-17.

5. *Carmen Astrologicum*, 306, 307. Synesius, quoted in L. Casson, *Travel in the Ancient World*, London: George Allen & Unwin Ltd. 1974, 161. See also C. Reynier, *Paul de Tarse en Méditerranée*, Paris: Les Éditions du Cerf 2006, 183-6. Dorotheus, *op.cit.*, 284. *Oxyrhynchus Papyri*, Vol. 31, London: Egyptian Exploration Society 1966, no. 2582; Vol. 36 (1970), no. 2777. Cf. Vol. 42 (1974), nos. 3053 and 3054. In the first of these, the owner of the slave is said to have no distinguishing marks, while the female slave has scars on the left side of her upper lip and a scar on her right knee. In the latter, the slave has 'white skin' – unusual for a man, even if one takes 'white' to mean 'pale' – a rather flat face, scanty eyebrows, a short nose, scars on the left forehead and eyebrow and jawline, and a slight squint. Cf. the description of recruits to the army, Vol. 7 (1910), no. 1022. Runaway slaves: Vol. 51 (1984), nos. 3616 and 3617. I have changed one or two words or phrases in the translation.

6. Holden, *A History of Horoscopic Astrology*, 32-3. Barton, *Power and Knowledge*, 120-2. On astrologers in Oxyrhynchus, see further P. Parson, *City of the Sharp-Nosed Fish*, London: Weidenfeld & Nicolson 2007, 185-8. Cicero, *Pro Quinto Roscio Comoedo* 7.20. Plutarch, *Moralia* (De facie in orbe lunae 28) 943A. Pliny, *Historia Naturalis* 2.108-10, 221; 32.55. Seneca, *Naturales Quaestiones* 2.32. Ptolemy, *Tetrabiblos* 3.13.4-5. Vettius Valens, another second-century

AD astrologer, attributes somewhat different parts of the body to most of the planets. See
Anthologies, 26-35. Beck, *Ancient Astrology*, 74-6.

4. The Imperial West *c*.100–*c*.200: Political Quicksands

1. Julius Marathus: Suetonius, *Vitae Caesarum, Augustus* 2.94.3. Asclepias of Mendes: *Ibid.*, 2.94.4.
   Nigidius Figulus: Dio Cassius, *Historiae* 45.3-4. Theogenes: Suetonius, *op.cit.*, 2.94.12. Nicolaus
   of Damascus: *Fragmenta historicorum graecorum*, ed. C. Müller, Vol. 3, (Paris: Ambrosio Firmin
   Didot 1849), 434 = fr. 101. Barton, 'Augustus and Capricorn', 37-8; quotations, 39, 44. She
   produces both natal and conception charts for Octavian, 41, 43. Cf. Abry, 'Auguste: le Balance
   et le Capricorne', 108. Manilius, *Astronomica* 2.507-9. Dwyer, 'Augustus and the Capricorn', 60-
   1, 66-7. Dicks, 'Astrology and astronomy in Horace', 70-2. Mamoojee, 'Quintus Cicéron et les
   douze signes du zodiaque', 247-8. Domenicucci, *Astra Caesarum*, 109-23.
2. This account is based on Abry, 'What was Agrippina waiting for?' 37-48. The two horoscopes
   are included at the end of her essay.
3. Juvenal, *Saturae* 6.553-4, 557-62. Plutarch, *Vitae Caesarum, Galba* 23.4. Tacitus, *Historiae* 1.22.
4. Cramer, *Astrology in Roman Law and Politics*, 249-51. Manilius, *Astronomica* 4. Thrasyllus:
   Campion, *The Dawn of Astrology*, 234-6. Tacitus, *Annales* 6.21. Suetonius tells a different story.
   Thrasyllus and Tiberius were strolling on top of a cliff when they caught sight of a ship.
   Thrasyllus declared it brought good news – as indeed it did, for it put in at Rhodes with
   instructions to recall Tiberius to Rome – and so Thrasyllus escaped the death which Tiberius
   had been meditating for him only a moment or so earlier, *Vitae Caesarum, Tiberius* 14; *Ibid.*,
   Caligula 57. Balbillus: Cramer, *op.cit.*, 112-31. Holden, *A History of Horoscopic Astrology*, 29-32.
   An example of Balbillus's work is given in Beck, *Ancient Astrology*, 121-2. Cramer, 'Expulsion of
   astrologers from Rome', 29-31. Suetonius, *Vitae Caesarum, Nero* 36. Cramer, *Astrology in Roman
   Law and Politics*, 137-8. Beck, *op.cit.* supra, 126-31.
5. The Augustan astrologer Manilius tells us that those born under Libra have a great capacity
   for friendship, *Astronomica* 2.616-19.
6. The drum-roll may signify their entry into the arena of an amphitheatre where they have been
   condemned to die as criminals. Taurus (i.e. a bull) and Leo (i.e. a lion) will thus prove fatal to
   them.
7. See Goold's introduction to his translation of Manilius. Volk, *Manilius and his Intellectual
   Background*, 1-6, 29-57, 226-46 (which contain a very useful discussion of Manilius's possible
   sources). So, too, Salemme, *Introduzione agli 'Astronomica' di Manilio*, 21-6 on his Hermetic
   influences. Holden, *A History of Horoscopic Astrology*, 23-6. Tester, *A History of Western Astrology*,
   30-48. Beck, *Ancient Astrology*, 62-7. Whitfield, *Astrology*, 39-55. Gain, *The Aratus ascribed to
   Germanicus Caesar*, 16-20. Possanza, *Translating the Heavens*, 7-10, 15-16, 219-43. Germanicus
   Caesar was not the only person to translate Aratus's poem. Cicero, too, had done so as a
   youthful exercise, remaining somewhat more faithful than Germanicus to the original, although
   'faithful' has to be understood in the light of his omissions and summaries. See J. Soubiran,
   Cicéron, Aratea, Fragments Poétiques, Paris: Les Belles Lettres 1972, 8-16, 87-93. E. Gee, 'Cicero's
   astronomy', *Classical Quarterly* 61 (2001), 520-36.

5. Jewish Traditions, Demons & Manuals *c*.100–*c*.200: An Astrological Legacy

1. Wise, *Thunder in Gemini*, 48, 50. Charlesworth, 'Jewish interest in astrology', 935-8. *Testament
   of Solomon*, 72, 74: translation by F.C. Conybeare, *Jewish Quarterly Review*, October 1898. Von
   Stuckrad, 'Jewish and Christian astrology', 17-21. Ness, *Written in the Stars*, 148-51. Carroll,
   'A preliminary analysis of the Epistle to Reheboam', 91-103: quotation, 94. On zodiacs in
   Palestinian synagogues, see Ness, *op.cit.*, 1-38. Drawnel, 'Moon computation in the Aramaic
   Astronomical Book (1)', 25, 32-4.

2. Firmicus Maternus, *Mathesis* 4.3.9. Ptolemy, *Tetrabiblos* 2.3. E.H. Merrill, *Qumran and Predestination*, Leiden: Brill 1975. Molnar, *The Star of Bethlehem*, 85-96, 101-9, 46-8. Molnar's general thesis is summarised by Chown, 'O invisible star of Bethlehem', 34-5. Earlier speculations that the star was a thrice-repeated conjunction of Jupiter and Saturn in Pisces in 7 BC are reviewed by Rosenberg, 'The star of the Messiah reconsidered', 105-9. See also Molnar, op.cit., 15-30. Denzey, 'A new star on the horizon', 207-21. Campion prefers to regard the star as a literary device used by St Matthew to emphasise to his readers the royalty and divinity of Jesus, *The Dawn of Astrology*, 249. See also Dorival, 'L'astre de Balaam et l'étoile des Mages', 93-111. Hegedus, *Early Christianity and Ancient Astrology*, 201-22.

3. For a notion of how bizarre the religious ambience in Alexandria must have been during the early Christian centuries, see S. Benko, 'The libertine Gnostic sect of the Phibionites according to Epiphanius', *Vigiliae Christianae* 21 (1967), 103-19.

4. Tatian, *Oratio ad Graecos*, 8. See also A. Yoshiko Reed, *Fallen Angels and the History of Judaism and Christianity*, Cambridge: Cambridge University Press 2005, 174-89. Campion, *The Dawn of Astrology*, 189-95. Barton, *Ancient Astrology*, 68-70. Thorndike, *History of Magic and Experimental Science* 1.353-6.

5. R.R. Newton, *The Crime of Claudius Ptolemy*, Baltimore & London: John Hopkins University Press 1977, 378-9.

6. Campion, *The Dawn of Astrology*, 208-17. Riley, *A Survey of Vettius Valens*, 1-3. Bara, *Anthologies, Livre I*, 13-14. Quotation: A-J. Festugière, *L'idéal religieux des Grecs et l'Évangile*, Paris 1932, 120-3. Riley, op.cit., 8-11: quotation, 3. Neugebauer & Van Hoesen, *Greek Horoscopes*, 176-85; quotation, 128-9. Climacterics: Riley, op.cit., 30-2; quotation, 32. Barton, *Ancient Astrology*, 73-6, 101-11. Beck calls Valens 'the pre-eminent empiricist', (p.101), on the grounds that 'the empirical method systematically tests effects against postulated causes', and that in composing a data-base of horoscopes, however limited in number, Valens was taking the first steps in using genethliacal charts to check his hypothesis of climacteric periods, (pp.101-2).

7. This is one explanation offered by Heilen, 'The Emperor Hadrian in the horoscopes of Antigonus of Nicaea', 57-60. But he also offers another which suggests that Antigonus 'was inspired by Hadrian's autobiography ... to analyse the Emperor's and some related individuals' horoscopes', (pp.60-5). See further Pingree, 'Antiochus and Rhetorius', 203-8. Holden, *A History of Horoscopic Astrology*, 64-5. Beck, *Ancient Astrology*, 83-4. On 'lots', see Paul of Alexandria, quoted in Holden, op.cit., 79-82. Heilen, op.cit., 49-67. Holden, op.cit., 60-4. Beck, op.cit., 124-5. Barnes, 'The horoscope of Licinius Sura?' 76-9. Heilen rejects Barnes's arguments and favours Acilius Attianus, one of Hadrian's enemies, op.cit., 56.

8. Cramer, *Astrology in Roman Law and Politics*, 181-2. Le Boeuffle, *Le ciel des romains*, 108-10. Kjeld de Fine Licht, *The Rotunda in Rome: A Study on Hadrian's Pantheon*, Copenhagen: Jutland Archaeological Publications 1968, 198-202.; quotation, 201. Aulus Gellius, *Noctes Atticae* 3.10.3-4, 6-7. Dio Cassius, *Historiae* 77.11.1.

6. A Christian Dilemma *c*.200–*c*.500: Theological Doubts & Popular Belief

1. On Maternus, see Jean Rhys Bram's introduction to her translation of the Mathesis. Holden, *A History of Horoscopic Astrology*, 66-79. Beck, *Ancient Astrology*, 97-100. Barton, *Ancient Astrology*, 114-25, which weds Maternus's astrology to the horoscope of Charles Windsor. Thorndike, *History of Magic and Experimental Science* 1.525-38.

2. Dodds, *Pagan and Christian in an Age of Anxiety*, 6-14. Origen, *Philocalia*, ed. J.A. Robinson, Cambridge: Cambridge University Press 1893, 187-98. Fédou, *Christianisme et Religions Païennes dans le Contre Celse d'Origène*, 432-7. Barton, *Ancient Astrology*, 74-5. Whitfield, *Astrology*, 78. Plotinus, *Ennead* 2.3.1-18; quotation, 7. Dillon, 'Plotinus on whether the stars are causes', 87-92. Campion, *The Dawn of Astrology*, 260-1.

3. Tertullian, *Apologeticum* 35. T.D. Barnes, *Tertullian: A Historical and Literary Study*, Oxford: Clarendon Press 1971, 33-4. Tertullian is, understandably enough, anxious to distance

Christians from professions of which he disapproves anyway, but which were also liable to fall under heavy Imperial displeasure because of the way they were used for political purposes. Cf. *Apologeticum* 43: 'I shall readily confess what sort of people can perhaps truly complain of the unprofitableness of Christians. First will come the procurers, the pimps, the bullies; then the assassins, the poisoners, the magicians; likewise the diviners, the soothsayers, the astrologers (*mathematici*). To be unprofitable to these is great profit'. Hegedus, *Early Christianity and Ancient Astrology*, 261-73.

4. *Historia Augusta: Severus* 3.9; *Geta* 2.6-7; *Severus* 15.5. Kelley, 'Astrology in the Pseudo-Clementine Recognitions', 610-11, 625-6, (Ross quotation, 624). Chadwick, *Priscillian of Avila*, 192, 194. Hegedus, *Early Christianity and Ancient Astrology*, 339-51. Ammianus Marcellinus, *Res Gestae* 28.4.24. Barton, *Ancient Astrology*, 64-7. St Augustine, *Confessions*, 34-5. See further O'Donnell's commentary in Vol. 2, Oxford: Clarendon Press 1992, 209-12. Tester, *A History of Western Astrology*, 108-12. St Augustine, *City of God*, 94-7. Thorndike, *History of Magic and Experimental Science* 1.513-21. Campion, *The Dawn of Astrology*, 280-4.

5. *Genesis* 49.9: 'Judah is the lion's cub. You have leapt upon the prey, my son. You have lain down, seeking rest like a lion, and, as in the case of a lioness, who will rouse him?'

6. *Luke* 10.19: 'Behold, I have given you the power to tread upon snakes and scorpions and upon the entire power of the Enemy, and nothing will harm you'.

7. Zeno, *Tractatus de duodecim signis ad neophytes* in *Corpus Christianorum*, Series Latina, Vol. 22, ed. B. Löfstedt, Turnhout: Brepols 1971, 105-6. Hübner, 'Das Horoskop der Christen', *Vigiliae Christianae* 29 (1975), 120-37. Sogno, 'Astrology, morality, the Emperor and the law', 168-72. Dagron & Rougé, 'Trois horoscopes de voyages en mer', 120-31. Campion, *The Dawn of Astrology*, 279, 287-8. Whitfield, *Astrology*, 82. On the roles played by Good and Evil in the Christianised cosmos, see M. Cristiani, 'La natura malata: il teatro delle passioni nelle cosmologie del Manicheismo antico e medievale', *Micrologus* 4 (1996), 207-29.

7. Islamic Speculation *c.*600–*c.*900: Fresh Insights, Transmission & Astral Magic

1. Translation of the Qu'ranic texts by N.J. Dawood, revised ed. London: Penguin Books 2000. In 15.16 I have altered Dawood's 'constellations' to 'zodiacal signs'. The word *burūj*, (plural of *burj* meaning 'castle' or 'tower') refers to these signs, as is clear not only from this verse but also from 36.6 and the opening verse of 85, a sūra itself entitled 'The Zodiacal Signs'.

2. Morony, *Iraq after the Muslim Conquest*, 393-4, 288-90, 409-10. Green, *The City of the Moon God*, 40-2, 57, 84 (Addai). Nothing now remains of the great temple to Sin, the moon god which the Emperor Theodosius destroyed in 382, perhaps because it was not actually in Harran but near the border with Persia. But there does seem to have been at least one temple to a moon goddess in or near the city. See further S. Lloyd & W. Brice, 'Harran', *Anatolian Studies* 1 (1951), 79-80, 90, 95-6. Thorndike, *History of Magic and Experimental Science* 1.661-3. On the Hermetic connection, see Alexander, 'Jewish traditions in early Islam', 24-6.

3. Severus's praise of Indian mathematics is partly sincere, partly a dig at Greeks (by whom he means Byzantines) 'who believe that they alone have arrived at the limit of knowledge because they speak Greek', as he wrote in a letter. Those who, like Severus, wrote in Syriac and, like Severus, had heterodox religious opinions, were persecuted by Constantinople. Hence, perhaps, Severus's animus. See Saliba, *Islamic Science and the Making of the European Renaissance*, 43.

4. Morony, *op.cit.* supra, 403-4. North, *Horoscopes and History*, 56-9, with illustrations of the working parts on pp.62-5; *Cosmos*, 124-73. Whitfield, *Astrology*, 93. Gunther, *Astrolabes of the World* 1.82-103. Neugebauer, 'The early history of the astrolabe', 242-5. Hartner, 'Asturlāb', 722-8. Sebokht, *Treatise on the Astrolabe*, Introduction. For a translation of the treatise by John Philoponos, see: *www.tertullian.org/fathers.john_philoponos_astrolabe_02_text.htm*

5. Pingree, 'The Byzantine translations of Māshā'allāh on interrogational astrology', 233. Pingree, 'Greek influence on early Islamic mathematical astronomy', 37-41. Pingree, 'Astronomy and

astrology in India and Iran', 242-3. See also E.S. Kennedy, 'A survey of Islamic astronomical tables', *Transactions of the American Philosophical Society*, new series 46, no. 2 (1956), 123-77. Holden, *A History of Horoscopic Astrology*, 107-11.

6. This is Pingree's date. Saliba gives 23 July, *op.cit.* supra, 15.
7. Pingree, 'Māshā'allāh', 159-62. Pingree, 'From Alexandria to Baghdād to Byzantium', 18-19: quotations, 30-1, 34-5. Pingree, 'Māshā'allāh's Zoroastrian historical astrology', 95-6. Thorndike, 'The Latin translations of astrological works by Messahala', 49-72. North, *History and Horoscopes*, 72-5.
8. Pingree, 'From Alexandria to Baghdād to Byzantium', 13-17. Holden, *A History of Horoscopic Astrology*, 104-7; quotation, 105-6. Mavroudi, 'Occult science and society in Byzantium', 87-9. Pingree, 'Indian and pseudo-Indian passages', 148-9. On zījes, see further North, *Cosmos*, 192-5.
9. Hand, 'A study in early house division', 1-4. North, *History and Horoscopes*, 75-81. Yamamoto & Burnett, *Abū Maʿshar on Historical Astrology* 1.xiii-xxii, 2-5. Holden, *op.cit.* supra, 115-26. Pingree, 'Abū Maʿshar', 32-9. An English translation of Abū Maʿshar's *Flores* can be found in Holden, *Five Mediaeval Astrologers*, 13-65. Thorndike, 'Albumasar in Sadan', 30, 31, 26, 28. One should enter a caveat that some of this information comes from Pietro d'Abano's Latin version of 'Sayings of Abū Maʿshar on the Secrets of Astrology', and may therefore lack a certain Gospel quality. Pingree, 'The Sabians of Harran', 26-9. For details of Abū Maʿshar's techincal discussions, see Tester, *A History of Western Astrology*, 164-8. Lemay, 'Des sages antiques aux astrologues médiévaux', 170-2.
10. Travaglia, *Magic, Causality and Intentionality*, 105-46. Jolivet & Rashd, 'Al-Kindī', 266. Quotation on incessant flow: Klein-Franke, 'Al-Kindī', 168. Quotation on knowledge of celestial harmony: *Risāla (De radiis)*, chap. 2. Tester, *op.cit.* supra, 159. Travaglia, *op.cit.*, 17-48, 97-101. Thorndike, *History of Magic and Experimental Science* 1.643-6.
11. *Liber Vaccae*: Pingree, 'The Sābians of Harrān and the Classical tradition', 33-4. Tardieu, 'Sābiens coraniques et Sābiens de Harrān', 11-38. Hämeen-Antilla, *The Last Pagans of Iraq*, 46-52. Pingree, *op.cit.*, 30. Saliba, *Islamic Science and the Making of the European Renaissance*, 48. Pingree, *op.cit.*, 35. Quotation from *De imaginibus*, chapter 5: Bobrick, *The Fated Sky*, 93-4. Ibn Wahshiyya also wrote a book containing alphabets for each planet and zodiacal sign. This type of book provided a source for anyone wanting to practise astral or talismanic magic. Hämeen-Antilla, *op.cit.*, 219, 258, 193, 138, 149, 186-7. Omidsalar, 'Magic in literature and folklore', 7, 9, 10.
12. Fierro, 'Bātinism in al-Andalus', 87-92, 97-102. An attempt by J. Thomann to suggest that 'Picatrix' is a translation of al-Majrītī's first name, Maslama, on the grounds that both mean 'prick' or 'sting', both have a feminine ending in their respective tongues, and Arabic personal names were sometimes translated into Latin, has not found universal favour, 'The name Picatrix', 289-96. Neither has the equation Picatrix = Biqrātīs = Hippocrates, recorded by Hartner, 'Notes on Picatrix', 438 and Kahane & Pietrangeli, 'Picatrix and the talismans', 575-7, where they prefer to suggest that Biqrātīs = Harpokratis/Harpokration. Pingree, 'Some of the sources of the Ghāyat al-Hakīm', 1-15. Yates, *Giordano Bruno*, 53-4.
13. The earliest Yemeni astronomer-astrologer about whom there is reliable information is the tenth-century al-Hamdānī who compiled a *zīj* which was still being used in the thirteenth century. On Yemeni practitioners of both sciences, see further King, 'Mathematical astronomy in Mediaeval Yemen', 62-4.
14. That is, the figure will not appear ghostly in the sense of semi-transparent, or merely as a head and shoulders. It will have the appearance of a real, solid person and will not be frightening or grotesque – hence 'seemly'.
15. Quotations from the *Picatrix* are taken from Pingree's edition of the Latin text. See further Thorndike, *History of Magic and Experimental Science* 2.813-21. Picatrix, ed. Backhouche, Fauquier, Pérez-Jean 35-8. On pseudo-Aristotelian works, see Burnett, *Magic and Divination in the Middle Ages*, III, 84-96. Byzantine amulets by no means always strayed into the realm of the demonic, or even possibly demonic. A sixth or seventh-century haematite amulet, for example, depicts Christ healing the woman with an issue of blood, (*Mark* 5.25-9), and is clearly meant

to be worn or carried by a woman suffering some similar disorder, who expected to benefit from the therapy it offered. This therapy was not necessarily magical in the sense that some exterior power used it as a channel to impart a cure, immediate or quick, which was beyond the normal ability of Nature to deliver. 'The curative powers of the amulet,' says Jacqueline Tuerk, 'lay in its power of signification to shape and even determine actuality. If there is magic here, it is the magic of signification itself.' 'An early Byzantine inscribed amulet and its narratives', Byzantine and Modern Greek Studies 23 (1999), 25-42; quotation, 40.

8. Byzantium & the Jewish Diaspora c.900–c.1200: Agreements to Disagree

1. R. Walzer, 'Al-Fārābī' in Encyclopaedia of Islam, new. ed. Vol. 2, Leiden & London: Brill & Luzac & Co. 1965, 778-81. M. Mahdi, 'Al-Fārābī' in Dictionary of Scientific Biography, Vol. 4, New York: Charles Scribner's Sons 1971, 523-6. D.L. Black, 'Al-Fārābī' in Nasr & Leaman, History of Islamic Philosophy 1.178-97. Quotation from T. Kukkonen, 'Averroes and the teleological argument', Religious Studies 38 (2002), 415. 'Uqlidisi quoted in Saliba, History of Arabic Astronomy, 58. Kennedy, Astronomy and Astrology in the Mediaeval Islamic World, XV, 12. Al-Bīrūnī, Chronology, quoted in Saliba, op.cit., 59. Book of Instructions, 101. S.H. Nasr, An Introduction to Islamic Cosmological Doctrines, Cambridge, Mass: Harvard University Press 1964, 163-5. Samsó, Astronomy and Astrology, VI, 588-92. M.S. Namus, 'Al-Bīrūnī, the greatest astrologer of the times' in H.M. Said (ed.), Al-Bīrūnī, Commemorative Volume, Karachi: The Times Press 1979, 545-57, and K.B. Nasīm, 'Al-Bīrūnī as an astrologer', Ibid., 578-81. A.I. Sabra, 'Ibn al-Haytham' in Dictionary of Scientific Biography, Vol. 6, New York: Charles Scribner's Sons 1972, 189-91. Saliba, Islamic Science and the Making of the European Renaissance, 97-108. E.R. Rowson, 'Ibn Sīnā' in Nasr & Leaman, op.cit. supra, 1-231-46. Saliba, History of Arabic Astronomy, 69. H. Corbin, Avicenna and the Visonary Recital, English trans., London: Routledge & Kegan Paul 1960, 162-4: quotation, 163. Mehren, Vues d'Avicenne sur l'astrologie, 5-6. Nofal, 'Al-Ghazali', 2, 9. W.M. Watt, The Faith and Practice of Al-Ghazālī, London: George Allen & Unwin 1953, 80-1. P.E. Walker, Early Philosophical Shiism: the Ismaili Neoplatonism of Abū Ya'qūb al-Sijistānī, Cambridge: Cambridge University Press 1993, 72-80, 87-94, 114-23. Marquet, 'La révélation par l'astrologie', 13: quotation, 15-16. Al-Asturlāabī quoted in F. Rosenthal, 'Al-Asturlābī and As-Samaw'al on scientific progress', Isis 9 (1950), 559.

2. Magdalino, 'Occult science and Imperial power', 123-6, 136. John's act of magic is perhaps a touch ironic, since he was the last and most notorious of the iconoclastic patriarchs. See further, Magdalino, L'orthodoxie des astrologues, 56-8, 82-3. Psellos, Chronographia, Englsih trans. London: Routledge & Kegan Paul 1953, 201-2, 93. Magdalino, 'Occult science', 137. Magdalino, The Empire of Manuel I Komnenos, 1143-1180, Cambridge: Cambridge University Press 1993, 377-80. Khoniates: O City of Byzantium: Annals of Niketas Khoniates, English trans. Detroit: Wayne State University Press 1984, 55-6, 124. Dall'Aglio, 'Magia e astrologia in Niceta Coniata', 570-2. George, 'Manuel I Komnenos and Michael Glykas', 15-16, 19-25, 31-6. Translation of Manuel's defence: Ibid., Part 2, 1-15. Translation of Glykas's reply: Ibid., Part 2, 16-28. See also Adler, 'Did the Biblical patriarchs practise astrology?' 245-63. Anna Komnena, Alexiad, English trans. Harmondsworth: Penguin Books 1969, 194. Magdalino, 'Occult science', 140-6; L'orthodoxie des astrologues, 91-132.

3. Symeon Seth: O. Temkin, 'Byzantine medicine: tradition and empiricism', Dumbarton Oaks Papers 16 (1962), 108-9. L-O. Sjöberg, Stephanites and Ichnelates, Stockholm: Almquist & Wiksell 1962, 87-101. Tihon, 'Les textes astronomiques importés à Byzance', 316-24. My discussion of the fourteenth century is based largely on Tihon, 'Astrological promenade in Byzantium', 273-90. Pingree, 'Gregory Chioniades and Palaeologan astronomy', 141. On other translations from Arabic or Persian manuscripts, see Ibid., 141-3, 145. Hermippus, De astrologia dialogus, 69-70.

4. R. Brody, The Geonim of Babylonia and the Shaping of Mediaeval Jewish Culture, New Haven & London: Yale University Press 1998, 146. Tihon, 'Astrological promenade in Byzantium',

289-90. Magdalino, *L'orthodoxie des astrologues*, 161-2. Pingree, 'The astrological school of John Abramius', 192, 196.

5. J. Dan, 'Shabbetai Donnolo' *Encyclopaedia Judaica* 6.168-70. Ruderman, *Jewish Thought and Scientific Discovery*, 23-9: quotation, 26. Holo, 'Hebrew astrology in Byzantine southern Italy', 301-8: quotation, 307. B. Kogan, 'Judah Halevi' in Nasr & Leaman, *History of Islamic Philosophy* 1.718-24. Schwarz, *Studies on Astral Magic*, 1-9, (quotations, 6, 5); 9-26, (quotation, 12); 27-54. A. Broadie, 'Maimonides' in Nasr & Leaman, *op.cit.*, 725-38. *Guide for the Perplexed*, English trans. 2nd revised ed., London: George Routledge & Sons Ltd. 1910, 333 – Part 3, chapter 37. *Epistle to Yemen*, English trans. New York: American Academy for Jewish Research 1952, xiii. Davidson, *Moses Maimonides*, 494-501. *Letter on Astrology*, English trans. (from Lerner & Mahdi, *Mediaeval Political Philosophy*, 227-36), 229, 230, 232, 234. See also Horowitz, 'Rashba's attitude towards science and its limits', 53-7.

6. Guttman, *Philosophies of Judaism: The History of Jewish Philosophy from Biblical Times to Franz Rosenzweig*, English trans. New York: Holy, Rinehart & Winston 1964, 217. Nahmanides: Ruderman, *op.cit.* supra, 35-41: quotation, 39. Schwarz, *op.cit.* supra, 55-68, especially 61-2, 66. Horowitz, *op.cit.* supra, 57-62L quotation, 59. D.C. Skemer, *Binding Words: Textual Amulets in the Middle Ages*, Pennsylvania: Pennsylvania State University Press 2006, 132. E. Ettlinger, 'British amulets in London museums', *Folklore* 50 (1936), 167. Schwarz, *op.cit.*, 81. G. Freudenthal, 'Gersonides: Luri ben Gershom' in Nasr & Leaman, *History of Islamic Philosophy* 1.739-54. Sirat, *History of Jewish Philosophy in the Middle Ages*, 280-308, especially 299-307. Ruderman, *op.cit.*, 41-4.

9. Mediaeval Europe *c*.1200–*c*.1300: The Inheritor of Traditions

1. Thorndike, 'John of Seville', *Speculum* 34 (1959), 20-38; *History of Magic and Experimental Science* 2.22, 40-2. Burnett, 'Adelard, ergaphalau and the science of the stars', 133-6. Thorndike, *History* 2.73-8, 82-3, 85-91. Lyons, *The House of Wisdom*, 103-24, 136-8, 140-1. C. Burnett & D. Pingree, introduction to Hugo of Santalla, *Liber Aristotilis*, 1-9. C.H. Hoskins, 'The translations of Hugo Sanctelliensis', *Romanic Review* 2 (1911), 1-15.

2. He also said he had profited *a Galippo mixtarabe*, 'a Mozarab, Galippus', who instructed him *in lingua Tholetana*, 'in Castilian'. Galippus was one of Gerard of Cremona's personal assistants, a Spanish Christian who agreed to observe certain Islamic rules and customs in return for religious freedom.

3. 'Thoz the Greek' refers to Egyptian Thoth, Greek Hermes, that is, 'Hermes Trismegistos', supposed author of the treatises which go to make up the *Corpus Hermeticum*. Aristotle did write a book on mirrors, so presumably this text will have been foisted upon him by someone anxious to lend his composition the weight of Aristotle's name.

4. Thorndike, *History of Magic and Experimental Science* 2.171-81. Abdukhalimov, 'Ahmad al-Farghānī and his Compendium of Astrology', Journal of Islamic Studies 10 (1999), 142-58. Silverstein, 'Daniel of Morley', 182-3. Bernardus Silvestris, *Cosmographia*, 98-104. Stock, *Myth and Science in the Twelfth Century*, 163-87, 227-37.

5. For a detailed overview of the earlier Tables, see G.J. Toomer, 'Survey of the Toledan Tables', *Osiris* 15 (1968), 5-174. My list of contents is taken from p.7. See also North, *Horoscopes and History*, 114-17; Cosmos, 227-31. Compilation of such tables became a matter of prestige for some monarchs. Hence, for example, *Las Tablas Astronómicas* put together for Pedro IV of Aragon by Jacob ben Isaac Carsono in *c*.1367. See further J.M. Millas Vallicrosa, *Las Tablas Astronómicas del Rey Don Pedro al Ceremonioso*, Madrid-Barcelona 1962, 11-84. On Alfonso's encouragement of learning, see further A. Ballesteros-Beretta, *Alfonso X El Sabio*, Barcelona-Madrid: Salvat Editores 1963, 243-53. J.F. Callaghan, *The Learned King: The Reign of Alfonso X of Castile*, Philadelphia: University of Pennsylvania Press 1993, 141-4. Roth, 'Jewish collaborators in Alfonso's scientific work', 59-71. Martin, 'Los intelectuales en la corte alfonsi', 1-23. Procter, 'The scientific works of the Court of Alfonso X', 12-29. The well-known chestnut that Alfonso

reproached God for making the celestial system too complicated and that everything would have been better done had he, Alfonso, been present at Creation, is no more than a political slander disseminated to discredit his Castilian ruling line. See M. Franssen, 'Did King Alfonso really want to advise God against the Ptolemaic system?' *Studies in the History of Philosophy and Science* 24 (1993), 313-25. On translators' difficulties in translating from Arabic, see T.E. Brown, 'Tafsīr and translation: traditional Arabic Qu'rān exegesis and the Latin Qu'rāns of Robert of Ketton and Mark of Toledo', *Speculum* 73 (1998), 703-32. On *Libro de las cruces*, see J. Samso, 'The early development of astrology in al-Andalus', 233-43.

6. Abattouy, Renn, Weinig, 'Transmission as transformation', 1-4, 5-9. Adelard of Bath, *Conversations with his Nephew*, ed. C. Burnett, Cambridge: Cambridge University Press 1998, 68. Whitfield, *Astrology*, 111. These objections were by no means new. Cf. a similar condemnation by the University of Paris in 1398. 'That our intellectual thought-processes and inward movements of the will are caused by the sky without its being a mediator: that such things can be known by some kind of magical transmission: and that through that [transmission] one may be permitted to come to reliable conclusions about them – error.' Wedel, *Astrology in the Middle Ages*, 71. Hubbard, *Michael Scot*, 12-13, 19. Tester, *A History of Western Astrology*, 190-2. Haskins, *Studies in the History of Mediaeval Science*, 272-98, especially 285-6. Cicero, *De natura deorum* 2.16.42: 'Since the stars are born in the upper regions of space (*in aethere*), it is reasonable [to think] that there exists in them a self-aware capacity to perceive by the sense and a degree of intelligence.' Cicero here seems to be reporting the opinions of Aristotle. St John of Damascus, quoted in Dales, 'The de-animation of the heavens', 533. St Augustine, as so often, was ambiguous on this point. My discussion on the background to the Condemnations of Paris is based on Dales's article cited above. Grosseteste, *Hexaëmeron* 5.8.1-5.11.1. See also Dales, 'Robert Grosseteste's views on astrology', 360-3. Tester, *op.cit.* supra, 179-80. St Thomas Aquinas, *Opuscula*, Venice 1508, 148-9; *Summa Theologiae* 1a.115.4 (responsio). St Thomas also noted, 'It is clear that a heavenly body acts via the medium of natural cause, and therefore its effects in this world are natural. It is impossible that any active power of a celestial body be the cause of things which happen here [on earth] by accident, either by mischance or good fortune. Consequently, one must say that things which do happen here by accident, either in Nature or in human affairs, are derived from some pre-ordaining cause: and that same [cause] is divine providence.' *Ibid.*, 1a.116.1 (responsio).

7. It is generally agreed that *Speculum astronomiae* is a genuine work by St Albertus. See Thorndike, *History of Magic and Experimental Science* 2.692-6. Zambelli, *The Speculum Astronomiae*, 33-42: quotations, 65, 67, 69, 208, 218. Grant, *Planets, Stars and Orbs*, 471-87, 523-68. Thorndike, *op.cit.*, 670-4. Wedel, *Astrology in the Middle Ages*, 71-5. Hackett, 'Roger Bacon on astronomy-astrology', 175-98. Conjunctions and religion: Sidelko, 'The condemnation of Roger Bacon', 73, 77.

8. Walker, 'The astral body in Renaissance medicine', 120-2. French, 'Foretelling the future', 468-9, 480. Jacquart, 'Bernard de Gordon et l'astrologie', 152-4. Prioreschi, *History of Medicine* 5.382-90. Demaitre, *Doctor Bernard de Gordon*, 162-4. R.S. Gottfried, *The Black Death*, London: Robert Hale 1983, 111. Cf. the observations of the astrologer Augustine of Trent on the outbreak of 1340, in which he argues that the illnesses of that year were and would be caused by the appearance of Mars in the sixth house of the zodiac, Thorndike, *History of Magic and Experimental Science* 3.224-8. Cf. also Geoffrey de Meaux on the outbreak of 1345, R. Horrox (ed.), *The Black Death*, Manchester: Manchester University Press 1994, 167-72. Whitfield, *Astrology*, 112-13. Thorndike, *op.cit.*, 284-93. Michael Scot, *Liber physionomie*, chap. 10. Talbot, 'A Mediaeval physician's vade mecum', 216, 222, 224, 228-9, 230. Thorndike, *op.cit*, 588, 855-7. Cf. Chaucer, *Prologue to the Canterbury Tales*, 'With us there was a Doctor of Physick/ In all this world there was no one like him/To speak of physick and of surgery,/ For he was grounded in astronomy./He kept his patient a full great deal. In hours by his natural magic'. Thorndike, *op.cit.*, 323. Anonymous alchemical treatise: Maxwell-Stuart, *The Occult in Mediaeval Europe*, 213.

9. Thorndike, *op.cit.* supra, 874-84, 888-901. Prioreschi, *op.cit.* supra, 375-82. Pietro d'Abano,

Conciliator, Pavia 1524, 14r-16r, 150v-152r, 218v-220r, 208r-209r: quotation, 208r. Thorndike, *op.cit.* refers to this passage, but reports the bull as a human being. The Latin *in auriculam tauri*, however, is quite clear. On D'Abando's trial, see Thorndike, 'Relations of the Inquisition to Peter of Abano and Cecco d'Ascoli', *Speculum* 1 (1926), 338-43. The text relating to the reasons for the trial is given there, p.342, note 1. Thorndike, 'Peter of Abano and the Inquisition', *Speculum* 11 (1936), 132-3. Text of the quotation, p.133, note 1. *Thorndike, History of Magic and Experimental Science* 2.938-47.

10. Thorndike, *History of Magic and Experimental Science* 2.948-68: quotation, 964. Wedel, *Astrology in the Middle Ages*, 75-7. H.C. Lea, *A History of the Inquisition in the Middle Ages*, Vol. 3, New York: Harper & Brothers 1887, 4414. Petrarch, *Letters of Old Age*, English trans. 2 vols. New York: Halica Press 2005, 1.32-3.

10. Astrology in Mediaeval Literature, Art & Architecture *c.*1300–*c.*1500

1. J. Holland Smith. *The Great Schism* 1378, London: Hamish Hamilton 1970, 135-54. Smoller, *History, Prophecy and the Stars*, 36-42. Text of quotations: 156 note 104, 157 note 111, 158 note 122, 159 note 132.

2. Haskins, *Studies in the History of Mediaeval Science*, 242-71: quotation, 293. Tester, *A History of Western Astrology*, 191-2. D. Abulafia, *Frederick II, A Mediaeval Emperor*, London: Pimlico 1988, 256-64. R. Kieckhefer, *Magic in the Middle Ages*, Cambridge: Cambridge University Press 1990, 123-4. Carey, *Courting Disaster*, 109. Thorndike, *History of Magic and Experimental Science* 3.585-9: quotation, 585. Bonatti's books were illustrated with examples of horoscopes. One, from his *Liber Introductorius*, can be dated to the siege of Lucca in 1261, and provides an answer to Guido Novello's question whether two armies were going to engage each other or not. Bonatti judged they would, and so it turned out. North, *Horoscopes and History*, 112-14. Holden, *A History of Horoscopic Astrology*, 137-42.

3. This allusion to her own genethliacal horoscope which is feasible to date to 1342 – the most likely year out of more than one possibility – makes her aged about forty at the time of the Canterbury pilgrimage.

4. The hot planets are Jupiter, Mars, and the sun. The cold planets are Saturn, Venus, and the moon. Mercury is neither but takes on the properties of the planet nearest to it.

5. Wedel, *Astrology in the Middle Ages*, 79. Kay, *Dante's Christian Astrology*, 2-9, 134-5, 249-50, 253-7. My discussion is largely based on Kay's work. Cf. Dante, 'The order of the houses is this, that the first they enumerate is that of the moon; the second is that of Mercury; the third is that of Venus; the fourth is that of the sun; the fifth is that of Mars; the sixth is that of Jupiter; the seventh is that of Saturn; the eighth is that of the stars; the ninth is one which is not visible except by [a certain] movement ... [This] they call the great crystalline sphere, diaphanous, or rather completely transparent', *Convivio* 2.4. Bemrose, *Dante's Angelic Intelligences*, 83-113. Brown & Butcher, *The Age of Saturn*, 34-5, 165-71, 190-204: quotation, 196. North, *Chaucer's Universe*, 289-303. Cf. Wood, *Chaucer and the Country of the Stars*, 172-80. North, *op.cit.*, 443-55, 38-86. Kitson, 'Chaucer's astrology', 79-84. Braddy, 'Chaucer and Dame Alice Perrers', 222-8. Curry, *Chaucer and the Mediaeval Sciences*, 94-107. Chaucer, *Treatise*, 12-17, 19-22. Wedel, *op.cit.*, 142-52.

6. A reference to the rape of Pasiphäe by Zeus in that form. Boccaccio means that sometimes passion may grow so great that controlling reason is abandoned and is replaced by animal lust.

7. Garth Carpenter as argued that there is a correlation between the twenty-four stories of the *Canterbury Tales* and the twelve signs of the zodiac, each take containing two oppositions – January and May: Capricorn/Aquarius/Saturn and Gemini/Cancer/Mercury, for example – to express the interplay of tensions between the principal characters, *Chaucer's Solar Pageant*, unpublished PhD thesis, Victoria University of Wellington, New Zealand, 1997. The text is available online at: *http://researcharchive.vuw.ac.nz/bitstream/handle/10063/946/thesis*

8. J. Burckhardt, *The Civilisation of the Renaissance in Italy*, English trans. London: Penguin Books

1990, 328. Petrarch, *Letters of Old Age* 3.1 (pp.75-91). Wedel, *Astrology in the Middle Ages*, 82-6. Tinkle, 'Saturn of several faces', 293-5, 302-6. Thorndike, *History of Magic and Experimental Science* 3.205-12, 191-200. Andalo di Negro: Blume, *Regenten des Himmels*, 105-11.Levarie Smarr, 'Boccaccio and the stars', 327-31, 312-17. Hollander, *Boccaccio's Two Venuses*, New York: Columbia University Press 1977, 53-65. Chaucer's reworking of the story of Palemon and Arcita in his *Knight's Tale* uses astrological themes and references in the same kind of fashion as Boccaccio. See W.C. Curry, 'Astrologising the gods', *Anglia* 47 (1923), 213-43.

9. Cf. the series of pictures in the Palazzo Schifanoia in Ferrara, mid-fifteenth century, showing the zodiacal signs and activities proper to each.

10. Folding almanacs: Murray Jones, *Mediaeval Medicine*, 53. Page, *Astrology in Mediaeval Manuscripts*, 56, 57. Murray Jones, *op.cit.*, 55. Page, *op.cit.*, 54, 60. Gleadow, *The Origin of the Zodiac*, 59-61. Gettings, *The Secret Zodiac*, 30-2, 97-117: quotation, 117. San Miniato also contains an arch, reached by a flight of steps, which has on each side of it friezes depicting demons and the fish symbol of Christ, echoing the identification of the Christian era as one under the rule of Pisces. Similarly, an arch known as the Porta dello Zodiaco because of its figures, can be seen at the top of the Scalone del Morti in the twelfth-century Sacra di San Michele, Val di Susa. Christ as Lord of light and dark, and therefore of time, is depicted at the centre of a twelfth-century zodiac. He holds the sun and moon in His hands, and is surrounded by the zodiacal signs with pictures of activities appropriate to each month in a wheel beyond them. B. Obrist, 'Cosmological iconography in twelfth-century Bavaria', *Studi Medievali*, 3rd series, 48 (December 2007), figure 24. Palazzo della Ragione: Blume, *Regenten des Himmels*, 70-85 and plates 70, 94-104, 146-52. Seznec, *Survival of the Pagan Gods*, 63-81.

11. Astrologers at Work *c*.1500–*c*.1600: The Stars in an Age of Reform

1. E. Eisdenstein, *The Printing Revolution in Early Modern Europe*, Cambridge: Cambridge University Press 1983, 7-17, 23, 32. M.J. Schretlen, *Dutch and Flemish Woodcuts of the Fifteenth Century*, reprint, New York: Hacker Art Books 1969, 7-21. A.M. Hind, *An Introduction to a History of Woodcut*, 2 vols. London: Constable & Co. Ltd. 1935, 2.649.

2. Both clocks, still extant and famous, have undergone much alteration. Münster's clock was completely destroyed in 1534-5. The present one is a reconstruction of 1542. Prague's clock was modified in 1490, its moving statues were added in the seventeenth century, and its Apostles in 1865-6. Fire damage in 1945 meant restoration of the wooden sculptures and the calendar dial face.

3. Richard of Wallingford, *Tractatus*, proposition 7, trans. J.D. North, *Richard of Wallingford*, 3 vols. Oxford: Clarendon Press 1971, 1.454. Bradbury & Collette, 'Changing times', 356-8. J. Gimpel, *The Mediaeval Machine*, English trans. London: Victor Gollancz Ltd. 1977, 155-65. Borst, *The Ordering of Time*, 97-8. Crosby, *The Measure of Reality*, 76-80, 83-6. North, *Stars, Minds and Fate*, 171-86; *Horoscopes and History*, 131-6: quotation, 136. Interestingly enough, it was quite frequently physicians who turned out to be mechanical engineers as well during the later Middle Ages. See L. White, 'Mediaeval astrologers and late Mediaeval technology' in L. White, *Mediaeval Religion and Technology*, Berkeley: University of California Press 1978, 301-10.

4. Thorndike, *History of Magic and Experimental Science* 3.602-10. Carey, *Courting Disaster*, 138-41: quotation, 141, Latin text, 214-15. Bobrick, *The Fated Sky*, 110, 124-7. Yates, *Giordano Bruno*, 45-7. Voss, 'The astrology of Marsilio Ficino', 36-40. Garin, *Astrology in the Renaissance*, 61-80. Campion, *Astrology, History and Apocalypse*, 56-61.

5. Cf. *Letters* 3.37 where he says he has written a book 'opposing the empty pronouncements of the astrologers' and goes on to enumerate his criticisms.

6. Ficino's letters, quite apart from his extensive philosophical compositions, are imbued with astrology and astrological references. Lovers are attracted to one another when the sun and moon are favourably aspected to each other, (1.29); Lorenzo de' Medici is a most fortunate man because his stars are favourable, as Ficino explains at length in a letter addressed to him, (4.46);

on the other hand, 'the last conjunction of Saturn and Mars in Virgo … the eclipses of the moon in Aquarius … [and] future eclipses of the sun in Leo', indicated that 'the next two years will be so miserable that it will be commonly believed that the utter destruction of the world is imminent', (5.9); and 'Saturn may have been the cause of my coming to you much later than usual last month, as he was retrograde the month before that, after moving in Capricorn to a trine aspect with the sun in Taurus', (7.66).

7. They are recorded in detail by Thorndike, *History of Magic and Experimental Science* 4.438-84.

8. Kaske & Clark, introduction to Ficino, *Three Books on Life*, 60-70. Catani, 'The polemics on astrology', 17; 'The dangers of demons', 45-6, 48-9. Ficino, *Three Books on Life*: quotation, 394-5. Thorndike, *History of Magic and Experimental Science* 4.440-2. Van Broecke, *The Limits of Influence*, 55-80. Thorndike, *op.cit.* 4.544-61. Catani, 'The danger of demons', 47-8; 'The polemics on astrology', 18-19. Holden, *A History of Horoscopic Astrology*, 159-62. Garin, *Astrology in the Renaissance*, 83-92. On the defence of astrology by eminent physicians, cf. the near constant support by Giovanni Garzoni, Professor of Medicine at Bologna from 1466 until 1505. P. Kibre, 'Giovanni Garzoni of Bologna', 508-12.

9. Luther, *Table Talk*, 458, 449, 173, 219-20. Brosseder, 'The writing in the Wittenberg sky', 558-9, 568-73. Thorndike, *History of Magic and Experimental Science* 5.378-405; 6.499-501. See also S. Kusukawa, 'Aspectio divinorum opera: Melanchthon and astrology for Lutheran medics' in O. Grell & A. Cunningham (eds.), *Medicine and the Reformation*, London: Routledge 1993, 33-56. Peucer, *Commentarius*, 59, 333. Del Rio, *Disquisitionum magicarum libri sex*, Book 4, chap. 3, question 1. Giovanni Pontano: Maxwell-Stuart, 'Representations of same-sex love', 168-9, 173. Gaurico: *Ibid.*, 170. Mizauld: *Ibid.*, 171. On Pontano's debts to Firmicus Maternus, see M. Rinalde, *Sic itur ad astra: Giovanni Pontano e la sua opera astrologica nel quadro della tradizione manoscritta della Mathesis di Giulio Firmico Materno*, Naples: Loffredo Editore 2002, Part 1. Thorndike, *op.cit.* 6.100-1. Maxwell-Stuart, *op.cit.*, 178. Whitefield, *Astrology*, 154-8.

10. Thordike, *History of Magic and Experimental Science* 5.167-8; 6.150; 5.252-3, 489, 256-9, 263-74. Brosseder, *op.cit.* supra, 564-6: quotation, 565. Azzolini, 'Reading health in the stars', 196-8. Thorndike, *op.cit.* 5.177, 180, 194-9, 202, 215-17, 210-11, 231. Grafton, *Cardano's Cosmos*, 9-10. On noble and royal employment of astrologers, see further North, *Stars, Minds and Fate*, 373-400 and Armstrong, 'An Italian astrologer at the Court of Henry VII', 433-54.

12. Questioning the Macrocosm *c.*1600–*c.*1700: The Pursuit of a 'Sane' Astrology

1. Copernicus also broadly accepted Ptolemy's system while modifying certain parts of it, as Thorndike explains. 'In large measure what Copernicus did was to attempt to derive and justify his own new hypotheses from the Ptolemaic data, devices and method by working them over from his own standpoint. He accepted the Ptolemaic observations of the heavens without question as the basis, along with further observations of his own, for his tables and conclusions. Indeed, it vexed him not a little when anyone else called them into question. His astronomical method still moved for the most part in the accustomed Ptolemaic grooves of eccentric and epicycle. He took little account of the criticisms and emendations and supplements to Ptolemaic theory which had been made in the closing Mediaeval centuries. His system was therefore still in large part Ptolemaic', *History of Magic and Experimental Science* 5.422.

2. Biskup & Dobrzycki, *Copernicus*, 102-10: quotation, 107-8. Kesten, *Copernicus and his World*, 175-90. North, *Stars, Minds and Fate*, 401-14, especially 405-6, 412: quotation, 405. Thorndike, *History of Magic and Experimental Science* 5.406-29. Lattis, *Between Copernicus and Galileo*, 61-85: quotation, 85. Guillaume de Salluste du Bartas, *La Sepmaine ou Création du Monde*, ed. V. Bol, Arles: Actes Sud 1988, 106. George Buchanan, *Sphaera*, Herborn 1586, 13-14. Bieńkowska, 'The heliocentric controversy in European culture', 127. Lattis, *op.cit.*, 181-2. D. Sobel, *Galileo's Daughter*, London: Fourth Estate 1999, 29, 52: quotation, 34. Rutkin, 'Various uses of horoscopes', 171-3.

3. Cf. Adam von Bodenstein (1528–77), a German physician and alchemist, who wrote a tract on

the relation of twelve herbs to the signs of the zodiac.

4. Biagoli, *Galileo Courtier*, 127-49. Scoggins, 'Wine and obscenities', 163-7, 178-9, 184-5. Agrippa, *De occulta philosophia* Book 1, chap. 22. On Agrippa and astral magic, see further C.I. Lehrich, *The Language of Demons and Angels: Cornelius Agrippa's Occult Philosophy*, Leiden: Brill 2003, 110-16. 'Paracelsus', *The Archidoxes of Magic*, 94-5. This work may actually have been written in *c*.1570 by Gerhard Dorn, a follower of Paracelsus.

5. 'Borage, Bugloss, Langue de Boeuf: They are all three herbs of Jupiter, and under Leo, all great cordials and strengtheners of nature' … 'Brank Ursine: It is an excellent plant under the dominion of the moon …. [a] decoction of the leaves applied to the place is excellent good for the King's Evil that is broken and runneth, for by the influence of the moon it reviveth the ends of the veins which are relaxed' … 'Germander: [It] is an herb of warm thin parts, under Mars, opening obstructions of the liver, spleen, and kidneys' …'Motherwort: Venus owns the herb, and it is under Leo', *Complete Herbal*, modern edition, London: W. Foulsham & Co. no date.

6. Thorndike, *History of Magic and Experimental Science* 5.328-9; 6.158-9, 406-8; 5.250-1. Paracelsus: Goodrick-Clark, *Paracelsus*, 26-7, 72-3, 75, 120-5, 128-9. Ball, *Paracelsus*, 245-6, 251-2, 297-8. Webster, *Paracelsus*, 142-6. See also John Christie's explanation of Paracelsus's remark about what it takes to be a good surgeon: 'He must not have a red beard'. 'The Paracelsian body', 274-6. Kassell, 'Simon Forman', 373-6. Traister, *The Notorious Astrological Physician of London*, 85, 104-7: quotation, 105-6. A detailed account of the work involved in astrological consultations is given in Grafton, *Cardano's Cosmos*, 22-37. Kassell, *Medicine and Magic in Elizabethan London*, 117, 188, 222-5. Cf. Traister, *op.cit.*, 99-101. Illustrations of Forman's sigils: Kassell, *Medicine and Magic*, 223 and Traister, *op.cit.*, 100. Summoning spirits: Kassell, *op.cit.*, 215-21:quotation, 221.

7. Thorndike, *History of Magic and Experimental Science* 5.127-38: quotation, 132. Morley, *Life* 2.138-9, 128 (both quotations), 145, 214-15, 319 (quotation). Dee, *Diaries*, 11, 23, 169, 233, 251, 232, 267, 239. French, *John Dee*, 6, 92 (quotation). Clulee, *John Dee's Natural Philosophy*, 77-96.

8. Gatti, *Giordano Bruno and Renaissance Science*, 98-114: quotation, 113. Spruit, 'Giordano Bruno and astrology', 238-49: quotation, 245-6. Yates, *Giordano Bruno*, 211-29: quotation, 217. Bruno, *De principiis*, 599; *De magia mathematica*, 493; *De magia*, 435-8. Rowland, *Giordano Bruno*, 117-20: quotations, 118, 12. Garin, *Astrology in the Renaissance*, 110-11. Yates, *op.cit.*, 325-7.

9. Firpo, 'Tommaso Campanella', 374-9, 389-97. Thorndike, *History of Magic and Experimental Science* 6.172-7. Yates, *Giordano Bruno*, 360-97. Campanella, *De siderali fato vitando*, chap. 7 and chap. 4, article 1.

10. The concept of a living or worshipping space overtly dedicated to and illustrative of astral influence was by no means uncommon among the noble classes. See further Quinlan-McGrath, 'The astrological vault of the Villa Farnesina', 92-104. Del Prete, 'Riflessioni sulla magia in Bruno e Campanella', 257, 260-6, 273. John Chamber: G.B. Harrison, *A Last Elizabethan Journal*, London & Boston: Routledge & Kegan Paul 1933, 221. Ephemera: Strauss, *The German Single-Leaf Woodcut* 1.190; 3.924, 1349, 888-9; 2.522-3, 525; 1.417-18; 3.1061.

13. Prophets & Sceptics *c*.1700–*c*.1800: Astrology Fighting Decline

1. Napier: MacDonald, *Mystical Bedlam*, 25-30, 173, 194, 210-11. Louis XIV's horoscope: Drévillon, *Lire et écrire l'avenir*, 117. Louis XIII: *Ibid.*, 104-5. Morandi: Dooley, 'The Ptolemaic astrological tradition', 530-48; *Morandi's Last Prophecy*, 154-61, (quotation, 162), 27-33, 85-91, 93-100, (quotations, 111, 125). Thorndike, *History of Magic and Experimental Science* 7.99-100. Barnes, *Prophecy and Gnosis*, 155-75.

2. Gaffarel: Thorndike, *History of Magic and Experimental Science* 7.291-3, 304-9. Lilly: Curry, 'William Lilly', 794-8. Parker, *Familiar to All*, 88-95. Capp, *Astrology and the Popular Press*, 39-66: quotation, 134. Geneva, *Astrology and the Seventeenth-Century Mind*, 100-2. Ovason, *History of the Horoscope*, 100-5, 108-9. Holden, *A History of Horoscopic Astrology*, 184-8. Curth, *English*

Almanacs, 105-16. Lilly, *History of his Life and Times*, 20-1, 48-50. Lilly, *Christian Astrology* Book 2, 135-42. Society of Astrologers: B. Woolley, *The Herbalist: Nicolas Culpeper and the Fight for Medical Freedom*, London: Harper Collins 2004, 251-2. Trusting Lilly more than God: Curry, *op.cit.*, 797. King of Sweden: Parker, *op.cit.*, 196. Plague and Fire: Parker, *op.cit.*, 226-32: quotation, 229-30. Butler: Nelson, 'Astrology, Hudibras, and the Puritans', 521-36. Stark, *Rhetoric, Science and Magic*, 66-7. Dryden's play was based on Thomas Corneille's *Le Feint Astrologue* which was, itself, based on Calderon's *El Astrologo Fingido*.

3. Pithoys, *Traitté curieux de l'astrologie*, Sedan 1641, preface. Bossuet, *Politique tirée des propres paroles de l'Écriture Sainte*, Paris 1709, Book 5, article 3. Saumaise, *De annis climactericis et antiqua astrologia diatribae*, Leiden 1648. Contrast the work of Andreas Argoli (1568/9–1651/57) on critical days, which is cast entirely in the mould of traditional astrologico-medical theory, Thorndike, *History of Magic and Experimental Science* 7.122-4. Pithoys and Mersenne: Thorndike, *op.cit.*, 7.102-4, 433-6. Brahe, *De disciplinis mathematicis oratio* = *Opera* 1.153. Kollerstrom, 'Kepler's belief in astrology', 164-6. See also Rabin, 'Kepler's attitude towards Pico and the anti-astrology polemic', 750-69. Thorndike, *op.cit.* 7.110-12. Jeake, *Astrological Diary*, 5-21. Morin: Thorndike, *op.cit.* 7.477-91. Drévillon, *Lire et écrire l'avenir*, 163-9. Tester, *A History of Western Astrology*, 235-8. Holden, *A History of Horoscopic Astrology*, 173-8. Gassendi: Thorndike, *op.cit.* 7.445-50. AL Lolordo, *Pierre Gassendi and the Birth of Early Modern Philosophy*, Cambridge: Cambridge University Press 2007, 24-33. Stark, *op.cit.*, 63 (quotation).

14. New Planets, Esotericism & Almanacs *c.*1800–*c.*1900: Astrology in the Post-Industrial World

1. Indian astronomers, for example, were resident in the Chinese capital in the seventh and eighth centuries AD, and Iranian influences were felt in some of the astronomical-astrological literature of these and the following century. Needham & Ling, *Science and Civilisation in China* 3.202-6.

2. Of three supernovae appearing in historical records, for example, one (1572) was observed and noted by Tycho Brahe, another (1604) by Johannes Kepler, but a much earlier one (1054) was recorded only in Chinese sources. Needham & Long, *op.cit.* supra, 3.426.

3. Pingree, however, is clear that 'astronomy and astrology in India are not indigenous sciences, but are local adaptations and developments of Mesopotamian, Babylonian, Graeco-Babylonian, and Greek texts', 'The Indian and pseudo-Indian passages', 142.

4. Needham & Ling, *op.cit.* supra, 2.351-9, 383-5: quotations, 352, 353, 379; 3.12, 189-90, 361-2, 378 note (a): quotations, 190, 442-3. W.K. Chu & W.A. Sherrill, *The Astrology of the I Ching*, London: Arkana 1993, 1-4, 11-57. For the impact of Chinese astrology on Japan, see S. Nakayama, *A History of Japanese Astronomy*, Cambridge, Mass: Harvard University Press 1969, 44-64. Sutton, *The Essentials of Vedic Astrology*, 1, 11, 168-73, 74-92. Powell, *History of the Zodiac*, 114-39: quotation, 114. Pingree, 'Astronomy and astrology in India and Iran', 231, 243-4; 'The Indian and pseudo-Indian passages', 155-7, 151.

5. These foreign appointments could be very lucrative. John Dee was offered a fortune by Tasr Boris Godunov in 1585 if he would enter his service, an offer Dee actually turned down.

6. Ryan, *The Bathhouse at Midnight*, 19-20, 340-7, 125, 22, 373-407: quotation, 69. Wigzell, *Reading Russian Fortunes*, 16, 21-3, 36-40.

7. Astrological almanacs were still popular in the States during the 1850s. See Davies, *Grimoires*, 197-204.

8. Ovason, *History of the Horoscope*, 87. Capp, *Astrology and the Popular Press*, 275-6. Stahlman, 'Astrology in colonial America', 558-61. Cerniglia, 'The American almanac and the astrology factor', 4-7. Butler, 'Magic, astrology and the early American heritage', 325, 327-34, 340-1; 'Thomas Teackle's 333 books', 458-9. Ames quotation: Cerniglia, *op.cit.*, 5. Guerra, 'Medical almanacs', 248, 245. Winthrop, Starkey, Browne, 'Scientific notes from the books and letters of John Winthrop, Junior, (1606-1676)', *Isis* 11 (1928), 326, 340. Butler, *Awash in a Sea of Faith*,

72, 74, 76, 82-3, 230. Nathaniel Ames: *Ibid.*, 80-1. Hamilton and the astrologer: *Ibid.*, 91. E.W. Baker, *The Devil of Great Island*, Basingstoke: Palgrave Macmillan 2007, 20. Quinn, *Early Mormonism and the Magic World View*, 22-4, 71-3, 76-91 and figure 29, 105-14, 166-7, 277-91.

9. C.A. Luboock (ed.), *The Herschel Chronicle*, Cambridge: Cambridge University Press 1933, 78, 95, 122-3, 201. Zadkiel, *Introduction to Astrology*, 53. John Varley: Holden, *A History of Horoscopic Astrology*, 201-2. Ovason, *History of the Horoscope*, 150-3, 145-8, 139-41. Swift, *Works* 4.305-30; 6.84-7. I. Ehrenpreis, *Swift, The Man, his Works, and the Age*, Vol. 2, *Dr Swift*, London: Methuen & Co. 1967, 198-209. Davies, *Cunning-Folk*, 43-5, 72, 90-1, 100. Holden, *op.cit.*, 190-1. Gaskill, *Crime and Mentalities in Early Modern England*, Cambridge: Cambridge University Press 2000, 116. Debus, 'Scientific truth and occult tradition', 266-8: quotations, 267, 274.

10. Pfaff: Oestmann, 'J.W.A. Pfaff and the rediscovery of astrology', 241-55. On Kepler's interest in astrology, see Campion, *A History of Western Astrology*, 136-42. J. Sharpe, *Instruments of Darkness*, London: Hamish Hamilton 1996, 282. Scott, *Letters on Demonology and Witchcraft*, Ware: Wordsworth Editions 2001, 202-5; *Guy Mannering*, ed. P.D. Garside, Edinburgh: University Press 1999, 19-20: quotation, 16-17. C.O. Parsons, *Witchcraft and Demonology in Scott's Fiction*, Edinburgh & London: Oliver & Boyd 1964, 89, 91. It is worth comparing the tone of the *Guy Mannering* passage with that of one from Jacques Cazotte's novel, *Le diable amoureux*, published in English translation in 1798.

'A loud gossiping drew me from my pensive state, and, in spite of myself, fixed my attention. I heard two voices behind me.

"Yes, yes," said one of them, "he is a child of the planet. He shall enter into his house. Look you, Zoradilla, he was born the third of May, at three o'clock in the morning."

"Ah truly, Lelagise," returned the other, "woe to the children of Saturn. This is under the ascendant of Jupiter, Mars, and Mercury, in a trine conjunction with Venus. Oh, what a handsome man! What natural advantages he is possessed of ! What expectations might he conceive! What a fortune he ought to come at!"

I was acquainted with the hour of my birth, and heard it mentioned with singular precision. I turned round to have a view of the two gossips. Who did I see but two old gipsies, not sitting, but squatting on their heels. Their complexion was of an olive colour, their eyes hollow and fiery; their paper lips, lanthorn jaws, and foreheads so low that their hair served instead of eyebrows, from which immediately projected a most formidable nose, faithfully inclining towards the chin: their bushy pericranium was encircled with a piece of blue and white stuff, which fell down upon their shoulders, and then went folding round their waists something after the manner of a scarf; so that the objects, however ridiculous or disgusting to the eye, were not absolutely naked', (pp.186-8).

11. Campion, *A History of Western Astrology*, 213-16. Ovason, *History of the Horoscope*, 176-8. Curry, *A Confusion of Prophets*, 46-108: quotation, 78. Whitfield, *Astrology*, 191-3. J. Devlin, *The Superstitious Mind*, New Haven & London: Yale University Press 1987, 93-4. Lévi, *Transcendental Magic*, London: Rider & Co. 1984, 147-54. Horniman and Gardner: A. Owen, *The Place of Enchantment: British Occultism and the Culture of the Modern*, Chicago & London: University of Chicago Press 2004, 158-61. Golden Dawn lecture: R.A. Gilbert (ed.), *The Sorcerer and his Apprentice*, Wellingborough: Aquarian Press 1983, 40-6: quotation, 42. I. Regardie, *The Complete Golden Dawn System of Magic*, Phoenix, Arizona: Falcon Press 1982, 4.46 (quotation); 3.26-9; 5.59; 9.4-5. Evangeline Smith Adams: Holden, *A History of Horoscopic Astrology*, 225-7. Crowley, *The Complete Astrological Writings*, 16 (quotation), 65.

12. Campion, *A History of Western Astrology*, 229-34. Curry, *A Confusion of Prophets*, 125-8. Davies, *A People Bewitched*, 107. Holden, *A History of Horoscopic Astrology*, 206-8.

15. Plus ça Change *c*.1900–2000: Facing the Future

1. Whitfield, *Astrology*, 200-1. Bobrick, *The Fated Sky*, 283-5. Holden, *A History of Horoscopic Astrology*, 257-8. I. Holst, *Gustav Holst*, London: Oxford University Press 1938, 43-4. M. Short,

Gustav Holst: The Man and his Music, Oxford: Oxford University Press 1990, 113, 120-2. Head, 'Astrology and modernism in "The Planets"', 1, 3-4. Campion, 'Sigmund Freud's investigation of astrology', 49-53. Hyde, *Jung and Astrology*, 36-7, 58. Bobrick, *op.cit.*, 279. Campion, *A History of Western Astrology*, 251-6: quotation, 255. Ovason, *History of the Horoscope*, 185-7, 207-8. Pluto was reclassified in August 2006 and astronomically is no longer considered to be a planet, at least in the same sense as Mars or Jupiter or Saturn. But astrologically it maintains its place in the influential and interpretive systems.

2. Campion, *A History of Western Astrology*, 259-62; *Astrology, History and Apocalypse*, 72-83. Bobrick, *The Fated Sky*, 274-5. Howe, *Astrology and the Third Reich*, 68-71, 80-1, 88-93: quotation, 90-1. Ovason, *History of the Horoscope*, 218-22. Howe, *op.cit.*, 104-18, 128-59, (quotation, 134), 160-5: quotations, 196 198. Wulff: Levenda, *Unholy Alliance*, 161-5. H. Trevor-Roper, *The Last Days of Hitler*, London: Macmillan & Co. Ltd, 1947, 93. Loog: T.W.M. van Berkel, 'Nostradamus, astrology and the Bible', Whitfield, *Astrology*, 198-9. One should also mention here that the Germans were not the only people to make use of astrology for propaganda purposes. The British employed Louis de Wohl (1903–61), a German astrologer of Hungarian and Austrian parentage, to work out what astrologers were likely to be saying to Hitler, Himmler, and the rest, and to provide false astrological information which could then be disseminated where it would do most damage. See further, Howe, *op.cit.*, 204-18. Bobrick, *op.cit.*, 286-8. Ovason, *op.cit.*, 216-18. *www.nostrodamusresearch.org/en/ww2/loog-info.htm*

3. It is interesting to see the language used in a report about de Wohl in a recent newspaper article. 'There is no doubt de Wohl was a charlatan – but his influence went all the way to the top. What's ironic about this is that British Intelligence were going down this cul de sac at the same time as people at Bletchley Park were doing amazing and useful scientific work', *The Scotsman*, Tuesday 4 March 2008, 16.

4. Campion, *A History of Western Astrology*, 271-5. Gauquelin, *Neo-Astrology*, 155, 160, 163, 166, (quotations). Bobrick, *The Fated Sky*, 291. Gauquelin, *The Truth About Astrology*, 27-36, 160, 46. Holden, *A History of Horoscopic Astrology*, 251. See also the detailed account of the Gauquelin researches in the West, *The Case for Astrology*, 230-327. Johnson, Payne, Wilson, 'Towards a contextualised astrological apologetic', IIA. Ovason, *History of the Horoscope*, 245-6. On the Indian sidereal zodiac, see further Powell, *History of the Zodiac*, 114-39. Holt, *Stars of India*, 60, 79-80. *The Scotsman*, Saturday 27 June 2009, 31. Campion, *op.cit.*, 280-1. Russian Astrologers: *www.mosnews.com/politics/2009/03/06/147*

5. The results are conveniently summarised in Heinrich Agrippa, *De occulta philosophia* Book 2, chap. 26.

6. Versluis, *The Esoteric Origins of the American Renaissance*, 184, 185. Harding, 'Astrology as a language game' in Campion, Curry, York, *Astrology and the Academy*, 179. Joost-Gaugier, *Measuring Heaven*, 35-6. Ilnitchi, 'Musica mundana', 44-5, 48-50, 55-64. Godwin, *Harmonies of Heaven and Earth*, 167-76, 143-8. Max Caspar: quoted in Godwin, *op.cit.*, 147.

Appendix: Horoscopes of Christ

1. Faracovi, *Gli oroscopi di Cristo*, 83-90, 61-82. Pseudo-Ovid, *De Vetula*, 594-9, 624-9, 631-3. North, *Horoscopes and History*, 163-4, 166-9. Thorndike, *History of Magic and Experimental Science* 5.78. Smoller, *History, Prophecy and the Stars*, 50-1. D'Ailly's horoscope of Christ: Faracovi, *op.cit.*, 157. On Edward VI's horoscope, see Girolamo Cardano, *Opera* 5.503-8. His 'later considerations' are on p.507. On the eye damage and parricide, *Ibid.*, 497, 502. Christ's horoscope: Shumaker, *Renaissance Curiosa*, 58-89: quotation, 74-5. Faracovi, *op.cit.*, 123-43. Ovason, *The History of the Horoscope*, 73-5. Whitfield, *Astrology*, 160-1. See also Vanden Broecke, 'Evidence and conjecture in Cardano's horoscope collections', 209-12, 218-21. Renaker, 'The horoscope of Christ', 213. Gay, 'Astrology and iconoclasm in Milton's Paradise Regained', 177-8, 182, 186-8: quotation, 178.

Bibliography

Aakhus P, 'Astral magic in the Renaissance: gems, poetry, and patronage of Lorenzo de' Medici', *Magic, Ritual, and Witchcraft* 3 (2008), 185-206

Abattouy M, Renn J, Weinig P, 'Transmission as transformation: the translation movements in the Mediaeval East and West in a comparative perspective', *Science in Context* 14 (2001), 1-12

Abdukhalimov B, 'Ahmad al-Farghānī and his Compendium of Astronomy', *Journal of Islamic Studies* 10 (1999), 142-58

Abry J-H, 'Auguste: la Balance et le Capricorne', *Revue des Études Latines* 66 (1988), 103-21

Abry J-H, 'What was Agrippina waiting for?' in G. Oestmann, H.D. Rutkin, K. von Stuckrad (eds.), *Horoscopes and Public Spheres*, q.v. 37-48

Abū Ma'šar, *The Abbreviation of the Introduction to Astrology*, ed. & trans. C. Burnett, K. Yamamoto, M. Yano, Leiden: Brill 1994

Adler W, 'Abraham's refutation of astrology: an excerpt from Pseudo-Clement in the Chronicon of George the Monk' in E.G. Chazon, D. Satran, R.A. Clements (eds.), *Things Revealed: Studies in Early Jewish and Christian Literature in Honour of Michael E. Stone*, Leiden: Brill 2004, 227-41

Adler W, 'Did the Biblical patriarchs practise astrology? Michael Glykas and Manuel Komnenos I on Seth and Abraham' in Magdalino & Mavroudi, *The Occult Sciences in Byzantium* q.v. 245-63

Albani M, 'Horoscopes in the Qumran scrolls' in P.W. Flint & J.C. Vanderkam (eds.), *The Dead Sea Scrolls After Fifty Years*, Vol. 2, Leiden: Brill 1999, 279-330

Al-Biruni, *The Book of Instruction in the Elements of the Art of Astrology*, trans. R.R. Wright, London: Luzac & Co. 1934, reprint 2006

Alexander P.S, 'Jewish tradition in early Islam: the case of Enoch/Idrīs' in G.R. Hawting, J.A. Mojaddedi, A. Samely (eds.), *Studies in Islamic and Middle Eastern Texts and Traditions*, Oxford: Oxford University Press 2000, 11-29

Allegro J.M, 'An astrological cryptic document from Qumran', *Journal of Semitic Studies* 9 (1964), 291-5

Allen D.C, *The Star-Crossed Renaissance: The Quarrel about Astrology and its Influence in England*, London: Frank Cass & Co. 1966

Al-Qabīsī, *The Introduction to Astrology*, English trans. London-Turin: Warburg Institute-Nino Aragno Editore 2004

Altman A, 'Astrology' in *Jewish Encyclopaedia* Vol. 3, Jerusalem: Keter Publishing House Ltd., 787-95

Alveni A, *People and the Sky: Our Ancestors and the Cosmos*, London: Thames & Hudson 2008

Andrews J, 'Richard Napier' in *Dictionary of National Biography*, Vol.40, Oxford: Oxford University Press 2004, 181-3

Armstrong C.A.T, 'An Italian astrologer at the Court of Henry VII' in E.F. Jacob (ed.), *Italian Renaissance Studies*, London: Faber & Faber 1960, 433-54

St Augustine, *Confessiones*, ed. J.J. O'Donnell, Oxford: Clarendon Press 1992

St Augustine, *The City of God against the Pagans*, ed. & trans. R.W. Dyson, Cambridge: Cambridge University Press 1998

Azzolini M, 'Reading health in the stars: politics and medical astrology in Renaissance Milan' in G.
Oestmann, H.D. Rutkin, K Stuckrad (eds.), *Horoscopes and Public Spheres* q.v. 183-205

Baigent M, *From the Omens of Babylon: Astrology and Ancient Mesopotamia*, London: Arkana 1994

Ball P, *The Devil's Doctor: Paracelsus and the World of Renaissance Magic and Science*, London:
William Heinemann 2006

Barnes R.B, *Prophecy and Gnosis: Apocalypticism in the Wake of the Lutheran Reformation*, Stanford:
Stanford University Press 1988

Barnes T.D, 'The horoscope of Licinius Sura?' *Phoenix* 30 (1976), 76-9

Barrenechea F, 'The star signs at Brundisium: astral symbolism in Lucan 2.691-2', *Classical
Quarterly* n.s. 54 (2004), 312-17

Bartlett R, *The Natural and the Supernatural in the Middle Ages*, Cambridge: Cambridge University
Press 2008

Barton T.S, *Ancient Astrology*, London & New York: Routledge 1994

Barton T.S, *Power and Knowledge: Astrology, Physiognomics, and Medicine under the Roman Empire*,
Ann Arbor: University of Michigan Press 1994

Barton T.S, 'Augustus and Capricorn: astrological polyvalency and imperial rhetoric', *Journal of
Roman Studies* 85 (1995), 33-51

Beck R, 'Mithraism since Franz Cumont', *Aufstieg und Niedergang der römischen Welt* II.17.4 (1984),
2002-115

Beck R, *Planetary Gods and Planetary Orders of the Mysteries of Mithras*, Leiden: Brill 1988

Beck R, 'The mysteries of Mithras: a new account of their genesis', *Journal of Roman Studies* 88
(1998), 115-28

Beck R, *A Brief History of Ancient Astrology*, Oxford: Blackwell Publishing 2007

Bemrose S, *Dante's Angelic Intelligences*, Rome: Edizioni di Storia e Letteratura 1983

Ben-Dov J, *Head of All the Years: Astronomy and Calendars at Qumran in their Ancient Context*,
Leiden: Brill 2008

Bernardus Silvestris, *Cosmographia*, English trans. New York & London: Columbia University
Press 1973

Biagioli M, *Galileo Courtier: The Practice of Science in the Culture of Absolutism*, Chicago & London:
University of Chicago Press 1993

Bianchi U (ed.), *Mysteria Mithrae*, Leiden : Brill 1979

Bieńkowska B, 'The heliocentric controversy in European culture' in B. Bieńkowska (ed.), *The
Scientific World of Copernicus*, Dordrecht: D. Reidel Publishing 1973, 119-32

Bloomfield M.W, 'The origin of the concept of the seven cardinal sins', *Harvard Theological
Review* 34 (1941), 121-8

Blume D, *Regenten des Himmels: Astrologische Bilder in Mittelalter und Renaissance*, Berlin:
Akademie Verlag GmbH 2000

Bobrick B, *The Fated Sky: Astrology in History*, New York: Simon & Schuster Paperbacks 2005

Borst A, *The Ordering of Time*, English trans. Cambridge: Polity Press 1993

Bottéro J, *Mesopotamia: Writing, Reasoning, and the Gods*, English trans., Chicago & London:
University of Chicago Press 1992

Bottéro J, *Religion in Ancient Mesopotamia*, English trans., Chicago & London: University of
Chicago Press 2001.

Bouché-Leclercq A, *Histoire de la divination dans l'Antiquité*, Grenoble: Editions Jérôme Millon 2003

Brack-Bernsen L, 'Empirie contra Theorie: Zur Entwicklung und Deutung der babylonischen
Astronomie', *Antike Naturwissenschaft und ihre Rezeption* 6 (1996), 7-15

Brack-Bernsen L & Hunger H, 'The Babylonian zodiac: speculations on its invention and
significance', *Centaurus* 41 (1999), 280-92

Braddy H, 'Chaucer and Dame Alice Perrers', *Speculum* 21 (1946), 222-8

Brosseder C, 'The writing in the Wittenberg sky: astrology in sixteenth-century Germany', *Journal
of the History of Ideas* 66 (October 2005), 557-76.

Brown P & Butcher A, *The Age of Saturn: Literature and History in the Canterbury Tales*, Oxford:
Basil Blackwood 1991

Bruno G, *Opera Latina Conscripta*, ed. F. Tocco & H. Vitelli, Vol.3, Stuttgart-Bad Cannstatt: Friedrich Frommann 1962

Brunsden G.M, 'Seventeenth- and eighteenth-century astrology and the Scottish popular almanac' in L. Henderson (ed.), *Fantastical Imaginations: The Supernatural in Scottish History and Culture*, Edinburgh: John Donaldson 2009, 47-69

Burnett C, *Magic and Divination in the Middle Ages*, Aldershot: Variorum 1996

Burnett C, 'Late antique and Mediaeval Latin translations of Greek tracts on astrology and magic' in Magdalino & Mavroudi, *The Occult Sciences in Byzantium* q.v. 325-59

Burns W.E, *An Age of Wonders: Prodigies, Politics and Providence in England, 1657–1727*, Manchester & New York: Manchester University Press 2002

Butler J, 'Magic, astrology, and early American religious heritage, 1600–1760', *American Historical Review* 84 (1979), 317-46

Butler J, *Awash in a Sea of Faith: Christianising the American People*, Cambridge, Mass: Harvard University Press 1990

Butler J, 'Thomas Teackle's 333 books: a great library on Virginia's eastern shore, 1697', *William and Mary Quarterly* 3rd series, 49 (1992), 449-91

Campanella T, *Opusculi Astrologici*, ed. G. Ernst, Milan: Biblioteca Universale Rizzoli 2003

Campion N, 'Sigmund Freud's investigation of astrology', *Culture and Cosmos* 2 (1998), 49-53

Campion N, *Astrology, History and Apocalypse*, London: Centre for Psychological Astrology 2000

Campion N, *The Dawn of Astrology: A Cultural History of Western Astrology*, Vol. I, London: Hambledon Continuum 2008; Vol. II, London: Hambledon Continuum 2009

Capp B, *Astrology and the Popular Press, 1500–1800*, London & Boston: Faber & Faber 1979

Cardano G, *Opera Omnia*, Vol.5, *Astronomica, Astrologica, Onirocritica*, Leiden 1663

Carey H.M, *Courting Disaster: Astrology at the English Court and University in the Later Middle Ages*, London: Macmillan 1992

Carmody F.J, 'The planetary theory of Ibn Rushd', *Osiris* 10 (1952), 556-86

Carroll S, 'A preliminary analysis of the Epistle to Rehoboam', *Journal for the Study of the Pseudepigrapha* 4 (1989), 91-103

Catani R, 'The danger of demons: the astrology of Marsilio Ficino', *Italian Studies* 55 (2000), 37-52

Cerniglia K.A, 'The American almanac and the astrology factor', *www.earlyamerica.com/review/2003_winter_spring/almanac.htm*

Chadwick H, *Priscillian of Avila: The Occult and the Charismatic in the Early Church*, Oxford: Clarendon Press 1976

Chanda S, *Astrologers and Palmists in Contemporary Society*, Kolkata: Anthropological Society of India 2002

Chapman A.A, 'Marking time: astrology, almanacs, and English Protestantism', *Renaissance Quarterly* 60 (2007), 1257-90

Charlesworth J.H, 'Jewish astrology in the Talmud, Pseudepigrapha, the Dead Sea Scrolls, and early Palestinian synagogues', *Harvard Theological Review* 70 (1977), 183-200

Charlesworth J.H, 'Jewish interest in astrology during the Hellenistic and Roman period', *Aufstieg und Niedergang der römischen Welt* II.20.2 (1987), 926-50

Charlier P, 'Splendeur et misère des courtesans: aspects du quotidien des divins à la cour des Sargonides' in R. Gyselen, *La science des cieux* q.v. 53-74

Chaucer G, *A Treatise on the Astrolabe*, Norman: University of Oklahoma Press 2002

Chown M, 'O invisible star of Bethlehem', *New Scientist*, December 1995, 34-5

Christie J.R.R, 'The Paracelsian body' in O.P. Grell (ed.), *Paracelsus: The Man and his Reputation, his Ideas and their Transformation*, Leiden: Brill 1998, 269-91

Clulee N.H, *John Dee's Natural Philosophy*, London & New York: Routledge 1988

Cowling T.G, *Isaac Newton and Astrology*, Leeds: Leeds University Press 1977

Cramer F.H, 'Expulsion of astrologers from ancient Rome', *Classica et Mediaevalia* 12 (1951), 9-50

Cramer F.H, *Astrology in Roman Law and Politics*, Philadelphia: American Philosophical Society 1954

Crosby A.W, *The Measure of Reality: Quantification and Western Society, 1250–1600*, Cambridge: Cambridge University Press 1997

Crowley A, *The Complete Astrological Writings*, ed. J. Symonds, London: Star Books 1987

Cryer F.H, *Divination in Ancient Israel and its Near Eastern Environment: A Socio-Historical Investigation*, Sheffield: Journal for the Study of the Old Testament Press 1994

Cumont F, 'Les noms des planètes et l'astrolatrie chez les Grecs', *L'Antiquité Classique* 4 (1935), 5-43

Curry P, *Prophecy and Power: Astrology in Early Modern England*, Princeton NJ: Princeton University Press 1989

Curry P, 'Astrology in early modern England: the making of a vulgar knowledge' in S. Pumfrey, P.L. Rossi, M. Slawinski (eds.), *Science, Culture, and Popular Belief in Renaissance Europe*, Manchester: Manchester University Press 1991, 274-91

Curry P, *A Confusion of Prophets: Victorian and Edwardian Astrology*, London: Collins & Brown Ltd. 1992

Curry P, 'Alan Leo' in *Dictionary of National Biography*, Vol. 33, Oxford: Oxford University Press 2004, 392-4

Curry P, 'William Lilly' in *Dictionary of National Biography*, Vol.33, Oxford: Oxford University Press 2004, 794-8

Curry W.C, *Chaucer and the Mediaeval Sciences*, revised and enlarged ed. London: George Allen & Unwin 1960

Curth L.H, *English Almanacs, Astrology and Popular Medicine, 1550–1700*, Manchester & New York: Manchester University Press 2007

Dagron G & Rougé J, 'Trois horoscopes de voyages en mer (5e siècle après J-C')', *Revue des Études Byzantines* 39 (1981), 117-33

Dales R.C, 'The re-animation of the heavens in the Middle Ages', *Journal of the History of Ideas* 41 (1980), 531-50

Dall'Aglio F, 'Magia e astrologia in Niceta Coniata' in Lucentini, Parri, Compagni (eds.), *Hermetism from Late Antiquity to Humanism* q.v. 569-76

Davidson H.A, *Moses Maimonides: The Man and his Works*, Oxford: Oxford University Press 2005

Davies O, *A People Bewitched: Witchcraft and Magic in Nineteenth-Century Somerset*, Trowbridge: Redwood Books Ltd 1999

Davies O, *Cunning-Folk: Popular Magic in English History*, London & New York: Hambledon & London 2003

Davies O, *Grimoires, a History of Magic Books*, Oxford: Oxford University Press 2009

Debus A.G, 'Scientific truth and occult tradition: the medical world of Ebenezer Sibly, (1751–1799)', *Medical History* 26 (1982), 259-78

De Callatay G, 'La grande conjunction de 1186' in Draelants, Tihon, Van den Abeele (eds.), *Occident et Proche-Orient* q.v. 369-84

Dee J, *Propaedeumata Aphoristica* (1558 and 1568), trans. W. Shumaker in W. Shumaker & J.L. Heilbron, *John Dee on Astronomy*, Los Angeles & London: University of California Press 1978

Dee J, *Diaries*, ed. E. Fenton, Charlburg: Day Books 1998

De Jong T & Worp K.A, 'A Greek horoscope from 373AD', *Zeitschrift für Papyrologie und Epigraphik* 106 (1995), 235-40

De Jong T & Worp K.A, 'More Greek horoscopes from Kellis (Dekhleh Oasis)', *Zeitschrift für Papyrologie und Epigraphik* 137 (2001), 203-14

Del Prete A, 'Riflessioni sulla magia in Bruno e in Campanella' I A. Ingengo & A. Perfetti (eds.), *Giordano Bruno nella Cultura del suo Tempo*, Naples: La Città del Sole 2004, 257-84

Demaitre L.E, *Doctor Bernard de Gordon: Professor and Practitioner*, Toronto: Pontifical Institute of Mediaeval Studies 1980

Denzey N, 'A new star on the horizon: astral Christologies and stellar debates in early Christian discourse' in S. Noegel, J. Walker, B. Wheeler (eds.), *Prayer, Magic, and the Stars in the Ancient and Late Antique World*, Pennsylvania: Pennsylvania State University Press 2003, 207-21

Dicks D.R, 'Astrology and astronomy in Horace', *Hermes* 91 (1963), 60-73

Dillon J, 'Plotinus on whether the stars are causes' in R. Gyselen, *La science des cieux* q.v. 87-93

Dobin J.C, *The Astrological Secrets of the Hebrew Sages*, Rochester, Vermont: Inner Traditions

International Ltd 1977

Dodds E.R, *Pagan and Christian in an Age of Anxiety*, Cambridge: Cambridge University Press 1965

Domenicucci P, *Astra Caesarum: Astronomia, Astrologia e Catasterismo da Cesare a Domiziano*, Pisa: Edizioni ETS 1996

Dooley B, 'The Ptolemaic astrological tradition in the seventeenth century: an example from Rome', *International Journal of the Classical Tradition* 5 (June 1999), 528-48 *Morandi's Prophecy and the End of Renaissance Politics*, Princeton, NJ & Oxford: Princeton University Press 2002

Dorival G, 'L'astre de Balaam et l'étoile des Mages' in R. Gyselen (ed.), *La science des cieux* q.v. 93-111

Dorotheus of Sidon, *Carmen Astrologicum*, trans. D. Pingree, Abingdon, MD: Astrology Centre of America 2005

Draelants A, Tihon A, Van den Abeele B (eds.), *Occident et Proche-Orient: Contacts Scientifiques au Temps des Croisades*, Turnhout: Brepols 2000

Drawnel H, 'Moon computation in the Aramaic Astronomical Book (1)', *Revue de Qumran* 89 (2007), 3-41

Drévillon H, *Lire et écrire l'avenir: l'astrologie dans la France du Grand Siècle, 1610–1715*, Seyssel: Champ Vallon 1996

Dwyer E.J, 'Augustus and the Capricorn', *Mitteilungen der Deutschen Archäologischen Instituts: Römische Abteilung* 80 (1973), 59-67

Fahd T, 'Ibn Wahshiyya' in *Encyclopaedia Islamica*, new ed. Vol.3, Leiden & London: Brill & Luzac & Co. 1971, 963-5

Fédou M, *Christianisme et Religions Païennes dans le Contre Celse d'Origène*, Paris: Beauchesne 1988

Ferrari L.C, 'Augustine and astrology', *Laval théologique et philosophique* 33 (1977), 241-51

Ficino M, *Letters*, English trans. 7 vols. London: Shepheard-Walwyn 1975-2003

Ficino M, *Three Books on Life*, ed. & trans. C.V. Kaske & J.R. Clark, Binghamton: State University of New York 1989

Fierro M, 'Bātinism in al-Andalus. Maslama b. Qāsim al-Qurtubi (d.353/964), author of the Rutbat al-Hakīm and the Ghāyat al-Hakīm (Picatrix)', *Studia Islamica* 84 (1996), 87-112

Firpo L, 'Tommaso Campanella' in *Dizionario Biografico degli Italiani*, Vol.17, Rome: Instituto Enciclopedia Italiana 1974, 372-401

Frea A, 'La peste astrological, ovvero il dibattito circa la scienza dei cieli tra Symphorien Champier e Giovanni Mainardi' in M. Bertozzi (ed.), *Alla Corte degli Estensi: Filosofia, Arte e Cultura a Ferrara nei secoli XV a XVI*, Ferrara: Università degli Studi 1994

French P.J, *John Dee: The World of an Elizabethan Magus*, London: Routledge & Kegan Paul 1972

French R, 'Foretelling the future: Arabic astrology and English medicine in the late twelfth century', *Isis* 87 (1996), 453-80

Gain D.B (ed.), *The Aratus Ascribed to Germanicus Caesar*, London: Athlone Press 1976

Garin E, *Astrology in the Renaissance: The Zodiac of Life*, English trans. London: Routledge & Kegan Paul 1983

Garin E, *History of Italian Philosophy*, Vol.1, English trans. London: Editions Rodopi BV 2007

Gasparro G.S, 'Il mitraismo nell'ambito della fenomenologia misterica' in U. Bianchi (ed.), *Mysteria Mithrae* q.v. 299-348 (including a résumé in English)

Gatti H, *Giordano Bruno and Renaissance Science*, Ithaca & London: Cornell University Press 1999

Gauquelin M, *The Truth About Astrology*, English trans. London: Hutchinson 1984

Gauquelin M, *Neo-Astrology: A Copernican Revolution*, English trans. Lodnon: Arkana 1991

Gay D, 'Astrology and iconoclasm in Milton's Paradise Regained', *Studies in English Literature, 1500–1900*, 41 (2000), 175-90

Genequand C, 'Idolâtrie, astrolâtrie et sabéisme', *Studia Islamica* 89 (1999), 109-28

George D, 'Manuel I Komnenos and Michael Glykas: a twelfth-century defence and refutation of astrology', *www.hellenisticastrology.com/articles/Demetra%20George%20-%20Manuel%20Komnenos%20Translation.pdf*

George D, 'A golden thread: the transmission of western astrology through cultures', *www.demetra-george.com/Transmission_Western_Astrology.pdf*

Geneva A, *Astrology and the Seventeenth-Century Mind: William Lilly and the Language of the Stars*, Manchester & New York: Manchester University Press 1995

Gettings F, *Dictionary of Astrology*, London: Routledge & Kegan Paul 1985

Godwin J, *Harmonies of Heaven and Earth: The Spiritual Dimension of Music from Antiquity to the Avant-Garde*, London: Thames & Hudson 1987

Goodrick-Clarke N, *Paracelsus: Essential Readings*, Wellingborough: Crucible 1990

Gordon R, *Image and Value in the Graeco-Roman World: Studies in Mithraism and Religious Art*, Aldershot: Ashgate Variorum 1996

Gleadow R, *The Origin of the Zodiac*, London: Jonathan Cape 1968

Grafton A, *Cardano's Cosmos: The Worlds and Works of a Renaissance Astrologer*, Cambridge, Mass: Harvard University Press 1999

Granbard M, 'Astrology's demise and its bearing on the decline of beliefs', *Osiris* 13 (1958), 210-61

Grant E, *Planets, Stars, and Orbs: The Mediaeval Cosmos, 1200–1687*, Cambridge: Cambridge University Press 1994

Green T.M, *The City of the Moon God: Religious Traditions of Harran*, Leiden: Brill 1992

Grosseteste R, *Hexaëmeron*, ed. R.C. Dales & S. Gieben, London: Oxford University Press 1982

Guerra F, 'Medical almanacs of the American colonial period', *Journal of the History of Medicine* 16 (July 1961), 234-55

Gunther R.T, *The Astrolabes of the World*, Vol.1, Oxford: Oxford University Press 1932

Gyselen R (ed.), *La science des cieux: sages, mages, astrologues*, Bures-sur-Yvette: Groupe pour l'étude de la civilisation du Moyen-Orient 1999

Hackett J (ed.), *Roger Bacon and the Sciences: Commemorative Essays*, Leiden: Brill 1997

Hackett J (ed.), 'Roger Bacon on astronomy-astrology: the sources of the Scientia Experimentalis' in J. Hackett, *Roger Bacon and the Sciences* q.v. 175-98

Hämeen-Antilla J, *The Last Pagans of Iraq: Ibn Wahshiyya and his Nabataean Agriculture*, Leiden: Brill 2006

Hand R, 'A study in early house division', *www.astrologer.com/aanet/pub/journal/jojul97.html*

Harari Y, 'The sages and the occult' in S. Safrai, Z. Safrai, J. Schwartz, P.J. Tomson (eds.), *The Literature of the Sages* Part 2, Assen: Royal Van Gorcum & Fortress Press 2006, 521-64

Harris W.V (ed.), *The Spread of Christianity in the First Four Centuries: Essays in Explanation*, Leiden: Brill 2005

Hartner W, 'Asturlāb' in *Encyclopaedia of Islam*, new ed. Vol.1, Leiden & London: Brill & Luzac & Co 1960, 722-8

Hartner W, 'Notes on Picatrix', *Isis* 56 (1965), 438-51

Haskins C.H, *Studies in the History of Mediaeval Science*, New York: Frederick Ungar Publishing 1960

Head R, 'Astrology and modernism in "The Planets"', *www.raymondhead.com/planets*

Hegedus T, 'The Magi and the star in the Gospel of Matthew and early Christian tradition', *Laval théologique et philosophique* 59 (2003), 81-95

Hegedus T, *Early Christianity and Ancient Astrology*, New York: Peter Lang 2007

Heilen S, 'Astrological remarks on the new horoscopes from Kellis', *Zeitschrift für Papyrologie und Epigaphik* 146 (2004), 131-6

Heilen S, 'The Emperor Hadrian in the horoscopes of Antigonus of Nicaea' in G. Oestmann, H.D. Rutkin, K. von Stuckrad (eds.), *Horoscopes and Public Spheres* q.v., 49-67

Hermetica, trans. B.P. Copenhaver, Cambridge: Cambridge University Press 1992

Hermippus, *De astrologia dialogus*, ed. W.Kroll & P. Viereck, Leipzig: Teubner 1895

Hippolytus, *Refutatio omnium haeresium*, ed. M. Marcovich, Berlin: De Gruyter 1986

Holden J.H, *A History of Horoscopic Astrology*, 2nd ed., Tempe, Arizona: American Federation of Astrologers 2006

Holo J, 'Hebrew astrology in Byzantine southern Italy' in Magdalino & Mavroudi, *The Occult Sciences in Byzantium* q.v.291-323

Holt P, *Stars of India: Travels in Search of Astrologers and Fortune-Tellers*, Edinburgh & London: Mainstream Publishing 1998

Horowitz D, 'Rashba's attitude towards science and its limits', *www.yutorah.org/_shiurim/TU30_Horowitz.pdf*

Horowitz W, *Mesopotamian Cosmic Geography*, Winona Lake, Indiana: Eisenbrauns 1998

Howe E, *Astrology and the Third Reich*, Wellingborough: Aquarian Press 1984

Hubbard T, *Michael Scot: Myth and Polymath*, Kirkcaldy: Akros Publications 2006

Huber P, 'Dating by lunar eclipse omens, with speculations on the birth of omen astrology' in J.L. Berggren & B.R. Goldstein (eds.), *From Ancient Omens to Statistical Mechanics: Essays on the Exact Sciences presented to Asger Aa boe*, Copenhagen: University Library 1987, 3-13.

Hübner W, 'Das Horoskop der Christen: Zeno 1.38L', *Vigiliae Christianae* 29 (1975), 120-37

Hübner W, *Raum, Zeit und soziales Rollenspiel der vier Kardinalpunkte in der antiken Katarchenhoroskopie*, München & Leipzig: K.G. Saur 2003

Hugo of Santalla, *The Liber Aristotilis*, London: Warburg Institute 1997

Hyde M, *Jung and Astrology*, London: Aquarian Press 1992

Idel M, 'Hermeticism and Kabbalah' in Lucentini, Parri, Compagni (eds.), *Hermetism from Late Antiquity to Humanism* q.v. 385-428

Ilnitchi G, 'Musica mindana, Aristotelian natural philosophy, and Ptolemaic astronomy', *Early Music History* 21 (2002), 37-74

Iqbal M, *Islam and Science*, Aldershot: Ashgate 2002

Jacquart D, 'Bernard de Gordon et l'astrologie', *Centaurus* 45 (2003), 151-58. Jeake S, *An Astrological Diary of the Seventeenth Century*, ed. M. Hunter & A. Gregory, Oxford: Clarendon Press 1988

Johnson P, Payne S, Wilson P, 'Towards a contextualised astrological apologetic, with a case study for Booth Ministry outreach', *www.areopagos.dk/lausanne/Toward%20Contextualized%20Apologetic%20Through%20 Astrology.doc*

Jolivet J & Rashed R, 'Al-Kindī' in *Dictionary of Scientific Biography*, Vol.15, Supplement 1, New York: Charles Scribner's Sons 1978, 261-7

Jones P, 'Celestial and terrestrial orientation: the origins of house division in ancient cosmology' in A. Kitson (ed.), *History and Astrology* q.v., 27-46

Joost-Gangier, *Measuring Heaven: Pythagoras and his Influence on Thought and Art in Antiquity and the Middle Ages*, Ithaca & London: Cornell University Press 2006

Juste D, 'Les doctrines astrologiques du Liber Alchandrei' in Draelants, Tihon, Van den Abeele (eds.), *Occident et Proche-Orient* q.v. 277-311

Kahane H & R, Pietrangeli A, 'Picatrix and the talismans', *Romance Philology* 19 (May 1966), 574-93

Kassell L, 'Simon Forman' in *Dictionary of National Biography*, Vol.20 Oxford: Oxford University Press 2004, 373-6

Kassell L, *Medicine and Magic in Elizabethan London; Simon Forman: Astrologer, Alchemist, and Physician*, Oxford: Clarendon Press 2005

Kauffmann C.M, 'John Varley' in *Dictionary of National Biography*, Vol.56, Oxford: Oxford University Press 2004, 146-9

Kay R, *Dante's Christian Astrology*, Philadelphia: University of Pennsylvania Press 1994

Kelley N, 'Astrology in the pseudo-Clementine Recognitions', *Journal of Ecclesiastical History* 59 (2008), 607-29

Kennedy E.S, *Astronomy and Astrology in the Mediaeval Islamic World*, Aldershot: Ashgate 1998

Kennedy E.S. & Pingree D, *The Astrological History of Māshā'allāh*, Cambridge, Mass: Harvard University Press 1971

Kesten H, *Copernicus and his World*, 2nd ed. London: Secker & Warburg 1946

Kibre P, 'Giovanni Garzoni of Bologna (1419–1505), Professor of Medicine and defender of astrology', *Isis* 58 (1967), 504-14

King D.A, 'Mathematical astronomy in Mediaeval Yemen', *Arabian Studies* 5 (1979), 61-5

Kitson A (ed.), *History and Astrology: Clio and Urania Confer*, London: Unwin Hyman Ltd. 1989

Klein-Franke F, 'Al-Kindī' in S.H. Nasr & O. Leaman (eds.), *History of Islamic Philosophy*, q.v.165-77

Koch-Westenholz U, *Mesopotamian Astrology*, Copenhagen: Museum Tusculanum Press 1995

Koch-Westenholz U, 'The astrological commentary Šumma Sîn Ina Tāmartīšu Tablet 1' in R.

Gyselen, *La science des cieux* q.v. 149-65

Kollerstrom N, 'Kepler's belief in astrology' in A. Kitson (ed.), *History and Astrology* q.v. 152-70

Kollerstrom N, 'The star zodiac of antiquity', *Culture and Cosmos* 1 (1997), 5-22

Kuhn T.S, *The Copernican Revolution: Planetary Astronomy in the Development of Western Thought*, Cambridge, Mass: Harvard University Press 1966

Kunitzsch P, 'Origin and history of Liber de stellis beibeniis' in Lucentini, Parri, Compagni (eds.), *Hermetism from Late Antiquity to Humanism*, q.v. 449-60

Kunitzsch P & Langerman Y.T, 'A star table from Mediaeval Yemen', *Centaurus* 45 (2003), 159-74

Lambert W.G, 'Babylonian astrological omens and their stars', *Journal of the American Oriental Society* 107 (1987), 93-6

Láng B, *Unlocked Books: Manuscripts of Learned Magic in the Mediaeval Libraries of Central Europe*, Pennsylvania: Pennsylvania State University Press 2008

Lattis J.M, *Between Copernicus and Galileo: Christoph Clavius and the Collapse of Ptolemaic Cosmology*, Chicago & London: University of Chicago Press 1994

Le Boeuffle A, *Le ciel des romains*, Paris: De Boccard 1989

Lehmann M.R, 'New light on astrology in Qumran and the Talmud', *Revue de Qumran* 8 (1975), 599-602

Leibovici M, 'Sur l'astrologie médicale néo-Babylonienne', *Journal Asiatique* 244 (1956), 275-80

Lemay R, 'Des sages antiques aux astrologues médiévaux. Falsafa et astrologie' in R. Gyselen, La science des cieux q.v. 167-82

Lemay R, 'Roger Bacon's attitude towards the Latin translations and translators of the twelfth and thirteenth centuries' in J. Hackett (ed.), *Roger Bacon and the Sciences* q.v. 25-47

Lerner R & Mahdi M (eds.), *Mediaeval Political Philosophy: A Sourcebook*, Canada: Collier-Macmillan Ltd. 1963

Levarie Smarr J, 'Boccaccio and the stars: astrology in the Teseida', *Traditio* 35 (1979), 303-32

Levenda P, *Unholy Alliance: A History of Nazi Involvement with the Occult*, 2,d ed. New York & London: Continuum 2002

Lilly W, *Christian Astrology*, Books 1 & 2, and Book 3, London 1647, reprint Bel Air MD: Astrology Centre of America 2004

Lippincott K, 'Two astrological ceilings reconsidered: the Sala di Galatea in the Villa Farnesina and the Sala del Mappamondo at Caprarola', *Journal of the Warburg and Courtauld Institutes* 53 (1990), 185-207

Long A.A, 'Astrology: arguments pro and contra' in J. Burns, J. Brunschwig, M. Burnyeat, M. Schofield (eds.), *Science and Speculation: Studies in Hellenistic Theory and Practice*, Cambridge: Cambridge University Press 1982, 165-92

Long A.A, *From Epicurus to Epictetus: Studies in Hellenistic and Roman Philosophy*, Oxford: Clarendon Press 2006

Lucentini P, Parri I, Perone Compagni V (eds.), *Hermetism from Late Antiquity to Humanism: Atti del Convegno Internazionale di Studi, Napoli, 20-24 Novembre 2001*, Turnhout-Belgium: Brepols 2003

Luther M, *Table Talk* = *Luther's Works* Vol.45, ed. T.G. Tappert & H.T. Lehmann, Philadelphia: Fortress Press 1967

Lyons J, *The House of Wisdom: How the Arabs Transformed Western Civilisation*, London: Bloomsbury 2009

MacDonald M, *Mystical Bedlam: Madness, Anxiety, and Healing in Seventeenth-Century England*, Cambridge: Cambridge University Press 1981

Magdalino P, 'Occult science and Imperial power in Byzantine history and historiography (9th – 12th centuries)' in Magdalino & Mavroudi (eds.), *The Occult Sciences in Byzantium*, q.v. 119-62

Magdalino P & Mavroudi M (eds.), *The Occult Sciences in Byzantium*, Geneva: La Pomme d'Or 2006

Mamoojee A.H, 'Quintus Cicéron et les douze signes du zodiaque', *Mélanges d'études anciennes offerts à Maurice Lebel*, Quebec: Éditions du sphinx 1980, 247-56

Manilius, *Astronomica*, ed. & trans. G.P. Goold, Cambridge, Mass & London: Harvard University Press 1977

Marcel P.Ch, 'Calvin and Copernicus' in R.C. Gamble (ed.), *Articles on Calvin and Calvinism*: Vol.12, *Calvin and Science*, New York & London: Garland Publishing 1992, 72-94

Marinatos N, 'The cosmic journey of Odysseus', *Numen* 48 (2001), 381-416

Marquet Y, 'La révélation par astrologie selon Abu Ya'qūb as-Sijistānī et les Ihwān as-Safā', *Studia Islamica* 80 (1994), 5-28

Martin G, 'Los intelectuales y la Corona: la obra histórica y literaria' in M. Rodriguez Llopis (ed.), *Alfonso X y su época*, Murcia: Carroggio 2002, 259-85

Mason Bradbury N & Collette C.P, 'Changing times: the mechanical clock in late Mediaeval literature', *The Chaucer Review* 43 (2009), 351-75

Massignon L. 'Les infiltrations astrologiques dans la pensée religieuse islamique', *Eranos-Jahrbuch* 10 (1943), 297-303

Maternus, Julius Firmicus, *Ancient Astrology, Theory and Practice: Matheseos Libri VIII*, trans. J. Rhys Bram, Bel Air: Astrology Classics 2005

Maxwell-Stuart P.G, *The Occult in Early Modern Europe*, Basingstoke: Macmillan 1999

Maxwell-Stuart P.G, *The Occult in Mediaeval Europe*, Basingstoke: Palgrave Macmillan 2005

Maxwell-Stuart P.G, 'Representations of same-sex love in early modern astrology' in K. Borris & G. Rousseau (eds.), *The Sciences of Homosexuality in Early Modern Europe*, Abingdon: Routledge 2008, 165-82

McIntosh C, *The Astrologers and their Creed: An Historical Outline*, London: Hutchinson 1969

Mehren A.F, *Vues d'Avicenne sur l'astrologie et sur le rapport de la responsabilité humaine avec le destin*, Louvain: Petters 1885

Mentgen G, *Astrologie und Öffentlichkeit im Mittelalter*, Stuttgart: Hiersemann 2005

Molland G, 'Roger Bacon' in *Dictionary of National Biography* Vol.3, Oxford: Oxford University Press 2004, 176-81

Molnar M.R, *The Star of Bethlehem*, New Brunswick, New Jersey & London: Rutgers University Press 1999

Morley H, *The Life of Henry Cornelius Agrippa von Nettesheim*, 2 vols. London: Chapman & Hall 1836

Morony M.G, *Iraq After the Muslim Conquest*, Princeton: Princeton University Press 1984

Murray Jones P, *Mediaeval Medicine in Illuminated Manuscripts*, revised ed. London: The British Library 1998

Nasr S.H & Leamen O. (eds.), *History of Islamic Philosophy*, Part 1, London & New York: Routledge 1996.

Needham J & Wang Ling, *Science and Civilisation in China*: Vol.2, *History of Scientific Thought*, Cambridge: Cambridge University Press 1956

Needham J & Wang Ling, *Science and Civilisation in China*: Vol.3, *Mathematics and the Sciences of the Heavens and the Earth*, Cambridge: Cambridge University Press 1959

Nelson N.H, 'Astrology, Hudibras, and the Puritans', *Journal of the History of Ideas* 37 (1976), 521-36

Ness L, *Written in the Stars: Ancient Zodiac Mosaics*, Warren Centre, Pennsylvania: Shangri La Press 1999

Neugebauer O, 'Demotic horoscopes', *Journal of the African and Oriental Society* 63 (1943), 115-27

Neugebauer O, 'The early history of the astrolabe', *Isis* 40 (1949), 240-56

Neugebauer O, 'Tamil astronomy', *Osiris* 10 (1952), 252-76

Neugebauer O & Van Hoesen H.B, *Greek Horoscopes*, Philadelphia: The American Philosophical Society 1959

Noegel S, Walker J, Wheeler B (eds.), *Prayer, Magic, and the Stars in the Ancient and Late Antique World*, University Park, Pennsylvania: Pennsylvania State University Press 2003

Nofal N, 'Al-Ghazali', *Prospects* 23 (1993), 519-42

North J.D, *Horoscopes and History*, London: Warburg Institute 1986

North J.D, *Chaucer's Universe*, Oxford: Clarendon Press 1988

North J.D, *Stars, Mind and Fate: Essays in Ancient and Mediaeval Cosmology*, London & Ronceverte: Hambledon Press 1989

North J.D, *Cosmos: An Illustrated History of Astronomy and Cosmology*, Chicago & London: University of Chicago Press 2008

Oestmann G, 'J.W.A. Pfaff and the rediscovery of astrology in the Age of Romanticism' in G. Oestmann, H.D. Rutkin, K. von Stuckrad (eds.), *Horoscope and Public Spheres* q.v. 241-57

Oestmann G, Rutkin H.D., Von Stuckrad K (eds.), *Horoscopes and Public Spheres: Essays on the History of Astrology*, Berlin-New York: W. de Gruyter 2005

Omidsalar M, 'Magic literature and folklore in the Islamic period', *www.iranica.com/newsite/articles/ot_grp7/ot_magic_islam_20050310.html*

Oppenheim A.L, 'Divination and celestial observation in the last Assyrian empire', *Centaurus* 14 (1969), 97-135

Oppenheim A.L, 'A Babylonian diviner's manual', *Journal of Near Eastern Studies* 33 (1974), 197-220

Ovason D, *The History of the Horoscope*, Stroud: Sutton Publishing 2005

Pseudo-Ovid, *De Vetula*, ed. P. Klopsch, Leiden & Köln: Brill 1967

Page S, *Astrology in Mediaeval Manuscripts*, Toronto: University of Toronto Press 2002

Page S, 'Hermetic magic in a monastic context' in Lucentini, Parri, Compagni (eds.), *Hermetism from Late Antiquity to Humanism* q.v. 535-44

Panchenko D, 'Who found the zodiac?' *Antike Naturwissenschaft und ihre Rezeption* 9 (1999), 33-44

'Paracelsus', *The Archidoxes of Magic*, trans. R. Turner, London 1656: modern edition, London: Askin Publishers 1975

Parker D, *Familiar to All: William Lilly and Astrology in the Seventeenth Century*, London: Jonathan Cape 1975

Parker R.A, 'Egyptian astronomy, astrology and calendrical reckoning' in C. Coulston (ed.), *Dictionary of Scientific Biography*, Vol. 4, New York: Charles Scribner's Sons 1971, 706-27.

Parpola S (ed.), *Letters from Assyrian Scholars to the Kings Esarhaddon and Assurbanipal*, Part 1: *Texts*, Neukirchener Verlag des Erziehungsvereins Neukirchen-Vluyn: Butzon & Bercker Kevelaer 1970

Peucer C, *Commentarius de praecipuis divinationum generibus*, Frankfurt 1607

Picatrix: The Latin Version of the Ghāyat al-Hakīm, ed. D. Pingree, London: The Warburg Institute 1986

Picatrix: Un traité de magie médiéval, trans. B. Bakhouche, F. Faquier, B. Pérez-Jean, Turnhout: Brepols 2003

Pico della Mirandola, Giovanni, *Disputationes adversus astrologiam divinatricem*, Firenze: Vallecchi Editore 1946

Pingree D, 'Astronomy and astrology in India and Iran', *Isis* 54 (1963), 229-46

Pingree D, 'Gregory Chioniades and Palaeologan astronomy', *Dumbarton Oaks Papers* 18 (1964), 135-60

Pingree D, 'Abū Ma'shar' in *Dictionary of Scientific Biography*, Vol.1, New York: Charles Scribner's Sons 1970, 32-9

Pingree D, 'The astrological school of John Abramius', *Dumbarton Oaks Papers* 25 (1971), 191-215

Pingree D, 'The Greek influence on early Islamic mathematical astronomy', *Journal of the American Oriental Society* 93 (1973), 32-43

Pingree D, 'Māshā'allāh' in *Dictionary of Scientific Biography* Vol.9, New York: Charles Scribner's Sons 1974, 159-62

Pingree D, 'Pseudo-Petosiris' in *Dictionary of Scientific Biography* Vol.10, New York: Charles Scribner's Sons 1974, 547-9

Pingree D, 'The Indian and pseudo-Indian passages in Greek and Latin astronomical and astrological texts', *Viator* 7 (1976), 141-95

Pingree D, 'Antiochus and Rhetorius', *Classical Philology* 72 (1977), 203-23

Pingree D, 'Some of the sources of the Ghāyat al-Hakīm', *Journal of the Warburg and Courtauld Institutes* 43 (1980), 1-15

Pingree D, 'Astrology and astronomy in Iran' in *Encyclopaedia Iranica*, Vol.2, London: Routledge & Kegan Paul 1987, 858-71

Pingree D, 'Theophilos of Edessa' in *Oxford Dictionary of Byzantium*, 3 vols. Oxford: Oxford University Press 1991, 3.2006-7

Pingree D, 'From Alexandria to Baghdād to Byzantium: the transmission of astrology', *International Journal of the Classical Tradition* 8 (Summer 2001), 3-37

Pingree D, 'The Sābians of Harrān and the Classical tradition', *International Journal of the Classical Tradition* 9 (Summer 2002), 8-35

Pingree D, 'Māshā'allāh's Zoroastrian historical astrology' in G. Oestmann, H.D. Rutkin, K. von Stuckrad (eds.), *Horoscopes and Public Spheres* q.v. 95-100

Pingree D, 'The Byzantine translations of Māshā'allāh on interrogational astrology' in Magdalino & Mavroudi, *The Occult Sciences in Byzantium* q.v. 231-43

Pingree D & Madelung W, 'Political horoscopes relating to the late ninth century 'Alids', *Journal of Near Eastern Studies* 36 (1977), 247-75

Pingree D & Kazhdan A, 'Astrology' in *Oxford Dictionary of Byzantium*, 3 vols. Oxford: Oxford University Press, 1.214-16

Plotinus, *The Enneads*, trans. S. McKenna, revised ed., London: Faber & Faber Ltd. 1956

Possanza D.M, *Translating the Heavens: Aratus, Germanicus, and the Poetics of Latin Translation*, New York: Peter Lang 2004

Powell R, *History of the Zodiac*, San Rafael, California: Sophia Academic Press 2007

Prioreschi P, *A History of Medicine*, Vol.5: *Mediaeval Medicine*, Omaha: Horatius Press 2003

Procter E.S, 'The scientific works of the Court of Alfonso X of Castille: the King and his collaborators', *Modern Language Review* 40 (1945), 12-29

Ptolemy, *Tetrabiblos*, trans. J. Wilson, London: William Hughes 1820 (?)

Ptolemy, *Tetrabiblos* in *Opera Quae Exstant Omnia*, Vol. 111.1 (*Apotelesmatika*), ed. W. Hübner, Stuttgart & Leipzig: Teubner 1998

Quinlan-McGrath M, 'The astrological vault of the Villa Farnesina: Agostino Chigi's rising sign', *Journal of the Warburg and Courtauld Institutes* 47 (1984), 91-103

Quinn D.M, *Early Mormonism and the Magic World View*, Salt Lake City: Signature Books 1998

Rabin S, 'Unholy astrology: did Pico always view it that way?' in G. Scholz Williams & C.D. Gunnoe (eds.), *Paracelsian Moments* q.v. 151-62

Rainer E, 'Fortune-telling in Mesopotamia', *Journal of Near Eastern Studies* 19 (1960), 23-35

Rainer E, *Astral Magic in Babylonia*, Philadelphia: The American Philosophical Society 1995

Renaker D, 'The horoscope of Christ', *Milton Studies* Vol.12 (1978), 213-34

Riley M, 'A survey of Vettius Valens', *http://www.csus.edu/indiv/r/rileymt/PDF_folder/VettiusValens.PDF*

Roberts T.J, 'John Dee' in *Dictionary of National Biography* Vol.15, Oxford: Oxford University Press 2004, 667-75

Robin S.J, 'Kepler's attitude towards Pico and the anti-astrology polemic', *Renaissance Quarterly* 50 (1997), 750-70

Robinson K, *A Search for the Source of the Whirlpool of Artifice: The Cosmology of Giulio Camillo*, Edinburgh: Dunedin Academic Press 2006

Rochberg F, 'Heaven and earth: divine-human relations in Mesopotamian celestial divination' in Noegel-Walker-Wheeler (eds.), *Prayer, Magic, and the Stars in the Ancient and Late Antique World* q.v., 169-85

Rochberg F, *The Heavenly Writing: Divination, Horoscopy, and Astronomy in Mesopotamian Culture*, Cambridge: Cambridge University Press 2004

Rochberg-Halton F, 'New evidence for the history of astrology', *Journal of Near Eastern Studies* 43 (1984), 115-40

Rochberg-Halton F, 'Babylonian horoscopes and their sources', *Orientalia* 58 (1989), 102-23

Rosenberg R.A, 'The star of the Messiah reconsidered', *Biblica* 53 (1972), 105-9

Rosenfeld B.A & Grigorian A.T, 'Thābit ibn Qurra' in *Dictionary of Scientific Biography*, Vol.13, New York: Charles Scribner's Sons 1976, 288-95

Roth N, 'Jewish collaborators in Alfonso's scientific work' in R.I. Burns (ed.), *Emperor of Culture:*

Alfonso X the Learned of Castile and his Thirteenth-Century Renaissance, Philadelphia: University of Pennsylvania Press 1990, 59-71

Rowland I.D, *Giordano Bruno: Philosopher, Heretic*, New York: Farrar, Straus & Giroux 2008

Ruderman D.B, *Jewish Thought and Scientific Discovery in Early Modern Europe*, New Haven & London: Yale University Press 1995

Rutkin H.D, 'Various uses of horoscopes: astrological practices in early modern Europe' in G. Oestmann, H.D. Rutkin, K. von Stuckrad (eds.), *Horoscopes and Public Spheres* q.v. 167-82

Rutkin H.D, 'Astrological conditioning of same-sexual relations in Girolamo Cardano's theoretical treatises and celebrity genitures' in K. Borris & G. Rousseau (eds.), *The Sciences of Homosexuality in Early Modern Europe*, London & New York: Routledge 2008, 183-99

Ryan W.F, *The Bathhouse at Midnight: Magic in Russia*, Stroud: Sutton Publishing 1999

Saliba G, 'The role of the astrologer in Mediaeval Islamic society', *Bulletin d'études orientales* 44 (1992), 45-68

Saliba G, *A History of Arabic Astronomy*, new. ed. New York: New York University Press 1995

Saliba G, *Islamic Science and the Making of the European Renaissance*, Cambridge, Mass: MIT Press 2007

Salemme C, *Introduzione agli 'Astronomica' di Manilio*, Napoli: Società Editrice Napoletana 1983

Samsó J, 'The early development of astrology in al-Andalus', *Journal of the History of Arabic Science* 3 (1979), 228-43

Samsó J, *Astronomy and Astrology in al-Andalus and the Maghrib*, Aldershot: Ashgate Variorum 2007

Saunders R, *The Astrological Judgement and Practice of Physick*, London 1677, modern reprint, Abingdon MD: The Astrology Centre of America 2003

Schechner Genuth S, *Comets, Popular Culture, and the Birth of Modern Cosmology*, Princeton NJ: Princeton University Press 1997

Schoeps H.J, 'Astrologisches im Pseudoklementinischen Roman', *Vigiliae Christianae* 5 (1951), 88-100

Scholz Williams G & Gunnoe C.D.(eds.), *Paracelsian Moments: Science, Medicine, and Astrology in Early Modern Europe*, Missouri: Truman State University Press 2002

Scoggins D, 'Wine and obscenities: astrology's degradation in the five books of Rabelais' in G. Scholz Williams & C.D. Gunnoe (eds.), *Paracelsian Moments* q.v. 163-86

Shumaker W (ed.), *Renaissance Curiosa*, New York: Binghamton 1982

Schwartz D, *Studies in Astral Magic in Mediaeval Jewish Thought*, English trans. Leiden: Brill 2005

Severus Sebokht, *Treatise on the Astrolabe*, English trans. In R.T. Gunther, *Astrolabes of the World* q.v. 1.82-103

Severus Sebokht, *Treatise on the Constellations*, English trans. *www.tertullian.org/fathers/severus_sebokht_constellations_02_trans.htm*

Seznec J, *The Survival of the Pagan Gods: The Mythological Tradition and its Place in Renaissance Humanism and Art*, English trans. New York: Pantheon Books 1953

Sidelko P.L, 'The condemnation of Roger Bacon', *Journal of Mediaeval History* 22 (1996), 69-81

Silverstein T, 'Daniel of Morley, English cosmologist and student of Arabic science', *Mediaeval Studies* 10 (1948), 179-96

Sirat C, *A History of Jewish Philosophy in the Middle Ages*, Cambridge: Cambridge University Press 1985

Small D.R, 'The raven: an iconographic adaptation of the planet Mercury' in U. Bianchi (ed.), *Mysteria Mithrae* q.v. 531-49

Smoller L.A, *History, Prophecy, and the Stars: The Christian Astrology of Pierre d'Ailly, 1350–1420*, Princeton NJ: Princeton University Press 1994

Sogno C, 'Astrology, morality, the Emperors, and the law in Firmicus Maternus's Mathesis', *Illinois Classical Studies* 30 (2005), 167-76

Spruit L, 'Giordano Bruno and astrology' in H. Gatti (ed.), *Giordano Bruno: Philosopher of the Renaissance*, Aldershot: Ashgate 2002, 229-49

Stahlman W.D, 'Astrology in colonial America: an extended query', *William and Mary Quarterly*

3rd series, 13 (1956), 551-63

Stark R.J, *Rhetoric, Science, and Magic in Seventeenth-Century England*, Washington: The Catholic University of America Press 2009

Steele J.M, 'Celestial measurement in Babylonian astronomy', *Annals of Science* 64 (July 2007), 293-325

Stock B, *Myth and Science in the Twelfth Century: A Study of Bernard Silvester*, Princeton: Princeton University Press 1972

Strauss W.L, *The German Single-Leaf Woodcut, 1550–1600*, 3 vols., New York: Abaris Books 1975

Sutton K, *The Essentials of Vedic Astrology*, Bournemouth: The Wessex Astrologer Ltd. 1999

Swerdlow N, 'On the cosmical mysteries of Mithras', (review article), *Classical Philology* 86 (1991), 48-63

Swerdlow N, *The Babylonian Theory of the Planets*, Princeton: Princeton University Press 1998

Swift J, *Works*, Vols. 4 & 6, Edinburgh and Glasgow: A. Kincaid, A. Donaldson, Yair & Fleming, and others 1756

Talbot C.H, 'A mediaeval physician's vade mecum', *Journal of the History of Medicine* 16 (1961), 213-33

Tardieu M, 'Sābiens coraniques et Sābiens de Harrān', *Journal Asiatique* 274 (1986), 1-44

Tatian, *Oratio ad Graecos*, ed. & trans. M. Whittaker, Oxford: Clarendon Press 1982

Tester J, *A History of Western Astrology*, Woodbridge: Boydell Press 1987

Thomann J, 'The name Picatrix: transcription or translation?' *Journal of the Warburg and Courtauld Institutes* 53 (1990), 289-96

Thomas K, *Religion and the Decline of Magic*, London: Penguin Books 1971

Thorndike L, 'A Roman astrologer as a historical source: Julius Firmicus Maternus', *Classical Philology* 8 (1913), 415-35

Thorndike L, *A History of Magic and Experimental Science* 8 vols. New York: Columbia University Press 1923–58

Thorndike L, 'Albumasar in Sadan', *Isis* 45 (1954), 22-32

Thorndike L, 'The Latin translations of astrological works by Messahala', *Osiris* 12 (1956), 49-72

Thorndike L, 'Adelard, ergaphalau, and the science of the stars' in C. Burnett (ed.), *Adelard of Bath: An English Scientist and Arabist of the Early Twelfth Century*, London: Warburg Institute 1987, 133-45

Tihon A, 'Les textes astronomiques arabes importés à Byzance aux xie et xiie siècles' in Draelants, Tihon, Van den Abeele (eds.), *Occident et Proche-Orient* q.v. 313-24

Tihon A, 'Astrological promenade in Byzantium in the early Palaiologian period' in Magdalino & Mavroudi, *The Occult Sciences in Byzantium* q.v. 265-90

Tinkle T, 'Saturn of the several faces: a survey of the Mediaeval mythographic traditions', *Viator* 18 (1987), 289-307

Toepel A, 'Planetary demons in early Jewish literature', *Journal for the Study of the Pseudepigrapha* 14 (3) 2005, 231-8

Traister B.H, *The Notorious Astrological Physician of London: Works and Days of Simon Forman*, Chicago & London: University of Chicago Press 2001

Travaglia P, *Magic, Causality, and Intentionality: The Doctrine of Rays in Al-Kindī*, Turnhout: Brepols 1999

Treitel C, *A Science for the Soul: Occultism and the Genesis of the German Modern*, Baltimore & London: The John Hopkins University Press 2004

Ulansey D, *The Origins of the Mithraic Mysteries: Cosmology and Salvation in the Ancient World*, Oxford: Oxford University Press 1989

Van Binsbergen W, 'The astrological origin of Islamic geomancy', *www.shikanda.net/ancient_models/BINGHAMTON%201996.pdf*

Vanden Broecke S, 'An astronomical and astrological commentary on an unknown horoscope by Johannes Kepler, 1619', *Lias* 27 (2000), 197-206

Vanden Broecke S, *The Limits of Influence: Pico, Louvain, and the Crisis of Renaissance Astrology*, Leiden: Brill 2003

Van de Vyver A, 'Les plus anciennes traductions médiévales (x-xi siècles) de traités d'astronomie et d'astrologie', *Osiris* 1 (1936), 658-91

Versluis A, *The Esoteric Origins of the American Renaissance*, Oxford: Oxford University Press 2001

Vettius Valens, *Anthologiae*, ed. D. Pingree, Leipzig: Teubner 1986

Vettius Valens, *Anthologies*, Livre I, ed. J-F. Bara, Leiden: Brill 1989

Volk K, *Manilius and his Intellectual Background*, Oxford: Oxford University Press 2009

Von Stuckrad K, 'Jewish and Christian astrology in late antiquity: a new perspective', *Numen* 47 (2000), 1-40

Voss A, 'The astrology of Marsilio Ficino: divination or science?' *Culture and Cosmos* 4 (Autumn-Winter 2000), 16-38

Walker D.P, 'The astral body in Renaissance medicine', *Journal of the Warburg and Courtauld Institutes* 21 (1958), 119-33

Walker D.P, *Spiritual and Demonic Magic from Ficino to Campanella*, London: Warburg Institute 1958

Waterfield R, 'The evidence for astrology in Classical Greece', *Culture and Cosmos* 3 (Autumn-Winter 1999), 3-15

Webster C, *Paracelsus, Medicine, Magic and Mission at the End of the World*, New Haven & London: Yale University Press 2008

Wedel T.O, *Astrology in the Middle Ages*, New York: Dover Publications 2005, reprint of 1920 edition.

Welkenhuysen A, 'A horoscope cast by Johannes Kepler, Linz, 3 June, 1619', *Lias* 27 (2000), 207-27

West J.A, *The Case for Astrology*, London: Viking Arkana 1991

Wigzell F, *Reading Russian Fortunes: Print Culture, Gender and Divination in Russia from 1765*, Cambridge: Cambridge University Press 1998

Whitfield P, *Astrology: A History*, London: The British Library 2001

Wise M.O, *Thunder in Gemini and Other Essays in the History, Language and Literature of Second Temple Palestine*, Sheffield: JSOT Press 1994

Wood C, *Chaucer and the Country of the Stars: Poetic Uses of Astrological Imagery*, Princeton, NJ: Princeton University Press 1970

Wright M.R, *Cosmology in Antiquity*, London & New York: Routledge 1995

Yamamoto K & Burnett C (eds.), *Abū Ma'shar on Historical Astrology*, 2 vols. Leiden: Brill 2000

Yates F, *Giordano Bruno and the Hermetic Tradition*, London: Routledge & Kegan Paul 1964

'Zadkiel', *An Introduction to Astrology by William Lilly*, London: George Bell & Sons 1881

Zafran E, 'Saturn and the Jews', *Journal of the Warburg and Courtauld Institutes* 42 (1979), 16-27

Zambelli P (ed.), *Astrologi hallucinati: Stars and the End of the World in Luther's Time*, New York: Walter de Gruyter 1986

Zambelli P (ed.), *The Speculum Astronomiae and its Enigma: Astrology, Theology and Science in Albertus Magnus and his Contemporaries*, Dordrecht: Kluwer Academic Publications 1992

Zeno of Verona, 'Tractatus de duodecim signis ad neophytes' in *Corpus Christianorum*, Series Latina, Vol.22, (ed. B. Löfstedt), Turnholt: Brepols 1971, 105-6.

Zoller R, *The Arabic Parts in Astrology: A Lost Key to Prediction*, Rochester, Vermont: Inner Traditions International Ltd. 1989

Available from March 2010 from Amberley Publishing

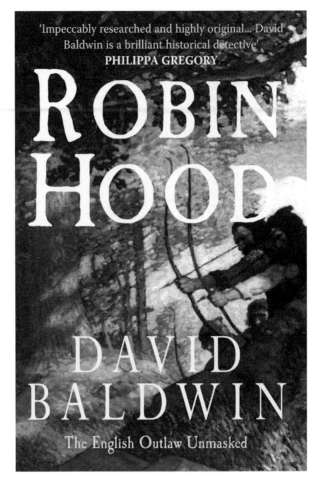

The identity of Robin Hood is one of the great historical mysteries of English history – until now

'Impeccably researched and highly original... David Baldwin is a brilliant historical detective'
PHILIPPA GREGORY

David Baldwin sets out to find the real Robin Hood, looking for clues in the earliest ballads and in official and legal documents of the thirteenth and fourteenth centuries. His search takes him to the troubled reign of King Henry III, his conclusions turn history on it's head and David Baldwin reveals the name of the man who inspired the tales of Robin Hood.

£20 Hardback
40 illustrations (20 colour)
320 pages
978-1-84868-378-5

Available from March 2010 from all good bookshops or to order direct
Please call **01285-760-030**
www.amberley-books.com

Available from March 2010 from Amberley Publishing

A major new history of the disaster that weaves into the narrative the first-hand accounts of those who survived

It was twenty minutes to midnight on Sunday 14 April, when Jack Thayer felt the Titanic lurch to port, a motion followed by the slightest of shocks. Seven-year old Eva Hart barely noticed anything was wrong. For Stoker Fred Barrett, shovelling coal down below, it was somewhat different; the side of the ship where he was working caved in.

For the next nine hours, Jack, Eva and Fred faced death and survived. They lived, along with just over 700 others picked up by 08.30 the next morning. Over 1600 people did not. This is the story told through the eyes of Jack, Eva, Fred and over a hundred others of those who survived and either wrote their experiences down or appeared before the major inquiries held subsequently.

£20 Hardback
40 illustrations
448 pages
978-1-84868-422-5

Available from March 2010 from all good bookshops or to order direct
Please call **01285-760-030**
www.amberley-books.com

Also available from Amberley Publishing

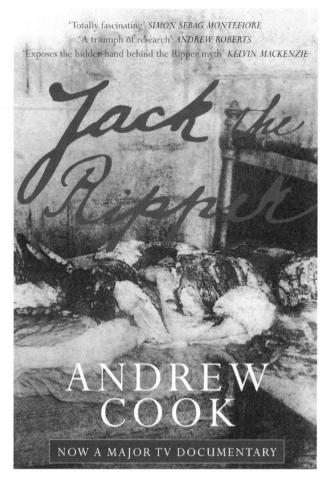

'Totally fascinating' *SIMON SEBAG MONTEFIORE*
'A triumph of research' *ANDREW ROBERTS*
'Exposes the hidden hand behind the Ripper myth' *KELVIN MACKENZIE*

ANDREW
COOK

NOW A MAJOR TV DOCUMENTARY

Finally lays to rest the mystery of who Jack the Ripper was

'Totally fascinating' SIMON SEBAG MONTEFIORE
'A triumph of research' ANDREW ROBERTS
'Exposes the hidden hand behind the Jack the Ripper myth' KELVIN MACKENZIE

The most famous serial killer in history. A sadistic stalker of seedy Victorian backstreets. A master criminal. The man who got away with murder – over and over again. But while literally hundreds of books have been published, trying to pin Jack's crimes on an endless list of suspects, no-one has considered the much more likely explanation for Jack's getting away with it... He never existed.

£9.99 Paperback
53 illustrations and 47 figures
256 pages
978-1-84868-522-2

Available from all good bookshops or to order direct
Please call **01285-760-030**
www.amberleybooks.com

Index